The Ulster Party

Irish Unionists in the House of Commons,
1884–1911

ALVIN JACKSON

CLARENDON PRESS · OXFORD
1989

Oxford University Press, Walton Street, Oxford OX2 6DP
Oxford New York Toronto
Delhi Bombay Calcutta Madras Karachi
Petaling Jaya Singapore Hong Kong Tokyo
Nairobi Dar es Salaam Cape Town
Melbourne Auckland
and associated companies in
Berlin Ibadan

Oxford is a trade mark of Oxford University Press

Published in the United States
by Oxford University Press, New York

British Library Cataloguing in Publication Data
Jackson, Alvin
The Ulster Party: Irish Unionists in
the House of Commons 1884-1911.
(Oxford historical monographs).
1. Northern Ireland. Political parties.
Ulster Unionist Party, 1884-1911
I. Title II. Series
324.2416
ISBN 0-19-822288-2

Library of Congress Cataloging in Publication Data
Jackson, Alvin
The Ulster Party: Irish unionists in the House of Commons,
1884-1911/Alvin Jackson.
(Oxford historical monographs)
Bibliography: p.   Includes index.
1. Northern Ireland—Politics and government. 2. Ulster Unionist
Party—History. 3. Ireland—Politics and government—1837-1901.
4. Ireland—Politics and government—1901-1910. 5. Great Britain.
Parliament. House of Commons—History. 6. Irish question.
I. Title. II. Series
DA990.U46J29 1989   941.6081—dc19   88-25321
ISBN 0-19-822288-2

Set by Dobbie Typesetting Limited, Plymouth, Devon
Printed and bound in Great Britain by
Biddles Limited, Guildford and King's Lynn

To Tom, Peggy, and Jane Jackson

PREFACE

I have incurred many debts in the writing of this book, and it is with pleasure that I may begin to make reparation.

For access to manuscript sources, and for permission to quote from them, I am grateful to the Duke of Abercorn, the Earl of Balfour, Birmingham University Library, Lord Bonham-Carter, Messrs Carleton, Atkinson and Sloan, the Master, Fellows and Scholars of Churchill College, Cambridge, the Trustees of the Chatsworth Settlement, Messrs Falls and Hanna, Kent Record Office, the Marquess of Londonderry, the Marquess of Salisbury, the Duke of Westminster and Francis Wyndham. I owe particular debts to Max Egremont for help with the Wyndham papers, and to R. M. Liddell, John McClintock, Sir William Moore, John Saunderson DSO, DFC, and Amanda Shanks for their generosity in the production of unpublished family records. Many people responded to my requests for help concerning the location or elucidation of source material, and I am indebted in this respect to the Earl of Antrim, Sir Walter Barrie, David Craig, Lord Deramore, John Grigg, Hector Kerr-Smiley, Lady Diana Lea, Mrs Jennifer Lyons, A. G. MacCaw, Robin Malcolm, Frank Millar and Lord Rathcavan. Messrs Faber and Faber have permitted me to use some lines of verse from *The Collected Poems of Louis MacNeice*. To owners of papers and owners of copyright whom I have been unable to locate, or whom I have omitted through oversight, I offer my apologies.

I am grateful to the long-suffering staff of many libraries and archives, but especially to Andrew Harrison, Anthony Malcomson, Trevor Parkhill and Roger Stronge at the Public Record Office of Northern Ireland, and to Ms K. M. Topping at the Kent Record Office, Robin Harcourt-Williams at Hatfield, and Ms Baker at Eaton, Chester.

Several institutions and funds have greatly aided the research and writing of this book. My thanks go to the Department of Education for Northern Ireland, the trustees of the A. M. P. Read Scholarship Fund at Oxford, the Warden and Fellows of Nuffield College, Oxford, and the Board of Management of the Institute of Irish Studies at the Queen's University, Belfast. The book was completed while I held a British Academy post-doctoral fellowship.

I have benefited very greatly from the help and encouragement of Paul Bew, Alastair Cooke, Perry Curtis, Roy Foster, David Harkness, David Hempton, Liam Kennedy, Martin Lynn, Tony Stewart, Brian Walker, Alan Ward and Allen Warren. Occasionally I have been sufficiently foolhardy to question the historical interpretations of a few of these, and other, scholars—but my reliance upon their stimulus will be self-evident. My colleague, Peter Jupp, bravely agreed to read the entire text, which is the better for his criticism. Patrick Buckland and Angus Macintyre examined the thesis upon which this monograph is based, and I am grateful to them for their advice, and their encouragement towards publication. The scholarly creditors to whom I owe the most are Michael Brock, Brian Harrison, Pat Thompson, and Philip Waller. The failings of this book are my own achievement.

A.J.

The Queen's University of Belfast,
January 1988.

CONTENTS

TABLES AND GRAPH

ABBREVIATIONS

ABP	Arthur Balfour Papers in the British Library
BL	British Library
BNL	*Belfast News Letter*
CAB	Cabinet Papers
DRO	Durham Record Office
ESP	Edward Saunderson Papers
ETUA	Papers of the East Tyrone Unionist Association
GWP	George Wyndham Papers
HLRO	House of Lords Record Office
ILPU	Irish Loyal and Patriotic Union
IT	*Irish Times*
IUA	Irish Unionist Alliance
JCP	Joseph Chamberlain Papers
JCUAI	Joint Committee of the Unionist Associations of Ireland
KRO	Kent Record Office
MSPH	Papers of the third Marquess of Salisbury at Hatfield
PRONI	Public Record Office of Northern Ireland
PUVA	Presbyterian Unionist Voters' Association
SACA	South Antrim Constitutional Association
UCL	Unionist Convention League
UJC	Unionist Joint Committee
UUC	Ulster Unionist Council
UVF	Ulster Volunteer Force
WJD	William Johnston Diaries
WLP	Walter Long Papers in the British Library

NOTE ON TERMINOLOGY

Note that contemporary usage has been followed in describing the parties and factions of late nineteenth-century Ireland. Where particular titles were (and, in some cases, still are) the subject of dispute, I have always accepted the case of the defendant, calling a party or political group what it called itself. Thus I have omitted inverted commas in referring to the Nationalist and loyalist movements, despite the fact that the former title was disputed by many Irish Unionists—and that the latter title is now sometimes treated within quotation marks. I have used 'Catholic' rather than 'Roman Catholic'. 'Ulster Party', 'Ulster members' and 'Irish Unionist Parliamentary Party' were interchangeable terms in the late nineteenth century; consequently each has been applied within this monograph to the body of Irish Unionist MPs.

1

Introduction

Why do we like being Irish? Partly because
It gives us a hold on the sentimental English
As members of a world that never was,
Baptised with fairy water.

MacNeice, *Autumn Journal* (1938)

1. *A Parliamentary Policy*

Although fifteen years have passed since the publication of Patrick
Buckland's pioneering research, the early history of Irish Unionism
remains comparatively underreported. A web of scholarship on
clearly defined episodes, generally the Home Rule controversies,
obscures any coherent image of the overall shape of the movement,
its centres of power, and directions of development. For the
historiography of Unionism remains a historiography of crisis,
minute analyses of developments in 1886, 1893, 1904–5, and
1912–14 offering only partial compensation for the lack of any
investigation of continuity. Unionism, then, has suffered from a
modest sensationalism; and the complex of reaction and mobilization
which characterized the Home Rule episodes emerges as a textbook
gloss on the broader nature of the movement.

This book began as an attempt to venture out from the laagers
of crisis and convention to a more general study of the early forms
of Unionist behaviour and organization. It gradually became clear
that much of the initiative within Unionism before 1912 lay not with
the organizational by-products of popular resistance to Home Rule,
but with a more stable and democratically constituted element of
the leadership: the MPs of the parliamentary Ulster Party. It was
with these men, either individually or collectively, that much of the
inspiration behind broader Unionist organization lay. Moreover,
their support lent credibility to other forms of political activity,
whether belligerent threats, popular conventions, or marches. The

movements spanned by the Home Rule crises never constituted a serious threat to the lasting ascendancy of the parliamentary party, partly because of the MPs' own contribution to popular organization—but also because these potential rivals proved to be too narrowly constituted or too ephemeral to pose as a credible alternative leadership. Thus the Loyal Irish Union, founded in 1885, collapsed ignominiously in 1885; and though the Irish Loyal and Patriotic Union, created in the same year, proved more sturdy, it never successfully colonized the crucial northern province, and retained a landed and élitist image. The Ulster Loyalist Union of 1886 survived until 1911; but it was never a mass organization, and it had to be supplemented by rival movements in 1892. It was deemed dispensable in a Unionist reorganization carried out in preparation for the third Home Rule Bill. None of the popular by-products of opposition to the Home Rule Bill of 1893—the Ulster Convention League, the Templetown Unionist Clubs—survived effectively beyond 1895.

David Fitzpatrick has described the Sinn Fein of 1917 as 'more a mood than an organisation'.[1] While there is a sense in which this epithet might be applied to Unionism, the organizational medium by which this creed was sustained *is* readily identifiable: the parliamentary Ulster Party and its constituency base. Local Unionist organization was naturally as vulnerable to popular apathy as the movements created in reaction to crisis; but at the very least such local organizations were revitalized at election times, and they sometimes survived with tenacity in the intervening years. However, the MPs of the movement generally represented its most conspicuous feature, and it was they, through public political activity—speeches, opening ceremonies—or through lobbying or exercising patronage (the 'oil' of the Irish Tory 'engine' in K. T. Hoppen's analogy), who effectively held Unionism together.[2] Their efficiency, or lack of it, reverberated more widely on support for Unionism; and their chairman, Edward Saunderson, was often referred to as the leader of the whole Unionist movement.

Thus, in so far as it is worthwhile applying labels, Unionism before 1911 may be described as a parliamentary movement. The British

[1] David Fitzpatrick, *Politics and Rural Life: Provincial Experience of War and Revolution, 1913–1921* (Dublin, 1977), 142.
[2] K. T. Hoppen, *Elections, Politics, and Society in Ireland, 1832–1885* (Oxford, 1984), 299.

House of Commons, and an alliance with a major British party, were as essential to the political calculations of Unionism as they were to contemporary, parliamentary Nationalism. This is not to deny that there was any form of extra-constitutional activity before 1911 (though on the other hand it is hard to agree with the suggestion that 'the actual extent of protestant military preparation at the time [1886] has been much underestimated'); nor is it to deny that there was serious constitutional activity after that date.[3] In late 1886 and 1892 there is some evidence suggesting provisional plans for military resistance; but these never came to fruition, and the evidence is in any case extremely ambiguous.[4] In fact it is reasonably clear that there was no organized and popular scheme for armed resistance in 1886 or in 1892. As James Loughlin has recognized, the militant activity of 1912 represented a new departure in Unionist politics, local organization and the real prospect of armed rebellion playing a larger role in the movement than the House of Commons and increasingly fruitless parliamentary debate.[5] Irish Unionist MPs served in the Asquith and Lloyd George coalition governments; moreover, it is a textbook commonplace that northern loyalists contributed extensively and, in the absence of Sinn Fein, effectively to key debates in the period 1918–20.[6] But this was a comparatively short parliamentary renaissance and, in any case, these MPs were now effectively harnessed to a variety of local organizations, the most significant of which was the Ulster Unionist Council, founded in 1905, and extended in 1918. The war also diverted numerous MPs from the Commons (including C. C. Craig, who served on the Western Front); one Ulster Unionist representative, Captain Arthur O'Neill, was killed in action on the Marne. And after partition Westminster came to occupy a relatively insignificant station in the loyalist landscape, for the Northern Ireland parliament now served as the constitutional stronghold of Unionism.

In brief, the period 1885 to 1911 represents a discrete phase of Unionist tactical and organizational development. And, since the chief focus of Unionism at that time was Britain and the British House

---

[3] A. T. Q. Stewart, *The Narrow Ground: Aspects of Ulster, 1609–1969* (London, 1977), 167.

[4] James Loughlin, *Gladstone, Home Rule and the Ulster Question, 1882–1893* (Dublin, 1986), 167–71.

[5] Loughlin, *Gladstone*, 292.

[6] Michael Laffan, *The Partition of Ireland, 1911–1925* (Dundalk, 1983), 62.

of Commons, the parliamentary Ulster Party emerges as a worthwhile means by which to approach the broader movement.

2. *Party, Class, and Nation*

Organized Unionism developed as a response to the peculiar demands of British and Irish politics in 1885–6, while the parliamentary party acted as precursor to a much more complex structure of resistance. But Unionism, defined simply as a commitment to the constitutional *status quo*, long predated the Home Rule crises, serving as an accepted element of the social and national consensus upon which most Irish Liberals and Tories fought out their policy battles. Unionism, therefore, represented a tacit link between disparate elements within Irish politics: it bound Church of Ireland and Catholic Tories in Dublin to Nonconformist Liberals in Ulster; it bound those with a northern regional identity to those who clung desperately to their Britishness, or to their Irishness. It united those who consciously felt that their general way of life or even, explicitly, their 'culture' would otherwise be threatened. Above all, Unionism was accepted by those who conceived their prosperity as being linked to the British economy. Thus Unionism was shared by northern and southern landowners, by Belfast industrialists and workers, by many urban professionals and farmers. Before 1886 Unionism was less a political creed than a flimsy and ill-defined expedient by which those who could not agree upon their national identity relegated questions of allegiance to financial and cultural survival: 'for the Protestant', Edward Moxon-Browne has argued in relation to contemporary Unionism, 'national identity is a pragmatic issue: it is based on perceptions of advantage'.[7] By the end of the nineteenth century 'Irish' Ireland confronted an amalgam of British nationalists, Ulstermen, and those who felt chiefly and sentimentally bound to Ireland, while fearing the personal, religious, and economic implications of such a connection. Founded upon a national evasion, Unionism in Ireland, as an organized political movement, could never really advance to any more positive creed without risking division. As will become clear, even when Irish Unionist MPs tacitly evolved

---

[7] Edward Moxon-Browne, *Nation, Class and Creed in Northern Ireland* (Aldershot, 1983), 8.

a wholly British-oriented political policy, organized Unionism in Ulster came close to collapse.

Thus, questions of social and economic relationships, and of regional and national identities, have been essential in interpreting the origins of organized Unionism. Peter Gibbon in his classic portrayal of the background to Unionist development has focused on the evolving economic hegemony of the Belfast Tory bourgeoisie, stressing the political implications of its strength.[8] The nature of industrialization in Ulster, export-oriented and concentrated in Belfast, created an economic and political foundation for the ascendancy of the Unionist creed. Industrialization accelerated the political strength of the Belfast manufacturing classes, and particularly of 'the mercantile faction', since an export economy must depend largely upon ease and quality of transportation. These classes, economically bound to Britain and the empire, held sway over a Protestant working class divided into a pliant labour aristocracy, centred on the shipyards, and more independent and vulnerable proletarian elements.

Reinterpreting the economic foundations of Unionist organization is not central to the ambitions of this study. However, the Gibbon hypothesis raises problems about the distribution of power within Unionism; and it conflicts with certain arguments fundamental to later portions of this book. Thus Gibbon sees the ascendancy of the Belfast bourgeoisie over landlordism as being a prelude to, or even a precondition of, Unionist organization. While there is no doubt that tensions between urban and landed Toryism are crucial in an understanding of early Unionism, the chronology of this conflict, and the circumstances of an urban bourgeois ascendancy, are rather more problematic. For example, as will become clear, the collapse of landed power within Unionism was not nearly so swift as Gibbon suggests. Nor was the Ulster Convention of 1892 the effective terminal point for this conflict, significant primarily as an aggressive display of Belfast strength. Henry Patterson has already convincingly challenged Gibbon's chronology of conflict; and it will be further argued here that the formation of the Ulster Unionist Council and the forms of resistance effected in 1912 were more significant

---

[8] Peter Gibbon, *The Origins of Ulster Unionism: The Formation of Popular Protestant Politics and Ideology in Nineteenth-Century Ireland* (Manchester, 1975), 143–6.

landmarks in the history of landlord–urban tension than either the 1892 Convention or any earlier event.[9]

Personal and economic bonds between an Irish and British landlord class were much more important in the evolving Unionist organization and in the maintenance of a parliamentary strategy than Gibbon has allowed. It has been suggested that the House of Commons was central to the strategy of Edwardian Unionism. That this was so depended largely on the survival of a strong landed corps among Unionist representatives—men who appear to have been better integrated within the House of Commons and more impatient of local responsibilities than their bourgeois counterparts. Indeed, the fact that the Unionist parliamentary leadership was held successively by two landlords and a landlord representative (Saunderson, Long, and Carson) suggests in itself the importance of this class—and condemns any unqualified argument for a precipitate landed demise.

The role of landlordism within Irish Unionism is linked to a second, significant, and problematic aspect of the movement: the distinctions between northern and southern Unionism and the evolution of an 'Ulster' political identity. Commentators as diverse as Gibbon and Buckland have recognized the political implications of the ties between northern and southern landowners; and from their observations it may be further contended that the bond between Ulster Unionism and the southern movement depended upon the relative strength of landlordism in the north. In other words, the overall strength of the Irish landlord class represented a significant unifying element within an all-Ireland Unionism. Thus as landlordism weakened its grip on Ulster Unionism, so the polarization of the two movements accelerated. This correlation is in fact implicit in Gibbon's work, since his questioning of landed influence in the development of northern Unionism is bound to a tacit dismissal of the general role of southern Unionism. Thus, for Gibbon, the events of 1892 demonstrated the subjugation both of landlordism and of southern Unionism by the Belfast mercantile élite.[10]

However, if one accepts the correlation between landlordism and 'Ulsterization', then the question of unity within Unionism hinges

    [9] Gibbon, *Ulster Unionism*, 130–3. Henry Patterson, 'Redefining the Debate on Unionism', *Political Studies*, xxiv (1976), 205–8.
    [10] Gibbon, *Ulster Unionism*, 131.

on the chronology of landed decline. D. C. Savage and others have emphasized the overlap between the forms and personnel of landlord organization in the 1870s and 1880s and those of early Unionism.[11] Landlord organizations, reflecting the coherence of the Irish landed élite, were generally Dublin-based, as indeed was Irish Toryism until the early 1880s. From this, and from the overall political strength of Irish landlordism in this period, one would expect a greater degree of assimilation between northern and southern Unionism than has hitherto been generally assumed for this period. And this is, in fact, reflected in the composition of the parliamentary 'Ulster' party, in financial bonds, and in the general organizational strength of the south in this period (as opposed to the comparatively weak and directionless north). As will become clear, 'southern' Unionism and 'southern' Unionists were a vital component of an all-Ireland movement: 'Ulster' Unionism only became a meaningful label between 1906 and 1912 with the creation of the Ulster Unionist Council and with greater northern flexibility on the principle of partition.[12]

The distinctions between southern and northern Unionism should therefore be understood primarily as questions of class rather than geography. If, however, the background to Unionist organization consists of northern and southern class co-operation and relative political assimilation, then this in turn bears on the related problem of Ulster identity (or nationality). Several theorists of nationalism, most recently John Breuilly, have recognized Unionism as 'to some extent a form of nationalism'.[13] Peter Gibbon has traced the emergence of a socially unified, territorially and culturally distinct 'Ulster' movement, which he, too, labels 'a form of nationalism'.[14] Other analysts of Northern Irish politics, including Edward Moxon-Browne and Michael Laffan, have shared this view: Laffan, for example, has suggested that northern Unionist politics after 1918 'conformed to a pattern of continental European nationalism'— though he has also identified a central paradox in noting that most loyalists would have been dismayed both by nationalistic parallels,

---

[11] D. C. Savage, 'The Irish Unionists: 1867–1886', *Eire-Ireland*, ii. 3 (1967), 96.

[12] See ch. 7.

[13] John Breuilly, *Nationalism and the State* (2nd edn., Manchester, 1985), 23; Anthony Alcock, *et al.*, *Ulster: An Ethnic Nation?* (Lurgan, 1986), *passim*.

[14] Gibbon, *Ulster Unionism*, 136.

and by the full implications of their own rhetoric and behaviour.[15] These and other comments invite speculation as to the political character of emergent Unionism: was Unionism a nationalist movement, reflecting in any sense the political aspirations of a distinct 'Ulster' nation? Were, then, Irish Unionists and Nationalists addressing each other in similar, if mutually incomprehensible, political terms?

There has never been any argument as to north-eastern distinctiveness, judged by religion, cultural, and political pursuits, or by language—whether the Ulster dialect of the Irish language, or the Ulster dialect of the English language. But, while there is agreement on the existence of regional distinctions, the significance of these, and in particular their political implications, have been areas of keener dispute. Thus both Gibbon and Loughlin, two of the most incisive contributors to this debate, have identified the development of a specific 'Ulster' identity, and Loughlin has commented on the academic origins of perceived Ulster racial distinctiveness.[16] However, while Gibbon places 'the Ulsterman' against a broader political and cultural profile, Loughlin sees the articulation of a north-eastern identity as being inseparable from British nationality, and a British political context. He rejects both the unequivocal assertions of Gibbon, and even the more circumspect hypothesis put forward by David Miller, who has posited a highly limited, contractual relationship between loyalism and the United Kingdom nation (while stopping short of arguing for the existence of an Ulster nationalism in the period 1885–1920).[17] Moreover, using the evidence of thirty speeches delivered by prominent loyalists in 1886, Loughlin argues that loyalism in general looked for a territorial identity beyond Ulster to the United Kingdom and to the Empire.

But Loughlin's assertions invite, in turn, a variety of counter-arguments. There are problems with his evidence.[18] First, the size of his sample precludes dogmatic generalization about complex issues of identity. Second, the limited timespan covered by Loughlin's

[15] Laffan, *Partition of Ireland*, 68; Moxon-Browne, *Nation, Class and Creed*, 1–15.

[16] Gibbon, *Ulster Unionism*, 136; Loughlin, *Gladstone*, 159–61.

[17] David W. Miller, *Queen's Rebels: Ulster Loyalism in Historical Perspective* (Dublin, 1978), *passim*, and esp. 43–121; Loughlin, *Gladstone*, 153–61.

[18] See e.g. the review article by Conor Cruise O'Brien in the *Sunday Times*, 11 Jan. 1987.

evidence suggests difficulties. Third, the particular timespan of his evidence—January to June 1886—is problematic. Ulster Unionist rhetoric at this time must surely be seen in context—in the context of British jingoism after Khartoum and in the midst of colonial wars in Burma and Egypt. Loughlin needs to demonstrate that loyalists were committed to an unpragmatic expression of principle at this time—since it may otherwise be contended that their speeches merely reflect ephemeral political needs. After all, it is prima facie likely that Ulster Unionists were tailoring their political statements to the condemnation of a specific Home Rule proposal within specific political conditions, rather than to the isolated expression of a coherent identity, or of a fundamental creed. Even leading Nationalists, like Redmond, were not above looking pragmatically to Empire and imperial sanction, or sculpting their demands according to imperial precedent. Yet this was not inconsistent with an Irish Nationalist identity.

Furthermore, the evidence of Irish Unionist contribution to debate taken over a longer period suggests that they were largely uninterested in British policy issues, and comparatively uninterested in imperial matters. Like Irish Nationalists, they devoted themselves to questions of Irish and local—Ulster—politics; like Irish Nationalists they were prepared to reject government policy if this conflicted with their own perceived interests.[19] The problems of northern imperial attitudes are thus more complex than has been suggested; and a fuller discussion is reserved for chapter 3. Here, however, it may be noted that there appears to be substance for the views of R. J. Lawrence, who has argued that 'the only aspect of [Ulster Unionist] policy after, say 1886, that could be called "imperialist" was their determination to maintain the political unity of the United Kingdom'.[20]

On the other hand, Loughlin is surely right in stressing the qualified and limited nature of United Kingdom nationality. He refers tellingly to the nationality embraced by Scotland, which (as he states) was consistent with distinctive local institutions. And he suggests further that Ulster Unionists, having less claim to separate national institutions, were no less bound to a United Kingdom nationalism:

---

[19] See ch. 4.
[20] R. J. Lawrence, *The Government of Northern Ireland: Public Finance and Public Services 1921–1964* (Oxford, 1965), 6.

'in this context the insistence of some Ulster Unionists that there was
a limit to their loyalty to the Westminster parliament could hardly
be described as aberrant behaviour'.[21]

But, while Loughlin is acutely aware of problems of definition,
these arguments take no account of distinctions between nation,
nationalism, and nationality.[22]Thus while he appears to accept that
a Scots 'nation' was compatible with United Kingdom nationality,
he does not explore the possibility that an Ulster 'nation'—a cohesive,
Protestant and particularist community in the north-east of Ireland—
might equally have embraced United Kingdom nationality. Instead,
Loughlin's argument is directed towards fixing north-eastern Irish
particularism within the general context of British regionalism and
British nationalism; but his definition of the latter is so flaccid that
it might conceivably include those Nationalists in Ireland who
professed themselves content with Gladstonian Home Rule. Thus,
partly through problems of nomenclature, Loughlin cannot prove
his case; and, through his choice of analogies, it is ultimately unclear
whether he sees Ulster loyalism as a purely regional identity within
a broader nationalism (like Yorkshiremen and English Nationalism),
or as a distinct nation bound to a broader constitutional unit
(Scotsmen and the United Kingdom).

One further aspect of this argument demands treatment. Loughlin
dates notions of an Ulster racial distinctiveness to the early 1850s;
but he binds this evidence to his central hypothesis by placing it
amidst a general Victorian preoccupation with British identity.[23]
But this is surely to ignore the extent to which notions of Anglo-
Saxon racial superiority are compatible with anti-British feeling, and
with alternative nationalisms (such as in the Populist movement of
late-nineteenth-century America). Loughlin's argument effectively
demonstrates merely that interests in racial identity were emerging
contemporaneously; and to place Nationalist Irish racial notions (the
features of the Gael) within a British context is as meaningful as the
emergence of an 'Ulsterman' with attendant Anglo-Saxon attributes
and Smilesian business virtues.

A crucial omission in several dissections of northern loyalist
identity, including those of Gibbon and Loughlin, relates to the
contribution of southern Unionism. It has been suggested that
Unionist expressions of allegiance in 1886 ought to be seen in the

---

[21] Loughlin, *Gladstone*, 159.   [22] Ibid. 153.   [23] Ibid. 160–1.

context of a need to formulate a broadly marketable opposition to the Home Rule Bill. The logic of Unionist single-mindedness in 1886 demanded that Ulster Unionism should be harnessed to the numerically insignificant, but politically and financially considerable southern movement. Southern Unionism possessed powerful organizational resources, it commanded influence within northern Unionism, as has been suggested; and it had a disproportionately great parliamentary and ministerial significance. Apart from these tangible attractions, southern Unionism offered the opportunity for sentimental capital—the opportunity to exploit images of a genteel and beleaguered loyalism threatened by a dark and menacing National movement. Thus, from the northern perspective, political pragmatism dictated that Gibbon's 'Ulsterman' be temporarily subsumed within a pan-Irish movement. Proclaiming an Ulster particularist identity implied the sacrifice, and risked the alienation of southern Unionists. Moreover, Irish loyalist division threatened the sanction of its British Unionist constituency. The political mobilization of the 'Ulsterman' was therefore effectively postponed until a future crisis.

The problematic relationship between Ulster Unionism and an Ulster regional identity may be considered within a further area of enquiry: whether or not an Ulster nation may be said to have existed by 1886. Anthony Smith has defined the nation as:

a large, vertically integrated and territorially mobile group featuring common citizenship rights and collective sentiments, together with one or more common characteristic(s) which differentiate its members from those of similar groups with whom they stand in relations of alliance or conflict.[24]

The later elements of this definition—common citizenship rights, collective sentiments, and common characteristics—present no difficulty of interpretation, though Smith's subsequent commentary may be mentioned to clarify the earlier part of the definition. 'Large' he defines flexibly, while suggesting obliquely that communities with membership of more than 500,000 qualify for consideration as 'nations' within the rest of the definition.[25] By 'vertically integrated'

---

[24] Anthony D. Smith, *Theories of Nationalism* (2nd edn., London 1983), 175. Alternative definitions occasionally refer to the idea of a common government—'either as a past memory, present reality or future aspiration': Moxon-Browne, *Nation, Class and Creed*, 1. This is not always an essential element of the definition, however.
[25] Smith, *Theories*, 188.

I understand vertical social and economic bonding. Smith's reference to 'territorial mobility' is evidently designed to preclude diaspora groups from consideration since these, 'lacking a territory, and often subject to residential restrictions cannot qualify for the status of nationhood'.[26]

In an earlier definition offered by Karl Deutsch, and exploited by David Miller in his *Queen's Rebels*, 'familiarity' and 'trust' within a community are held to be significant prerequisites for the determination of nationhood. Miller interprets this definition as 'the aspect of nationality which musters diffuse support for a democratic state . . . one assumes that even if one disagrees strongly with the government of the day it will not invade one's basic rights for it is composed of people "like" oneself'.[27] This emphasis is roughly analogous to Anthony Smith's reference to 'collective sentiment'.

Late-nineteenth-century Ulster loyalism would appear to conform to most of these criteria for nationhood (Smith calls for conformity with all the elements of the definition). The community was large in Smith's calculation; and, as Gibbon has argued, it was comparatively well integrated in terms of potential social and economic cleavage. It possessed a distinctive, Protestant-based culture: while membership of the Orange Order, though developing in the 1880s, still constituted only a fraction of the adult male loyalist population, Orange festivals, Orange songs and cultural objects— jugs, plates, tokens, and badges with the portrait of William III— affected a much wider audience. The Order may have been essentially reactionary in origins; but, with the passage of time, heroes were accumulated, a martyrology devised, and organizational structures and trappings developed and diversified. Like the evolution of certain aspects of Scottishness, the growth of Orangeism represented the speedy invention of tradition; even so, and despite its vital bond with anti-Catholicism, the appeal and significance of the Order ultimately transcended its origins, its specific membership, and questions of religious definition.[28]

[26] Smith, *Theories*, 175.

[27] Miller, *Queen's Rebels*, 66, Karl Deutsch, *Nationalism and Social Communication: An Enquiry into the Foundations of Nationality* (2nd edn., Cambridge, Mass., 1966).

[28] Hugh Trevor-Roper, 'The Invention of Tradition: The Highland Tradition of Scotland', in E. J. Hobsbawm and T. Ranger (edd.), *The Invention of Tradition* (Cambridge, 1983), 15–41.

The issue of citizenship rights has attracted greater scholarly attention—and is central both to the work of David Miller, and to the critique of James Loughlin. Miller has argued that, since nationality is partly a matter of trust and shared citizenship, then the Ulster Protestant's British nationality was significantly impaired by the actions of British government in Ireland. But Miller distils the broad problem of citizenship rights and community trust into one narrow area of investigation: 'for the purposes of this analysis the crucial right of the citizen was the right of free expression throughout his state's territory'.[29] Since British administrations restricted both Protestant and Catholic religious and political demonstrations, all Irishmen, in Miller's hypothesis, possessed a second-class—and therefore unviable—British citizenship. But by harnessing his argument to this one legislative theme, Miller significantly weakened his case. For Loughlin has had no difficulty in pointing to similar restrictions on contemporary English political and religious movements—restrictions which do not appear to have compromised British national feelings or citizenship. Given that the rights of the nineteenth-century British citizen were so generally circumscribed, Loughlin can persuasively question the extent to which such infringements should alone have produced a loyalist distrust for British nationality.[30]

But the problems with Miller's choice of case-study do not disprove his primary contention. Perceived variations in the quality of British citizenship extended far beyond the admittedly important issue of marching rights. Thus, it was the breadth and recurrence of loyalist grievance which represented a more devastating blight on British citizenship and national feeling in Ulster than the problems associated with any one issue. Miller and others have identified 'the [British] state's drift towards neutrality between the religions' in Ireland—a movement perceptible, for example, in the development of constructive Unionism between 1885 and 1905.[31] Such neutrality antagonized loyalists who expected the principle of partisanship, rather than pragmatic government tailored towards Irish exigency. Moreover, the Home Rule debates always contained the perceived threat that the British electorate or their representatives would not

[29] Miller, *Queen's Rebels*, 68.
[30] Loughlin, *Gladstone*, 154 ff.
[31] Miller, *Queen's Rebels*, 67–8; Andrew Gailey, 'The Unionist Government's Policy Towards Ireland, 1895–1905', Ph.D. thesis (Cambridge, 1983).

merely deprive loyalists of their residual rights as British citizens, but effectively support their political, religious, and cultural annihilation. Thus, after 1886 loyalists looked at Liberal election victories as evidence of general British unreliability; and indeed their organizational initiatives in 1885–6, 1892, 1905, and 1910–11 may be seen as a measure of their lack of trust in the British nation.

Loyalists' occasional and self-proclaimed 'Britishness' reflected both political necessity and their unhappiness with the government's definition of their citizenship. A British identity coexisted with a sense of Irishness and—a particular feature of this period—a developing Ulster identity. As has been argued, the clarity with which this identity was articulated had much to do with the overall significance of southern Unionism. Thus literature celebrating 'Ulster' and the ('honest') 'Ulsterman' only flourished after the creation of a popular northern organization in 1905, and with the effective acceptance of partition in 1912 (in the form of the Agar–Robartes amendment to the third Home Rule Bill). The domination of the North in the campaign against this measure contrasted with the comparative lack of territorial differentiation which had characterized the campaigns of 1886 and 1892–3. Thus, the Ulster Unionist Convention, which is frequently cited as evidence for the uniqueness of northern activity was in fact merely the sister meeting to a similar convention for Leinster, Munster, and Connacht, also held in June 1892 and attended by northern representatives.[32] Only after 1912 was the plausible fiction of an all-Ireland Unionism dropped, and consequently—or at any rate contemporaneously—an Ulster political and literary culture received a stimulus. Unionist apologists and others emphasized a plantation tradition, and the apparently peculiar features both of Ulster life and of Ulstermen. Novelists like St John Ervine and George Birmingham, northerners then unsympathetic to Ulster Unionism, distinguished an Ulster type in their work. Literary preoccupation with Belfast and the Belfast man effectively emerges at this time, a theme developing in works like Birmingham's *Red Hand of Ulster* (1912), through Ervine's *Mrs. Martin's Man* (1914), to Hugh Shearman's *A Bomb and a Girl* and *The Bishop's Confession* (1943). An Ulster history was discovered and elucidated in anti-

---

[32] Gibbon, *Ulster Unionism*, 131. See also *Unionist Convention for the Provinces of Leinster, Munster and Connaught (June 1892): Report of the Proceedings, Lists of Committees, Delegates, etc.* (Dublin, 1892).

Home Rule tracts like Peter Kerr-Smiley's *The Peril of Home Rule* (1911) and Lord Ernest Hamilton's *The Soul of Ulster* (1917); this was developed in Ramsay Colles's four volume *History of Ulster* (1919–20) and, later, by Cyril Falls in his *The Birth of Ulster* (1936). Northern Ireland was given a contemporary historical defence in McNeill's *Ulster's Stand for Union* (1922).[33]

All this is not to suggest that perceptions of an Ulster identity did not exist in the early 1880s—since these long predated the Home Rule controversy.[34] Rather the political, literary, and general development of this identity was bound to the evolution of the Home Rule debate, and particularly to the debate on the third Home Rule Bill. Before 1886 an Ulster Unionist possessed a local identity, but this coalesced with a measure of ambiguity concerning his nationality. Many loyalists defined themselves as simultaneously Irish and British in the same way that a Scotsman might have defined himself as Scots and British. But, in practice, as we have seen, their claim to British nationality suffered through distrust, and through their own exaggerated demands on British citizenship. Thus, while in the early 1880s an Ulster 'nation' (in textbook definition) may have been evolving, this did not immediately produce an Ulster nationalism. Even though Ulster Unionists and Irish Nationalists were certainly bound by a peculiarly productive tension, exchanging organizational forms and political rhetoric, loyalism was ultimately tailored to a negative end, the defeat of Home Rule, rather than to the positive expression of an identity.

The choice of national identity within Unionism may, again, have been bound less to circumstances of geographical location than to class. For much of the period covered by this book Unionism was governed by economic élites, whose wealth was originally based on land, but who ultimately gave way to business and professional interests. It will become clear that these latter groups proved willing to repudiate a parliamentary policy, and indeed to repudiate Britain. Miller has commented that 'for a few—a very few—members of a Protestant élite, the United Kingdom indeed became the "nation"'; and it may be possible to equate these 'very few' with the dominant landed elements amidst the leadership of parliamentary Unionism.[35]

[33] Miller, *Queen's Rebels*, 108–21.
[34] See e.g. A. T. Q. Stewart, *The Ulster Crisis* (London, 1967), 26–33.
[35] Miller, *Queen's Rebels*, 80.

Despite rabble-rousing origins, and despite early contractarian formulations of nationality, Edward Saunderson and his like, were for the greater part of their careers constitutional West Britons— men who were more at home in the Carlton club or in the House of Commons, than with the idiosyncrasies and brashness of Belfast Unionism.[36] They pursued largely British political careers, binding Unionism to parliament and to the English campaign trail. Saunderson was self-consciously Irish (as indeed was the landlord representative, Carson); but this identity had probably less to do with self-assessment than with the expectations of British politicians.[37] Contrasting with this landed élite was a popular Unionism, more frankly Anglophobic, and irritated by their representatives' collusion with an unsatisfactory British administration in Ireland.[38] While their leadership appears to have been well-integrated within the United Kingdom governing classes (certainly much better integrated than has been hitherto assumed), most northern Unionists lacked both the desire for, and the means to achieve Anglicization; and this in turn heightened their sense of their own uniqueness, while damaging any bond with British citizenship and British nationality. Richard Rose and Edward Moxon-Browne have demonstrated a similar correlation between economic privilege and Britishness for a more recent period of Unionist development: 'upper class Protestants are more likely to accept a British national identity; and the lower socio-economic groups are more attached to an Ulster allegiance'. Of the Protestants who responded to a survey carried out in 1968, some 32 per cent claimed an 'Ulster' identity, mostly in low status occupational categories.[39]

Early Unionism may have rested partly on an Ulster nation, but it offered no clear expression of national allegiance. The movement was not at this time an Ulster nationalism. Class considerations as well as the relative significance of southern Unionism emerge as

[36] See my *Edward Saunderson and the Evolution of Ulster Unionism, 1865–1906* (Belfast forthcoming).

[37] 'A sort of Sir Lucius O'Trigger' was the epitaph on Saunderson offered by the Liberal *Westminster Gazette* on 4 Mar. 1909. For a view of Carson's self-conscious Irishness see St John Ervine, *Sir Edward Carson and the Ulster Movement* (Dublin and London, 1915), 47.

[38] Henry Patterson, *Class Conflict and Sectarianism: The Protestant Working Class and the Belfast Labour Movement, 1868–1920* (Belfast, 1980), 45.

[39] Moxon-Browne, *Nation, Class and Creed*, 6–7. Moxon-Browne uses figures from Richard Rose, *Governing Without Consensus* (London, 1971), 485.

relevant to any consideration of Irish Unionist identity. But the abiding impression is one of ambiguity. For, if there were two, or even three nations in late-nineteenth-century Ireland, it would appear that each of these (and every combination) was represented within loyalism.

3. Unionist Roots

If Unionism was more than the political expression of a regional identity, and yet not quite a nationalism, then its structural origins were equally unfocused. Indeed, the vitality and longevity of Unionism lay in the strength and complexity of its roots. The movement drew on a long heritage of Irish Protestant organization, spanning the entire island, and bridging conventional political parties. Many of its founding fathers had a prolonged grounding in the politics of crisis and reaction, whether as embattled landlords, or as embattled champions of the Church of Ireland. Irish Toryism, both populist and landed, was a well-established and crucial progenitor of Unionism, bequeathing personnel, political structures, and social and sectarian attitudes. Thus there was essentially nothing new about the movement which emerged in the 1880s. Organized Unionism was merely the rearrangement of traditional political concerns within an old but now overt constitutional creed.[40]

The quiet acceptance of the Irish Free State by southern Unionists, and their developing flexibility after 1912 has perhaps led to an exaggeration of the qualitative distinctions between northern and southern Unionism.[41] In fact, though the disproportionately propertied nature of southern Unionism implied a greater moderation of tone, Irish Unionism as a whole drew on an Orange and militant tradition: as K. T. Hoppen has recognized, 'the first great centre of organised working class Protestantism was Dublin, not Belfast'.[42] Unionism emerged from Toryism; and Irish Toryism, whether in

---

[40] Hoppen, *Elections*, 285.

[41] This has probably been influenced by Patrick Buckland's important research on northern and southern Unionism, which was published in two separate volumes— one for the north (*Irish Unionism, ii. Ulster Unionism and the Origins of Northern Ireland* (Dublin, 1973)) and one for the south (*Irish Unionism, i. The Anglo-Irish and the New Ireland* (Dublin, 1972)).

[42] Hoppen, *Elections*, 312.

the north or south of the island, sustained vital bonds with evangelical Protestantism. Thus one of the earliest organs of the party was the Irish Protestant Conservative Society of 1831—an unequivocal titular expression of its perceived constituency. Though this sectarian identity was dropped in 1836, when a new label, the Irish Metropolitan Conservative Society, was adopted, this did not reflect any fundamental shift in the organization's support or political tone. The Central Conservative Society of 1853 ('perhaps the single most important development in the history of the party's electoral and political machinery') was significantly patronized by leading Orangemen, like the Grand Master of the Order, Lord Enniskillen.[43] Moreover, the first attempts at a separate Ulster Tory Organization, like the Ulster Constitutional Union of 1880, received similar Orange sanction. And while, as Peter Gibbon has argued, the later significance of the Orange Order as an institution was comparatively slight, at any rate until 1912, individual Orangemen and fiery Protestantism remained influential elements within organized Unionism.[44]

Thus, evangelical Protestant ministers were active agents both of Edwardian Unionism and of mid-Victorian populist Toryism. The forebears of the Revd R. R. Kane, the politico-spiritual director of late-nineteenth-century Belfast Unionism, were Henry Cooke and, for the southern party, the celebrated, if idiosyncratic, Revd T. D. Gregg, who preached no-popery and one-nation Toryism to mid-Victorian Dublin. For each of these men, political and religious creeds coalesced. Each represented a significant level on popular Tory opinion, without being tools of leadership. Each upheld the Protestant ideology which reconciled social and economic tensions within Toryism and Unionism. Their message was central, therefore, to the viability of the party which they embraced.[45]

The debate over Church of Ireland establishment in 1868–9 gave point to an angrily defensive Toryism, and resulted in the provocation of measures and personalities which foreshadowed organized Unionism. Thus, just as Irish and Ulster Protestants formed separate, if interconnected Unionist bodies in 1885–6, so Tory defenders of the Church of Ireland reacted to the threat of disestablishment with a Central Protestant Defence Association and an Ulster Protestant

---

[43] Hoppen, *Elections*, 280–1, 284, 286.
[44] Gibbon, *Ulster Unionism*, 9, 131.   [45] Hoppen, *Elections*, 289, 309–16.

Defence Association. In May and August of 1868 meetings were held at St James's Hall and the Crystal Palace, London, meetings promoted by prominent Tories like Lords Erne and Crichton, and Lord Claud Hamilton. As D. C. Savage has pointed out, these men were also among the progenitors of organized Unionism; and both the general forms of their resistance and their specific venues were inherited by Unionist demonstrators in 1886.[46]

Appeals to Protestantism were also a feature of northern opposition to the Land and National Leagues between 1880 and 1885. Yet, reiterating a politico-religious orthodoxy was by itself an insufficient spur to action, since other influences—economic pressures, the nature of a given threat—still commanded Protestant opinion. For example, agricultural depression in the 1870s, and the crop failure of 1879 reactivated an independent tenant-right tradition within Ulster; and in the west of the province, where conditions were particularly bad, Protestant farmers joined the Land League in considerable numbers. Furthermore, the Orange Order's response to the spread of the League—a programme of counter-demonstrations beginning in November 1880—appears to have been comparatively unsuccessful. What ultimately disarmed farmer opinion was rather the Land Act of 1881, and the narrowing constitutional ambitions of Land League activists.[47]

On the other hand, economic well-being was a significant, but not the only influence on northern political orientation. The Protestant Land Leaguers of western Ulster were no less Unionist for being immune to Orange tribalism. Furthermore, landlord political activity does not appear to have been wholly contingent on economic circumstances. The landed role in organized Unionism was considerable, but this was by no means a simple response to economic threats from the League or from Gladstone. Apart from the momentary aberration of support for the Home Government Association, the landlord class of nineteenth-century Ireland was predominantly and statically Unionist. Thus the response to the Home Rule Bill need not be judged solely in the context of the preceding land agitation. And the overlap between propertied activists and the progenitors of Unionism reflects not so much the

[46] Savage, 'Irish Unionists', 90.
[47] Paul Bew and Frank Wright, 'The Agrarian Opposition in Ulster Politics, 1848–1887', in S. Clark and J. S. Donnelly (edd.), *Irish Peasants; Violence and Political Unrest 1780–1914* (Manchester, 1983), 213–27.

evolution of landlord strategy as more general continuities within the Irish conservative leadership. While vocal landowners like the Viscount Crichton or Arthur Smith-Barry, graduated naturally into the Unionist hierarchy, an ultimately more influential squire, Edward Saunderson, offered a supine response to the growth of the Land League, and only renewed his public political activity after the Phoenix Park murders.[48] In fact, Saunderson's early career as a Unionist was built upon a systematically ambiguous response to farmer demands, complemented by a strong stand on law and order. His popular credibility probably hinged upon these evasions, for in later life, when Saunderson had evolved into a more unequivocal landlord proponent, his political influence was significantly impaired.[49]

If the Orange campaign of 1880 had developed against an unpromising background, then the circumstances of a later reaction, in 1883, were altogether different. The more explicit ambitions of the new National League, allied to the disarming effects of Phoenix Park and of the Gladstone Land Act, meant that Orange Toryism was confronting a largely altered political opponent within a largely altered political context. Thus, in June 1883, when Tim Healy seized one of the County Monaghan seats for Home Rule, and launched his 'Invasion of Ulster', Toryism and Orangeism were able to draw on a much broader section of Unionist opinion than hitherto. Indeed, Orange leaders like Saunderson specifically appealed to a cross-party, and even—less ingenuously—to a cross-sectarian, constituency, advocating a movement founded on loyalty, and cemented by class arbitration. Their rhetoric recognized an embattled Ulster, identifiable against the uniform anarchy and political eccentricity of the three southern provinces. Analogies were drawn with 1689: Derry and Enniskillen stood once again besieged, their morale sustained only by the precedent of an earlier victory. Through loyalism, it was said, Ulster could again rescue Ireland, just as she had once provided a springboard for the forces of William III.[50]

Thus the reaction to Healy provoked the characterization of a distinctive Ulster political role; and though in 1883 this was linked to a wholly Irish context, it looked forward to the concerns and

---

[48] Reginald Lucas, *Colonel Saunderson, M.P.: A Memoir* (London, 1908), 65–6.
[49] See my *Edward Saunderson*, ch. 8.2.
[50] See Edward Saunderson, *Two Irelands: Loyalty versus Treason* (London and Dublin, 1884), 29.

expressions of Ulster Unionism. But the campaign of 1883 supplied more than rhetoric, for it inspired both new leaders and an ostensibly non-partisan character. The Rosslea Incident of October 1883 created a loyalist martyr in the unlikely frame of the fifth Lord Rossmore; more important, it brought to public attention one of Rossmore's lieutenants, Edward Saunderson.[51] When, through the Reform and Redistribution measures of 1884–5, the spectre of Tory treachery intermingled with the threat of Home Rule ascendancy, Saunderson and the other loyalists of 1883 would pursue the goals of that year with greater urgency and more obvious effect. Thus, Unionist mobilization in 1885–6 built upon earlier political conditions and rhetoric, exploiting a mood among northern Protestants which was no less febrile for being so comparatively recent in origin.

The shape of organized Unionism was determined by the nature of its Tory antecedents, by campaigns for the Church of Ireland, and by the concerns of landlordism. It exploited a developing north-eastern identity. But, one of the fundamental implications of this heritage was that Unionism was at least partly reactionary, in the neutral sense that it developed by responding to Nationalist (or British) challenge. Unionist organizations were tailored to, and countered those of the Irish opposition. Political initiatives often originated in the identification of external threat. Unionist missionaries travelled to Britain, and to North America, following in the footsteps of their Nationalist adversaries. Racial and sectarian slurs were exchanged; accusations of criminality were deployed. Given this dependence, and given a more fundamental need to sustain political debate, one might expect a loyalist reaction within every forum of Nationalist activity. Thus, if the diversity of popular Nationalism was focused and articulated within a parliamentary organization, then one would expect a collateral Ulster parliamentary party and policy. This expectation is examined in the remaining chapters of this book.

[51] See my *Edward Saunderson*, ch. 2.

2

Parliamentary Origins, 1884–1886

The Parnellite Party owe whatever success they have secured in no little measure to their united action in Parliament, and loyalty to their leader, and if we are not to be swallowed up by that party before long, it behoves us to take a leaf out of their book.

Revd J. J. Browne, Rector of Toome, (1886)

The original and determining personal factor in Lord Salisbury's opposition to Home Rule was his overmastering sense of an honourable national obligation towards the minorities in Ireland—landholding, Protestant and loyalist—who depended on English protection. Considerations of imperial security or of Ireland's economic solvency came later.

Gwendolen Cecil, *Life of Robert, Marquess of Salisbury* (1931)[1]

1. *Introduction*

Irish loyalism owed much to Parnell—for Home Rule catapulted its representatives and concerns from provincial insignificance to a central role in the Conservative world-view. Before 1885 loyalism lacked parliamentary cohesion and a credible political cause; Parnell inspired both. Here the effects of this inspiration are reinterpreted: the emergence of Irish Unionist organization is charted, and a revised account is offered of the standing and effectiveness of the first Ulster parliamentary party.

Between 1867 and 1885 Irish Conservative MPs were little more independent than any other group of Tories possessing a geographically distinct base. Although local party organization lurked

---

[1] *BNL*, 6 Jan. 1886. Lady Gwendolen Cecil, *Life of Robert, Third Marquess of Salisbury* (4 vols; London, 1921–32), iii. 150–1.

outside British control, there was no permanent Irish caucus, and consequently no exceptional influence over the British leadership. Moreover, while there were occasional efforts to co-ordinate the local movement with action in the House of Commons, Irish Tories lacked any distinct and lasting parliamentary organization.[2] Like many of their British colleagues, there were landed gentlemen; like many British Tories, they supported their front bench regularly but not systematically. Statically conservative and fervently Protestant, Irish Tories baulked at the leadership of a Peel (but, then, so ultimately did many of their British co-partisans); and, in any case, they eventually found a more sympathetic spirit in the shape of the fourteenth Earl of Derby. There were other occasional independent gestures (for example, their support for the Land Act of 1881) but, at a time when party discipline was not yet absolute, such truculence was scarcely exceptional.[3] What is more, they were generally well represented among the national leaders of the Party—Edward Gibson and Earl Cairns both enjoyed promotion at the hands of Disraeli.

But after 1886, with Home Rule, the nature and organization of Irish loyalist representation changed. Wild Orangemen, who looked forward to ferociously resisting Gladstone, came to be cultivated by mild-mannered British Tories; Irish squires, with no aspirations to political subtlety, found themselves in conclave with cabinet ministers. In private some British Tory leaders still trivialized loyalist politicking, but many remained sensitive to the Irishmen's capacity for making trouble. Indeed, Parnell had demonstrated the efficacy of parliamentary truculence—and loyalist Members, as in so much else, were quick to imitate his example. Defying their British command, they seized the structures of political independence in 1885-6.

However, Irish loyalists still skulk at the sidelines of research into late-nineteenth-century parliamentary politics. In part this stems from the frequency with which a stereotype of Irish, and especially Ulster, Toryism is accepted—a stereotype, which, though sometimes founded in reality, blurs divisions within the movement, and

[2] K. T. Hoppen, *Elections, Politics, and Society in Ireland, 1832-1885* (Oxford, 1984), 284-5.

[3] B. M. Walker, 'Pride, Prejudice and Politics: Society and Elections in Ulster, 1868-1886' (unpublished draft), 260-1. A. B. Cooke, 'A Conservative Party Leader in Ulster: Sir Stafford Northcote's Diary of a Visit to the Province, October 1883', *Proceedings of the Royal Irish Academy*, lxxv, sect. c.4 (Sept. 1975), 67-8.

consequently misrepresents the complexity of British and Irish party relations.[4] Such an image is exploited in a number of works, but an outline of its main features may be distilled from one of the most important studies of late Victorian high politics, A. B. Cooke and John Vincent's *The Governing Passion* (1974). This presents a uniform image of loyalist behaviour, Ulster Tories never graduating beyond 'rabid speeches', delivered under the leadership of an 'Orange bigot'. They emerge as the dupes of Randolph Churchill, briefly exploited by him through his Belfast visit, and thereafter deserted.[5] These unlovely politicians were evidently more likely to attract disparagement and, in the most recent and compelling accounts of the period, they stand systematically condemned and snubbed by the Tory leadership.[6]

Certain features of this image are undoubtedly true to life, reflecting both the attitudes of some Tories and the behaviour of some of their Irish clients. But whether loyalists were generally 'a cross the English party had to bear' is harder to prove.[7] Moreover, the use of a stereotype is often related to an assumption that loyalists could not have been a considerable influence on government policy—because they were not a credible political force. But this circular argument is not beyond question. These problems of credibility and influence, with other aspects of the orthodox perspective on loyalist activity in 1885–6, are explored in the remaining sections of this chapter.

Here it is suggested that Irish Tories were not wholly beyond the political pale in 1885–6, and were therefore a credible parliamentary force when, in January 1886, Conservative leaders had to decide on a long-term policy for Ireland. In pursuing Irish loyalist behaviour, the evolution of an independent Irish Unionist parliamentary party is traced; an analysis is offered, too, of the ways in which local

---

[4] Clare O'Halloran, *Partition and the Limits of Irish Nationalism: An Ideology under Stress* (Dublin, 1987), 29–56. James Loughlin also considers the Nationalist use of an 'Orange' loyalist stereotype: Loughlin, *Gladstone, Home Rule and the Ulster Question, 1882–1893* (Dublin, 1986).

[5] A. B. Cooke and John Vincent, *The Governing Passion: Cabinet Government and Party Politics in Britain 1885–1886* (Brighton, 1974), 114, 160.

[6] R. F. Foster, *Lord Randolph Churchill: A Political Life* (Oxford, 1981), 256–8. R. F. Foster, 'To the Northern Station: Lord Randolph Churchill and the Prelude to the Orange Card', in F. S. L. Lyons and R. A. J. Hawkins (edd.), *Ireland under the Union: Varieties of Tension* (Oxford, 1980), 277–80.

[7] Cooke and Vincent, *Governing Passion*, 160.

political movements were influenced by the nature of their MPs' communication with British party leaders. The chapter offers, therefore, an alternative assessment of the relationship between Irish back-bench and British front-bench, and of the implications for loyalist activity in the House of Commons and Ireland.

2. *Irish and British Tories, 1884-1885*

Irish Conservatives first demonstrated their capacity for independent parliamentary initiative not, as suggested by D. C. Savage, through direct reaction against Home Rule, or against Conservative dalliance with Parnell, but in uniting against the Arlington Street compact on franchise reform and redistribution.[8] Through this agreement Gladstone and Salisbury both effectively sacrificed their immediate party interests in Ireland.[9] For his part, Salisbury was unwilling to press Irish Tory claims because these conflicted with his personal interests, and with those of the English party. Thus, though extending the householder and lodger franchise to county constituencies was likely to weaken Irish Conservatism (by effectively increasing the proportion of Catholic electors), Salisbury accepted the reform because it did not threaten English constituency support in the same way; and in any case there were tactical difficulties in opposing a principle which had already been conceded once by a Conservative government (in 1867). Furthermore, from a personal perspective, Salisbury had no interest in defending Irish Conservative claims. He could long recall with bitterness Irish Tory support for Gladstone's Land Act of 1881.[10] And he had suffered a personal slight over the Arrears Bill of 1882—when Irish peers had withdrawn support from his wrecking amendments, thereby leaving him isolated and humiliated.[11] But, more important, Salisbury's interest in Irish Toryism was influenced by its association with his party rival, Sir Stafford Northcote.

---

[8] B. M. Walker, 'Parliamentary Representation in Ulster, 1868-1886', Ph.D. thesis (Dublin, 1976), 525. D. C. Savage, 'The Origins of the Ulster Unionist Party, 1885-1886', *Irish Historical Studies*, xii. 47 (Mar. 1961), 191.

[9] Andrew Jones, *The Politics of Reform, 1884* (Cambridge, 1972), 25, 81-2.

[10] Salisbury to Churchill, 16 Nov. 1885, quoted in Cooke and Vincent, *Governing Passion*, 160.

[11] Jones, *Politics of Reform*, 81.

The Irish Conservative case had been tentatively adopted by Northcote while visiting Ireland in 1883, after the Nationalist 'Invasion of Ulster'.[12] From the loyalist point of view this proved to be a not unmixed blessing, since one probable consequence was the abandonment of their cause, both in Salisbury's campaign tour of the late summer of 1884, and at the Downing Street conferences on redistribution. Salisbury focused the Conservative case on a defence of the constitutional function of the House of Lords—and not on the future electoral decimation of Northcote's Irish allies. Northcote himself half-heartedly took up the Irish brief before the first of the redistribution conferences, but he brought forward no detailed scheme of protection before any of the sessions. On 20 October 1884 he demonstrated the insubstantial nature of his sympathy through having to ask Edward Gibson if he knew of the existence of any plan of salvation for Irish Toryism. Gibson prevaricated, Northcote's request was pigeon-holed, and the Irish Tory case collapsed.[13]

Thus, British Conservatives were not unmindful of the needs of their Irish party; typically, however, the Irish case was sacrificed in the internal wrangling of the national leadership. That this case could be adopted by a moderate leader suggests that it held a broader potential appeal in the party than Lord Randolph's later association might otherwise suggest. That the loyalist claim was abandoned at the redistribution conferences reflects the leadership's tactical priorities and Northcote's personal failure, rather than the intrinsic British lack of interest in Ireland identified by A. B. Cooke and John Vincent.

But, crucially, this analysis did not form part of the view from Belfast in January 1885. Irish Conservatives felt abandoned by their British party, and particularly by their newly acquired ally, Northcote. Angry at, but accepting, the Franchise Bill, they invested their remaining hopes in a sympathetic scheme of redistribution. However, publication of the plan at the beginning of December finally indicated how far their claims had been relegated—that is, the extent to which Northcote had been superseded. Irish seats *were* to be redistributed, but along the same lines as in Britain: this included

<hr />

[12] See Cooke, 'Northcote's Diary', 61–84; also Andrew Lang, *The Life, Letters and Diaries of Sir Stafford Northcote, First Earl of Iddesleigh* (2 vols.; Edinburgh and London, 1890), ii. 251–63.

[13] Jones, *Politics of Reform*, 72.

the disfranchisement of boroughs of less than 15,000 inhabitants—a particular threat to Irish loyalists, since it meant the loss of a disproportionately large number of seats. At the beginning of 1885, when the progress-reports of the Boundary Commission began to filter through to local Conservative leaders, an independent Irish campaign developed for the amendment of the Redistribution Bill; and this included the first attempt to create a separate Irish Conservative party within the House of Commons.

Anger briefly focused on Salisbury: an *Irish Times* editorial at the beginning of February condemned him alone for abandoning his party's Irish support.[14] Yet perhaps Salisbury did not so much abandon as miscalculate—for there is evidence to suggest that both he and Northcote believed Irish loyalist interests would be adequately protected by appropriately partisan boundary commissioners.[15] Thus, having first deprived Northcote of the opportunity to exploit his Ulster popularity by a stand on Ireland, then playing the commanding mother hen to Northcote's chick at the redistribution conferences, Salisbury at last revealed an interest in Irish Conservatism. In mid-December 1884 he approached Lord Arthur Hill, MP for County Down, and one of those who had invited Northcote to Ulster, asking for Irish party opinion on the nature of the composition of the Irish Boundary Commission.[16] At the end of the month he followed this up with a letter to the Apprentice Boys of Derry, expressing his conviction that the position of Irish Tories depended greatly on the Boundary Commission: how it was constituted, and how impartially it performed its duties. Indeed, this attitude gained credibility through the faith of certain loyalist leaders in a partisan Commission.[17]

Thus, when Salisbury wrote to the Apprentice Boys, he had already obtained a declaration from the Conservative boss in Belfast, E. S. Finnegan, expressing complete satisfaction with the Commission. Finnegan wrote on 23 December:

The Irish Boundary Commission is . . . a fair one, and much fairer than we had hoped for. Macpherson is a Conservative and an Orangeman, and he is in charge of Ulster arrangements. The boundaries published by the

[14] *IT*, 19 Feb. 1885, 4.
[15] PRONI, Erne Papers, D 1939/21/10/10, Northcote to Crichton, 17 Dec. 1884.
[16] MSPH, E. S. Finnegan to Lord Arthur Hill, 23 Dec. 1884.
[17] *IT*, 5 Jan. 1885, 5.

Commissioners for County Down are so fair that we do not propose to make any real opposition.[18]

Finnegan, in turn, misconstrued the evidence of Salisbury's concern as an indication that Irish loyalists might expect some concession when the Redistribution Bill entered Committee in the House of Commons. Modifying earlier images of Salisbury as traitor, he depicted him to a Larne audience on 3 January as ready to admit the justice of Irish Conservative claims.[19] Thus, though Finnegan had been disappointed with the Commissioners' work, he could still reasonably hope for redress from both Northcote and, now, Salisbury.

This attitude embodied not only a provincial recognition of Northcote's faltering position, but also a miscalculation and anticipation of Salisbury's concern for the Irish minority. Salisbury would demonstrate his concern—but only when loyalists finally detached themselves from Northcote, and only when their interests were not at odds with those of the British party. His overtures of December 1884 suggest in principle some sympathy with Irish Conservatives, but this did not extend, as they had hoped, to support for their amendments to the Redistribution Bill—amendments which would probably have been rejected by Gladstone, allowing Liberals the luxury of appealing to the country on the basis of an extended franchise alone.

Irish Tories were first disabused of their illusions when they lobbied the party leadership directly in February 1885. These meetings, and their aftermath, provided a greater boost to the evolution of an independent Irish loyalist movement, both in parliament and the constituencies, than later fears of leadership equivocation on Home Rule. Encouraged by Northcote's long-standing commitment to Irish loyalty, and by distinct signs of sympathy from Salisbury, they felt reasonably assured of concession. It was the efficiency with which this modest confidence was dispelled that shocked northern loyalists into self-reliance.

On 14 January 1885 a meeting of the Political Committee of the Ulster Constitutional Club was held, chaired by Viscount Crichton, Tory MP for County Fermanagh.[20] This meeting agreed on preliminary arrangements for an interview with Salisbury and

---

[18] MSPH, Finnegan to Hill, 23 Dec. 1884.   [19] *IT*, 5 Jan. 1885, 5.
[20] *IT*, 15 Jan. 1885, 5.

Northcote, identifying grievances for presentation to the leaders: the over-representation of Ireland in general, and of Leinster in particular, and the under-representation of the urban population in relation to the rural. Significantly, a parliamentary committee was then appointed to construct appropriate amendments, and to present them to the House of Commons; this represented the first move towards the organization of a separate parliamentary group. Significantly, too, the press reported a discussion on the future of Liberalism in Ireland.[21] Those at the meeting recognized that Gladstone's abandonment of his Irish support was more complete than Salisbury and Northcote's abandonment of Irish Toryism. And in this they identified the possibility of recouping electoral ground lost to them by their British leaders—and also the opportunity for increased parliamentary leverage over Gladstone, or, potentially, over their own leadership, if recalcitrant. Indeed, one Tory MP, James Porter Corry, hinted at earlier efforts to combine with Irish Liberals, 'but he could not say that he had been very successful [in his overtures]'.[22] Thus, possibly as early as the autumn of 1884, when the Franchise Bill had been conceded in principle, Irish Tories had begun to project an electoral alliance with local Liberals—as a defensive manœuvre to minimize both the likelihood and the potential liability of rejection by their own national party.

Speculation on recasting Irish Toryism into a loyalist parliamentary alliance only became meaningful when it could be demonstrated that the British parties would ultimately concede Parnellite claims. Both Irish Conservatives and Liberals suspected that they might be relegated, but this suspicion was slow to develop into conviction. On the other hand, some Irish Tories and their sympathizers were quickly aware that, once the Franchise Bill had passed into law, the likelihood of any serious concession to their demands on redistribution was remote. Lord George Hamilton admitted this to Salisbury in December 1884.[23] Hamilton's brother, Lord Claud, evidently shared this opinion, for, addressing a County Tyrone Orange meeting in January 1885, he looked forward to Protestant Liberal and Roman Catholic support in an anti-Parnell coalition. Hamilton studiously avoided any criticism of the Conservative

[21] Ibid.   [22] Ibid.
[23] MSPH, Lord George Hamilton to Salisbury, 18 Dec. 1884. Quoted in Jones, *Politics of Reform*, 214.

leadership—since there was just the possibility that the projected meetings might inspire some agreement. But his speech was primarily designed to prepare the ground in Tyrone for loyalist union: he was calculating already on the failure of negotiation.

Hamilton saw the short-term tactical need to avoid accusing the Conservatives of desertion, for his equivocation was rooted in Irish ignorance of their leaders' tactics, rooted in the suspension of communication between Irish Tories and Northcote. But as time passed, and no commitment to amendment was given by Salisbury, or by Northcote, Irish Tories became less ambiguous in their public declarations. On 12 February, a week before the planned meeting with Northcote, the *Irish Times* felt able to say that:

It is only by becoming troublesome to both parties, by taking a leaf out of the book of their opponents, that the Irish minority can assert any position whatever . . . what they mostly want to press effectively is the independent Irish loyalist leadership which will refuse to sell the interests of the Irish minority to any party . . .'[24]

To some extent this was a rhetorical pose, calculated for an English audience, and calculated to improve the Irish bargaining position with Northcote. But it was also a demonstration of alarm at the apparent divergence in Irish and British Tory thinking, alarm at British failure to communicate in response to Irish fears.

The Irish Tories' meetings with Northcote (18 February) and with Salisbury (25 February) confirmed their suspicions of isolation— since neither leader would offer any commitment of support.[25] But, while Salisbury proffered his regrets to a small group of Ulster leaders during a private interview, Northcote was involved in a set piece, confronting over forty Irish representatives, and left by Salisbury with no room for manœuvre; Edward Saunderson, who acted as one of the loyalist spokesmen, assured his wife that he 'had put it [the loyalist case] very straight to Sir Stafford'—though to no avail.[26] The loyalists left St James's Place, knowing that their only immediate defence against Parnell lay within the internal structure of Irish politics. Since, for the foreseeable future, nothing was to be expected from contact with the Conservative leadership, overtures

[24] *IT*, 12 Feb. 1885, 4.   [25] *IT*, 21 Feb. 1885, 5.
[26] ESP, T 2996/2/257, Saunderson to his wife, 18 Feb. 1885, quoted in Reginald Lucas, *Colonel Saunderson M.P.: A Memoir* (London, 1908), 79, and Walker, 'Parliamentary Representation', 525.

to Irish Liberals and the development of independent action had to become less restrained. A phase of discreet conferences, cautious constituency speeches, and inconsequential speculation ended with Northcote's platitudes.

However, independent action was still essentially a parliamentary phenomenon—at least until the evolution of the Irish Loyal and Patriotic Union in the summer of 1885. On the day following the interview with Northcote, leading Irish Conservatives met again to consider future action.[27] Urged on by Saunderson, two well-established and respected Tories, the Marquess of Hamilton and Sir Thomas Bateson, moved and seconded a resolution establishing 'an independent Irish Conservative party'. Saunderson defined the nature and purpose of the new body as being:

an independent constitutional party in the House of Commons entirely free to act for the good of Irish loyalty, unfettered by party ties. The result will be in future the Conservative leaders will no longer find an unswerving support as they have been accustomed to do in the past. Our party will give its support for the government that does most for the true interests of Ireland.[28]

But the force both of the resolution and of Saunderson's subsequent definition was directed towards the relationship with Toryism: the new body was professedly an independent Irish 'Conservative' party, even though, according to Saunderson, it might act for the good of a non-partisan Irish loyalty. There was still resistance to the relegation of a Tory within a loyalist identity; and indeed there were even local Orange grumbles that an Irish Tory party should be formed which might oppose a Tory ministry.[29] Thus, by the élitist nature of their independence, Irish loyalists had for the present declared against a substantive connection with Gladstonian Liberalism. Short-term tactical combinations were theoretically feasible; in practice, Irish loyalists in defining their indépendence, had highlighted its limitations.

This was recognized by the *Irish Times*, and became increasingly clear to the MPs of the new 'independent constitutional party': time and again cool resolutions embodying a rejection of the Conservative leadership dissolved into, at most, patchy abstention during divisions.

[27] ESP, T 2996/2/259, Saunderson to his wife, 21 Feb. 1885.   [28] Ibid.
[29] Revd T. Ellis, *The Actions of the Grand Orange Lodge of the County of Armagh (and the Reasons thereof) on the 6th July 1885* (Armagh, 1885), *passim.*

Moreover, this hesitation was encouraged by sympathetic, if insubstantial, handling by Salisbury and W. H. Smith. On 23 February 1885 the second meeting of the independent Irish Conservative party was held: MPs agreed on a boycott of the gathering of Conservative MPs at the Carlton, declared in favour of a reduction in the number of Irish members, and offered support for Sir John Lubbock's motion on proportional representation—this last was a gesture of solidarity with Irish Liberals.[30] But loyalist braggadocio was swiftly deflated. J. P. Corry, one of the members for Belfast, held a series of 'private conversations' with Smith which left him impressed by the Conservative leaders' strength of sympathy with the Irish Tory case.[31] The meeting with Salisbury on 25 February may have confirmed this impression, for though no details ever reached the press, this very silence (in contrast to the bitter aftermath of the Northcote interview) suggests that Salisbury had succeeded in mitigating a little of the Irish anger.

The immediate object of leadership concern was the Sudan censure vote on 27 February, in which Irish Tories had threatened to support the government, or to abstain, rather than enter the Opposition lobby behind Northcote.[32] And this object was attained, for Salisbury and Smith's overtures appear to have thwarted any plans for rebellion.[33] The collapse of loyalist resistance indicated the value placed on contact with the leadership, for their resolve had weakened after the most intangible assurances. This collapse underlined, too, the pointlessness of any attempt to defy party leadership in a polarized parliament. Though Irish Tories could make gestures of revolt, satisfactory settlement could ultimately be made only inside the Conservative party—if complete isolation were to be avoided; and indeed this was stated quite explicitly by local Orangemen. The pose of independence was only of value in determining the nature of any settlement. In this limitation lay the strength of the leaders' position.

Thus, loyalists in practice rarely committed themselves to outright parliamentary revolt. Few were moved to speak in the Committee debates on redistribution, and those who did betrayed considerable disagreement in their attitude towards the Conservative leadership. The maverick firebrand, John Ellison-Macartney, member for County Tyrone, denounced a front-bench conspiracy to block Ulster

---

[30] *IT*, 24 Feb. 1885.   [31] *IT*, 25 Feb. 1885, 4.
[32] Ibid.   [33] House of Commons Divisions Lists, 1885, no. 30.

amendments; enraged by failure, Ellison-Macartney, like Carson on the Land Bill of 1896, loudly abandoned the effort of even arguing for concession.[34] Henry Bruce, MP for Coleraine, and (according to his grandson) an equally wild and Orange Tory, deplored 'the manner in which he and his Hon. Friends had been deserted by their leaders'.[35] But others were less embittered: C. E. Lewis, for example, denied that Ulster members intended to act in rebellion against their front-bench, and pleaded that Conservative support be given to loyalist amendments.[36]

If there was anger, then Northcote, stranded on the opposition front-bench, was its focus. Yet, in one sense, his developing role as Ulster bogey helped further to stabilize the relationship between the Tory command and its Irish support. For Northcote's earldom and loss of leadership to Salisbury, removed from the Commons the Conservative most closely associated with resistance to Irish Tory demands; and this offered a chance to reassess the bond between British and Irish Toryism. Once they were effectively detached from Northcote, Salisbury, as the new Prime Minister, could re-establish contact with erring Irish Tories, and offer some tangible evidence of good faith.

D. C. Savage, writing in 1961, posited a highly strained relationship between Irish Tories and Salisbury's first administration. 'The attitude towards Ireland', he wrote, 'of some of the leading Conservatives of Salisbury's government, provoked the Ulstermen [in parliament] to consider some form of separate organisation.'[37] Both the implicit suggestion of tension, and the explicit connection between the first parliamentary organization and fears of Conservative policy on Ireland, are open to question. It has been demonstrated that independent parliamentary organization was originally planned in response to the Redistribution Bill, in February 1885. Once the Bill passed into law the immediate source of Ulster anger in parliament disappeared. There is little evidence to suggest that Irish Tory reaction to the June government was substantially different to that prevailing among other MPs namely, a muted welcome, based on a recognition of the difficulties created by its dependence on Parnellite votes.[38]

---

[34] Hansard, 3rd ser., (1885), ccxcv. 1474.   [35] Ibid. 773.   [36] Ibid. 802.
[37] Savage, 'Ulster Unionist Party', 191.
[38] Lord George Hamilton, *Parliamentary Reminiscences and Reflections 1868–1885* (London, 1916), 277–8. R. E. Quinault, 'Lord Randolph Churchill and Home Rule', *IHS*, xxi. 84 (Sept. 1979), 394.

Indeed, they had good reason to be cautiously sympathetic: seven of their number held office, and one, Edward Gibson, was in the cabinet as Lord Chancellor for Ireland.[39] They possessed a further cabinet sympathizer in Lord George Hamilton, whose father, the Duke of Abercorn, effectively controlled Conservative politics in County Tyrone. Moreover, those Ulster Tories not given office by Salisbury were otherwise won to the government. Appointments to the Privy Council and other honours constituted a serious effort to provide assurance at the personal level, which, given reliance on Parnell, could not be provided wholly by policy. Accordingly, even if Irish Tories had serious doubts about the new government, these were never given unequivocal expression—either in parliament or in Ireland. Thus, at the 12 July celebrations the new government won considerable Orange endorsement.[40] If doubts did exist, they were demonstrated, not through sustained denunciation of the government, but in the development of local politics.

Salisbury's handling of his Irish party support in June 1885 betrayed more sensitivity than his abrupt dismissal of their claims in 1884. By June the survival of the caretaker government (and, conceivably, success at a general election) depended on Parnell; but Salisbury showed no signs of wanting a long-term alliance with Irish Nationalists, even though both Liberals and Tories had come to accept the usefulness of the Parnellites as a path to the stable government of Ireland.[41] Short-term Conservative advantage, if only that of keeping options open, lay rather in governing Ireland by consent—the 'consent both of Orangemen and Nationalists'.[42] Thus, Salisbury did not want to goad Irish Tories into developing the substance of the independence which they had first assumed in February—for, although this had possessed little immediate significance in terms of parliamentary support, it remained a potential embarrassment. In reality, and despite the later accusations of Herbert Gladstone, the government was pursuing no consistent policy on Ireland, and displaying concurrently different and incompatible

[39] A. B. Cooke and A. P. W. Malcomson, *The Ashbourne Papers, 1869-1913: A Calendar of the Papers of Edward Gibson, First Lord Ashbourne* (Belfast, 1974), p. xvii.

[40] *BNL*, 15 July 1885, 6-7.

[41] Alan O'Day, *Parnell and the First Home Rule Episode, 1884-1887* (Dublin, 1986), 55.

[42] Cecil, *Third Marquess of Salisbury*, iii. 154.

Irish sympathies within the flexible bounds of a commitment to the Union and to landlordism.[43]

Salisbury's developing relationship with the Irish Tories confirms this analysis. Thus he indicated his new interest in their concerns by granting a loyalist representative, Edward King-Harman, an interview when he was otherwise deeply preoccupied with the formation of his ministry (16 June).[44] On the following day, 17 June, Irish Tories held a meeting at which King-Harman reported on his conversation with Salisbury. The details of this, and of King-Harman's interview in Arlington Street, do not survive; but it is clear that both King-Harman and a substantial proportion of those present were satisfied with whatever assurances and arguments Salisbury had been able to offer.[45] The issue on which Irish Conservatives consistently offered an uncompromising stand, law and order, was apparently glossed over; for, though Irish loyalists subsequently united to extort coercive measures from the government, in June 1885 they were largely content to leave the matter in Salisbury's hands.[46] This was a compromise formula, indicating an important division of opinion among Irish Conservative MPs.

The Maamtrasna debate of July 1885, used by several historians to demonstrate unity of loyalist opposition to Salisbury's hesitant law and order policy, in reality reveals the extent of their disagreement—and this in turn merely reflected disunity within the Tory administration.[47] On 3 July, C. E. Lewis, the Londonderry City MP, who was Randolph Churchill's chief antagonist during the debate, made a plea for coercion. On the same day, however, Lord Arthur Hill, addressing his County Down constituents, declared that he and the 'majority of Conservatives in Ireland accepted that a firm administration of the ordinary criminal law was sufficient without any renewal of coercion'.[48] When, later in July, Parnell brought the Maamtrasna murder case before parliament, demanding an inquiry into the Spencer administration, the issue at stake remained the same: the commitment of the Conservative government, or lack of it, to a tough crimes policy. Lord Randolph proclaimed that the

---

[43] Cooke and Vincent, *Governing Passion*, 71. O'Day, *First Home Rule Episode*, 27, 56, 79.

[44] *IT*, 17 June 1885, 6.   [45] *IT*, 18 June 1885, 6.   [46] Ibid.

[47] Quinault, 'Lord Randolph Churchill', 394; Savage, 'Ulster Unionist Party', 192; Foster, 'Northern Station', 265. Cooke and Vincent, *Governing Passion*, 276–8.

[48] *IT*, 4 July 1885, 4.

government would be 'foredoomed to failure, if they go out of their way unnecessarily to assume one jot or tittle of responsibility for the acts of the late administration'.[49] But the confidence of this plea did not obscure a more general ministerial caution. Thus there could be no decisive loyalist stand against the attitude of the government—because there was no clear policy to stand against. And even Churchill's attitude was not wholly unsatisfactory, since Spencer had been unpopular with certain loyalists: certainly his even-handed, if severe, regime had brought him into conflict with Orange opinion over the Rosslea Incident and over the dismissal of the loyalist hero William Johnston from the Fisheries Inspectorate. Churchill's declaration did not provoke, therefore, any united Irish Tory condemnation of the government. Criticism of the policy on law and order was not widespread, and focused on Lord Randolph himself.

The Maamtrasna debate contained only two Irish Tory contributions—from C. E. Lewis, and from John Ellison-Macartney.[50] Even Lewis, who had placed himself at the extremity of loyalist opinion, was careful to distinguish Lord Randolph's statement from what he believed was the bulk of government and British party opinion.[51] And, given his earlier extremism, the violence of this condemnation was probably unique. Ellison-Macartney's contribution to debate has an even more limited significance; offering no serious rebuttal of Churchill, he rose to speak in reaction to the taunts of the maverick John Gorst, the Solicitor General.[52] Churchill later repudiated Gorst's reference to the 'reactionary Ulster members', soothing their ruffled pride by some complimentary allusions in a speech at Sheffield.[53] Other ministers were equally, though more privately, dismayed by Gorst's outburst.[54]

---

[49] Hansard, 3rd ser. (1885), ccxcix, 1098.

[50] Quinault, 'Lord Randolph Churchill', 394–5. Hugh Holmes, the Irish Attorney General, named the chief die-hards as St John Brodrick, Edward King-Harman, A. L. Tottenham, and Lewis. It is probable that Holmes, writing in 1901, and immediately after the death of his wife, is inaccurate: King-Harman refuted Lewis's demands for coercion at the beginning of July 1885. See A. B. Cooke and John Vincent, 'Ireland and Party Politics, 1885–1887: An Unpublished Conservative Memoir (1)', IHS, xvi. 62, (Sept. 1969), 158.

[51] Hansard, 3rd ser. (1885), ccxcix, 1111.   [52] Ibid. 1149.

[53] Foster, Lord Randolph Churchill, 229.

[54] O'Day, First Home Rule Episode, 71. Cooke and Vincent, Governing Passion, 278.

The ambiguity of government Irish policy—the anxiety to avoid being seen to offer partisan commitment in Ireland—extended even to the celebrated interview between the Conservative viceroy, the Earl of Carnarvon, and Parnell in August 1885. Herbert Gladstone saw a causal connection between the Hill Street meeting and Salisbury's ambiguous references to Ireland and federation in his Newport manifesto. The pieties of Gladstone's *After Thirty Years* have long since been called into question, but the neglected Irish Tory dimension confirms doubts about the broader significance of this meeting as evidence for the drift of Conservative policy.[55] Carnarvon had originally agreed with Salisbury that the Irish Tory cabinet minister, Lord Ashbourne (Edward Gibson), should be present as a third party at this interview. In the event, for some reason, probably Gibson's well-developed regard for his own political security, he neglected to attend; Lady Gwendolen Cecil recalled her father's dismay at the failure of this arrangement.[56] National prominence had, to some extent, distanced Ashbourne from his Dublin Tory roots—but Irish loyalists still treated him as an ally. Thus, for Salisbury, Ashbourne's presence at Hill Street would serve as a guarantee of the meeting's limited function. If there were general tactical advantages in the presence of a second Conservative, these were enhanced by his being an Irish Tory.

The ambiguity of Salisbury's Irish policy reached an appropriate climax at Newport on 7 October—for his speech there offered encouragement to an embarrassingly wide range of thought on Ireland. While a minority of Orange firebrands were worried by the elements which encouraged Parnell and some Liberals, many moderate Unionists, like the editor of the *Irish Times*, drew comfort from soothing sentences stressing the integrity of the empire.[57] More surprising, the editor of the *Belfast News Letter* was ecstatic, hailing the speech as a 'masterly exposition . . . [which] will be read with satisfaction throughout the country'.[58] Irish disunity here, as in their general response to the government, was fitting testimony to the ambivalence of Salisbury's strategy. For it was now clear that

[55] L. P. Curtis, *Coercion and Conciliation in Ireland, 1880–1892: A Study in Conservative Unionism* (Oxford and Princeton, 1963), 50; Cooke and Vincent, *Governing Passion*, 72.

[56] Cecil, *Third Marquess of Salisbury*, iii. 157. O'Day, *First Home Rule Episode*, 64, 75–7.

[57] *IT*, 9 Oct. 1885, 6.   [58] *BNL*, 8 Oct. 1885, 4.

he had succeeded in assuaging the alarm among Irish Tories, created when they had been ditched over redistribution. Moderates were impressed by his apparent sincerity, and by the extent to which he appeared to take Irish loyalists into his confidence. Extremists were aggrieved by the relationship with Parnellism, but they were never given a substantive grievance like redistribution upon which to focus their anger.

Thus, even the most embittered Irish Tories never reached the depths of antipathy plumbed in February 1885. What had angered them then had been the revelation that, all things being equal, British Tories would look after British Tory interests before their own. While the experience of this hard truth remained unchallenged, Salisbury was able to demonstrate that there need not be any lasting conflict between the interests of the English and Irish parties. This involved very little practical cost: occasional verbal assurances, appointments to minor office, avoiding any cast-iron commitment to an inimical policy. These were sufficient to calm fears, and to undermine Irish loyalist unity. In this way the first attempt to develop an independent Irish Tory parliamentary party was frustrated; so long as the leadership was friendly, independence, as defined in February 1885, was deprived of purpose.

However, though Salisbury's role was important, Tory unity also depended upon an Irish recognition of the futility of opposition. Salisbury inspired confidence—but he was not the government, as the *News Letter* specifically declared in early January 1886.[59] Opinion among the more embittered Orange elements expressed both respect for the Prime Minister and also alarm at what one Orange peer characterized as 'the eccentricities of [the government's] more irresponsible members', that is, Lord Randolph Churchill.[60] But this was never systematically conveyed to the House of Commons: Irish Tories did not set themselves up to be deserted on the wild periphery of right-wing politics, even though—predictably—they did try the patience of a maverick conciliationist like Carnarvon.[61] Desertion had seemed a likely fate in February, but by the autumn local political activity and careful handling by Salisbury had exhausted Irish Tory rage, and downgraded open revolt to mere truculence. For, if loyalist equivocation was partly a recognition of temporary parliamentary

---

[59] *BNL*, 5 Jan. 1886, 4.   [60] *IT*, 13 Aug. 1885, 6.
[61] O'Day, *First Home Rule Episode*, 95.

impotence, then local politics were more fluid, and offered compensating strength. Irish Tories sought to exploit this room for manœuvre both against Nationalism, and as a source of increased leverage on their own leadership.

3. *Organization in Ireland, 1885*

Local organization took two forms: developing central movements for registration and propaganda, and creating an electoral alliance with the Liberals. Before the Home Rule Bill the success of the latter was at best patchy: relations between a predominantly landed party and popular tenant Liberalism took long to develop, and remained bitter, even after the evolution of Liberal Unionism.[62] But this bitterness was less marked in southern Ireland where Liberals were weaker and more Whiggish—and where considerations of electoral advantage were largely irrelevant. It was in the Dublin area that the first gestures of solidarity were perceptible, one of the first combinations of Liberal and Tory occurring at Rathmines in March 1885. Significantly, the basis of this unity, as with the parliamentary organization, was not always direct opposition to Parnell, but rather shared fears of betrayal by the parties' respective English commanders: 'they had followed their leaders blindfolded . . . and they found that they had been betrayed', declared one speaker at Rathmines.[63] Uniting Irish Liberals with Irish Conservatives in parliament and constituency would, it was thought, lessen the likelihood of repudiation when redistribution was enacted. Thus, an *Irish Times* editorial declared, obliquely acknowledging the debt to Parnellism, that 'it is only by becoming troublesome to *both* parties . . . that the Irish minority can assert any position whatever'.[64]

In Ulster the relative strength of Liberalism meant that, in the short term, Conservative gestures of alliance were treated with extreme suspicion. In South Tyrone, where there was a large number of Liberal tenant farmers, Conservative and Liberal recrimination allowed the seat to fall to a Home Ruler, William O'Brien. Similar

---

[62] Thomas Macknight, *Ulster as it is, or Twenty Eight Years' Experience as an Irish Editor* (2 vols.; London, 1896), ii. 157 (and *passim*).
[63] *IT*, 16 Mar. 1885, 6.   [64] *IT*, 12 Feb. 1885, 4.

disagreement in West Belfast, where Protestant and Catholic were fairly evenly divided, brought a second Nationalist victory.[65] Under the patronage of the Marquess of Hamilton, electoral co-operation was rather more successful in the far west of the province—as D. C. Savage has demonstrated.[66] Moreover, under Hamilton's pressure, a secret meeting was held in Belfast on 14 November 1885 in order to seek a broader alliance in preparation for the general election.[67] But, despite the blessing of Lord Hartington, Hamilton's initiative failed, and in the bitter aftermath of the general election, the Ulster Reform Club warned against any further disingenuous Conservative overtures. In the long term, however, electoral annihilation in December, and the presentation of a Liberal Home Rule Bill, weakened the obstructionist case. On 19 March 1886 a majority of Unionist Liberals broke away from the Gladstonian party, and fought the general election of July in an uneasy, if lasting, alliance with Ulster Conservatives.[68]

The development of a constituency Unionist alliance was complemented at a provincial level by the creation of campaign organization—but here, too, partisan jealousies were slow to die. The Loyal Irish Union, founded in August 1885, suffered in this way. Its function was defined as missionary: 'to inform and train in political affairs and bring into active service in the constitutional cause electors of all classes'; 'to promote and spread constitutional principles in Ireland by means of the platform and press and by social and political associations'.[69] In keeping with the studied moderation of much of Irish Tory politicking at this time, the Union declared a commitment to the suppression of all religious, racial, and class prejudice. But these pious aspirations rang hollow, given the inaccessibility of the more fundamental goal of party unity. W. R. Young, present at the inaugural meeting, recalled that a cantankerous Scots Liberal—possibly T. W. Russell—had inflamed divisions through a provocative address. Only by subtle diplomacy were the effects of this rodomontade concealed from public view; and the progenitors of the Union were ultimately happy to kill the project rather than let its failings compromise any future initiative. Thus

[65] *IT*, 5 Jan. 1886, 4.

[66] Savage, 'Ulster Unionist Party', 190; though there remained problems—see Walker, 'Parliamentary Representation', 400.

[67] WJD, 14 Nov. 1885; *IT*, 16 Nov. 1885, 4.

[68] Savage, 'Ulster Unionist Party', 198-9   [69] *IT*, 10 Aug. 1885, 6.

the Ulster Loyalist Union, founded as an alternative co-ordinating body in January 1886, was able to annex the programme of the LIU, without acquiring any legacy of schism; and though its general significance has been overestimated, the new grouping was an important source of non-partisan opposition to the Home Rule Bill.[70]

Concern to avoid a sectarian identity was similarly high among the priorities of the southern and Dublin-based Irish Loyal and Patriotic Union. Like the Loyal Irish Union, the ILPU was formed in the aftermath of the failure of Irish Tory tactics over redistribution. As with the Loyal Irish Union, many loyalist MPs were represented within the ILPU structure. Though founded discreetly in May 1885, the ILPU announced its existence only on 26 October, through a tripartite manifesto, appealing under different headings to 'the people of Ireland', 'Irishmen', and to 'citizens of the empire'.[71] In cautious and strategic language this confirmed the dignity of nationality, its compatibility with a great empire (and with government by the 'united parliament' of that empire); Parnellism, on the other hand, was rejected as a criminal mutation of nationality. Unlike the Loyal Irish Union, which was a largely Tory movement, the ILPU disclaimed a specific party allegiance; unlike the Loyal Irish Union, it sought to run loyalist candidates in as many constituencies as it could afford—indeed this, for the first years of its existence, was its chief occupation.

The success of the ILPU owed much to the final collapse of traditional party distinction in the south of Ireland; conversely, the failure of the Loyal Irish Union had much to do with its clumsy effort to adopt loyalism as a Conservative monopoly. Given that there was demonstrably little to gain for either party by remaining divided in the south, the ILPU's pose was easily assumed: parliamentary candidates were selected with only a general pledge to support the Union, and to sit, if elected, 'on whatever side of the House they think proper'.[72] Since there was virtually no chance of any ILPU candidate winning a seat, this pious indifference to party was fundamentally a sham. But it impressed both the north, and more

[70] PRONI, W. R. Young Papers, D 3027/7/8-11, 'Recollections of 75 Years in Ulster' (unpublished memoir, Nov. 1931), 139-41. Savage exaggerates the importance of the Ulster Loyalist Union—which was not 'the central core of the Unionist Party in Ulster': Savage, 'Ulster Unionist Party', 194-5.
[71] *IT*, 26 Oct. 1885, 6.   [72] Ibid.

important, English Conservative opinion, which solemnly approved the manifesto, and the rejection of party for principle which it ostensibly embraced.[73]

The evolution of the Liberal alliance and popular organization are important in the parliamentary context because Irish Tory and Unionist MPs were intimately involved. As has been argued, local developments also indicated that loyalists were not obtaining political satisfaction within the Commons. Moreover, these movements displayed ostentatious moderation; Orangeism and no-popery were discreetly veiled, Catholic participation being explicitly encouraged. And it seems probable that Irish Toryism and Unionism gained by association with such conspicuous, if self-conscious, restraint. Thus the assumption that loyalist MPs were, through their uniform extremism, a negligible force in parliament at this time, is open to serious doubt. The actual influence of these representatives is a separate issue which will be broached in the following section of the chapter; but it may be stressed here that there was little in the attitude of Irish loyalists as a whole which automatically rendered them doubtful allies or advisors. If in practice Conservative leaders still occasionally referred to them disparagingly, then this disparagement was as much a commonplace of political rhetoric as any other form of ritual denunciation in contemporary high political correspondence.

From a different perspective, Irish Tory members gained by association with an apparently popular movement largely beyond the control of British party management. How much the prospect of growing loyalist independence worried the leadership is extremely difficult to assess. There is no surviving record of any substantial discussion between Conservative leaders concerning these developments in Ireland. This suggests complete indifference, but there are a number of problems in assuming this. Some evidence does survive, indicating that Salisbury was concerned with Irish loyalist independence. Writing to Lord Randolph in November 1885, he confessed: 'I am afraid that I am not competent to quell the Irish Orangemen . . . their loyalty to the party is not a very great passion just now, and if I tried to interfere, I should be told to mind my own business. They are troublesome and unreliable allies . . .'[74] This

---

[73] *IT*, 27 Oct. 1885, 5, reviewing the British press.
[74] Salisbury to Lord Randolph Churchill, 16 Nov. 1885, quoted in Cooke and Vincent, *Governing Passion*, 160.

letter has generally been cited to illustrate Salisbury's low opinion of Irish Toryism. Yet, while Salisbury certainly is scathing, the thrust of the letter indicates his concern with loyalist independence; and, though 'troublesome', loyalists were unequivocally 'allies'. If Salisbury was rude, he was also worried—and it is this dimension of his response which has been hitherto largely neglected.

Lord Salisbury's principal contact in Ulster was Lord Arthur Hill, one of the party whips, and it is probable that, through Hill, Salisbury kept in touch with developments in Ulster loyalist politics, exercising some limited and discreet influence. Thus, it is reasonably clear that Hill was deputed by Salisbury and the British party hierarchy to organize the elections in Ulster: newspaper reports and some surviving correspondence on the South Antrim election confirm this.[75] What is not clear from the sources is the exact nature of this commission—*how* Salisbury wanted the elections managed.

To some extent, however, this is perceptible from Hill's tactics. His importance as a loyalist manager is hard to overestimate: he lurks everywhere, participating in most of the crucial, or potentially significant, events of the winter of 1885-6. Hill evidently sought to limit the dimensions and implications of loyalist independence—to keep restless Irish Tories more firmly in the Conservative camp. This aim was pursued in two different ways: by aligning Irish Tories in general sympathy with the government, and behind specific items of policy, and in thwarting any precipitate alliance with Irish Liberals. He was one of the leaders of the loyalist lobby rejecting coercion in July 1885; he identified himself with the predominantly Tory Loyal Irish Union, chairing its first meeting in August.[76] Furthermore, despite his general importance, Hill played little part in the evolution of an independent parliamentary party in January 1886. Indeed, he may have set himself up as a counter to Edward Saunderson; at any rate his political demise followed Saunderson's ascent to leadership.[77]

By keeping faith with Hill in the mid-1880s, Salisbury retained some limited influence over Irish Tory affairs. His interest in, and reaction to, developments in Ulster was not confined, therefore, to

[75] MSPH, Lord Arthur Hill to Salisbury, 23 Aug. 1885; *IT*, 19 Aug. 1885, 4.
[76] *IT*, 1 Sept. 1885.
[77] Press reports suggest that Saunderson and Hill may have had differing personal support among Ulster MPs: *IT*, 29 Jan. 1886, 5. Also Cooke, 'Northcote's Diary', 72, n. 49; and Walker, 'Parliamentary Representation', 530.

occasional complaints and impotent malice. Through Hill he had access to the Ulster political scene; and there are indications both that he was concerned with developments there, and exploited what limited resources for influence he possessed.

For a number of reasons, then, Irish Tories may have had more influence in high politics than has been supposed. They were not uniformly Orange and militant; they had not rejected Salisbury's first government *en bloc*, even though many were alarmed at the prospect of a Parnellite alliance. Organization and limited independence had provided a new strength; attempts at union with Liberals had given them a favourable press image for sincerity and principle. There is some persuasive evidence suggesting that the Conservative leadership took note of these developments, and was impressed by the potential threat which was emerging.

The last section of this chapter seeks to examine Conservative government in January 1886, in the light both of this revised image of a politically more marketable Irish Toryism, and in the light, too, of their reformulation of a semi-independent parliamentary stand. In January 1886 the nature of the Conservative opposition and alternative to Home Rule was determined. Given the problems with existing interpretations, the role of loyalism in the definition of this alternative may now be reassessed.

4.   *Organization in the Commons, January 1886*

The Unionist ginger group which emerged in the Commons in January 1886 differed fundamentally from its predecessor of 1885. Firstly, it became a permanent feature of the House of Commons: the Ulster Unionist members of the present parliament trace an unbroken ancestry back to Edward Saunderson's group of 1886. Secondly, it was more cautious in its attitude to the Conservative Party: its members paid lip-service to the leadership, yet maintained sufficient distance to be able to threaten opposition. Thirdly, and consequently, it exercised a perceptible influence on the leadership.

As early as December 1885, Edward Saunderson, the newly elected Conservative representative for North Armagh, was planning a revival of a distinct loyalist parliamentary group, and acting as spokesman for 'the Ulster members'.[78] It was probably Saunderson,

---

[78] ESP, T 2996/2/281, Saunderson to his wife, 18 Dec. 1885.

and not (as is sometimes suggested) Lord Claud Hamilton, who was the chief driving force behind the bid for independence and reorganization.[79] Benefiting by the experience of failure in February 1885, Saunderson now effectively placed the limits of his party's action within a Conservative context. Before parliament met at the end of January, he embarked upon a speaking tour throughout loyalist Ireland—establishing his claim to lead the Irish Tory group, and offering a definition of the relationship between that group and government. His language varied according to the nature of his audience, but the principle of a bond with Conservatism was consistent. Thus, at Lurgan, where sectarian division was acute, Saunderson indulged his audience with rip-roaring threats of defiance: the Orangeism of the Irish Tory group was emphasized, as was the spectre of British betrayal—but both themes were primarily rhetorical, part of the well-defined formula for a successful militant loyalist address.[80] In reality probably only ten of Saunderson's putative party were Orangemen; and, even in addressing this fiery Protestant audience, he stressed that rebellion of the Ulster MPs was a last resort.[81] Speaking to the rather more sedate Irish Loyal and Patriotic Union on 8 January, Saunderson was appropriately moderate in tone.[82] He expressed satisfaction at government assurances on the Home Rule question; he was doubtful about the desirability of the Education and Local Government bills, which were thought to be impending, but did not commit himself to rejecting either of these measures in defiance of the government. And, on 11 January, addressing a County Cavan audience, he was unrestrained in praise of the Conservative party, and of Salisbury, 'whose patriotism, integrity and honesty would prove an unflinching obstacle in the way of any concession to Home Rule . . .'.[83]

On the whole, therefore, Saunderson demonstrated a personal and party commitment to Salisbury and this reflected a wider sympathy within contemporary loyalism, held even by the moodily suspicious editor of the *Belfast News Letter*.[84] Moreover, this affection was seen to be reciprocated—when on 19 January 1886, Salisbury met a large deputation of loyalist representatives, who were petitioning for a firm policy on law and order.[85] Salisbury gave every indication

[79] Savage, 'Ulster Unionist Party', 193.
[80] *IT*, 8 Jan. 1885, 5.
[81] Ibid.   [82] *IT*, 9 Jan. 1885, 5.
[83] *IT*, 12 Jan. 1886, 5.
[84] *BNL*, 5 Jan. 1886, 4.
[85] *BNL*, 20 Jan. 1886, 5.

of being moved by the Irishmen's pleas, and though—two days before
the Queen's Speech—he declined to offer specific commitments, his
overall tone was sympathetic, and his parting words offered hope
of redress. At any rate, as Churchill subsequently discovered and
informed the Prime Minister, the loyalist delegates had been delighted
by his words and evident consideration.[86] In private, to leaders like
the duke of Abercorn, Salisbury was equally diplomatic. Inviting
Abercorn to move the Loyal Address, he affirmed that 'your
[Abercorn's] undertaking this duty would greatly comfort the
loyalists of the north of Ireland, whom we wish extremely to reassure
as to the intentions of the government.'[87] Thus if, in January 1886,
Saunderson and other loyalist leaders still grasped the bond with
Toryism, then this had much to do with their faith in Salisbury. More
than any other single factor, the Prime Minister's tactful and emollient
leadership ultimately bound Irish Tories to the British party.

On 14 January 1886 Saunderson and six other Irish Tories
met in St Stephen's Club in order to organize a parliamentary
Ulster Party.[88] On the following day, Saunderson learned of plans
to found a rival group which was to include not only Irish
Tory members, but also any English sympathizers.[89] Fearing that
incorporating English MPs would further neutralize any independence which the party might claim, Saunderson persuaded its
promoters, Edward King-Harman, and R. U. Penrose-Fitzgerald,
to abandon their separate efforts. On 22 January press reports
announced a Carlton Club meeting for 24 January, whose purpose
was to found 'a loyalist party in the House of Commons to watch
over the interests of the minority of Ireland, and to take independent
action on Irish questions generally'.[90] Saunderson, working
incessantly to recruit Irish Tories—both those sitting for English as
well as Irish constituencies—calculated on winning some twenty-six
adherents.[91] The new 'party' declared foremost its repudiation of
Home Rule: 'it was also resolved to give the government a cordial
support in any measure they might consider necessary for restoring

---

[86] Churchill College Cambridge, Papers of Lord Randolph Churchill, 1/11/1307b,
Churchill to Salisbury, 20 Jan. 1886 (copy).

[87] PRONI, Abercorn Papers, D 623/A/331, Salisbury to Abercorn, 7 Jan. 1886.

[88] WJD, 14 Jan. 1886; Walker, 'Parliamentary Representation', 529.

[89] ESP, T 2996/1/61, Saunderson to his wife, 15 Jan. 1886.

[90] IT, 22 Jan. 1886, 4, quoting from the Standard, 22 Jan. 1886.

[91] ESP, T 2996/1/66, Saunderson to his wife, 23 Jan. 1886.

law and order to Ireland'.[92] This was a thinly veiled demand for a renewal of a Crimes Bill: the consciously delicate phrasing indicates again the group's desire to remain in communication with, and bound to, the Conservative leadership. In their anxiety to defend a narrow and local political interest, Irish loyalists remained aware of the consequences of alienating the cabinet through harangue. Independent loyalism in January 1886 represented principally an allusion to lobby strength; Irish loyalists still hoped that the reality would never have to be tested.

Such hope implied an element of confidence in the ultimate goodwill of the leadership, and this was confirmed by frequent contact with cabinet ministers. Formal set pieces such as the Salisbury interview were important as a means of soothing loyalist nerves; but there were other, more discreet, and no less productive meetings. In January Saunderson and his colleagues lurked at the periphery of government, a shadowy presence, exercising an uncertain influence.

The members of the Ulster Party sought to carry the demand for coercion by stressing their indispensability to the minority government—and they made this point both through public speeches, such as that delivered by Saunderson at Lurgan—and through approaches to government ministers. Thus on 23 January Saunderson spelt out to Michael Hicks-Beach the possible consequences of Ulster recalcitrance, although subsequently a more fertile opportunity emerged in which the loyalist leader could argue his case.[93] For the usefulness of the loyalists, both as lobby fodder and as prolix debaters, was borne in upon Hicks-Beach when the government narrowly avoided an unexpectedly early defeat on a Liberal amendment to the Address on 25 January. During the debate, Saunderson was asked to go to Hicks-Beach's office; there he found the Leader of the House and Randolph Churchill 'in a state of trepidation', fearing collapse, and begging Saunderson to organize his Ulster members to speak until an adjournment.[94] In the event, Ulster party votes were not needed since Hartington and his Whig members voted with the government. But the incident was a useful demonstration of the potential significance of loyalist dissent.

Within the government the cry for coercion was taken up by Ashbourne, the Dublin Tory, and by Cranbrook—and won majority

[92] *IT*, 26 Jan. 1886, 5.
[93] ESP, T 2996/1/66, Saunderson to his wife, 23 Jan. 1886.
[94] ESP, T 2996/1/68, Saunderson to his wife, 26 Jan. 1886.

support; but at a cabinet held on 16 January four ministers, including Churchill and Hicks-Beach, still dissented from any statutory suppression of the National League.[95] This recalcitrance focused divisions and brought the adjournment of discussion. Though Churchill retreated a little later that day, a rallying letter from Hicks-Beach forced the temporary acceptance of a weak compromise on law and order hammered out in cabinet on 18 January.[96]

If, as is sometimes suggested, Lord Randolph's principal preoccupation in January 1886 was tactical preparation for a Liberal alliance, then he was also being made aware of a threat from within Toryism.[97] Having met Saunderson at Howth in December, Churchill began in early January to canvass opinion on a proposed visit to Ulster, and on his aspirant Ulster allies. The early feedback was encouraging (Lord George Hamilton thought the idea of a visit 'excellent' and Saunderson 'a clever fellow'); and, on the basis of this, Churchill remained accessible to loyalist leaders for the rest of the month.[98] He held at least three recorded conversations with Saunderson in the last fortnight of January, culminating in his renewed offer of 27 January to speak at Belfast. Details of these meetings are scant, but it is clear from a reference to the first, on 17 January, that Churchill was offering unequivocal encouragement to the Ulstermen's demand for coercion.[99]

Between 16 and 23 January Lord Randolph and Hicks-Beach were converted from opposition to immediate, statutory coercion into accepting a hard line. It is generally argued that for Churchill, at any rate, the more sympathetic attitude of the Whigs towards coercion influenced this change of heart.[100] But Ulster Party lobbying of the two cabinet rebels may (given the peculiar significance of Ulster lobby support at this time) have had an abnormally great influence. Thus, although Churchill had rejected coercion in cabinet

[95] Nancy E. Johnston (ed.), *The Diary of Gathorne Hardy, Later Lord Cranbrook, 1866–1892: Political Selections* (Oxford, 1981), 590.

[96] Johnston, *Cranbrook Diary*, 591; Cooke and Vincent, *Governing Passion*, 302–3.

[97] Foster, *Lord Randolph Churchill*, 247; Cooke and Vincent, 'Ireland and Party Politics', 167.

[98] Churchill Papers, 1/11/1235, George Hamilton to Churchill, 2 Feb. 1886. Foster, *Lord Randolph Churchill*, 253.

[99] ESP, T 2996/1/62, Saunderson to his wife, 17 Jan. 1886.

[100] Foster, *Lord Randolph Churchill*, 250. Savage in fact suspected this to be the case—though at that time the evidence was not available to substantiate his belief: Savage, 'Ulster Unionist Party', 194.

on 16 January, he responded sympathetically to Saunderson's overtures of 17 January. The loyalist leader left Churchill on that occasion clearly expecting the immediate suppression of the National League.[101]

On the other hand, Hicks-Beach gave no indication of relaxing his opposition to coercion before Sunday, 24 January. Salisbury was then able to tell the Queen that 'the recalcitrant members of the cabinet have changed their minds about coercion *under party pressure*, and a bill will probably be introduced in two or three days'.[102] Hicks-Beach apparently registered no opinion on coercion at the cabinet meeting of 23 January, though Lord Randolph for the first time acknowledged 'the mistaken course in which he had joined'.[103] Thus, Hicks-Beach's volte face occurred in the wake of the new cabinet alignment. Sometime on 23 January, probably after the cabinet meeting, Saunderson lobbied Hicks-Beach on behalf of the Ulster group; and he described this interview to his wife later, on the same day:

[our] party has now swelled to 26 so we are now quite a power in the House. I have just had an interview with Sir M. Hicks-Beach & pointed out to him clearly the course I should have felt bound to adopt, and those who act with us, in case the government did not give us some definite assurance that they intended to act with vigour and promptitude . . .'[104]

The content and outcome of Saunderson's overture are uncertain, since he omitted any reference to Hicks-Beach's reaction, but his report to his wife implies that he had threatened the minister with Irish defections. That this may well have been given considerable weight by Hicks-Beach is suggested by several pieces of evidence. Salisbury's subsequent allusion to a change of mind brought about by 'party pressure' may refer specifically to loyalist lobbying, since there is no other evidence of well-organized pressure on ministers. The new weight which Hicks-Beach placed on the Ulster group in parliament is indicated by his attempt on 25 January—only two days after the Saunderson interview—to secure their co-operation in debate. Saunderson himself believed that his meeting on 23 January

---

[101] ESP, T 2996/1/62, Saunderson to his wife, 17 Jan. 1886.
[102] G. E. Buckle (ed.), *Letters of Queen Victoria, 1886–1901*, 3rd ser. (3 vols.; London, 1932), i. 17.
[103] Johnston, *Cranbrook Diary*, 593.
[104] ESP, T 2996/1/66, Saunderson to his wife, 23 Jan. 1886.

had been decisive in winning the government to coercion. 'I have no doubt', he wrote, 'that it was owing to the determined stand I made with Hicks-Beach that the government decided to proclaim the League . . .'.[105] The likelihood is, therefore, that Hicks-Beach's conversion to special crimes legislation was precipitated by Irish Unionist lobbying. If there were other strategic considerations, the imminent loss of twenty-six votes was in itself persuasive. Conservative Irish policy still needed an Irish-based support, and unless Salisbury risked outbidding Gladstone by embracing Home Rule—an unlikely scenario—then the only source of that support lay with Irish loyalism.

5. Summary

Except for Salisbury's long-standing commitment to the interests of Irish loyalists, January 1886 saw an emergence of the framework of Conservative policy on Ireland for the next twenty years. After seven months of equivocation, the party committed itself to coercion and therefore to an irrevocable break with Parnellism.[106] The direct role of Irish loyalists in these developments is ultimately incalculable: the one Irish Tory in the cabinet, Ashbourne, was losing influence at this time both with his colleagues and with his political base.[107] Another minister with Irish Tory connections, Lord George Hamilton, though identifying himself sentimentally with loyalism, in practice appears to have played little role in the formulation of Irish policy.[108]

Irish loyalist participation in events consisted, rather, in the influence exercised indirectly through friends, and in direct approaches to the Prime Minister, Randolph Churchill, Hicks-Beach, and Ashbourne. It is reasonably clear that Salisbury kept in touch with Irish Tory politics through Lord Arthur Hill. On the evidence of Gwendolen Cecil, and of the meetings with loyalist representatives, he appears to have sympathized with the prospective plight of Unionists under Home Rule—though this sympathy did not survive

---

[105] ESP, T 2996/1/70, Saunderson to his wife, 28 Jan. 1886.
[106] Curtis, *Coercion and Conciliation*, 89.
[107] A. B. Cooke and John Vincent, *Lord Carlingford's Journal: Reflections of a Cabinet Minister, 1885* (Oxford, 1971), 128, n. 2.
[108] *IT*, 19 Jan. 1886, 4.

conflict with clear personal and British party advantage (as over parliamentary reform).[109] Furthermore, Salisbury was probably impressed by loyalist organization, and was in turn deeply respected by loyalists. Whether this mutual regard materialized in specific Conservative legislation is incapable of conclusive demonstration; but it is important to indicate the nature of this interest, and to note its existence as one further possible influence over policy formulation. Similarly with Ulster Party lobbying: the nature and limitations of the available evidence mean that it is difficult to prove beyond all doubt any causal linkage between back-bench pressure and executive action. Again, it is important to note the existence of channels of communication between Ulster members and government, and to point to the evidence suggesting the effectiveness of this contact.

One aim of this chapter has been, therefore, to call into question any facile dismissal of the Irish Tory role in the high politics of 1885-6. This is partly a matter of interpreting otherwise undisputed evidence. For example, Cooke and Vincent illustrate the leadership's disregard by referring to the absence from loyalist parliamentary meetings in early 1886 of Tory ministers.[110] But this is surely to overlook the extent to which these meetings were purposely designed as an expression of independence. Edward Saunderson, as chairman of the Ulster group, defined its role as being the independent representation of loyalist opinion, and he was conscious even of comparatively minor challenges to the successful fulfilment of this task. The presence of a minister would have been a contradiction of the very purpose of these meetings—and none were in fact invited to attend. Thus the composition of these meetings implies little about ministerial attitudes towards loyalism, whereas it does illuminate the attitude of loyalists towards Tory ministers.

But there are other, factual contentions. Thus, to suggest, as has been done, that there was 'no trace of contact' between Ulster loyalists and British Tory leaders in early 1886 is demonstrably incorrect, even excluding the Churchill visit to Belfast.[111] The Saunderson papers in the Public Record Office of Northern Ireland contain numerous references to such contact, as indeed does Reginald Lucas's biography of the loyalist leader. There is also the evidence of the

---

[109] Cecil, *Third Marquess of Salisbury*, iii. 150-1.
[110] Cooke and Vincent, *Governing Passion*, 159.
[111] Ibid. Cooke and Vincent cite the Saunderson papers in their bibliography.

interview between loyalist delegates and Salisbury held on 19 January 1886. However one interprets it, whether as an exchange of genuine concerns, or as a consummate display of theatrical emotion, this meeting was clearly one element of a relatively sustained process of communication between the Tory leadership and its loyalist support.

A second aim of this chapter has been to observe the impact of Conservatism on the development both of an independent Irish Unionist parliamentary party, and of the broader loyalist movement. Again there are conflicts with the existing historiography. Thus, it has been suggested here that loyalist parliamentary independence was originally a response to the prospect of betrayal over reform and redistribution, and not, as was argued by D. C. Savage, to the equivocal attitudes of the first Salisbury government. More generally, it may be noted that Irish loyalist independence was related to British responsiveness, and not simply to the threat of Home Rule. When Conservatives disregarded loyalist colleagues—when high political communication was proving ineffective—Irish Tories looked to exploit their own local political resources. Deprived temporarily of any private means of influencing the Conservative leadership, they declared their opinions openly. But, even when loyalist ease of access to leadership was greatest, and when their respective opinions coincided (the two are connected), Ulster Party parliamentary organization remained intact, if quiescent.

This dependence indicates how far the pose of a separate 'Fourth Party' was a sham, for the Ulster group could exist only within the broad confines of Conservatism. 'Independence' in practice meant sporadic complaints to the leadership, and occasional lobby dissent. But Irish loyalists believed in their charade; and Irish Protestant political vanity was invested in the trappings of parliamentary independence. It was fortunate for loyalists' self-esteem, therefore, that the Conservative leadership could never really call their bluff—so long as Ireland determined the nature of British party divisions.

3

The Parliamentary Party, 1885–1910

Torn before birth from where my fathers dwelt,
Schooled from the age of ten to a foreign voice,
Yet neither western Ireland nor southern England
Cancels this interlude; what chance misspelt
May never now be righted by my choice.

MacNeice, *Carrick Revisited* (1945)

1. *Party Personnel*

Fighting Home Rule in 1886 brought a restoration of the alliance between British and Irish Unionism. Britons now referred piously to the virtues and plight of Irish loyalty, while Irishmen developed a tactical amnesia, forgetting the spite and angry posturing of 1885. Though their independent organizational structures survived, and were developed, Irish Unionists were temporarily content to be bound within the British party; and indeed, the greater flexibility of attitude permitted by parliamentary opposition meant that their rehabilitation was the more readily achieved.

Yet, what contemporaries remembered in their published diaries and autobiographies about the Irish Unionist members was not so much their formal relationship with the British party as their personal, or—more rarely—their generic distinctiveness. Thus, Saunderson's quintessential Irishness attracted notice—and not his status as chairman of a parliamentary pressure group, or the nature of his bond with Lord Salisbury. For the Liberals, A. E. Pease recorded that Saunderson's nickname was the 'Dancing Dervish'; his wit and panache impressed, but not the substance of his political contribution, or the nature of his political pretensions.[1] Even Reginald Lucas, Saunderson's biographer, in recalling a personal

---

[1] Alfred E. Pease, *Elections and Recollections* (London, 1932), 133.

acquaintance with his subject, remembered above all the colourful violence of the Colonel's rhetoric, and his hibernian passion for laughter and practical jokes.[2]

In part this emphasis may reflect the restraints of a literary medium, the political memoir, where anecdotes were at a premium, and where there was a tendency to invest every acquaintance mentioned with the trappings of a 'character'. It may also reflect the priorities of battle-weary parliamentarians, for whom personal qualities had come to mean more than party political distinctions. Yet even allowing for these influences, it remains striking that contemporaries should have classified both Unionists and Nationalists as being sources of good-natured fun, and that they should have associated particular qualities with the Irish Unionist group (temperance, and, para-doxically—given the humour association—dourness).

But the frivolity of this form of reminiscence raises more fundamental political issues. Despite the need to entertain, it may be that authors like Pease, or Lucas, were accurately reflecting an isolated and idiosyncratic loyalist parliamentary party—and that they were provoked to caricature rather through xenophobia than fond friendship. How personally distinct, then, was the Irish Unionist group in the late Victorian and Edwardian period? Did these attitudes reflect unthinking national stereotyping—or some more substantial distinction between Irish Unionists and British Tories? This chapter is a response to these problems. It offers an analysis of the personnel of the Irish Unionist parliamentary party, while seeking to illuminate the extent of their assimilation within the framework of British party politics.

The Irish Unionist presence, measured whether by their political influence or by their impact on fellow members, was always more significant than their bald numerical strength might suggest. The number of Unionist MPs returned by Irish constituencies never exceeded twenty-three during the period 1885–1918—though, on the other hand, this figure never fell below nineteen. Such stability, even at a low level of representation, provided strength and cohesion to the group. It reflected the absence of any prolonged and serious threat within the Unionist heartland, and it meant that the British Conservative leadership was faced with a more or less permanent ginger group among its ranks. Irish Unionist pressure could not be

[2] Reginald Lucas, *Colonel Saunderson M.P.: A Memoir* (London, 1908), 226.

TABLE 3.1. *The Numerical Strength of the Irish Unionist Parliamentary Party*

Year	No. of Irish Unionist members	Percentage of Total Unionist strength	No. of Southern Unionist members
1880*	25	11	7
1885*	18	7	2
1886	19	5	2
1892	23	7	4
1895	21	5	4
1900	21	5	2
1906	20	13	3
1910 (J)	21	8	3
1910 (D)	19	7	2
1918	26	8	3

*Conservatives only considered before 1886

Source: Brian M. Walker, *Parliamentary Election Results in Ireland, 1801–1922* (Dublin, 1978).

obviated by being ignored—because Irish Unionists did not go away. Their numbers held with a dreary consistency, equalled only by the nature and permanence of their complaints.

Even with a core of a little over twenty members, Irish Unionists could still exercise numerical punch. Though twenty Irish Unionists in 1900 might be overwhelmed in a tide of British MPs, by 1906 almost the same number represented a substantial fraction of Unionist representation. With rather more than one in eight members of the Unionist parliamentary party an Irish loyalist, the party leadership had to recognize their strength and susceptibilities; in fact, the Chamberlains were anxious to curry favour with the Ulster group in February 1906 and thereafter.[3] It seems reasonable to suggest that the trenchant Unionism represented by Walter Long, which characterized the British party's public stand between 1906 and 1910, had much to do with the disproportionately great Ulster influence on the Opposition benches.

Unionists sitting for Irish seats were strengthened, in theory, by a number of compatriots representing British constituencies (table 3.2). Their numbers were never large, generally hovering around

[3] ESP, T 2996/3/13, Austen Chamberlain to Saunderson, 7 Feb. 1906. For Saunderson's reply see Ronan Fanning, 'The Unionist Party and Ireland, 1906–1910', *Irish Historical Studies*, xv. 58 (Sept. 1966), 150, n. 9.

TABLE 3.2. *Irish Unionists sitting for British Constituencies*

Year	Number	Percentage of total Unionist strength
1880	12	5
1885	16	6
1886	14	4
1892	5	2
1895	8	2
1900	8	2
1906	4	3
1910 (J)	12	4
1910 (D)	11	4
1918	18	5

Source: M. Stenton and F. Lees, *British Members of Parliament, 1832–1969*, 4 vols. (Brighton and Hassocks, 1976–81); R. H. Mairs (ed.), *Debrett's Illustrated House of Commons and the Judicial Bench*.

4 per cent of the Conservative and Unionist parliamentary total. Nor is it altogether clear how closely these emigrant MPs co-operated with the Ulster Party—though scattered evidence is provided by private diaries and press reports. For example, Edward Saunderson recorded in January 1886 that twenty-six members had attended a preliminary meeting of his Party, and since only eighteen Irish loyalists had been returned at the general election, the remaining eight almost certainly came from among the sixteen British Tories of Irish background sitting in the Home Rule parliament.[4] After 1886 enthusiasm for the parliamentary party among both Irish and English loyalists waned perceptibly, but a small number of the latter were consistently associated with the Ulster Party—men like Arthur Smith-Barry, J. G. Butcher, and R. U. Penrose-Fitzgerald in the 1890s; and Ronald McNeill in the period after 1910.[5] However, though these men rose to relative political prominence by promoting the Irish Unionist cause, they constituted only a small minority within a more passive English group. Some emigrants may have deliberately sought political and national assimilation; the links of others with Protestant

[4] ESP, T 2996/1/66, Saunderson to his wife, 23 Jan. 1886.   [5] See ch. 4.

TABLE 3.3. *The Ulster Party: Occupational Background (As a Percentage of the Total Membership)*

Year	1[a]	2	3	4	5	No Data	Total Elected
1880	60	24/24	16	—	—	—	25
1885	50	33/33	11	—	6	—	18
1886	53	26/26	11	5	5	—	19
1892	35	43/35	22	—	—	—	23
1895	33	48/33	19	—	—	—	21
1900	33	43/33	24	—	—	—	21
1906	25	20/20	50	5	—	—	20
1910 (J)	19	38/38	43	—	—	—	21
1910 (D)	16	42/42	42	—	—	—	19
1918	4	46/27	35	—	12	4	26

[a] 1: Landowners, and those deriving their income directly from land ownership; 2: Upper Professionals/Lawyers; 3: Merchants, Industrialists and Rentiers; 4: Lower Professionals; 5: Wage Earners, Tenant Farmers, and Farm Labourers.

Sources: Stenton and Lees, *Who's Who of British Members of Parliament*; *Debrett's Illustrated House of Commons*; *Who's Who*.

Ireland may have been too tenuous to have had any political significance. The Ulster Party could never, therefore, call on its full complement of emigrant support though the commitment and verve of MPs like Smith-Barry and McNeill offered compensating strength.

Categorized according to occupation, Ulster Party membership appears to have developed rapidly between 1880 and 1918 (table 3.3).[6] As in contemporary Britain, the landlord element was decimated, claiming 60 per cent of members in 1880 and only 4 per cent in 1918. The merchant/industrial and professional classes, especially lawyers, were clearly the chief beneficiaries of this decline where few low-grade professionals and wage-earners were elected before 1918. In particular, the fall in landlord representation was associated with measures of franchise reform and constituency redistribution—important drops occurring in 1885 and 1918; but

---

[6] Cf. J. P. Cornford, 'The Parliamentary Foundations of the Hotel Cecil', in R. Robson (ed.), *Ideas and Instiutions of Victorian Britain: Essays in Honour of George Kitson Clark* (London, 1967), 282; and Jane Ridley, 'Leadership and Management in the Conservative Party in Parliament, 1906–1914', D.Phil. thesis (Oxford, 1985), 17 ff.

it may also have been associated with constant farmer pressure on the leadership in the late 1880s, and with the reorganization of Unionist machinery in 1904–6. Already by 1891 John Ross was complaining that though 'there will be some pretty good N[orth] of Ireland seats open at the general election . . . our best class [of candidate] are excluded through their interest in the land'.[7] The upward trend in lawyer numbers was also interrupted significantly in 1906. T. W. Russell's land campaign, conducted during this period, directed attention to inefficient landlord and lawyer representation, and the subsequent fall in their numbers may reflect local Unionist sensitivity on this score.

The general trend, however, was towards a growth in lawyer representation, and there were sound parliamentary reasons for this.[8] The increasing complexity of Irish legislation, particularly on land, demanded technical legal skills which the old squire-politicians did not possess. The records of the Irish Loyal and Patriotic Union, for example, contain frequent references to the hire of solicitors—for the interpretation of recondite acts, or for drafting amendments on behalf of friendly MPs. Consequently, lawyers like D. P. Barton, Carson, Ellison-Macartney, and William Moore were able to dominate the Irish Unionist contribution to debate on the land bills; where an Edward Saunderson, lacking technical mastery of land law, struggled with the details of legislation, and preferred general indictment to specific and reasoned criticism. Reginald Lucas recalled the aftermath to Saunderson's speech on the Second Reading of the 1896 Land Bill:

When he [Saunderson] sat down, he said to his colleague beside him, as a speaker often does, 'Was that all right?'. 'Excellent', was the answer, 'but you might have said something about the Bill'. 'How could I? I never read it.'[9]

Such studied ignorance may have made for lively (if uninformative) debate—but Irish Unionism, to survive, needed greater dialectical skills than Saunderson and his kind could provide. Lawyers became the new knights errant of Unionism, and were rewarded with a large share of the limited number of parliamentary seats available to the cause.

---

[7] ABP, Add. MS 49848, fo. 69, Ross to Balfour, 21 Feb. 1891.

[8] Ridley, 'Leadership and Management', 15, 46. For her 'professionalisation of politics' argument: Ibid. 34.

[9] Lucas, *Saunderson*, 251, paraphrased in Edward Marjoribanks and Ian Colvin, *Life of Lord Carson* (3 vols.; London, 1932–6), i. 160. The novelist George Birmingham identified loyalism's new enthusiasm for legal acumen: Birmingham, *Benedict Kavanagh* (London, 1907), 50–1.

Lawyers, therefore, were scarcely losers by their usefulness to Unionism. Parliament provided a catalyst for the careers of the ambitious, accelerating promotion to the judicial bench. William Moore was surely not alone in perceiving this, though his candour was certainly refreshing: 'he never made any secret or mystery of why he went into parliament', his daughter recalled, 'it was the way to get promotion at the bar'.[10] Not all were as fortunate as John Ross (member for Londonderry City, 1892–5) who in 1896, at the age of forty-three, was appointed a Judge of the Irish High Court: Moore had to wait until 1917, when he was fifty-three, before gaining a similar appointment.[11] But most lawyer-MPs of reasonable ability could look forward to promotion to one of the Irish law offices, and thence to the judiciary. The Irish Attorney-General and Solicitor-General in Unionist governments were always recruited from the seven or eight lawyers of the Ulster Party. With a one-in-four chance of winning office, these members were peculiarly favoured in the parliamentary promotion stakes.

Unlike Irish Nationalists (and contrary to the suggestion of F. S. L. Lyons), the Ulster Party was able to win new commercial wealth to its ranks.[12] Great employers, like the linen manufacturer William Ewart, and the shipbuilders Edward Harland and G. W. Wolff, might sit for their home constituencies in Belfast. Wolff represented the eastern division (where his yards were situated and his labour recruited) for eighteen years. Successful merchants like Sir Daniel Dixon, who owned a timber and shipping business, or Sir James Haslett, a retail chemist, also held Belfast constituencies. Businessmen with smaller, local firms, or rural family connections, might represent one of the county seats. John Brownlee Lonsdale, a wealthy merchant and banker, had roots in Mid Armagh, which seat he held between 1900 and 1918. Henry Liddell represented West Down, where his family had a linen business, between 1905 and 1907.

[10] Private possession, Diary of Nina Patrick (daughter of William Moore, MP), v. 7. Cf. Cornford, 'Hotel Cecil', 289.

[11] Sir John Ross, The Years of My Pilgrimage: Random Reminiscences (London, 1924), 120–3.

[12] K. T. Hoppen, Elections, Politics, and Society in Ireland, 1832–1885 (Oxford, 1984), 308. F. S. L. Lyons, The Irish Parliamentary Party, 1890–1910 (London, 1951), 175. Lyons, in his original research, greatly underestimated the number of Ulster business members: 'Irish Parliamentary Representation, 1891–1910', Ph.D. thesis (Dublin, 1947), 129.

These businessmen-members did not share any single perception of their function as MPs. Some had inherited their wealth, and were able to devote as much time as they chose to politics. James Craig, member for East Down (1906–18), was by training a stockbroker, and the son of a millionaire distiller, and, on election, became virtually a professional politician.[13] Henry Lyle Mulholland, member for North Londonderry (1885–95), inherited his seat, and (ultimately) a peerage and an estate worth £580,000 from his father, a linen manufacturer; but economic security and social status did not promote political commitment.[14] This was also true of Henry Liddell, son of a linen baron, who was as negligent a politician as he was a businessman. His working day at the family's London office began well at 8.30 a.m., but swiftly petered out:

At 9.30 a.m. he would go to the barber to be shaved, and shortly after 11 o'clock a friend or customer would generally call to see him, when they would adjourn to a room in the basement of the office where a supply of liquor was kept. They would reappear at 12.45 p.m. and leave for lunch, and Harry Liddell would not be seen in the office again that day.[15]

Liddell had been pressured into standing for parliament by his rather more vital brother, Robert, chairman and managing director of the family firm.[16] But, if Robert had calculated on directing his brother into politics, or at least on diverting him from the firm, then he was disappointed, for in 1907, after a singularly uneventful parliamentary career of two years' duration, Harry took the Chiltern Hundreds.

Liddell was uniquely insouciant; but, for many of the self-made, politics were an unwelcome diversion from the more serious business of money-making. Since their political standing—in the frequently conspicuous absence of any parliamentary ability—depended on financial strength, this was, on the whole, a wise calculation of priorities.[17] But, as always, there were exceptions, and some effective politicians were spawned from the otherwise drab entrepreneurial ranks. T. W. Russell, the son of a Fifeshire stonemason, created a successful hotel business, and won political

[13] St John Ervine, *Craigavon: Ulsterman* (London, 1949), 69.
[14] Vicary Gibbs, H. A. Doubleday and Lord Howard de Walden (edd.), *The Complete Peerage*, (13 vols.; London, 1912–59), iv. 541.
[15] Private possession, typescript memoir of H. Liddell (n.d.), 4.
[16] R. M. Liddell to author, 17 June 1985.
[17] Cf. Cornford, 'Hotel Cecil', 285.

pre-eminence, both in Ireland and at Westminster. Supremely energetic, and a depressive, Russell juggled his commitments with agility—and was equally prepared to discuss technical local government legislation, or the state of the hotel trade.[18] Hugh Thom Barrie, member for North Londonderry (1906-22), was a similar exception. Barrie borrowed £100 from his father and, at the age of nineteen, started a produce business; by 1906 he had become a successful grain merchant, and was poised to embark on a distinguished parliamentary career.[19] Later in life, he led the Ulster Unionist delegation at the Irish Convention, earned the respect of Lloyd George, and won appointment to Horace Plunkett's old position of Vice-President at the Irish Department of Agriculture.[20]

For Barrie, as for many businessmen-members, political involvement came almost by accident, and was certainly not—at least to begin with—an end in itself. In a conservative society, wealth alone was not respectable—except in so far as it could be used to illustrate the moral worth of its creator. However, wealth could be rendered respectable, as in England, by being clothed in a more old-fashioned and recognizable form. Thus, businessmen, like John Mulholland, could buy land, and adopt the trappings of squiredom, including its political functions. Many were impressed by the MP's status, and, having won election, were careful to preserve what they viewed as the dignity of the office.[21] Harry Liddell, for example, sacrificed his beloved open motor car in order to acquire a landaulette—this later being, apparently, more appropriate to his new rank as member for West Down.[22] For businessmen, therefore, parliament was a means of demonstrating their success and consolidating their social position. And with the retreat of landlordism, parliament was a progressively realistic ambition.

The decline in the landlord group is associated with a similar fall in the number of Oxbridge graduates among members of the Party.

---

[18] John Vincent (ed.), *The Crawford Papers: The Journals of David Lindsay, Twenty-seventh Earl of Crawford and Tenth Earl of Balcarres, 1871–1940, during the Years 1892 to 1940* (Manchester, 1984), 61. For Russell's career see my 'Irish Unionism and the Russellite Threat, 1894–1906' *IHS.*, xxv. 100 (Nov. 1987).

[19] Sir Walter Barrie to author, 10 May 1985.

[20] Patrick Buckland, *Irish Unionism*, i. *The Anglo-Irish and the New Ireland, 1885–1922* (Dublin and New York, 1972), 122.

[21] Cf. W. L. Guttsman, *The British Political Elite* (London, 1963), 173.

[22] Liddell, Memoir, 3. For the popular perception of the MP's stature, see Alexander Irvine, *The Souls of Poor Folk* (London, 1921), 40–1.

TABLE 3.4. *University Graduates within the Ulster Party (as a Percentage of the Total Membership).*

Year	Oxbridge	TCD	Queen's Colleges	Military College	Non-graduates	Total elected
1880	36	8	—	—	56	25
1885	22	22	6	11	39	18
1886	21	21	—	11	47	19
1892	26	30	9	—	35	23
1895	19	29	10	—	42	21
1900	19	24	14	10	33	21
1906	10	15	5	—	70	20
1910 (J)	5	24	14	19	38	21
1910 (D)	11	21	21	—	47	19
1918	12	31	12	8	37	26

Source: Stenton and Lees, *British Members of Parliament*; *Who's Who*.

In an age of élitist politics, an Oxbridge education was a desirable component of an ambitious and able young Irishman's political training. For landlords, with greater ease of access to the English social élite, and with perhaps a greater sense of supra-national class solidarity than local lawyers or businessmen, Oxbridge provided a useful badge of rank, and cemented social and class bonds. But with the popularization of Irish politics came localization, and loyalist members needed to stay in close contact with the development of local opinion. Against the background of Russellism, labour politicking, and Presbyterian agitation, constituency knowledge was at a premium, and thus any form of tertiary education in England became a liability. One of James Craig's greatest political assets, according to his first biographer, was that he had been preserved from an English public school and university:

To be removed at a formative stage of life from the influences and impressions of home, and to be subjected for a long period to the stronger and less subtle impacts of an alien communal institution, makes it very hard for a young [Ulster] man to take up normal work again later in life in his original home surroundings. . .[23]

---

[23] Hugh Shearman, *Not an Inch: A Study of Northern Ireland and Lord Craigavon* (London, 1942), 50. It should be said that St John Ervine took issue with Shearman: Ervine, *Craigavon*, 33–4.

TABLE 3.5. *Irish Unionist Members' Form of Secondary Education (as a Percentage of the Total Number Elected).*

Year	Clarendon	English public and grammar schools	Irish schools	Total elected
1880	32	16	8	25
1885	28	6	17	18
1886	26	5	11	19
1892	35	13	13	23
1895	33	14	10	21
1900	29	10	5	21
1906	20	25	15	20
1910 (J)	29	19	19	21
1910 (D)	26	14	21	19
1918	15	12	31	26

Source: Stenton and Lees, *Who's Who of British Members of Parliament*; *Debrett's Illustrated House of Commons*; *Who's Who*.

More generally, professional men tended to regard education in a functional light, and consequently the intangible advantages of a liberal arts education in England paled besides the more solid merits of the law and medical schools at Trinity College, Dublin. Particularly for aspirant lawyers, Trinity brooked no rival. Oxbridge offered a training for the English legal system, but few Irishmen took advantage of it, preferring a less competitive career in their home country.

All forms of Irish education underwent expansion during the period. More Irish Unionist members were recruited from Trinity and Queen's College, Belfast, and more claimed wholly Irish secondary education. These increases mirror, again, developments in the occupational backgrounds of the members: more professional men, more merchants and industrialists, were being elected, filling the vacuum created by the departure of the landlords. Unionist professionals, certainly lawyers, were almost by definition Trinity graduates for the first half of the period under consideration, although Queen's Belfast claimed an increasing number of alumni, especially in the sciences—men who took their skills into industry and commerce, and thence into parliament.

A fall in the educational attainments of party members seems to be associated with both measures of parliamentary reform and with the party reorganization preceding 1906. Significant falls in the numbers of Oxbridge graduates, and of old boys from the élite Clarendon schools occur in 1885, 1918, and also in 1906. This may simply reflect the preferences of an expanded electorate (or perhaps the party's conception of popular preferences); but in 1918, with a growth in the number of winnable constituencies, there was also a need to recruit (and speedily) more candidates. The popularization of the 1906 party, revealed by the figures for occupation, is confirmed by a breakdown of its educational background. Fewer graduates than ever were elected, and for the first time a Unionist was returned who had received only primary education (T. H. Sloan, member for South Belfast, 1902-10). With the restoration of a Liberal government and the Home Rule threat, loyalist constituency dissent weakened: the balance between occupational and educational attainments, temporarily upset in 1906, was restored (though long-term trends continued apace).

Parliamentary reforms and constituency redistribution also promoted the recruitment of inexperienced politicians to the Ulster Party. Table 3.7 reveals that the members elected in 1885 and 1918 had less parliamentary experience than after any other general election in the period examined (except 1886, when the party of 1885 was returned virtually intact). Under the more stable constitutional conditions of 1885-1918, the parliamentary experience of the party

TABLE 3.6. *Irish Unionist Members with Primary and Private Education (as a Percentage of the Total Number Elected).*

Year	Primary only	Private	Number elected
1880	—	4	25
1885	—	6	18
1886	—	11	19
1892	—	13	23
1895	—	10	21
1900	—	14	21
1906	5	20	20
1910 (J)	—	14	21
1910 (D)	—	11	19
1918	12	4	26

Source: Stenton and Lees, *Who's Who of British Members of Parliament*; *Debrett's Illustrated House of Commons*; *Who's Who*.

TABLE 3.7. *Irish Unionist Members' Parliamentary Experience on Election*

Year	Average Experience (years)
1880	7
1885	4
1886	4
1892	6
1895	7
1900	8
1906	9
1910 (J)	7
1910 (D)	7
1918	3

Source: Stenton and Lees, *Who's Who of British Members of Parliament.*

developed progressively, reflecting the absence of any significant political threat for most of the period. Out of the peak total of twenty-three seats won by Irish Unionists in 1892, only four were in any sense marginal; the remainder more or less consistently returned Unionists between 1885 and 1918. Personal circumstances rather than electoral defeats were, therefore, by far the most significant cause of retirement. Death, sickness, and career influences caused the majority of resignations, though some members took more flamboyant paths of departure. Edward de Cobain, member for East Belfast, was expelled from the Commons in 1892, 'having been charged with having committed gross and criminal acts of indecency'.[24] Henry Liddell retired in 1907 when he discovered— from a legal colleague, William Moore—that his wife had, for eleven years, received secret payments from a former lover.[25]

Comparative electoral stability is reflected in the slight overall ageing of the Party. If there was no lasting political threat to Unionism after the polarization of Irish politics, then MPs could retain their seats at whim. Many grew old in parliament: James Haslett, William Johnston, Thomas Waring, and William Ewart

[24] M. Stenton and S. Lees, *Who's Who of British Members of Parliament, 1832-1979* (4 vols.; Hassocks and Brighton, 1976-9), ii. 93.
[25] Liddell, Memoir, 3.

TABLE 3.8. *The Ageing of the Ulster Party*

Year	Average Age (Years)	Age Range
1880	48	28–68
1885	46	27–68
1886	46	28–69
1892	46	36–64
1895	51	40–67
1900	50	31–71
1906	52	35–72
1910 (J)	50	26–76
1910 (D)	50	31–72
1918	51	35–68

Source: Stenton and Lees, *Who's Who of British Members of Parliament*.

were each over seventy when death interrupted their constituency tenure; Robert Thompson, who sat for North Belfast (1910–18), died a member of parliament—aged over eighty. And, if the party venerables were becoming increasingly antique, there was no compensating injection of youth at the other end of the age scale. Local associations opted increasingly for middle-aged candidates, where formerly they had been prepared to adopt men in their late twenties. After 1886, with one exception, no new member was under thirty-one—and in 1895 the youngest member whom the party could sport was aged forty.

This caution on the part of Unionist selectors was partly a by-product of a popular debate on the quality of Ulster representation (which raged through the late 1890s and into the new century). Public discontent was registered with ineffectual MPs: farmer spokesmen like T. W. Russell, Presbyterians like T. L. Corbett, and sectarian populists like T. H. Sloan presented their separate complaints which, in combination, represented a devastating critique on the Ulster Party.[26] Local Unionist managers responded to this by playing safe with selections, choosing men of local status and experience rather than young unknowns. The last exceptionally precocious MP before partition was Bryan Ricco Cooper, son of a major Sligo landowner, who was elected in 1910, at the age of twenty-six for South County

[26] See ch. 5.

Dublin. But he was a maverick, moulded by the preternaturally crusty Tories of the Kildare Street Club, and elected for a largely urban constituency where Unionism was fighting for survival. In the gerontocratic north, he would have been an improbable candidate.[27]

Running an Irish Unionist constituency was costly—and there was therefore an independent financial compulsion on selectors to opt for older, and wealthier, candidates. Previously, however, wealth had been more readily compatible with youth, for young candidates had been almost exclusively scions of the great landlord families. Viscount Castlereagh, later the sixth Marquess of Londonderry, was returned for County Down in 1880 at the age of twenty-eight; Lord Ernest Hamilton, brother of the second Duke of Abercorn, was thrust as 'an unwilling victim' upon the electors of North Tyrone in 1885, at the age of twenty-seven.[28] With the break-up of the great estates, and the growth of popular agitation on land questions, such candidates came forward more rarely, and stood a diminishing chance of being elected. New forms of wealth provided less contentious, if also less youthful, candidates before partition.

The Ulster Party emerges as quite different in occupational composition from the Nationalist Party. The number of landowners sitting as Nationalist members dropped dramatically at the 1885 general election—and never rose subsequently above 9 per cent of the total membership. Tenant farmers, on the other hand, though a negligible force in the party of 1880, greatly increased their representation in 1885, and grew thereafter from strength to strength.[29] Within the Ulster Party, landlord numbers were also falling off—but from a much greater initial strength; and this decline was also symptomatic of a readjustment in the ratio of rural to urban members. Landlords were not, as in the Nationalist Party, replaced by farmers; instead lawyers and businessmen filled this gap. Irish Nationalists had generally a weaker lawyer contingent—though even then lawyers were overrepresented in relation to businessmen.[30]

[27] See Lennox Robinson, *Bryan Cooper* (London, 1931), 70.
[28] Lord Ernest Hamilton, *Forty Years On* (London [1922]), 203 (quoted by Cornford, 'Hotel Cecil', 269).
[29] C. C. O'Brien, *Parnell and His Party, 1880-1890* (2nd edn., Oxford, 1964), 18, 152.
[30] Lyons, *Irish Parliamentary Party*, 169, 174-5.

Lawyers were, of course, necessary to Nationalist parliamentary success, but they lacked the opportunities for promotion possessed by their colleagues in the Ulster Party. A parliamentary seat, therefore, was a much more equivocal career asset.

Moreover, the Nationalist Party failed singularly to attract big business into its ranks. In 1892, of eighty Parnellite and anti-Parnellite members elected, only nine were businessmen of substance; by 1910, when eighty-three Nationalists of varying descriptions were returned, a single MP represented the Irish business community. The feebleness of the party's business lobby deprived it of prestige and wealth, and weakened its claim to embrace all sections of Irish society.[31] Irish Unionists, on the other hand *were* able, with negligible effort, to recruit the linen barons and shipbuilders who together dominated Ulster industry.

Journalists—from local hacks to figures of national importance (like T. P. O'Connor)—constituted a significant element within the Nationalist parliamentary party. Its leaders were keenly alive to the value of a sympathetic press, and owners of even comparatively minor provincial papers were recruited to serve in the Commons.[32] Irish Unionist members like Horace Plunkett and Walter Long were also aware of the value of press backing: both were involved in negotiating the purchase of established papers.[33] Yet journalists and proprietors did not feature significantly in the Ulster Party, at least before 1918. Three local press magnates were returned at the Coupon Election: R. J. Lynn, editor and managing director of the *Northern Whig*, Peter Kerr-Smiley, chairman of the *Whig*, and Thomas Moles, editor of the *Belfast Telegraph*. Kerr-Smiley had held his seat since January 1910; hitherto the only Irish Unionist member connected with the newspaper industry had been H. O. Arnold-Forster—and even he, by 1900, had become effectively a career politician. In part this degree of representation may be connected with the extreme social conservatism of the pre-1918 Ulster Party—a party controlled by wealthy landowners, lawyers, and businessmen (though with token, and tame, populists like William Johnston). Before 1918 the

[31] Lyons, *Irish Parliamentary Party*, 175.
[32] Ibid. 174. See also Alan O'Day, *The English Face of Irish Nationalism: Parnellite Involvement in British Politics, 1880-1886* (Dublin, 1977), 20.
[33] Margaret Digby, *Horace Plunkett: An Anglo-American Irishman* (Oxford, 1949), 81; A. M. Gollin, The Observer *and J. L. Garvin 1908-14: A Study in a Great Editorship*, (Oxford, 1960), 15.

party included very few low-grade professionals, wage-earners or small farmers. Mavericks of doubtful social standing (like T. H. Sloan) might slip into the ranks, but Unionist selectors on the whole preferred wealthy candidates to those with more democratic credentials.

The Nationalist Party had always a broader social base, and between 1892 and 1910 the numbers of working-and lower-middle-class members grew. By January 1910, where no Irish Unionist member was recruited from the lower professional and wage-earning ranks, these classes provided 46 per cent of the Irish Nationalist Party's membership.[34] But if this made for accessibility and popularity in the constituency, a party dominated by small shopkeepers and farmers was an alien and unnatural component of a gentrified House of Commons. Nationalists' parliamentary effectiveness was undoubtedly impaired by both their unfamiliar nationality and their unfamiliar class origins.[35] If loyalist MPs could not always overcome the barriers of nationality, then they were not separated from their English allies by class.

In terms of educational background Irish Unionist and Irish Nationalist parties were no less dissimilar. In the 1890s around one third of Nationalist members were university graduates, mostly from the Queen's Colleges, Trinity College Dublin, and the Catholic University.[36] Twice as great a proportion of the Irish Unionist party were graduates, mostly from Oxbridge and Trinity College, Dublin. A substantial proportion (generally 25-30 per cent) of the Irish Unionist group had been to a Clarendon public school in England; most Irish Nationalists received an exclusively Irish secondary education.[37] Where only maverick loyalists (Tom Sloan, for example) had received no secondary education, as many as 14 per cent (in 1892) of the Irish Nationalist Party were similarly disadvantaged.[38]

On the other hand, like its Irish Unionist equivalent, the Conservative Parliamentary Party of 1900-10 was predominantly middle class, containing few—if any—working men. Like the Irish Unionist party, a substantial number of Conservative MPs were recruited from the professions; and almost exactly the same

[34] Lyons, *Irish Parliamentary Party*, 169.   [35] Ibid. 171-2.
[36] Ibid. 166; Lyons, 'Parliamentary Representation', 114. O'Day suggests a larger proportion of Parnellite graduates (41%) in the early 1880': *English Face*, 22-3.
[37] Lyons, *Irish Parliamentary Party*, 167.   [38] Ibid. 165.

proportion (30 per cent) of each party comprised businessmen.[39] A large number of Irish Unionists enjoyed private incomes, this reflecting a relatively great number of landlords. The 'miscellaneous' category, as defined by Michael Rush in his essay 'The Members of Parliament', and including wage-earners and most lower-middle-class occupations, captured a negligible section of both Conservative and loyalist parties.[40]

Compared with the occupational background of the Edwardian Liberal Party, the Irish Unionist group emerges again as broadly similar. The professional sector of the Liberal Party was close to the proportionate strength of its Ulster Party equivalent.[41] The Liberals boasted more businessmen than either the Conservatives or loyalists; but the difference between the parties was quite small (around 7 per cent).[42] Both Liberals and Irish Unionists contained close to the same negligible number of working men—though slightly more Liberals were recruited from the lower-middle-class occupations embraced by the 'miscellaneous' category.[43] The chief claim of the Irish Unionist Parliamentary Party to distinction was again the relatively large number of its members with private incomes: that is, the relatively strong (if declining) landlord contingent.

Comparing the educational attainments of Irishmen and Englishmen poses more serious problems. Irishmen, it might be expected, would be more likely to receive education in Irish institutions; and, in the absence of a public school tradition, the nature of Irish educational attainment might be expected to defy comparison with any English model. F. S. L. Lyons had in mind both the quantity and quality of Irish Party education when he argued that the isolation and aloofness of Nationalists owed much to their distinctively un-English educational experience.[44]

Yet despite the arguments for presupposing discontinuity, the Edwardian Ulster Party emerges as quite similar in educational experience to the English parties—particularly with the Liberal party. More Conservatives, sitting between 1900 and 1910 had enjoyed a university education (64 per cent to the Ulster Party's 53 per cent); and, consequently, more Irish Unionist members had experienced

[39] Michael Rush, 'The Members of Parliament', in S. A. Walkland (ed.), *The House of Commons in the Twentieth Century: Essays by Members of the Study of Parliament Group* (Oxford, 1979), 101.
[40] Ibid.   [41] Ibid. 106.   [42] Ibid.   [43] Ibid.
[44] Lyons, 'Parliamentary Representation', 113.

only secondary education. But the number of members in both parties who had either received only elementary education, or who were autodidacts, was negligible.[45] For the pre-university stages of educational experience, the Edwardian Ulster Party was very similar to the Liberals. The proportion of autodidacts and those with only elementary schooling was small in both parties; and though Irish Unionists again appear with fewer graduates, the difference between the parties was slight (53 per cent of the Ulster Party to the Liberals' 58 per cent).[46]

A substantial difference emerges, admittedly, in the nature of loyalist and Conservative secondary education: where 51 per cent of Conservative members were Clarendon products, only 25 per cent of Ulster members had received similar schooling. The majority of loyalists were given a 'private' or 'non-public' education in Ireland, only 35 per cent receiving an English public school education (as against 75 per cent of Conservative members).[47] On the other hand, Irish Unionist education at the secondary level closely echoed the Liberal parliamentary party. Similar proportions had attended the Clarendon schools: indeed, a rather higher proportion of Irish Unionists were thus advantaged.[48] Discrepancies arise in the relative ratios of public : non-public-school products, originating again in the absence of any English-style public-school system in Ireland. But the proportion of those in the two parties who were privately educated was virtually the same.[49] Furthermore, given both the relative cost of maintaining a son in England and the fine reputation of many Irish schools, it is surprising that so many members of the gentry and upper middle classes should have sent their offspring to English public schools. And, while twice as many Conservative members had been to public school in England, the fact remains that over one third of the Ulster Party had experienced a similar education.

Pressures to remain in Ireland were even greater at the university level. For the reasons outlined earlier, young Irishmen aspiring to professional, especially legal, careers found it more convenient to remain for training at Irish universities. Some 35 per cent of the total Party membership went to Trinity, or to one of the Queen's Colleges—generally Queen's College, Belfast. Yet a not insubstantial proportion (15 per cent) shared the Oxbridge education enjoyed by

---

[45] Rush, 'Members of Parliament', 99.   [46] Ibid. 105.
[47] Ibid. 99.   [48] Ibid. 105.   [49] Ibid.

some 49 per cent of their Conservative contemporaries.[50] Similar proportions of the Liberal and Ulster Parties were Oxford graduates; but, where there was a slight preference among Liberals for Cambridge, the Edwardian Ulster Party could only sport one graduate of the younger university (Peter Kerr-Smiley, member for North Antrim).[51]

Thus, even allowing for geographical distinctions, Irish Unionists' education was much more akin to that of their British than Irish contemporaries. There remained a hard core of Irish Unionists who shared the Clarendon and Oxbridge education of most Conservatives. The assimilating value of these members for loyalism defies quantification: but there are good reasons for supposing that they helped to promote contact between the British and Irish wings of the Unionist party. Some, like Horace Plunkett (University College, Oxford, matriculated 1873) slunk through their Oxbridge careers, but several made a mark on their school and university contemporaries. D. P. Barton (exhibitioner, Corpus Christi College, Oxford, matriculated 1873) held the presidency of the Oxford Union while H. O. Arnold-Forster (commoner, University College, matriculated 1874) gained a fine 'First' in History.[52] Even Ulstermen with comparatively undistinguished educational careers might possess a bond with English contemporaries, by virtue of sharing the same school tie. Writing in 1953 of his colleagues in Baldwin's first government, L. S. Amery remembered Ronald McNeill, an Ulster Unionist who sat for Canterbury, not as an Irishman, but first and foremost as an old Harrovian.[53]

This occupational and educational similarity points to the likelihood of personal compatibility within Conservatism at Westminster. Assessing whether this was translated into reality—whether Ulster members, unlike Nationalists, *were* assimilated—must depend on a more subjective assessment of their capacity to form close friendships with members of other parties. Their degree of assimilation can also be estimated from the reactions of British contemporaries—though these are much harder to interpret than has generally been supposed.

---

[50] Rush, 'Members of Parliament', 99   [51] Ibid. 105.

[52] Digby, *Horace Plunkett*, 16-18. Thomas Fowler, *The History of Corpus Christi College, Oxford, With Lists of Its Members* (Oxford, 1893), 436. J. Foster (ed.), *Alumni Oxoniensis: The Members of the University of Oxford, 1715-1886* (4 vols.; London, 1887-8).

[53] L. S. Amery, *My Political Life* (3 vols.; London, 1953-5), ii. 426.

Nationalists members, recalled T. P. O'Connor, were, on the whole, poor men, and their poverty isolated them from contemporaries in the British parties.[54] Though they were sociable, it was not within the framework of London clubland. Some had joined the National Liberal Club under the Union of Hearts, but 'fraternization', of this kind was discouraged: political as well as personal factors militated against assimilation.[55] For members of the Ulster Party the reverse was true. The party was generally wealthy, and could afford club fees, but, more important, its fundamental political conviction encouraged social integration.

Thus, club membership in the Ulster Party was high, never falling below an average of two clubs for each member. Membership was rising through the period, reaching a peak with the party elected in January 1910. As with other aspects of the Party's composition, the reforms of 1884-5 and 1918 appear to have had a democratizing effect on the membership: the average number of clubs per MP fell after the general elections in 1885 and 1918. The Carlton was always the most important club among Irish Unionists, followed, after 1900, by the Constitutional and the Ulster Club in Belfast. The expansion of the latter seems to have been at the expense of Dublin's Kildare Street Club, and perhaps reflects the gradual 'Ulsterization' of the Irish Unionist movement.

For a variety of reasons, therefore, Ulster members liked and respected clubs. Edward Carson, as prospective candidate for Trinity College, Dublin, in October 1891, sought membership of the Carlton 'as it would assist me in the event of a contest'.[56] Clubs provided contacts for ambitious politicians as well as enterprising businessmen, and the general rise in membership may well be linked to the influx of business representatives into the party. Barrie, the successful grain merchant, sought recommendation to 'an inexpensive first class club in London'—even before his presence there had been guaranteed by victory at the North Derry election of January 1906.[57] Barrie, a

[54] T. P. O'Connor, *Memoirs of an Old Parliamentarian* (2 vols.; London, 1929) ii. 426. However O'Day has warned against the uncritical acceptance of an image of 'the lone isolated Irishman': *English Face*, 30.

[55] F. S. L. Lyons, *Ireland Since the Famine* (2nd edn., London, 1972), 194.

[56] Whittingehame, Arthur Balfour Papers, TD 83/113/31, Edward Carson to Balfour, 25 Oct. 1891.

[57] Private possession, William Moore Papers, H. T. Barrie to Moore, 26 Dec. 1905.

TABLE 3.9. *Club Membership within the Ulster Party*

Year	Average No. of clubs per MP	No. of MPs with no club	Most popular clubs[a]
1880	2.3	—	C, K, A, S, C
1885	2.1	11	C, K, CO, U
1886	2.1	5	C, K, U
1892	2.3	4	C, K, JC
1895	2.6	5	C, K, JC
1900	2.4	5	C, CO, U
1906	3.0	5	C, CO, U
1910 (J)	3.1	—	C, CO, U
1910 (D)	2.7	—	C, CO, U
1918	2.5	15	C, CO, U

[a] A: Athenaeum; C: Carlton; K: Kildare Street; S: St Stephen's; U: Ulster; CO: Constitutional; JC: Junior Constitutional.

Sources: *Who's Who*; McCalmont's *Parliamentary Poll Books*; Stenton and Lees, *British Members of Parliament*.

parvenu, with (as yet) no permanent London home, recognized that a club might provide an entrée into political and commercial society.

Clubbability is a personal characteristic, and while Ulster members appeared generally clubbable, there were individual extremes. Some, like John Lonsdale and James Campbell, took club membership seriously, exploiting it as an adjunct to more conventional forms of political or personal advancement. Lonsdale, secretary to the Ulster Party, was a *habitué* of the Carlton, and rose to a position of considerable eminence within its committee structure; the thrusting Campbell was one of only twenty-four MPs to win election to F. E. Smith's 'Other Club' in 1911.[58] James Craig was elected to the Committee of the Constitutional Club in 1906.[59] 'Jemmy' McCalmont, MP for East Antrim, and Harry Liddell, MP for West Down, embraced a rather more flamboyant form of sociability: both were unrepentant sybarites, never allowing parliamentary, or any other responsibilities to interfere with their enjoyment of life. McCalmont once scribbled a note to the Conservative whip, Akers-Douglas,

[58] Sir Charles Petrie, *The Carlton Club* (London, 1955), 152; John Campbell, *F. E. Smith, First Earl of Birkenhead* (London, 1983), 268.
[59] PRONI, Diary of Lady Craigavon, D 1415/B/38, 8 Mar. 1906.

offering—grudgingly—to attend a division; but he confessed that he would rather not move from the Ascot enclosure of the Coaching Club.[60] Liddell's biography contains several references to his fondness for alcohol and good company, and provides a memorable vignette of Liddell, supporting the bar of the Eccentric Club, 'armed with a double scotch and the inevitable cigar'.[61] At the other extreme were the teetotallers, T. L. Corbett and William Johnston. Teetotalism may not have been an insuperable barrier to participation in high political society—but it can scarcely have been an advantage: Corbett was a member only of the two 'regulation' political clubs, the Carlton and Constitutional, and had a reputation for worthy, if unsmiling, faddism; Johnston had no club membership.

Johnston had individual political friends (like Wilfrid Lawson and Coningsby Disraeli), and a wide range of contacts in the temperance and Orange movements. But, as an impecunious landowner, he had not the means with which to sustain a place in political society. Where several Irish Unionist members—Carson, Saunderson, Plunkett, Lonsdale—had prestigious London houses, and the financial capacity to entertain, Johnston occupied two-room lodgings on Vauxhall Bridge Road (at a rent of £1 a week, 'fire and light included').[62] Whatever his personal characteristics, Johnston's poverty precluded parliamentary assimilation. In this, ironically, he had much more in common with Irish Nationalists than with members of his own party.

Irish Unionist prowess in the dinner circuit, therefore, varied. Celebrities like Carson and Saunderson were lionized: Saunderson was a noted raconteur, a friend of the Prince of Wales, while Carson, having come to prominence in the courts, was swiftly ensnared in Theresa Londonderry's social net.[63] But where Saunderson could dominate an Osborne House luncheon, and Carson a party at Wynyard or Mountstewart, William Johnston's social success peaked with temperance soirées.[64] And there is no evidence to suggest that other maverick populists—like E. S. W. de Cobain and T. H. Sloan—ever infiltrated political high society.

[60] KRO, Papers of Aretas Akers-Douglas, First Viscount Chilston, C 355/1, J. M. McCalmont to Akers-Douglas, n.d.

[61] Liddell, Memoir, 7.   [62] WJD, D 880/2/39, 27 Jan. 1887.

[63] H. Montgomery Hyde, Carson: The Life of Sir Edward Carson, Lord Carson of Duncairn (London, 1953), 124–5.

[64] Sir Almeric Fitzroy, Memoirs, (2 vols.; London, [1925]), i. 9; WJD, D 880/2/39, 11 Mar. 1887 (referring to Saunderson's social contact with the Prince of Wales); and passim for Johnston's own social exploits.

Irish Unionists, whether social lions or not, were not themselves prolific hosts. As has been noted, the majority of the Party were wealthy, and a number had fine London houses. Yet there were other obstacles: while both Carson and Saunderson entered happily into London society, their wives were more hesitant. Mrs Saunderson spent more time at the principal family home in County Cavan than in London, and the first Lady Carson shared this Anglophobia, finding London uncongenial and Londoners 'reserved and even superior compared with Irish standards'.[65] Leading an effectively bachelor existence for most of the parliamentary session, neither Saunderson nor Carson could entertain adequately in their homes. Irish Unionists, like James Craig and H. O. Arnold-Forster, who married English wives, appear to have established a social base in London with greater ease. But, on the whole, to paraphrase Maurice Bowra, it seems that Irish Unionist members were more dining than dined against.

From their socializing, Irish Unionists forged various firm friendships with English members. Saunderson was a particular friend of both Walter Long and the Burdett-Coutts family—the Baroness and her MP husband.[66] Carson and F. E. Smith were close friends, though their bond was shaken somewhat by F. E.'s tampering with devolution in 1910, and his final apostasy in 1921. Of the Ulster second rank, William Moore, MP for North Armagh after Saunderson's death, befriended the young Stanley Baldwin: the venerable Earl Baldwin of Bewdley recalled in 1946 that Moore had been 'consistently a kind and helpful friend to me in those far off [Edwardian] days'.[67] Horace Plunkett was an intimate of both Arthur and, especially, Gerald Balfour. Gerald's wife, Lady Betty, provides a rare portrait of Plunkett in domestic surroundings, both in his own mansion at Foxrock, County Dublin, and in the Balfour's home at Woking.[68] She also describes another family friend, S. H. Butcher, an Irish Unionist sitting for Cambridge University, and a future President of the British Academy, in unfamiliar pose:

He [Butcher] has given us such a delightful Sunday—making himself quite at home with all the [Balfour] children, and winning them as no outsider

[65] Hyde, *Carson*, 157.   [66] Lucas, *Saunderson*, 256, n. 1.
[67] Moore Papers, Earl Baldwin to William Moore (son), 10 Aug. 1946.
[68] Whittingehame, Papers of Gerald Balfour, TD 83/133/140, Betty Balfour to Gerald, [*c*.1903].

ever does. They acted to him Saturday evening—historical scenes, which neither he nor I could guess. On Sunday they made him play a paper game with them . . .[69]

By way of postscript, it may be noted that a number of leading Irish and British Unionists shared a bond in Freemasonry. The first and second dukes of Abercorn were successive Grand Masters of Irish Masonry; Aretas Akers-Douglas and his junior whip, Lord Arthur Hill, were each active masons—Hill occupying the Provincial Grand Mastership of Down. Other loyalist members, like William Johnston, held less exalted rank in the craft.[70] Whether Masonry had any, even indirect, political significance, is unclear; but, at the very least, it represented a potential aid to loyalist assimilation, which most Nationalist members, given the disapproval of the Irish hierarchy, could not exploit.

Against the evidence suggesting successful integration should be set the numerous complaints of English Unionists about their Irish colleagues. These complaints have generally been treated uncritically as evidence of blanket suspicion and alienation, but, in reality, they have a much more limited bearing on the Irish–British Unionist relationship.

All the memorable British slurs occur after demonstrations of Irish Unionist spleen, or independence. For example, the development of loyalist qualms, and a distinct loyalist movement in 1885–6, provoked a harsh Conservative reaction, characterized at its most extreme by Randolph Churchill's well-known reference to the 'foul Ulster Tories'.[71] Ulster members' campaign against George Wyndham won a bitter response from some British Unionists, not least from Wyndham himself. 'My contact with the Ulster members is like catching an "itch" from park pests', he wrote in August 1904; 'it is very unpleasant, not your fault, but still degrading.'[72] A friend, Henry Bellingham, complained after Wyndham's resignation that loyalists were 'the most selfish and narrow minded clique that ever

[69] Gerald Balfour Papers, TD 83/133/273, Betty Balfour to Gerald, [c.1906].
[70] Samuel Leighton, *The History of Freemasonry in the Province of Antrim, Northern Ireland* (Belfast, 1938), 223, 226, WJD, D 880/2/38, 19 June 1886.
[71] R. E. Quinault, 'Lord Randolph Churchill and Home Rule' *IHS*, xxi. 84 (Sept. 1979), 394, referring to A. B. Cooke and John Vincent, *The Governing Passion: Cabinet Government and Party Politics in Britain, 1885–6* (Brighton, 1974), 278.
[72] GWP, Wyndham to his wife, Sibell Grosvenor, 13 Aug. 1904.

existed, and are really Radicals by origin'—this last being the most damning accusation in his vocabulary of abuse.[73] Arthur Balfour's most unequivocal repudiation of his Irish support came after their trouble-making in the autumn of 1906.[74]

That British vituperation should be associated with loyalist misdemeanour suggests that any alienation, far from being permanent, was rather wholly ephemeral. The depth of British reaction, furthermore, argues rather the seriousness with which Irish Unionist dissent was treated—than the ease with which they were dismissed. As evidence of the fundamental Irish–British Unionist relationship, this vituperation is therefore as ambiguous as the public eulogies showered on Ulster members—when (as in 1893) they could contribute to the British party's success.

Generic criticism of Irish Unionists was not incompatible with regard for individuals. George Wyndham, of all leading Unionists in the period, expressed the most consistent hostility for 'uncouth' loyalism. Yet he and Carson sustained mutual respect at least until 1904: Wyndham had a high opinion of Carson's parliamentary effectiveness, and Carson reciprocated—as his elegant compliment on Wyndham's appointment to the Irish Office suggests: 'I need not say what gratification it [the appointment] is to your former friends in Ireland—and I almost feel sorry in some ways that I am only an English law officer.'[75] Nor was Wyndham so distanced from the Ulster Party that he could not appoint William Moore as his Parliamentary Private Secretary. Arthur Balfour developed a similar haughtiness towards Irish Unionist members in general, and this, again, was compatible with loyalty and respect for individuals (Carson, Ellison-Macartney, Penrose-Fitzgerald, Plunkett).

Given that the most suspicious of British critics maintained such a qualified hostility, it is important to decide what they meant by their criticism—and who exactly fell victim to their bile. Though British Unionists like Wyndham might condemn the Ulster Party out of hand, they were also prepared to elaborate a more careful case. Ulster Party trouble-making was, as has been noted, a constant focus of complaint. Their extremism offended: Wyndham was angered by 'Orange uncouthness', and Balfour condemned their unharnessed

[73] GWP, Henry Bellingham to Sibell Grosvenor, 9 Mar. 1905.
[74] See Blanche E. L. Dugdale, *Arthur James Balfour, First Earl of Balfour, KG, OM, FRS &c* (2 vols.; London, 1936) i. 421.
[75] GWP, Edward Carson to Wyndham, 5 Nov. 1900.

suspicions.[76] Ulster sectarianism was alien: certain British Unionists—in particular, Balfour's circle of friends and clients—alluded frequently to 'Orange bigotry'.

It should be emphasized, however, that British Unionists on the right wing of the Party very rarely offered criticism of this or, indeed, any type. Furthermore, those who were most ready to dismiss Irish Unionists on these grounds, were themselves targets of their colleagues' malice. William Hayes-Fisher wrote an oddly ambiguous letter of congratulation to Wyndham on his appointment to the Irish Office, referring to 'certain early prejudices on comparatively trifling matters' which had 'caused so many good judges of men to deny your aptitude for the House of Commons, and your capacity for statesmanship'.[77] Arthur Lee, never sparing in his judgements, identified more specific causes of Wyndham's unpopularity:

The rank and file had never cottoned to his dandified and over-polished parliamentary manners, which led one old Tory member to mutter in my hearing after one of Wyndham's Burke-conscious perorations, 'Damn that fellow; he pirouettes like a dancing master'. His ambitions were overweening, and he had undoubtedly marked himself down as the coming leader of the Unionist Party—a role for which he was entirely inadequate and temperamentally unfit.[78]

Asquith, an untiring observer of his political contemporaries, shared this judgement.[79] The representative importance of Wyndham's prim and self-conscious repudiation of loyalism has to be gauged against this evidence of his own unpopularity. It seems likely that the uncouthness and parochialism which Wyndham identified in Irish Unionist members also distanced him from similarly uncouth and parochial English members. What was alien to the Commons was not so much Irish Unionists' lack of finesse as Wyndham's preternatural refinement.

Moreover, the complaints of Balfour and others ought to be considered in the context of a generally poor relationship between the Unionist front- and back-benches. In 1895 Lord Balcarres noted

[76] J. W. Mackail and Guy Wyndham (edd.), *The Life and Letters of George Wyndham* (2 vols.; London, [1924], ii. 459. Dugdale, *Balfour*, i. 421.

[77] GWP, William Hayes-Fisher to Wyndham, 10 Nov. 1900.

[78] Alan Clarke (ed.), *'A Good Innings': The Private Papers of Viscount Lee of Fareham, PC, GCB, GCSI, GBE* (London, 1974), 128-9.

[79] The Earl of Oxford and Asquith, *Fifty Years in Parliament* (2 vols.; London, 1928), ii. 24. Cf. Vincent (ed.), *Crawford Papers*, 605.

the 'singular rarity' of any close acquaintanceship, shared by a minister and rank-and-file MP; back-benchers complained that they were treated merely as lobby fodder.[80] These grumbles appear to have been well founded, for leaders like Balfour could, in private, be genially dismissive of others: Balfour and Wyndham shared a rather prissy literary and conversational style which embodied its own mode of abuse. Irish Unionists were only one group of back-benchers among a number of others who suffered in this way, and, even then, it is by no means clear how seriously such cattiness was treated by its authors.[81]

British criticism of Irish Unionist politicians should also be seen in the context of internal loyalist wrangling. When British politicians criticized Ulster members, they had specific vices in mind, and often specific individuals: Saunderson, Johnston, and to a lesser extent, Moore, were particular objects of attack from British politicians. Yet these same Irish Unionist MPs were also dismissed scathingly by more moderate Ulster colleagues. Johnston, though secretary to the parliamentary party by default, was treated by many as an amiable simpleton: William Ellison-Macartney could refer mockingly to 'Ballykilbeg's' anti-Catholicism in letters to Balfour.[82] Edward Saunderson was recognized even by sympathetic Unionists as a light-weight, though few were as dismissive as H. O. Arnold-Forster, member for West Belfast: 'Saunderson . . . is sure to be wrong, if there is a chance'.[83] Even one of Saunderson's loyalist friends, J. Mackay Wilson, described the Ulster leader as 'absolutely devoid of business capacity'.[84] Many Irish Unionists (including Saunderson) were alienated from William Moore's increasing extremism in and after 1905: Anthony Traill, Provost of Trinity, dismissed him as an 'ass'; Murray Hornibrook reported to George Wyndham that he had heard a Protestant bishop say 'the tone of William Moore's speeches made one feel ashamed to be a northerner'.[85] Irish Unionists

[80] Vincent, (ed.), *Crawford Papers*, 31.

[81] All the Irish suffered from Balfour's bile: MSPH, E/Balfour/461, Balfour to Salisbury, 24 Dec. 1892.

[82] ABP, Add MS. 49845, fo. 38, W. G. Ellison-Macartney to Balfour, 23 Sept. 1889.

[83] Trinity College Dublin, H. O. Arnold-Forster Papers, TCD 5000/222, Arnold-Forster to Florence O'Brien, 24 Dec. 1896.

[84] WLP, Add. MS 62410, J. M. Wilson to Long, 2 Feb. 1906.

[85] PRONI, Edward Carson Papers, D 1507/A/2/10, Anthony Traill to Carson, 12 May 1908. GWP, Murray Hornibrook to George Wyndham, 17 Feb. 1907. WLP, Add. MS 62409, Edward Saunderson to Walter Long, 11 Nov. 1905.

therefore often shared the personal judgements of their English leaders; so that when Wyndham or Balfour disparaged Saunderson or Johnston, they were merely articulating prejudices held by other Ulster members and loyalists.

In sum, the evidence of British disparagement proves very little about the parties' general relationship; and it certainly cannot be used uncritically to document any hypothesis claiming that British and Irish Unionists were irremediably divided. On the contrary, examination of this evidence reveals, if anything, some similarities between Irish Unionist and Conservative back-bench opinion. In particular, George Wyndham's hostility reflects as much his distance from British back-benchers as from the parliamentary Ulster Party, and this, to a lesser extent, is also true for Arthur Balfour.

The Edwardian Irish Unionist Parliamentary Party was broadly similar in social composition and educational experience to its British contemporaries. Ulster members made friends in other parties; their leaders were fêted in Conservative society. They were often clubbable—sometimes, as in the case of 'Jemmy' McCalmont, rather too clubbable for the good of their constituents. This is not to deny that the Ulster Party was distinct from other parties, judged not only by the nature of its political resolve, but also by perceptions of ethnic identity. For example, loyalist Irishness was occasionally identified as a defining characteristic, and indeed both Edward Saunderson and William Moore acknowledged this with pride. Ulster members were—or were thought by some Englishmen to be—alien in temperament, by virtue of their place of birth. But all the evidence suggests that these potential sources of division never really operated as such. There was no loyalist parliamentary ghetto to rival that of Irish Nationalists. Loyalists *qua* loyalists were excluded neither from government, nor, in the case of lawyers, from professional advancement; no more were they excluded from society.

In combination with this partial social assimilation, Irish Unionist distinctiveness carried political weight, rather than, as has sometimes been suggested, the reverse. When Irish Unionists complained, they were not isolated voices crying in a right-wing wilderness, for they harnessed quirky prejudices and concerns to an immense financial and political support, supplied by social and business contacts, by school and club friendships, and by loyalties of class and creed. Irish Unionists were, therefore, true West Britons in the sense that their educational and economic background was of greater significance within Toryism than their Irishness—however evident the latter might have been in the minds of contemporaries.

2. Contribution to Debate

A *bon raconteur*, an accomplished sportsman, a fluent platform speaker: Edward Saunderson appeared to contemporaries as an indispensable asset of late Victorian Unionism. With his wealth, he could sustain a parliamentary career; with his social gifts, his castle in County Cavan, and West End mansion, he had the wherewithal to beguile and entertain political associates. He seemed the epitome of loyalist integration within the structure of the British power élite. Yet some observers had suspicions: Almeric Fitzroy found it difficult to reconcile the image of influence with the reactionary, blustering reality.[86] Most historians, reviewing Saunderson's extravagant performances in parliament, have assumed that he was a comic and frothy fraud—with some of the trappings, and none of the reality of political power.[87]

If Irish Unionists, like Saunderson, were similar in educational and occupational background to British Conservatives, this did not in itself guarantee influence. For, it is conceivable that party members, while socially similar to British MPs, acted in a fashion so alien to the House of Commons as to surrender all political credibility. It is important, therefore, to establish the nature of loyalists' parliamentary interests, and to assess their level of parliamentary ability, and behaviour. If they pursued eccentric concerns in a consistently unparliamentary manner, then it may be argued that the influence provided by social bonds was undermined. If, on the other hand, Irish Unionists combined social *and* political assimilation, they emerge as a more impressive parliamentary force than historiographical myth has allowed.

The following survey is based on an analysis of every contribution made by members of the Ulster Party, and the few independent Irish Unionists, to parliamentary debate between 1895 and 1905 (table 3.10).

---

[86] Fitzroy, *Memoirs*, i. 9.
[87] See e.g. the characterization by R. F. Foster in *Lord Randolph Churchill: A Political Life* (Oxford, 1981), 247, 257-8. Saunderson is 'markedly eccentric', restrained from excess and errors of judgement by Lord Randolph.

Three additional years (1890, 1893 and 1910) have been included for comparative purposes.[88] In presenting this data, the intention is not, primarily, to represent the simple bulk of Irish Unionists' contribution—but, rather to identify the areas of policy which commanded their interest. No account, therefore, was taken of loyalist participation on select and standing committees, since these were largely nominated: and participation here, even less than in debate, did not truly reflect voluntary interest. Similarly, Irish Unionist members who served in government were not considered, since their contributions reflected only departmental preoccupations. The second section of the chapter contains a more qualitative assessment of the nature of the Irish Unionist contribution. Their parliamentary ability and their impact, as parliamentarians, on colleagues of other parties are each assessed.

Even discounting committee participation, there were other, structural, pressures determining the Party's contribution. Governments exercised considerable control over the Commons time-table, and Irish Unionists, like other back-benchers, generally had to discuss what was thrust before them. Ideally, for a survey of this kind, MPs should have been able to contribute what they wanted, when, and as often as they wanted. But freedom of contribution for members, though confined, remained significant. Governments' choice of legislation was not carried out on an isolated plane without reference to popular and parliamentary pressures. Furthermore, individual members could decide whether to contribute to a given debate. And, though the Ulster Party's intensive parliamentary involvement coincided with government legislation, this intensity varied—reflecting a gradation of interest in different measures. Other outlets existed for a member's initiative. A loyalist member was free to articulate his concerns during ministerial question time; he was free to attempt to pass motions of adjournment, and to introduce amendments to bills before the House. He could also attempt to introduce private bill legislation under Commons Standing Orders 10 (1888)—The Ten Minute Rule—and 72 (1902). Each of

---

[88] Table 3.10 is based on the total number of Irish Unionist interventions—contributions to debate, motions, and questions—on each subject in any year. Each intervention was classified according to the main theme of the speaker: long, rambling speeches which dealt with several topics were classified under the speaker's chief concern, judged both by the amount of time devoted to it, and by its relevance to the topic supposedly under debate.

TABLE 3.10. *Irish Unionist Members' Contribution to Debate, 1890–1910 (Number of Interventions)*

Year	1890	93	95	96	97	98	99	1900	01	02	03	04	05	10
Irish Topics														
Local government	54	21	72	46	24	205	10	8	21	24	13	25	22	13
Land	60	74	62	201	69	22	31	36	63	50	152	82	92	168
Law and order	44	412	35	22	32	16	15	33	43	59	21	89	118	285
Economy	8	29	3	3	17	11	4	8	6	7	8	12	12	16
Local	12	50	13	53	15	27	10	26	32	46	23	58	78	60
Education[a]	5	39	25	22	46	12	15	10	34	32	22	44	78	110
Administration[b]	50	586	36	43	42	33	23	23	18	29	21	92	130	82
British Topics														
Colonial	7	6	29	8	13	4	5	1	6	5	3	5	2	7
Defence	1	25	38	22	23	44	36	47	17	12	2	7	3	55
Economy	5	4	4	0	0	1	1	2	1	5	0	0	0	35
Foreign	4	9	7	7	9	2	2	0	1	0	3	4	0	4
Domestic/Commons[c]	26	160	69	36	38	41	22	17	51	17	14	33	49	123
Totals														
Questions[d]	114	706	199	145	163	132	78	105	126	177	106	327	360	785
Debate contrib.	147	652	181	278	143	262	93	105	164	94	158	122	212	166
Motions	15	57	13	40	22	24	3	1	3	15	18	2	12	7
Total annual contribution	276	1415	393	463	328	418	174	211	293	286	282	451	584	958

[a]Educational Issues; [b]Issues of Castle Administration; [c]All matters relating to internal British affairs, including problems of parliamentary procedure. [d]Parliamentary questions.

these forms has been considered in preparing the statistics of contribution.

These statistics reveal that Irish Unionist activity peaked in years when the threat of Home Rule re-emerged (1893, 1905, 1910). Contentious legislation provoked intensive debate: the number of contributions rose in 1896 (because of the Land Bill) and in 1898 (because of the Local Government Bill). The level of contribution was also rising in the last years of George Wyndham's Chief Secretaryship. In 1904—*before* the devolution scandal broke—Irish Unionists were sufficiently angry to contribute more than in any year since 1896. No important Irish Bill was before parliament in 1904, so that the number of contributions principally reflects Irish Unionist unhappiness with the Wyndham regime. It would appear, thus, that Irish Unionist concern over devolution, expressed in 1905, merely concluded an older process of alienation.

Considering the loyalist contribution by type, it appears that their level of questioning (as a proportion of the total contribution) rose dramatically when they were in opposition—and also, significantly, in 1902 and 1904–5. Interrogation, as a parliamentary technique, seems, therefore, to be associated with rejection of an administration. For example, John Lonsdale, MP for Mid Armagh, established a parliamentary record in 1907, by tabling 370 questions to ministers of the unpopular Liberal government—mostly on questions of Irish law and order.[89] A correlation exists, on the other hand, between a high level of contribution to debate and important Unionist legislation for Ireland (as in 1896, 1898, and 1903—with the Land Bill).

Even though it has been sometimes suggested that, in terms of self-perception, loyalists were conventionally British, they contributed comparatively little on British issues in parliament. They were largely uninterested in matters relating to the economy and finance, and to British foreign relations, though non-financial domestic and parliamentary issues roused greater enthusiasm. Contribution to these debates (as a proportion of the total) rose during years when Irish legislation did not dominate the timetable, falling when a major Irish measure was under discussion; and this correlation indicates fairly

[89] Patrick Buckland, *Irish Unionism*, ii. *Ulster Unionism and the Origins of Northern Ireland* (Dublin and New York, 1973), 42.

conclusively the nature of loyalist priorities. Unrest with Wyndham after 1902 drove British issues further to the periphery of their concern.

On the other hand, some Irish Unionists *were* enthusiastic about British domestic and parliamentary concerns, particularly those who had long-standing ties with Britain and the House of Commons. Several—H. O. Arnold-Forster, Walter Long, T. L. Corbett, J. A. Rentoul, T. W. Russell—were either Englishmen or Scots, through birth or prolonged residence. In addition, veteran MPs like William Johnston and Edward Saunderson (first elected in 1868 and 1865, respectively) naturally acquired a knowledge of, and interest in, parliamentary procedural matters. And a few more junior and clubbable Party members were concerned with the Commons recreational facilities: one of Colonel 'Jemmy' McCalmont's three parliamentary contributions in 1902 was a heart-felt plea for an improvement in the smoking-room accommodation provided for members.[90] Irish Unionist contribution on defence issues was similarly high, though certain members contributed a disproportionate amount. H. O. Arnold-Forster's interest in defence was idiosyncratically intense and long-standing, and is already apparent in the contribution figures for 1893, when he had been in the House for only one year. Work on defence promoted an interest in colonial affairs—and Arnold-Forster's contributions under that category are similarly well above the average for the Party.

This imperial interest was shared most prominently by William Johnston, Edward Saunderson, and other unreconstructed Orange Tories, for whom Empire had a very local significance. Some explored a parallel between the colonist's role in the grimmer corners of Empire, and loyalist responsibilities in Ireland. For example, Richard Dane, MP for North Fermanagh, argued in 1893 that the native Irish were tainted with a residual barbarism. Ulstermen, on the other hand were 'Men of English and Scottish descent, with English and Scottish blood in their veins, descendants of men who were sent over to Ireland three hundred years ago to civilise it . . . so far as it was possible.'[91] Such rhetoric was intermittently associated with the bitter extremes of loyalism, though it was also encouraged by English sanction (such as in Salisbury's 'Hottentots' speech of May 1886) and by barbed Nationalist references to a loyalist

---

[90] Hansard, 4th ser. (1902), cviii. 435.   [91] Hansard, 4th ser. (1893), viii. 157.

colonial garrison. The comparative decline in jingoism following the Boer War, combined with the less provocative attitudes on loyalism associated with Griffith's Sinn Fein, deprived such imperial chauvinism of purpose; and the parallels between Ireland and Empire were gradually dropped from loyalist rhetoric.

Thus the loyalist stand on Empire has to be seen partly in the context of the need to market Unionism. Certainly Edward Saunderson's imperial attachments effectively functioned as a useful adjunct to his ideology of Union—even if this involved a sleight of hand, wherein a minority and provincial cause became identified with dynamic jingoism. The general corollary to these attitudes was a belief that Irish Nationalism, uninterested in the world beyond the Kingstown ferry (except as a source of income), was both parochial and retrograde. But the bond with the Empire could also be exploited for non-partisan argument, in occasional and ritual demonstrations of moderation. For the Empire was also a matter of broader Irish pride and prosperity, as Saunderson suggested in May 1904, speaking in favour of a proposed monument to Lord Salisbury:

It is not simply as an Irishman but as something higher still to my view than even an Irishman—and that is as a subject of the head of this great Empire . . . without which we [in Ireland] would be but a miserable waif among the nations of the world—that I revere Lord Salisbury's memory.[92]

Similarly pragmatic arguments in favour of an imperial or Commonwealth connection were subsequently forwarded (albeit in less emotive and tendentious language) by pro-Treatyite Nationalists like Ernest Blythe or Desmond Fitzgerald.[93]

Despite occasional forays into exotica, loyalists were more confident in treating of local concerns, being chiefly interested in Irish land, law and order, and problems of Castle administration. An emphasis on law and order was sustained throughout the period, but developed under Liberal governments—and under the Wyndham administration. A similar distribution of interest holds true for constituency issues (which assumed great importance in the final years of Wyndham's rule) and for general administrative problems; disputes relating to Castle patronage dominated the loyalist contribution in 1904-5. However, other Irish issues commanded

[92] Hansard, 4th ser. (1904), cxxxv. 56.
[93] D. W. Harkness, *The Restless Dominion: The Irish Free State and the British Commonwealth of Nations, 1921-31* (London, 1969), 25-6.

slighter attention. Interest in local government remained steady at a low level, peaking in 1898, with the passage of Gerald Balfour's Local Government Bill. The Irish economy inspired even less debate—even though the Party sported a growing number of businessmen qualified to contribute on technical commercial matters: Horace Plunkett noted in 1904 that politically active businessmen held back from registering their interests and opinions.[94] Education only interested loyalists in the context of a Catholic University: their otherwise weak contribution peaked in 1897, and under George Wyndham—years when, because of government initiatives, the University question occupied popular attention.

Irish Unionists contributed on Irish matters partly because they were effectively a permanent opposition to the Nationalists. They alone had the local knowledge so often necessary to undermine Nationalist attacks on Conservative government; only they could counter local Nationalist grievance with local Unionist grievance, and attempt to deflate Nationalist pretensions to represent the whole Irish people. It seems, therefore, that the comparative neglect of British concerns by Irish Unionists (who were otherwise anxious to identify themselves with Britain), was as much an enforced response to Nationalist activity as a voluntary choice of priorities.

Irish Unionists were imperturbably concerned with law and order, even though there was no major bill relating to the issue in the period under survey. It appears rather that they voiced their concerns by close questioning of successive Chief Secretaries, for there is a clear correlation between the number of contributions made by Party members on law and order issues, and the overall number of questions tabled. On the other hand, no obvious correlation exists between the figures for crime and members' interest in law and order. In 1893, Irish Unionists were unprecedentedly vocal on law and order—despite a significant drop in agrarian crime between 1890 and 1893 (there was a slight rise in the total crime statistic, but this bears little relation to the amount of loyalist excitement). And between 1900 and 1902 there was an overall decline in both sets of crime figures which is associated with a large increase in the number of loyalist complaints.

It would appear, then, that in both 1893 and 1902 Irish Unionists were exploiting the issue of law and order to embarrass an unpopular

[94] Sir H. C. Plunkett, *Ireland in the New Century* (London, 1904), 68.

Irish administration. In 1902 it did not escape the attention of Irish Unionists that the discrepancy between the amount of recorded crime and the intensity of their concern might reflect on the credibility of their indictment. William Ellison-Macartney, who led the assault on Wyndham's government, admitted: 'that the statistics of agrarian crime last year and at the present moment were, when compared with those of 1887, of a favourable character, and if he (Macartney) believed that those statistics presented any accurate indication of the state of some parts of Ireland, he would not have troubled the House with a speech . . .'.[95] But John Dillon probably came closer to the truth in suggesting that:

The main grievance of Irish Unionism is the question of office and the question of rent, and you will notice from the speech of the Right Honourable Gentleman who has just sat down [Macartney] that nothing that the Chief Secretary . . . could do in the direction of the maintenance of law and order . . . would satisfy honourable gentlemen opposite, if the Chief Secretary so far strays from the paths of political virtue as by chance to give office to one of the majority of the Irish people.[96]

If law and order was fundamentally a genuine loyalist concern, then the intensity with which this was expressed hinged on other factors. Proving to parliament that a government had failed in this basic responsibility of Irish administration aroused greater support for loyalist disquiet than complaints about patronage and discrimination. Thus Irish unrest emerged as a useful tool with which to bludgeon a more generally unacceptable administration.

Irish Unionists were more directly concerned with agrarian questions. Problems of purchase and rent assessment agitated Irish—and Ulster—farmers throughout the period and Unionist governments, recognizing the political threat which this unrest represented, legislated accordingly. As landlords, as lawyers dependent on landed patronage, and as representatives of rural seats, Irish Unionists MPs had an interest in the land debate (though, as is suggested in chapter 4, there was no single, identifiable loyalist stand). Yet, despite internal differences, their overall contribution on land issues rose in sessions when important measures were before the Commons, as did their number of contributions to debate (as a proportion of their total contribution). Loyalists dropped their

[95] Hansard, 4th ser. (1902), ci. 814.   [96] Ibid. 829.

tactic of hostile questioning, therefore, in favour of a more constructive form of contribution.

In addition, the Party had a comparatively good record on local and constituency issues. Though loyalists represented more than a quarter of the population of Ireland, they generally held less than one fifth of the number of parliamentary seats; and thus, particularly in the context of Nationalist claims, they were under a constant obligation to remind the House of the full significance of their political support. This meant, too, that northern MPs felt compelled to bring before parliament the problems and interests of southern Unionists (who would otherwise have been unrepresented). This obligation was unequivocally acknowledged by H. O. Arnold-Forster (whose sister was in fact married to a southern Unionist squire). 'I am anxious', he wrote in 1892 to Cox of the Irish Unionist Alliance, 'that you should understand that, as far as my small powers of rendering service in the House of Commons go, I consider myself almost as much bound to the loyalists of the South and West . . . as I do to my own constituents in West Belfast.'[97] But, while this commitment was sustained, its relative significance wavered as northern representatives were increasingly compelled to articulate northern grievances. This was a further way in which the popular agitations in Ulster at the turn of the century contributed to the creeping isolation of the southern movement.

But, if the south came to suffer relative neglect, then the general commitment of the Ulster Party to local issues was reaffirmed under these new pressures. T. W. Russell, the Independent Orange movement, and labour politicians each demanded a more efficient and responsible Ulster Party; and George Wyndham's administration offered a number of local issues with which to satisfy this clamour.[98] Constituency grievances were, therefore, aired with greater frequency after 1900, particularly through the medium of the parliamentary question: both the number of contributions on constituency issues, and the number of questions rose in the period of Wyndham's reign in Ireland. Local grievances were used at this time to interrogate a government whose legislative ambitions, and central administrative policy, were judged to be inimical to Irish

---

[97] PRONI, IUA In-Correspondence, D 989, Arnold-Forster to Cox, 25 Aug. 1892.
[98] See ch. 6.

Unionist interests.[99] The grievance of a sub-postmaster might be used to illustrate an iniquitous trend in central government. Individual questions on alleged discrimination against Irish Unionists, and alleged maldistribution of funds, fitted into a broader indictment of Castle government. Extrapolation of high political generalities from constituency specifics was practised more extensively by Irish Unionists than any other parliamentary group (except, perhaps, the Nationalists); and no other group used the technique so antagonistically against its own government.

In terms of what they said in parliament, Irish Unionists were scarcely typical of their British colleagues. They were far from being yes-men, obsequiously following nominal British leaders. All the characteristics of their behaviour in opposition are evident under George Wyndham's administration, particularly in 1904–5; and they were more generally keen on interrogating ministers. Moreover, they differed, not only in their truculence of technique, but also in concentrating on wholly Irish concerns. Though they were interested in British domestic and parliamentary issues, their first loyalty was to their constituency, with its parochial and—from the British perspective—bizarre preoccupations. Judged, then, by their contribution to parliament, Irish Unionist members were (as many stated openly) Ulstermen or Irishmen first—and Unionists second.

If Irish Unionists pursued quixotic parliamentary interests, then they did so with reasonable ability and with surprising industry. Despite all the factors militating against a permanent presence at Westminster, Irish Unionist MPs, on the whole, fulfilled their duties with diligence. Only by the turn of the century, did the political incapacity of some Party members begin to attract public notice.

Few British members of the Commons had to manage political bases so remote from the centre of government: even a highly efficient politician, like H. O. Arnold-Forster, found the journeys between London and Belfast wearisome, and at least once he had to make the return trip four times within seven weeks.[100] Frequent attendance brought the expense of a London establishment where many English

---

[99] The novelist George Birmingham mocked this dour concern for local trivia: Birmingham, *Benedict Kavanagh* (London, 1907), 50. For a local perspective see R. B. Robson, *Autobiography of an Ulster Teacher* (2nd edn., Belfast, 1937), 109.

[100] Arnold-Forster Papers, TCD 5000/188, Arnold-Forster to Florence O'Brien, 5 Nov. 1893.

members either already possessed a London house, or could commute to Westminster from the country. Parliamentary attendance for both Irish Unionists and Nationalists demanded disruption of marriages, temporary exile in a strange country, and neglect of business

TABLE 3.11. *Irish Members' Average Attendance during Parliamentary Divisions by Party, 1886-1910 (as a Percentage of the Total Number of Divisions in any Session)*

Year	Anti-Parnellite*	Parnellite	Unionist
1886	60.7		50.6
1887	50.4		49.8
1888	43.3		51.8
1889	27.3		49.3
1890	41.0		52.9
1891	23.5	12.4	41.7
1892	30.2	18.5	53.6
1893	81.8	62.7	64.0
1893W	49.1	7.5	24.7
1894	52.8	19.4	30.9
1895	45.2	13.6	64.2
1896	25.2	15.7	34.5
1897	24.5	12.5	44.5
1898	20.3	21.5	45.4
1899	18.6	7.2	38.3
1900	19.8	—	40.3
1901	64.5		49.4
1902	36.1		34.5
1903	18.4		38.0
1904	44.1		47.9
1905	55.5		47.1
1906	51.8		37.0
1907	30.3		35.1
1908	27.8		36.0
1909	22.7		33.9
1910	42.3		42.9

*The figures for 1886-90, and for 1901-10, represent the average attendance of the united Nationalist party.

Sources: Constitutional Year Books for 1886 to 1892; F. S. L. Lyons, 'Irish Parliamentary Representation, 1891-1910' (Dublin Ph.D. thesis 1947), 342, for 1893 to 1910.

commitments. But, unlike Nationalists, Unionist members had a political obligation to show that these obstacles could be overcome, and that the Irish public could be adequately represented by a London parliament.

Thus, Irish Unionists, throughout the period 1886-1910 faithfully attended parliamentary divisions. Occasionally their diligence wavered—especially when their party was out of power—but, on the whole, they sustained a consistently higher attendance than their Nationalist opponents.[101] Peak attendance occurred always under Unionist governments, the overall average being boosted by high individual totals from junior ministers like William Ellison-Macartney and T. W. Russell. Other members who were obliged to attend divisions, and did so with equal regularity, included William Johnston (who was in the pay of the Unionist party), and Lord Arthur Hill (who had served as a Conservative whip).

Though frequent voting satisfied the Party managers, it was not always sufficient for an MP's constituents. Division records were published at the end of each session, but they had less popular impact than detailed accounts of an MP's speech, and they carried less weight than an MP's reputation for diligent constituency work. Persistent, silent parliamentary attendance was not widely esteemed as a political virtue; so that when Ulster members were under local pressure—even when they were accused of neglecting parliament—they worried about their constituency presence rather than legislative responsibilities. Thus, at the height of T. W. Russell's agitation, one of the themes of which was the inefficacy of Ulster representation, loyalist attendance—paradoxically—dropped.

Division attendance is therefore an unhelpful guide to popular perceptions of an MP's usefulness. Most contemporaries, both within British Unionism and in Ulster constituencies, were interested in the substance of a loyalist member's concerns, and how well and how freely they were articulated, rather than in the drab record of his diligence. Thus, the final section of the chapter seeks to offer comment on the different quantities and qualities of contribution made by individual members of, and social groupings within the Party. The nature of the data (number of interventions, subdivided by type) renders exact comparison impossible, since a voluble member might occupy a great deal more parliamentary time over

[101] Lyons, 'Parliamentary Representation', 343.

an involved question than a more taciturn member offering a short interjection. And within categories one member may occupy much more parliamentary time than another. Most of William Johnston's (rather large) tally of contributions to debate comprise short interruptions: 'his annals are scanty', observed Henry Lucy of *Punch*, for 'his contributions were rather interjectionary than prolonged'.[102] On the other hand, most of Edward Carson's contributions to debate, or those of T. W. Russell, represent substantial speeches. Yet the classification does reveal, in broad terms, who contributed most to parliament. Though there may be discrepancies in the length of individual speeches, an alternative, and less ambiguous, basis for comparison exists with the number of questions tabled.

Little is proved by a professional breakdown of the main parliamentary contributors within the Ulster Party—beyond the predictable revelation that the occupational groups with the largest numbers of members also produce the largest number of industrious parliamentarians. Lawyers feature largely: they had experience at public speaking, and the technical skill necessary for effective contribution to debate. But, taken as a whole, lawyers were not particularly vocal—for if they had aptitude for parliament, then they had also professional and business responsibilities which kept them outside the House. J. H. M. Campbell, member for Dublin University, could decline a request to contribute to debate because of his court commitments. Carson's professional career prevented him contributing much to the parliament of 1895–1900, although he did return for debates on matters of keen concern (the Land Bill of 1896, for example).

Wealthy landowners, as an important occupational group within the Party, also feature among its more frequent contributors: men like E. M. Archdale, Edward Saunderson, Thomas Waring. In theory, the class had the leisure and wealth to pursue a parliamentary career, but in practice, for many, other distractions proved more tempting. The Hon. R. T. O'Neill represented Mid-Antrim for twenty-five years (1885–1910), only retiring through serious illness.[103] In the main sample years, O'Neill made a total of eight substantive contributions to debate, and tabled one motion. He was a reluctant and ill-equipped parliamentarian, and obituarists were

---

[102] Henry W. Lucy, *The Balfourian Parliament* (London, 1906), 191.
[103] Terence O'Neill, *The Autobiography of Terence O'Neill* (London, 1972), 5.

at a loss to find anything worthy of comment in his career beyond his (otherwise unsubstantiated) skill as a string-puller.[104] His nephew, A. E. B. O'Neill, an equally ineffectual politician, succeeded him in the representation of the division.

The Hill Family provides further evidence of landed inactivity. Lord Arthur Hill, son of the fourth Marquess of Downshire, and member for West Down, made four parliamentary contributions in the sample years 1895–8, all brief statements arising from his post as Comptroller of the Royal Household. Yet—with the support of William Johnston, as an influential Orange colleague—he was able to secure the succession of his twenty-five-year-old son to the seat.[105] For the seven years in which he represented West Down, Captain Hill did not speak in parliament, and took part in only 106 divisions. The *Belfast News Letter*, normally tolerant of the shortcomings of Unionist politicians, was moved to complain in September 1900:

His programme, as disclosed by his Address, is all right. He confesses that he is not an experienced politician, and asks his electors to extend to him a renewal of the confidence which for generations has been invariably given to those who bear the name of Hill. This we think is hardly sufficient recommendation . . . our members must assert themselves, and every one of them should be able to do so by voice as well as vote . . .[106]

Installed in the House of Commons through sense of family duty (or through devotion to clubland and political society), MPs like Hill were tolerated only so long as constituents' parliamentary needs were as insubstantial as their leaders' abilities. Such men could only flourish when Home Rule was in abeyance.

Dynastic tenure of representation (such as that enjoyed by the O'Neills) placed little compulsion on the landlord-member to make any parliamentary impression. Such MPs rarely had overweening personal ambitions: representation of the division fell naturally into their (frequently reluctant) possession, and not after long and careful campaigning on behalf of principle or self. Thus, Lord Ernest Hamilton, member for North Tyrone, was allotted the constituency after an Abercorn family conclave in 1885. A wholly unenthusiastic

[104] *BNL*, 29 July 1910.
[105] WJD, D 880/2/50, 20 May 1898. See ch. 5.4.
[106] *BNL*, 29 Sept. 1900.

MP (as he confessed in his autobiography of 1922), he made no contribution to parliament in the sample year 1890.[107]

If no simple correlation exists between a member's activity and his occupation, parliamentary diligence emerges as a more consistent characteristic of the populist members of the Party. Both tenant-farmer representatives (T. L. Corbett, R. M. Dane, and T. W. Russell) and urban populists (William Johnston and Tom Sloan) feature among the Party's greatest contributors to Commons debate. Each group was responsible to reasonably well-organized batteries of opinion: farmer representatives to tenant associations; urban members to the Orange Order, and to opinion focused through specifically urban concentrations of employment (in the shipyards, engineering, and textile industries, and in large schools). However, otherwise conventional Unionist representatives might be goaded into activity through similar pressures, focused within their constituency. J. B. Lonsdale, who sat for the farming constituency of Mid Armagh, systematically scrutinized rural opinion, tailoring the nature and extent of his parliamentary contribution to meet local fears.[108] William Moore, in North Antrim, may have sustained a similarly high political profile in reaction to farmer opinion.[109]

Lonsdale's concern was political survival—but the demotic Unionists had more extensive and constructive political ambitions. For a conviction politician like Russell, there was a close correlation between, on the one hand, mollifying and exploiting mass opinion, and, on the other, achieving influence over government. Moreover, like T. L. Corbett and T. H. Sloan, Russell had entered parliament in the trail of a campaign directed against the sloth of traditional Ulster members. Thus the need for an energetic parliamentary presence was tied to a fundamental issue of credibility.

The quality of Irish Unionist contribution also varied but, as with attendance, the small size of the Party meant that members were subject to greater scrutiny, and inadequate members more easily harried, than in the English parties. Quality, therefore, was comparatively high. Poor speakers frequently offered compensating

[107] Hamilton, *Forty Years On*, 203. For an English parallel see P. F. Clarke, 'British Politics and Blackburn Politics, 1900–1910', *Historical Journal*, xii. 2 (1969), 304–5.

[108] PRONI, Joshua Peel Papers, D 989/4C/6, letter book for 1900–10.

[109] J. R. B. McMinn, 'The Reverend James Brown Armour and Liberal Politics in North Antrim, 1869–1914', Ph.D. thesis (Belfast, 1979), 353.

political virtues (influence with British leaders, for example, or within the Orange Order) to mitigate criticism.

Possessing a large number of lawyers, the Ulster Party had a core of experienced debaters, boasting a detailed knowledge of legislation. Earl Winterton, whose parliamentary career began in 1905, considered Edward Carson to be the one member of the Party who could match the debating skills of the most able Nationalists: J. H. M. Campbell he considered 'a good debater'—and Jack Sandars, Balfour's *alter ego*, agreed.[110] Henry Lucy regarded Carson's early speeches as unattractively reminiscent of court-room cross-examination; Joseph Chamberlain, *The Times*, and others thought differently.[111] Other lawyers attracted notice: William Moore won a reputation for debating skill through the MacDonnell debates of February 1905.[112] D. P. Barton was chosen to move the Queen's speech in 1892, and impressed Arthur Griffith-Boscawen by his ability.[113] John Atkinson, Irish Attorney General (1895–1905), had a detailed knowledge of the Castle administration, which was exploited by three Chief Secretaries: Atkinson carried out the duties of Chief Secretary after Wyndham's breakdown, and was at last offered the post by Arthur Balfour.[114] Talented lawyers, like William Kenny, were recruited to serve as Solicitor-General for Ireland.

Non-lawyers were capable of effective contribution, particularly in their individual fields of interest or experience. T. W. Russell complemented a formidable reputation as a platform speaker by his parliamentary performances. Henry Lucy, in reviewing the contributions of new members to the parliament of 1886–92, singled out the young member for East Fife, H. H. Asquith, and Russell for special attention—the latter possessing 'conspicuous debating power', and rising occasionally 'to the height of eloquent declamation'.[115] During the passage of the second Home Rule Bill,

---

[110] Earl Winterton, *Orders of the Day* (London, 1953), 39. DRO, Papers of Theresa, Lady Londonderry, D/Lo/C671/21, J. S. Sandars to Theresa Londonderry, 6 Dec. 1908.

[111] Marjoribanks and Colvin, *Lord Carson*, i. 267.

[112] A. S. T. Griffith-Boscawen, *Fourteen Years in Parliament* (London, 1907), 324.

[113] Ibid.

[114] Bodleian Library, Oxford, J. S. Sandars Papers, c749, fo. 100, John Atkinson to Sandars, 11 Mar. 1905.

[115] Henry W. Lucy, *A Diary of the Salisbury Parliament* (London, 1892), 430.

Russell consolidated this reputation: in April 1893, Gladstone confided to Charles Hobhouse that he considered the speeches of Chamberlain, John Redmond, and Russell the best which he had heard on the Bill.[116] Other political opponents conceded his ability: John Morley thought Russell the most effective member of his Select Committee on Land (1894).[117] When he was sacked from his Parliamentary Secretaryship in 1900, at least one influential Conservative, Griffith-Boscawen, believed 'that it would have been wiser to have retained him in office, thus curtailing his independence, and making use of his talents'.[118]

Though not a naturally gifted speaker (a failing recognized by individuals as diverse as the Catholic Bishop of Limerick, William Johnston and, not least, by himself), Horace Plunkett was capable of effective and stimulating contribution on the agricultural and educational subjects which interested him.[119] Lucy referred, not unkindly, to 'those simple, business-like addresses with which the member for County Dublin occasionally varies the ordinary business of speech-making in the House of Commons'.[120] Other of his contemporaries in the Party contributed effectively to specialized or technical discussion, most prominently H.O. Arnold-Forster on naval and defence issues. The Belfast shipbuilders, Edward Harland and Gustav Wolff, shared this interest, contributing engineering the business expertise to naval debate.

Against the effect of this ability should be set the mitigating influence of other aspects of the loyalist parliamentary contribution. The humour inspired, consciously or otherwise, by some Party members had an ambiguous influence on the collective prestige. John Ross, member for Londonderry City (1893–5), believed that his maiden speech had been spared an indifferent reception through an unconsciously humorous slip of the tongue: this won him the laughter and future attention of the House.[121] But, though a humorous speech had a certain social value, which occasionally might bring a more tangible political gain, there was a potential disadvantage: a

[116] Edward David (ed.), *Inside Asquith's Cabinet: From the Diaries of Charles Hobhouse* (London, 1977), 20.
[117] Viscount Morley, *Recollections* (2 vols.; London, 1917) i. 351.
[118] Griffith-Boscawen, *Fourteen Years*, 172.
[119] Digby, *Horace Plunkett*, 53. WJD, D 880/2/44, 22 Dec. 1892.
[120] Henry W. Lucy, *Later Peeps at Parliament* (London, 1905), 26.
[121] Ross, *Years of My Pilgrimage*, 76.

member might find that he was tacitly regarded as unofficial jester to the Commons, as Lord Hugh Cecil warned the future Lord Brabazon of Tara in 1918.[122]

Edward Saunderson was a celebrated parliamentary humorist. Henry Lucy, writing in 1892, lauded Saunderson's ability to entertain; Saunderson himself recognized this ability, and was gratified by a parliamentary audience receptive to his sly humour.[123] But—as Nationalist critics readily understood—what he gained in popularity was often to the disadvantage both of his personal credibility, and to that of his cause. Recalling the Edwardian Ulster Party in 1932, the Earl of Selborne offered a damning judgement on Saunderson's comic performances:

Saunderson was the leader of the Ulstermen; Carson was not then in the House. The style of the two men was totally different. Saunderson never could refrain from joking even when he felt most deeply. Carson's style was, and is, almost gloomy; but he was much the biggest man of the two.[124]

Moreover, Saunderson shared this unfortunate facility for generating humour with other members of the Party, notably the veteran Orange leader, William Johnston. The sombre, patriarchal member for South Belfast provoked the merriment of the House generally, and the not unfriendly wit of Nationalists in particular. Johnston maintained the forms of traditional hostility, but with his eccentric concerns, and outrageously partisan interjections, he scarcely constituted a serious political challenge to any but his own party. Paid a salary of £200 a year by Conservative Central Office, Johnston, as a parliamentarian, represented doubtful value for money.[125]

Loyalists, in common with all Irish members, were associated with verbal 'bulls'—inadvertent mixed metaphors and other errors of expression which were seized on with relish by parliamentary reporters anxious to enliven their copy. Henry Lucy recounted in laboured detail several such lapses (Saunderson's reference to Nationalist 'gorilla' warfare, for example).[126] 'Bulls' were central to

[122] Lord Brabazon of Tara, *The Brabazon Story* (London, 1955), 112.

[123] Lucy, *Salisbury Parliament*, 430.

[124] Bodleian Library, Oxford, Papers of William Waldegrave Palmer, Second Earl of Selborne, cxci. 49, Some Reflections in My Old Age [1932-3].

[125] For a more charitable account of Johnston's political career, see Aiken McClelland, 'Johnston of Ballykilbeg', M.Phil. thesis (Coleraine, 1978).

[126] Henry W. Lucy, *A Diary of the Unionist Parliament, 1895-1900* (Bristol and London, 1901), 319.

the humour culture of the late Victorian parliament, and Irish Unionists like Saunderson were numbered among the chief perpetrators. This association, as with intentional humour, tended to the discredit of Party members: Cadogan, the Irish viceroy, recorded a 'foolish *lapsus linguae*', committed by Saunderson in February 1900, which had wholly spoilt the effect of a violent speech.[127]

The verbal humour associated with some members of the Ulster Party may also be related to a question of accent. Not all Irish Unionist MPs can have possessed a regional lilt, partly because many were educated in England, but also because landlords often regarded the Irish brogue with apprehension: Brian Inglis has recalled the neuroses of his class on this score.[128] However, contemporary cartoons of several leading Irish Unionist politicians were occasionally accompanied by captions expressed in a grotesque language. Both Saunderson and Carson appear to have retained an Irish accent, and this was certainly seized on by humorists (in much the same way that the pronounced accents of more recent loyalist leaders have been a target for television satire). Yet, as with the general entertainment value of particular loyalist representatives, the specific issue of accent and its relation to loyalist effectiveness is hard to interpret. On the one hand, an alien brogue can hardly have been an aid to assimilation; and yet, despite what was sometimes described as a cultivated Irishness, Carson for long survived at the heart of British Toryism.[129] Saunderson achieved widespread celebrity in late Victorian Britain through sustaining a similarly pronounced Irish identity. He, too, actively cultivated this. It seems, then, that these conventional attributes of Irishness, far from alienating British audiences or being perceived as a political millstone, made loyalist speakers more accessible. And this paradox is probably to be explained in terms of British expectations of Irish behaviour— expectations shaped by popular stage entertainment and comic literature.

The Ulster Party owed its place within the humour culture of parliament not only to verbal fun, but also to occasionally eccentric

[127] Gerald Balfour Papers, TD 83/133/111/11, Cadogan to Gerald Balfour, 5 Feb. 1900.
[128] Brian Inglis, *West Briton* (London, 1962), 23-4.
[129] St John Ervine, *Sir Edward Carson and the Ulster Movement* (Dublin and London, 1915), 47.

and unfamiliar parliamentary behaviour. Their passion for melodrama was consistently bewildering, and sometimes amusing. Sharing, perhaps, the same frustrations as Nationalists, some loyalist members indulged in belligerent rhetoric, and, occasionally, in eccentric or aggressive behaviour.[130] A bemused grandson recalled that H. H. Bruce (member for Coleraine 1862-74, 1880-5) had a habit of standing on his seat in the Commons, and 'crowing like a cock' whenever a Liberal or Home Ruler rose to speak.[131] In 1896, Carson's theatrical exit from the Commons during the Committee Stage of Gerald Balfour's Land Bill surprised and offended more staid English contemporaries.[132] Irish Unionist members, like Nationalists, were sometimes associated with parliamentary 'scenes', particularly when in Opposition; like Nationalists, they were riled by comparative numerical weakness and impotence, reacting with aggression. Saunderson was at the heart of a celebrated Commons brawl in July 1893, and—worse—admitted afterwards that he had enjoyed himself.[133] Ronald McNeill, the Canterbury MP and Ulster Unionist, threw the Order book which struck Winston Churchill, during debate on the third Home Rule Bill.[134]

If violent acts were comparatively few, violent language was a commonplace of the Party's contribution to debate. Dour and alien threats of armed resistance were laughed down in the House, both in 1886 and 1893. Frequent repetition of the threat further invalidated it; so that when, in April 1914, guns were landed in Ulster, a Liberal Prime Minister, lulled by years of laughable Irish Unionist bluster, could regard the event as merely a novel twist in a very old political theme.[135]

The core in the Irish Unionists' problem of parliamentary presentation lay in resolving two mutually incompatible demands on their loyalty—from government and from constituency. That they

---

[130] Lyons, *Irish Parliamentary Party*, 224.

[131] H. J. Bruce, *Silken Dalliance* (London, 1947), 23.

[132] Lucy, *Unionist Parliament*, 98. Lucy describes Carson's exit as 'pettishly melodramatic'.

[133] Lucas, *Saunderson*, 200-1.

[134] A. T. Q. Stewart, *The Ulster Crisis* (London, 1967), 67.

[135] See Patricia Jalland, *The Liberals and Ireland: The Ulster Question in British Politics to 1914* (Brighton, 1980), 264. For an impression of Asquith's equanimity after the Larne episode, see Michael and Eleanor Brock (edd.), *H. H. Asquith: Letters to Venetia Stanley* (Oxford, 1982), 71 (letter 66).

indulged occasionally in parliamentary gestures of defiance satisfied local opinion; at the same time, it embarrassed and worried their Conservative allies and damaged their parliamentary credibility. In certain ways, therefore, Irish Unionists were alien to a British parliament: they sometimes exhibited a rhetorical and behavioural extravagance more frequently attributed to their Nationalist compatriots than English Conservatives. What Irish Unionists said was sometimes alarming; the gap between what they said and what they meant was worryingly indefinable. They were unpredictable and unreliable allies. Though the Party contributed much to parliament, its members were comparatively uninterested in British affairs. In sum, these factors reduced the effectiveness of the Party before a British audience: the un-Englishness of certain Irish Unionists separated them from this audience. Britons might laugh off some of the differences causing this separation, but laughter often only masked incomprehension and embarrassment.

Yet the occasional strangeness of Irish Unionist political behaviour has to be set in the context of both the personal and social integration described earlier. An ally like Walter Long might feel pained by some of the more ridiculous expressions of loyalist wrath.[136] But pain did not develop into any more serious breach—constituting, rather, a paternal concern for erring allies. Salisbury reacted to the violence of his landlord allies with similarly benign condescension.[137] This tolerance was facilitated by the fact that, though Irish Unionists might act strangely, they were, as a group, highly talented parliamentarians. They had technical knowledge; some were able debaters; a large proportion had ministerial experience.

Irish Unionists combined, therefore, ability with connections in high places: they combined occasional parliamentary eccentricity with social conformity. That they did not always act as their British counterparts was never doubted by contemporaries: less certain was whether British back-benchers would be more strongly motivated by respect for individual loyalists, or by outrage at their collective misdemeanours. This ambiguity lay at the heart of the parties' relations; it created despair among those Unionist leaders who felt little in common with certain loyalists, yet who could never quite

[136] Theresa Londonderry Papers, D/Lo/C/666/9, Walter Long to Lady Londonderry, 6 Aug. 1907.
[137] Lady Gwendolen Cecil, *Biographical Studies of the Life and Political Character of Robert, Third Marquess of Salisbury* (London [1948]), 17, 25.

decide whether they might be defied. No British Unionist could afford, therefore, to dismiss Irish Unionist parliamentary opinion (however odd); very few did.

3. Party Discipline

The pinched features of Edward Saunderson and the vacant magnanimity of the sixth Marquess of Londonderry were not, perhaps, calculated to please; and it was scarcely surprising, therefore, that the newly-elected member for South County Dublin should have reacted with distaste.[138] Veiled in diffidence, Horace Plunkett scanned his assembled colleagues of the Ulster Party on 30 January 1893, and pronounced that: 'I like [them] not . . . they are altogether too narrow, and it is only a question of time how long they will exist as an active party'.[139]

But Plunkett, as in so many other judgements on contemporaries, was quite wrong. The Irish Unionist Parliamentary Party survived, accommodating faddists like himself, because it claimed no iron authority over its membership. Like the more rigorous Nationalists, it possessed disciplinary structures, but these perhaps had more to do with satisfying the political vanity of loyalist politicians than fulfilling any systematic regulating function. Combination *was* occasionally considered necessary, but it was generally accepted that members 'had perfect freedom of action in political matters', the Union being defined as more than a mere 'political' matter.[140] The Ulster Party was therefore an appropriate parliamentary billet for many forms of political rebel: successive mavericks (T. L. Corbett, John Gordon, and—for a time—Tom Sloan) were swiftly integrated, and found that the Party's easy discipline allowed sufficient parliamentary independence, while offering some of the advantages of combination.

Within the grimy splendour of Palace Chambers, Westminster, in the offices of Irish Unionist Alliance, the Ulster Party held its sessional meetings.[141] It possessed a chairman, and one, occasinally two,

---

[138] WJD, D 880/2/45, 30 Jan. 1893.

[139] Plunkett Foundation, Oxford, Horace Plunkett Diaries, 30 Jan. 1893.

[140] ESP, T 2996/2/D1, Saunderson to Plunkett, 21 Feb. 1896 (copy).

[141] Irish Loyal and Patriotic Union, *Report for 1886*, 5; Irish Unionist Alliance, *Report for 1893*, 48. The Party also used House of Commons Committee Rooms: WJD, D 880/2/53, 15 Jan. 1901.

secretaries, who also acted as whips. William Johnston presided over some early meetings of the embryonic loyalist group; but, once it had been formally constituted, Edward Saunderson emerged as the first effective leader.[142] According to Johnston, Colonel Saunderson 'objected to take the chair *en permanence*'; nevertheless, the elections which were held each session, while salving the Colonel's modesty, brought forward no rival, and he held the chair until his death in 1906.[143] His relative indolence and failing health gave colleagues the opportunity of deputizing: acting chairmen were generally chosen from among the older members of the Party, William Johnston, J. M. McCalmont, and W. E. H. Lecky each serving in this capacity.[144] Deference to age and experience was also reflected in the choice of Saunderson's successor; otherwise, Walter Long, as an Englishman with only tenuous family connections in Ireland, was a curious candidate—and it is likely that the then Secretary, J. B. Lonsdale, had been the Party's first choice, and had declined promotion.[145]

The Chairman had responsibility for presenting his Party's opinion in debate. Indeed, Saunderson's position within his Party arose partly from the widespread belief that 'he had the ear of the House', and he frequently opened presentations of the Irish Unionist position. He was responsible, too, for negotiation between the Ulster Party and British government—though pushy junior members, and those enjoying a special relationship with individual ministers, might communicate independently. Chairmen, by definition, also presided over party conclaves, though it seems that they enjoyed no special role in decision-making, by virtue of their office alone. With the formation of the Ulster Unionist Council, however, the influence of the parliamentary Chairman within Unionism was consolidated, for he was given wide powers of nomination to the Council's governing body.[146]

The Party Secretary kept minutes—badly for the most part. William Johnston, who held the Secretaryship from the evolution of the office until his death in 1902 was evidently as terse in recording

[142] WJD, D 880/2/38, 14 Jan. 1886, 20 Jan. 1886.

[143] WJD, D 880/2/38, 20 Jan. 1886.

[144] WJD, D 880/2/45, 7 Feb. 1893; D 880/2/51, 27 June 1899.

[145] Joshua Peel Papers, D 889/4C/3/fo. 601, Joshua Peel to J. B. Lonsdale, 27 Oct. 1906.

[146] John Harbinson, *The Ulster Unionist Party, 1882-1973: Its Development and Organisation* (Belfast, 1973), 24.

the proceedings of his Party as he was in contributing to debate. In the 1890s the office was sometimes held jointly, Johnston sharing his minimal responsibilities with veteran nonentities like 'Jemmy' McCalmont.[147] If this innovation was designed to circumvent Johnston's inefficiency, then Party members must have been disappointed, for no improvement was forthcoming. The standard of records barely changed under Johnston's more able colleague and successor, William Ellison-Macartney; but when Ellison-Macartney retired in 1903, John Brownlee Lonsdale brought to the office the virtues of a meticulous business mind. Party minutes were kept more fully, and Lonsdale's discreet industry lent both himself and the Secretaryship an ever-widening influence.[148]

The Party Secretary supervised membership of the Party and election to its offices, issued whips, and planned debating strategy: Lonsdale, for example, was credited with having devised the Ulster Party's campaign against Antony MacDonnell and George Wyndham.[149] Only one Party whip survives (among the papers of Edward Saunderson), though there is evidence of others having been issued.[150] But, Ulster Conservatives also received whips from the British party, for these survive among various loyalist archives.[151] Sometimes the views of the Ulster and British managers coincided: a bemused Colonel Thomas Waring wrote to Aretas Akers-Douglas when he received two overlapping directives (from Ellison-Macartney, and from Akers-Douglas himself).[152] But it seems more probable that Ulster Party whips were generally issued in rejection of the British managers, rather than as an unnecessary confirmation

[147] WJD, D 880/2/49, 26 Feb. 1897.

[148] The Party minute books have disappeared. In 1960 Charles Curtis Craig, brother of Viscount Craigavon, presented a set of Edwardian minute books to Unionist Party headquarters in Belfast. Persistent enquiries and research over five years suggest that these records were destroyed in one of several bomb attacks carried out on the building. All the information in the text concerning the standard of minute-keeping was derived from ESP, T. 2996/6/3, William Moore to Reginald Lucas, 25 Nov. 1907. Lonsdale's abilities were recognized by, among others, the veteran Colonel J. M. McCalmont, BNL, 3 Dec. 1904, 10.

[149] For procedural matters see WLP, Add. MS 62415, Long to Lonsdale, 8 Feb. 1910; also TCD, W. E. H. Lecky Papers, 1834/2288, Lonsdale to Lecky, 20 Feb. 1903. Gibbs, The Complete Peerage, xiii. 272.

[150] ESP, T 2996/3/33, copy of whip signed by Edward Saunderson [August 1896].

[151] Moore Papers, copy of a parliamentary summons, signed by Arthur Balfour, 8 Feb. 1909.

[152] Akers-Douglas Papers, C 537/2, Waring to Akers-Douglas, n.d.

for British tactics: the single surviving Ulster Party whip, for example, was a call to defy the government by supporting the Lords' amendments to the Irish Land Bill of 1896.[153]

On the other hand, conflict between the parties within the voting lobby was comparatively rare, and the Ulster Party Secretary issued very few commands to his members. Even loyalist die-hards like Johnston and J. M. McCalmont willingly accepted orders from the British Conservative Chief Whip, McCalmont on one occasion offering (albeit grudgingly) to sacrifice Ascot for an important division.[154] Relations between Ulster Party officers and their Conservative counterparts were therefore amicable, despite the independent disciplinary machinery. Ulster members never continuously or systematically repudiated the authority of the British Party, and respected their membership of a broad and powerful parliamentary alliance: thus, Edward Saunderson cast aside the rhetoric of loyalist autonomy in complaining to Alexander Acland-Hood that Tom Sloan, as a suspected heretic, still received the privilege of the British whip.[155] Furthermore, by keeping favour with the British whips (and ministers), Ulster members could expect a greater influence over the evolution of parliamentary strategy, over patronage, and over the allocation of parliamentary time: in August 1904, for example, Acland-Hood co-operated with John Lonsdale in assigning time for discussion of the controversial Constable Anderson case.[156]

Despite intricate party machinery, meetings of the Ulster group attracted, on average, only ten or eleven members from a theoretical strength of (at times) well over twenty MPs.[157] Enthusiasm and internal discipline—predictably—were at a peak shortly after the party's evolution, when the Home Rule threat still inspired conformity. Attendance at the first party conclave reached twenty-five members; at that time Saunderson could still plausibly threaten an obdurate member with constituency pressure unless he fell into line by attending meetings.[158] But such rigour was short-lived.

[153] See n. 150.

[154] Akers-Douglas Papers, C 355/1, J. M. McCalmont to Akers-Douglas, n.d.

[155] ESP, T 2996/3/34, Saunderson to unrecorded, n.d. Internal evidence suggests Alexander Acland-Hood as the recipient, and a date of c.Jan. 1906.

[156] Hansard, 4th ser. (1904), cxxxvii. 1040.

[157] WJD, D 880/2/52, 1 Feb. 1900 (ten present); D 880/2/49, 16 Mar. 1897 (ten present).

[158] ESP, T 2996/1/66, Saunderson to his wife, 23 Jan. 1886; T 2996/1/61, Saunderson to his wife, 15 Jan. 1886.

Where, in the mid-1880s laziness was interpreted as a sell-out to Nationalism, a decade later nobody much cared whether an Ulster member attended the gatherings of his party or not. A member's popularity among colleagues had more to do with his *joie de vivre* than grim diligence. Thus, a charming reprobate like J. M. McCalmont could occupy the Party Secretaryship, or act as chairman, while contributing little to the House of Commons beyond a zest for the good life.

Ten years of existence had reformed the tenor of party organization. Members had less responsibility to the corporate body of their Party, and even Horace Plunkett could generally speak and vote according to personal whim, and against the consensus prevailing among his peers. In February 1896 Plunkett pronounced in favour of an amnesty for the Fenian dynamitards, a provocation so serious as to demand a response from the normally unflappable Party convocation. Saunderson was deputed to berate the erring Plunkett, and his letter reveals the broad parameters of the conformity appropriate to party membership. He wrote:

The opinion of the Committee was this, that though each member of the Party had perfect freedom of action in political matters, it was expected that before taking a grave step on public policy the Committee should be informed beforehand, and thus be enabled to take counsel together. It was felt that without this mutual confidence it would serve no useful purpose to continue the existence of a separate Irish Unionist Party.[159]

Within British Conservatism, in contrast, the might of the Party machine was used to threaten or crush dissent: Lord Balcarres recalled frightening 'conversations' held between the awesome Chief Whip, Acland-Hood, and miserable back-benchers and junior ministers.[160] Itself a party engaged in modest rebellion, the Ulster group had neither moral authority nor numerical strength sufficient to do more than browbeat dissidents. According to Saunderson's disciplinary catechism, the party demanded at most, not conformity, but merely prior knowledge of rebellion.[161]

Internal unity was not therefore an overriding objective of party organization; and, where Party functionaries bothered to deal with rebels, they were emollient and coaxing. Accepting that a small party placed on a permanent war-footing could generally achieve

[159] ESP, T 2996/2/D1, Saunderson to Plunkett, 21 Feb. 1896 (copy).
[160] Vincent (ed.), *Crawford Papers*, 85.   [161] See n. 159.

comparatively little, this laxity ultimately worked to the advantage of Irish Unionism. Effective independence *was* sacrificed: MPs absented themselves from Party meetings, and occasionally defied their peers, thus thwarting any identifiable loyalist parliamentary stand. On the other hand, generally good relations were sustained within an alliance which embraced a wide span of personal and political eccentricity. The Ulster Party assimilated dissent, because it had not the strength to crush it; but this meant that, when a truly important threat (like Home Rule) emerged, there were few distracting animosities to challenge the unity of the Party's resistance.

The laxity of the Party's disciplinary procedures is clearly demonstrated by an examination of its voting pattern over the period 1880–1910. Table 3.12 suggests a highly fissile party where a split is defined as one or more members dissenting from the majority line. The definition employed by Hugh Berrington, following A. L. Lowell—that a level of dissent above 10 per cent of the total party

TABLE 3.12. *The Voting Pattern of Irish Unionist Members, 1880–1910*

Session	Total No. of divisions	No. in sample[a]	% of split votes	% of split votes with 1 or 2 rebels
1880[b]	216	54	11	72
1884/5[b]	289	72	11	100
1886[b]	189	47	19	83
1887	485	121	22	75
1890	262	65	18	84
1893/4	450	112	9	90
1895	178	45	29	100
1898	310	77	16	54
1900	298	74	9	70
1903	263	66	39	77
1905	362	90	55	75
1907	466	116	15	98
1910	159	40	8	100

[a]The divisions examined were based on a random sample of one quarter of the total divisions in any year.
[b]Only Conservative voting patterns were considered for divisions before 1887.

Source: House of Commons Division Lists.

strength constituted a 'non-party vote'—was held to be inappropriate in the context of the Ulster group, given its numerical weakness.[162] The data reveal that the overwhelming majority of split votes were created by only one or two Party rebels. This level of dissent, disproportionately significant in a small parliamentary group, would have been obscured by using the Lowell–Berrington definition.

Table 3.12 suggests several determinants of Party unity. After 1886 the number of divisions producing a split loyalist vote increased quite substantially. It is likely, therefore, that the creation of the Ulster Party allowed loyalist members greater opportunities for self-expression: they could vote more readily in accordance with personal whim, rather than continually submit their consciences to the exigencies of party management. Through their semi-independence, Ulster loyalists were able, therefore, to defy the trend towards rigorous discipline, discernible within other parliamentary parties.[163]

Under Conservative administrations Irish Unionists could afford to indulge their fads in the voting lobbies: Home Rule was comatose, and more divisive issues could occupy their minds. Thus, there is a correlation between periods of Conservative government and the level of loyalist disunity. Whatever the rhetoric of their independence, Irish Unionists' only reliable ally was the Conservative Party; and, as an ally, it was much more susceptible to individual or factional bullying, than Liberalism.

Apart from the general circumstances of division, there were specific recurring lines of fissure within the Ulster Party. Its unity could be disrupted by the unflappable loyalty of office-holders when all their colleagues were in revolt. But it would be misleading to suggest that there was any simple relationship between possession of place or pension, and unwavering commitment to Conservatism; loyalty among Ulster office-holders depended, rather, on the less tangible circumstance of the individual's desire to maintain his tenure. Thus, conviction politicians—like T. W. Russell, William Ellison-Macartney, and William Johnston—displayed comparatively little regard for the places and pensions which they enjoyed. Russell, though an efficient and able junior minister, was more devoted to

---

[162] Hugh Berrington, 'Partisanship and Dissidence in the Nineteenth-Century House of Commons', *Parliamentary Affairs*, xi. 4 (Autumn 1968), 340.
[163] Ibid. 348.

the interests of his political base, than to Salisbury's third government, of which he was a member. He alarmed Walter Long in 1896 by his loud support for the Nationalist point of view on Gerald Balfour's Land Bill; and he sacrificed promotion in 1900 by coming out in favour of compulsory land purchase.[164] His bitter enemy, William Ellison-Macartney, as Financial Secretary to the Admiralty in 1898, threatened the First Lord, Goschen, with resignation—should the Cabinet commit itself to a Catholic University.[165] William Johnston, who was privy to Ellison-Macartney's threat, was a client of the Conservative Party, enjoying a stipend of £200 a year: when his paymaster, Lord Arthur Hill, attempted to reprimand him for a maverick vote, he offered a characteristically obdurate response: 'Lord Arthur Hill spoke to me at [W.H.] Smith's instance about my adverse vote; alluding to my expenses being paid, and the help recently given to Ina [his ailing wife] in April, I offered to resign. If I did, I should stand again, and appeal for funds . . .'.[166] While benefiting from government patronage, Irish Unionists could be unwilling to accept its responsibilities. For the Conservative managers it was a strange and sad feature of the loyalist psyche that many should seek in this way to subordinate party politics to the demands of conscience.

However, even allowing for the occasional supremacy of principle, office-holders voted with the government more consistently than their loyalist colleagues, and there were several members whose appetite for advancement outweighed any loyalty to Party. Cynical self-interest was popularly held to be a generic attribute of the lawyers among the Irish Unionist Parliamentary Party: this prejudice gained currency both in contemporary fiction (in the work of George Birmingham, for example), and in the allegations of political opponents, like T. W. Russell.[167] William Moore's frankness on this score has already been cited.[168] But the single most unrepentant legal careerist was, perhaps, J. H. M. Campbell, MP for Trinity College, Dublin, between 1903 and 1917. In 1899 he urged his claims on a vacant judgeship. Later, in October 1900, Campbell complained that he had been passed over in the appointment of a Unionist Solicitor-General for Ireland; in 1905 he pressed shamelessly

---

[164] Ervine, *Craigavon*, 101–2. Griffith-Boscawen, *Fourteen Years*, 192.
[165] WJD, D 880/2/50, 9 Feb. 1898.   [166] WJD, D 880/2/39, 6 July 1887.
[167] Birmingham, *Benedict Kavanagh* (London 1907), 29–55.
[168] Diary of Nina Patrick, v. 7.

for promotion to the Bench.[169] In 1916 he was again on the search for title, pestering the hapless Bonar Law with his claims on the Irish Lord Chancellorship.[170] Campbell was an able man, serving the Unionist Party well in the difficult years after 1906, but he had an unattractively sure sense of his personal merit. This, however, worked to the advantage of the British party leaders, for Campbell (unlike Macartney, Russell, and Johnston) never jeopardized his career in the interests of loyalist independence.

A second significant line of fissure within the Ulster Party occurred between the radical Unionists, T. W. Russell and Thomas Lea, and more conservative colleagues. Their dissent from the majority line on the Land Bill of 1887 explains the high level of division recorded for that year. In the late 1890s Lea's health failed, and he retired in 1900—but Russell maintained his defiance, gradually drifting outside the Ulster Party, particularly after the land agitation of 1894–5, and his inclusion in Salisbury's third ministry. In 1902–3 Russell successfully ran his own independent parliamentary candidates; he and his acolytes remained, albeit heretical, Unionists until 1905, and for this reason they were included in the calculations for Table 3.12. But, as Lord Balcarres noted glumly in 1904, the Russellite ginger group consistently voted against the Unionist whip (whether British or Ulster) and this more or less permanent rebellion boosted the number of split votes in 1903 and 1905.[171]

A third, and less serious, cause of division were the fads and adopted causes of individual loyalist MPs. Exploiting the relative freedom offered by Party membership, temperance advocates (like William Johnston and T. L. Corbett), and reforming populists (like T. H. Sloan) recorded independent votes in those divisions affecting their special interests. But individual enthusiasms were happily tolerated, and the dissent which they promoted was short-lived, and insignificant. Of these mavericks, only Tom Sloan was driven from

[169] Sandars Papers, C. 732, fo. 90, J. H. M. Campbell to Balfour, 21 Oct. 1900; WLP, Add. MS 62409, J. H. M. Campbell to J. S. Sandars, 28 Nov. 1905 (copy). HLRO, Cadogan Papers, CAD 1685/2, Campbell to Ashbourne, 7 Dec. 1899.

[170] Robert Blake, *The Unknown Prime Minister: The Life and Times of Andrew Bonar Law, 1858–1923* (London, 1955), 254–5.

[171] Vincent, *Crawford Papers*, 70. See my 'Irish Unionism and the Russellite Threat', *passim*.

the Party, and for reasons unconnected with his quixotic reforming zeal.[172]

The divisions which racked British Unionism at this time had an equally slight effect on the Ulster Party. Most loyalist members supported Chamberlain and imperial preference; and a number attended the meeting of Tariff Reform MPs, held at Westminster in April 1905.[173] But the arguments over Preference inspired comparatively little excitement in a Party preoccupied with the electoral threat posed by T. W. Russell, and with rumours of devolution and a government sell-out. There were no bitter internal wrangles, therefore; as with most other basically English issues and disputes, Irish Unionists expressed their opinions, but invested little emotional energy in defending them.

Concentrating on Party divisions should not obscure its essential unity. Ulster members, with the exception of one year (1905) were more likely to be united than divided on an issue; and 'division' of the Party meant, in general, one or two members dissenting from the stand maintained by the rest of the group. Furthermore, the Ulster Party very rarely offered any comprehensive programme on which to unite (or to divide). It claimed to represent the parliamentary interests of Irish loyalism, but—beyond a consensus that these interests hinged on the Union—the Party offered no clear definition of its purpose. Each of its members, therefore, voted as he saw fit on a particular issue; no colleague much minded a dissentient vote (except on a few, crucial Irish divisions) since all enjoyed the same flexibility of voting choice.

This laxity reflected on the Party's parliamentary function. It was not an efficient pressure group: discipline was too haphazard for loyalists, as a body, to succeed in maintaining a constant check on all aspects of Conservative policy. Since they were concerned only with the Union, it was only on matters directly relating to the Union that they could effectively bind together.

[172] Sloan effectively broke with 'official' Unionism after the Magheramorne Manifesto of July 1905. See J. W. Boyle, 'The Belfast Protestant Association and the Independent Orange Order, 1901–1910', *IHS*, xiii. 50 (Sept. 1962), 134–6.

[173] Birmingham University Library, Joseph Chamberlain Papers, JC/20/4/20, a list of 142 MPs present at a Commons Tariff Reform meeting, 13 April 1905. T. L. Corbett, C. C. Craig, John Gordon, J. B. Lonsdale, and William Moore of the Ulster Party attended.

For the most part, then, Irish Unionists were left by their Party to their own devices. Horace Plunkett was free to rail, unattended, against his colleagues; T. W. Russell (until, at any rate, 1895) and T. H. Sloan (until 1905) were both able to demonstrate their populist credentials. And William Johnston, racked by the spectre of Romish conspiracy, could stoutly resist her enticements within the sanctity of the division lobby. Possessing little discipline, the Ulster Party only rarely recognized rebellion; but, for this reason, it survived—in defiance of Plunkett's scepticism.

4

The Ulster Party, the Tories, and a Policy for Ireland, 1886–1906

The Conservative Party never yet took up a cause without betraying it in the end

William Harcourt[1]

1. *Introduction*

Perhaps the most dramatic feature of Irish Unionist development before 1912 was the relative decline in importance of both the loyalist parliamentary party and the movement's parliamentary strategy. Different aspects and causes of this localization are explored throughout the book, but it will already be clear from the initial chapters that the behaviour of the English Tory leadership was an important influence. In 1884–5 the spectre of Tory betrayal helped to inspire the first attempts at independent loyalist organization, both within the House of Commons, and, more haphazardly, within Ulster. When the Tories rallied around Unionist orthodoxy in 1886, part of the purpose of their Irish party's independence was undermined. Accordingly, and despite the vitality of the Nationalist threat, many aspects of loyalist organization had fallen into abeyance by the late 1880s.

On the evidence of party relations in 1884–6 it may be further suggested that the viability of a loyalist parliamentary policy depended largely upon the achievements of Ulster MPs in the Commons, and that these in turn depended upon the pliability of Tory government. Thus, if the government resisted Ulster Unionist pressure, it discredited loyalist parliamentary representatives, and undermined the function of parliament within loyalism. The extent

---

[1] Edward Marjoribanks and Ian Colvin, *Life of Lord Carson*, (3 vols.; London, 1932–6) i. 163–4.

to which this sequence of reactions was a feature of the period 1885–1905 is explored in what follows.

Clearly, given the emotions raised by reform in 1884, the near collapse of the Unionist alliance under the Chief Secretaryship of George Wyndham was not unprecedented.[2] But, if the parties' bond had always contained snags, then relations grew perceptibly more warped after the Home Rule crises. Although the bitterness of 1884–5 was succeeded by ostentatious displays of amity in 1886 and 1893, the partnership seems to have been subsequently, and indelibly, marred. At any rate, the unity of the parties in 1912 was much less complete than in the earlier Home Rule controversies, judged both by the new reliance of Ulster Unionists on military organization, and by the vitality of their suspicions concerning Tory loyalty.[3] During most of the period before 1905 Unionist administrations were in power, and it may be inferred that their policies played a role in chilling the parties' relationship, and in sculpting the forms of Ulster Unionist evolution.

Thus, this chapter is concerned with the development of the Unionist partnership, and primarily in the context of Tory government. The Home Rule crises are taken as a starting point, because it is here that one might expect the unity of the parties, and the contrast with the last years of Wyndham's Chief Secretaryship to be most complete. In fact, this unity was less than absolute, and when the Unionists returned to government in 1895, inaugurating a period of extensive reform, any incipient distrust was given free rein. All the same, it should be emphasized that the notorious disputes between British and Irish Unionists in 1905 were not wholly about the repudiation of constructive Unionism, and it is highly misleading to assume that there was any simple loyalist reaction to reform. Indeed, it will become clear from the later sections of this chapter that, even within the parliamentary Ulster Party, the reaction to individual constructive measures varied very greatly. If constructive Unionism helped to prise the parties apart, then there was no even crescendo of animosity, as reform succeeded reform. Constructive Unionism certainly created difficulties—but less through what it achieved than through what it symbolized: the relegation of partisan government in Ireland, and the relegation of Irish Unionism, in favour of keeping peace between the natives. Constructive Unionism

[2] See ch. 6.   [3] See ch. 7.

was simply a more than usually expensive and progressive programme of colonial government; and it was partly the recognition of this which inspired resentment among loyalists.[4]

2. Home Rule

Only in a superficial sense was the relationship between Irish Unionist and British Conservative closest when a Home Rule Bill threatened. There was certainly greater social and public political contact between the parties, and leading loyalists like Edward Saunderson found themselves in demand both as dinner guests and as public speakers.[5] But for all Irish Unionist representatives, the political and social popularity inspired by Home Rule was a painfully transient phenomenon, and those loyalists who were heroes to English Unionism in 1886 soon found themselves dethroned. English audiences who had been moved by the plight of valiant Ulster, swiftly tired of their Irish wards, and the lugubrious affection which they had once displayed often degenerated into embarrassment and impatience. Given this outcome, how substantial can the unity of the parties have been in 1886 and 1893?

In 1886, and (probably to a lesser extent) 1893, interest in Ulster peaked, and Conservative leaders sought to identify themselves as closely as possible with loyalist opinion and, by implication, with British sympathy. Conservative speeches often echoed the sabre-rattling threats uttered by some Irish Unionists. But, while bellicosity was more or less a constant rhetorical theme within the extreme elements of Irish Tory Unionism, British Conservatives generally

[4] ABP, Add. MS 49852, fo. 105, T. M. Healy to Balfour, 28 May 1897. (Healy suggested that Ireland might as well be declared a crown colony.)
[5] PRONI, ESP, T 2996/1/70, Saunderson to his wife, 28 Jan. 1886 ('It seems queer to me to become suddenly a political personage')—quoted by Reginald Lucas, *Colonel Saunderson, M.P.: A Memoir* (London, 1908), 96. For Saunderson's sudden social success, see Lucas, *Saunderson*, 142-3. See also Bodleian Library, Alfred Milner Papers, dep. 63, Diary for 12 Feb. 1893. Milner found himself lunching with Saunderson at Londonderry House on the eve of a debate on the second Home Rule Bill. References to Edward Saunderson's speaking commitments at the time of the Home Rule bills may be found in KRO, Akers-Douglas Papers, C 481/3, Saunderson to Akers-Douglas, 14 Nov. 1890; C 387/2, Lord Mountedgcumbe to Akers-Douglas, 6 April 1889. Also ESP, T 2996/2/343, Saunderson to his wife, 16 Feb. 1887 (quoted in Lucas, *Saunderson*, 368); ESP, T 2996/2/379, Saunderson to his wife, 23 Feb. 1889.

adopted this tone only when in opposition. The *locus classicus* of Conservative incitement was Lord Randolph Churchill's Ulster Hall speech of 22 February 1886, but Salisbury's defence of Orange resistance in his Crystal Palace speech of 2 March 1886 was scarcely less uncompromising.[6] Salisbury adopted an equally defiant tone in his more famous St James's Hall address of 15 May 1886: responding to a call for 'three cheers for Lord Salisbury, and three cheers for Ulster!', he sanctioned the use of violence by Irish loyalists in defence of their political faith.[7] Arthur Balfour offered similar encouragement, both during the 1892 election campaign (in a Midlothian address), and—an echo of the Churchill visit—to a Belfast audience in April 1893.[8]

Extravagant verbal commitments arose partly from the infectiousness of what would later be described as 'Ulsteria'; more importantly, they were a consequence of the Conservative leadership's need to rally support around a popular cause—and to hold together a potentially fissile coalition between their own party support, and Liberal and Ulster Unionists. In adopting the cause, they had to defend its excesses; and, so long as they were free from the compromising responsibilities of Irish government, such a defence posed few problems. Indeed, later Unionist leaders faced the same tactical demand, and offered a similar response. Andrew Bonar Law was merely repeating the substance of older commitments in declaring at Blenheim Palace in July 1912 that he could 'imagine no length of resistance to which Ulster can go, in which I shall not be prepared to support them'.[9] What is surprising about Bonar Law's Blenheim Pledge is thus not so much that it should have been given, as that it should have been treated by contemporaries as outside the context of traditional Conservative rhetoric on Ireland.

The corollary of rhetorical identification with extreme loyalism was the appearance of Conservative leaders in loyalist Ireland. Public visits of Conservative leaders to Ulster and Dublin are associated, again with the Home Rule crises (Lord Randolph in 1886, Balfour

---

[6] *IT*, 4 Mar. 1886, 5. R. F. Foster, *Lord Randolph Churchill: A Political Life* (Oxford, 1981), 255-6.

[7] Quoted in A. L. Kennedy, *Salisbury, 1830-1903: Portrait of a Statesman* (London, 1953), 175.

[8] Kenneth Young, *Arthur James Balfour: The Happy Life of the Politician, Prime Minister, Statesman, and Philosopher 1848-1930* (London, 1963), 128-9.

[9] Quoted, for example, in Robert Blake, *The Unknown Prime Minister: The Life and Times of Andrew Bonar Law, 1858-1923* (London, 1955) 130.

and Salisbury in 1893, Bonar Law in 1912), though less important figures might grace loyalist platforms in the intervening periods (Walter Long and Austen Chamberlain in 1906, Cawdor in 1909). These visits had a twofold function. In a general sense they represented an encouragement of essential Irish support and such encouragement, even when bitterly partisan, was seen by many leaders as having a cathartic function for restless Orange opinion.[10] An earlier visitor to Ulster, Stafford Northcote, considered that his presence 'may have added a little to the excitement, but it let off more steam than it generated'.[11] Distinguished tourists like Northcote brought in train British and continental pressmen to Protestant Ireland, and gave loyalists an opportunity to demonstrate to their fellow-Britons the sterling virtues which they claimed as a monopoly. The brooding restraint of Unionist crowds in 1912 was designedly impressive; but even when Lord Randolph journeyed to Belfast, and harangued a loyalist audience in the Ulster Hall, there was little violence as a direct consequence, and spectators reported favourably on the order and discipline displayed.[12] Mary Leslie, writing to Alice Balfour of her brother's 1893 Belfast visit, described 'the comfort and calm [inspired] . . . by the genuine belief that came into our hearts from the ring with which he read and seconded Lord Salisbury's telegram that he *was* England's messenger, and authorised us to hope'.[13] Mary Arnold-Foster was an eyewitness to the same demonstration and reported her awe of 'the quiet orderliness and sobriety of the crowd'.[14]

[10] Not all Irish Unionists were encouraged, especially those in predominantly Nationalist areas: Private Possession, Cochrane Papers, R. Lippon to Capt. E. Cochrane, 21 May 1893.
[11] Andrew Lang, *The Life, Letters and Diaries of Sir Stafford Northcote, First Earl of Iddesleigh* (2 vols.; Edinburgh and London, 1890) ii. 262. For a fuller (and more accurate) account of Northcote's Irish tour, see A. B. Cooke, 'A Conservative Party Leader in Ulster: Sir Stafford Northcote's Diary of a Visit to the Province, October 1883', *Proceedings of the Royal Irish Academy*, lxxv, sect. C.4 (Sept. 1975), 61-84.
[12] R. E. Quinault, 'Lord Randolph Churchill and Home Rule', *Irish Historical Studies*, xxi. 84, (Sept. 1979), 397-8. See also Churchill College, Cambridge, Lord Randolph Churchill Papers, RCHL. 1/12/1380, R. Fitzgibbon to Churchill, 22 Feb. 1886.
[13] Whittingehame, Arthur Balfour Papers, TD 83/133/32/37, Mary Leslie to Alice Balfour, 3 Mar. 1893.
[14] Trinity College Dublin, H. O. Arnold-Foster Papers, TCD 5000/178, Mary Arnold-Foster to Jane Forster, 6 Apr. 1893; TCD 5000/179, Mary Arnold-Foster to Florence O'Brien, 8 Apr. 1893.

From an English perspective, these visits also offered Conservative leaders sentimental capital—the opportunity to identify themselves with an isolated and embattled community, and to pose as their champions against the threat of Home Rule. 'So long as I live', wrote Mary Leslie, 'I shall never get over that pathetic giant, the Ulster people, stretching out its hands, brown, strong, toil-worn, and sorely tried, towards your brother [Arthur Balfour] . . . I suppose he is tired of being called, "a still, strong man in a blatant land".'[15] The 'pathetic giant', whose plight inspired Swinburne and Kipling, could also engage the emotions and votes of the lugubrious middle classes. Through loyalism Balfour could pose as a Tennysonian saviour, while even Northcote might play at popular leadership in competition with Churchill.[16]

But, though the Home Rule crises appeared to heighten the Conservative commitment in terms of rhetoric and personal contact, the reality, as displayed by the debates on each bill, was rather more complex. Irish Unionists could not agree, either internally or with British Conservatives, in defining precisely what they were defending, or how it should be defended. Lacking unity among themselves, Irish Unionists, as a party, were unable to achieve complete harmony with their British allies, even over the issue which determined their very political existence.

The Home Rule debate quickly acquired, and tenaciously retained, an imperial dimension. Unionist statements on the issue resolved down to a fundamental belief that Home Rule for Ireland promoted the disintegration of the Empire—both as a precedent for constitutional concession through agitation, and through the threat that a semi-independent Ireland might represent to imperial security. For many English Conservatives, considerations of Empire promoted a merely tangential concern for Ireland and the prospective plight of the loyalist minority.[17] Indeed, Peter Marsh has gone so far as to suggest (contradicting Lady Gwendolen Cecil) that Salisbury's true

---

[15] Whittingehame, Arthur Balfour Papers, TD 83/133/32/37, Mary Leslie to Alice Balfour, 3 Mar. 1893.

[16] Cooke deems Northcote 'perhaps the most active stump orator in the party', 'Northcote's Diary', 69.

[17] Argued perceptively (in relation to a later period) by D. G. Boyce, *Englishmen and Irish Troubles: British Public Opinion and the Making of Irish Policy* (London, 1972), 103-4. For an 18th-cent. parallel see John W. Derry, *Castlereagh* (London, 1976), 41.

commitment was to the Empire, and that 'there was more utility than conviction to his defence of the Union'.[18] Joseph Chamberlain, among the Liberal Unionists, shared these priorities, consistently viewing the problem of Irish government in an imperial context, and offering plans for administrative reform which encompassed, not merely Ireland, but the entire United Kingdom.[19]

Irish loyalist MPs posed as imperialists but, in attacking the proposals of the Home Rule Bills, the true nature of their imperialism, and of the gulf separating them from British Conservatives became quite apparent. If leading Conservatives and Liberal Unionists thought of Home Rule primarily as a threat to Empire, then loyalists were unequal to the detachment which a similar point of view demanded from Irishmen: they thought of Ireland fundamentally in terms of local partisan division, and exploited imperial rhetoric partly as a ready source of communication with English Conservative sentiment. Thus, the focus of loyalist thought on the Empire had little to do with broader concerns of imperial unity—although in the more tranquil conditions of the late 1890s individual leaders like Saunderson would seek a more objective definition of their Unionism as an imperial cause.[20]

In 1886, when general imperial arguments were aired to a much greater extent than in 1893, Irish loyalists gave no serious consideration to the implications of Home Rule for the Empire. Their concerns centred rather on the more parochial fear that Home Rule would downgrade their homeland to the status of a colony, with themselves, one-time members of an imperial governing race, as mere colonials. On 8 April 1886 Colonel Thomas Waring followed Gladstone's opening speech on the Home Rule Bill with a fundamentally local and partisan plea, conveyed in spuriously jingoistic language. 'Irish loyalists', he declared, 'were now part and parcel of one of the greatest Empires of the world . . . and were

---

[18] Peter Marsh, *The Discipline of Popular Government: Lord Salisbury's Domestic Statecraft, 1881–1902* (Hassocks, 1978), 276. Lady Gwendolen Cecil, *Life of Robert, Third Marquess of Salisbury*, (4 vols.; London, 1921–32) iii. 151.

[19] Richard Jay has, however, questioned the view that Chamberlain's opposition to Home Rule was primarily based upon fears of imperial disintegration. Richard Jay, *Joseph Chamberlain: A Political Study* (Oxford, 1981), 123–8. See also C. H. D. Howard, 'Joseph Chamberlain and the Irish Central Board Scheme', *IHS*, viii (1953), 324–61.

[20] Lucas, *Saunderson*, 264–78. David W. Miller, *Queen's Rebels: Ulster Loyalism in Historical Perspective* (Dublin, 1978), 118–20.

utterly determined that they should not be changed into colonials
. . . at the mercy of those from whom they differed politically.'[21]
Waring's imperial fervour resolved simply into a distaste for colonial
status, and opposition to Parnellite government. The former was an
odd repudiation for one who otherwise apparently glorified the
purpose and structure of Empire, while the latter argument embodied
Waring's fundamental concern. This subsequently became clear
when, in reviewing the alternatives open to Gladstone, Waring
abandoned his earlier jingoism: he confessed that he thought the
prospect of complete independence for Ireland more attractive than
the British-sponsored Parnellite domination threatened by the Home
Rule Bill.[22]

Later Irish Unionist speakers echoed Waring's arguments, seeking
an artificial equation between the Act of Union, which was their real
concern, and the unity of the Empire, which they tacitly identified
as a broader Conservative preoccupation.[23] C. E. Lewis, member
for Londonderry City, abandoned all circumlocution and stated this
bluntly: 'We have no alternative to propose but a united Empire;
there is no other alternative; and I put the matter in this way—you
want to break the Union—it is our duty to maintain it.'[24] Thus,
Irish Unionists, offering no justification, and receiving no serious
Liberal challenge, barely disguised a narrowly Irish political cause
under the guise of a disinterested faith in imperial unity.

In 1886 the Irish Unionist interest in imperialism probably owed
more to a perception of the state of British opinion one year after
the death of Gordon, and in the midst of continuing colonial warfare
in Egypt and Burma, than to any truly deep-rooted faith in Empire.
Nor were loyalist MPs alone in identifying the marketability of
the call 'The Empire in danger' at the time.[25] In 1893, however,
imperial arguments played a slighter role in Irish Unionists'
presentation of their case before parliament, as indeed the Church
of Ireland bishop of Clogher observed.[26] The most substantial
reversion to an imperial plea was an effective exploitation of the
concept of empire as a Unionist surrogate for the appeal of
nationality. David Plunket, senior member for Trinity College,

---

[21] Hansard, 3rd ser. (1886), ccciv. 1088.   [22] Ibid.
[23] See e.g. Hansard, 3rd ser. (1886), ccciv. 1089.
[24] Hansard, 3rd ser. (1886), cccv. 677.   [25] Jay, *Chamberlain*, 128.
[26] PRONI, Hugh de Fellenberg Montgomery Papers, D 627/428/230, bp. of
Clogher to Montgomery, 18 Mar. 1893.

Dublin, defined two types of Irish patriotism: the vulgar 'green flag' variety, and the less parochial patriotism of Irish loyalists, who saw Ireland glorified rather than denigrated by participating in a world-wide empire.[27] But, as with earlier loyalist interest in Empire, even Plunket's eloquent appeal embodied an Irish argument alien to British Conservative thought. Plunket promoted Empire only as a vehicle for Irish patriotism, attempting to reconcile an Irish national pride, which most loyalists accepted and shared, with rule by a parliament at Westminster.

The ambiguity of the loyalist commitment to Empire was betrayed by a strand of their thought which, paradoxically, favoured the complete independence of Ireland, rather than the Gladstonian half-way house. This argument maintained that the loyalist minority in Ireland stood a better chance of defending its interests in an independent state than under a Home Rule parliament, protected and maintained by British power. One of its fullest expositions was given in a letter written in March 1908 by the former North Derry MP, John Atkinson, to Walter Long. Atkinson specifically stated what few loyalists dared to suggest in public—that their fear of Home Rule was not in any real sense bound to a concern for the integrity of the British Empire. Irish loyalists' interests lay rather in the total abandonment of the imperial connection. He wrote:

It is a delusion to suppose that a desire for Imperial Supremacy with Home Rule is a law of the being of the Irish Protestant. If I were a young man, and Home Rule were carried, I'd join Sinn Fein, and advocate separation, and a republic, with all the power that I possess—[but] not from pique, or a sense of wrong, or a feeling of having been deserted or betrayed—that's the English delusion . . .[28]

Atkinson argued that the strength of the Protestant minority in an independent Ireland was in itself sufficient guarantee against majority repression. Home Rule, on the other hand, involved the real possibility of acts of oppression, since the Home Rule parliament would be backed by British force and British troops might be used to put down any minority rebellion. English opinion would lose all interest in the fate of the minority, once Home Rule was granted, and repression (unless wildly barbarous) might well be ignored. 'In short', Atkinson concluded, 'an independent Ireland means for the

---

[27] Hansard, 4th ser. (1893), x. 1863.
[28] WLP, Add. MS 62413, Atkinson to Long, 28 Mar. 1908.

minority such tyranny and wrong as the majority itself could inflict—
Home Rule means tyranny . . . maintained by the aid of English
troops.'[29]

Atkinson's political testament was in no sense that of a maverick,
or deviant, loyalist—for subsequent Irish political debates brought
forward others thinking along similar lines.[30] These radical theorists
were unwilling to alienate any temporarily sympathetic Conservative
opinion by a blunt confession of loyalist self-interest, but they said
sufficient to reveal that they did not regard Ireland's imperial link
as a necessary, or permanent, connection. Colonel Thomas Waring
declared on 8 April 1886, at the beginning of the debate on the first
Home Rule Bill, that he considered a grant of complete independence
for Ireland 'an intelligible course to take, and an honest one—for,
by taking it, an opportunity would arise for the minority . . . to take
care of themselves'.[31] Several other Irish Unionist members attacked
the Bill on the grounds that it offered 'an integral part of the Empire'
merely colonial status, and not compensating independence.[32]
Edward Macnaghten stressed the limitations of the Bill's conception
of Irish self-government.[33] Loyalist criticism was often directed, not
so much against the principle of legislative independence, as against
its Gladstonian form, and the threat of Parnellite supremacy. 'Half the
difficulties of Home Rule', declared T. W. Russell, during the Second
Reading of the 1893 Bill, 'would be got rid of if it were not for the
Home Rulers. There is as much objection to the Home Rulers
themselves as there is to Home Rule.'[34]Edward Saunderson had
used the same argument in May 1886, employing a phrase which
found its way into a host of late Victorian parliamentary memoirs—
'I can assert 85 reasons why this House should not consent to this Bill.
They are not abstract, but concrete reasons—and they are to be found
sitting below the gangway opposite.'[35]

The Irish loyalist case, as presented to the House of Commons,
had little to do with a moral commitment to the Union and to the

---

[29] Ibid.

[30] See Richard Davis *Arthur Griffith and Non-Violent Sinn Fein* (Dublin, 1974),
60–1, for evidence of Protestant and Unionist support for Sinn Fein and its separatist
ambitions; Richard Davis, 'Ulster Protestants and the Sinn Fein Press, 1914–1922',
Eire-Ireland, xv. 4 (1980), 60–85.

[31] Hansard, 3rd ser. (1886), ccciv. 1089.   [32] Ibid. 1091.   [33] Ibid.

[34] Hansard, 4th ser. (1893), xi. 63.

[35] Hansard, 3rd ser. (1886), cccv. 1772. Quoted e.g. by Marjoribanks and
Colvin, *Lord Carson*, i. 160.

British Empire—contrary to a recent suggestion.[36] What bound Irish loyalists to British Conservatives was neither faith in a shared imperial destiny, nor positive affection for Westminster, but rather an overwhelming fear of Nationalist tyranny. This was one measure of the insubstantiality of their alliance.

A second measure existed in the problem, for British Conservatives, of Orange bluster. British Conservatives found themselves closely allied with extremists whose rhetoric was not merely alien to their own, but also a source of embarrassment—particularly before a Commons audience. Yet, as allies, Conservatives felt compelled to offer a defence for even the worst excesses of Orange bravado.

Throughout April and May 1886 reports of armed loyalist resistance filtered through to the press in England.[37] The *Belfast News Letter* carried advertisements inviting tenders for large numbers of Snider rifles, and seeking drill instructors: such calls captured the imagination of the English papers, and this indeed may have been their sole purpose.[38] A leading Orange member of parliament, William Johnston, announced at two public meetings—the Maze (on 26 April) and Dungannon (6 May)—plans for Ulster's military resistance.[39] At Dungannon Johnston informed his Orange audience that Field Marshal Lord Wolseley ('the great grandson of Colonel Wolseley who fought at Newtownbutler') and one thousand other officers had pledged themselves to resign their commissions, and to lead the Ulster Protestants' defiance of the prospective Dublin parliament.[40] The *Pall Mall Gazette* carried the story of Johnston's revelations on 8 May, and was able to offer corroborating evidence of his claims regarding Wolseley in its edition of 10 May.[41] The *Gazette* of 1 June carried an interview with the loyalist member for East Belfast, Edward de Cobain, in which he embroidered Johnston's earlier tales with claims of an Orange army muster roll of 120,000

[36] R. J. Lawrence, *The Government of Northern Ireland: Public Finance and Public Services 1921–1964* (Oxford, 1964), 6. James Loughlin, *Gladstone, Home Rule and the Ulster Question, 1882–1893* (Dublin, 1986), 153–61.

[37] The *Irish Times* carried extensive quotations from the English press throughout April and May 1886. Loughlin, *Gladstone*, 153–67.

[38] D. C. Savage, 'The Origins of the Ulster Unionist Party 1885–1886', *IHS*, xii. 47 (Mar. 1961), 202–4. Loughlin, *Gladstone*, 167–71.

[39] *IT*, 27 Apr. 1886, 6; 7 May 1886, 5.   [40] *IT*, 7 May 1886, 5.
[41] *Pall Mall Gazette*, 8 May 1886, quoted in *IT*, 10 May 1886, 5.

men.[42] Edward Saunderson was interviewed for the *Gazette*'s
2 June number, and he confirmed and defended the preparations for
resistance. The Orangemen's loyalty, he declared, in vindicating their
action, was to 'the crown of an absolute monarch, not to the crown
of a monarch acting through representative institutions'.[43] In this
way Saunderson defined the extent of his commitment to the rule
of Westminster.

Orange MPs echoed these threats before the House of Commons.
Some were circumspect in their language: Colonel Waring (Grand
Master of the County Down Orangemen) referred vaguely to the
potential need to 'take such steps as might be advisable to save their
connexion'.[44] In a rare parliamentary appearance, R. T. O'Neill,
member for Mid Antrim, declared with rather less restraint that
Ulster Protestants were determined to protect themselves 'by all
means in their power', if a Dublin parliament were created by
Gladstone.[45] It was left, however, to William Johnston to abandon
all circumlocution and to repeat to a sceptical Commons the
substance of his Ulster tirades. With blood-curdling directness he
conveyed to the House the reality, as he saw it, of Ulster's
preparations for war. Resistance, he warned, would be offered 'at
the point of the bayonet'.[46] However, the irony implicit in the
heroic pretensions of an otherwise respectable elderly gentleman was
not lost on the House. As the Liberal member for Bethnal Green
commented: 'For a gentleman of a disposition so pacific, [Johnston]
adopted remarkably sanguinary language. He thought he could only
say of the hon. Member that he seemed to be "the mildest man who
ever cut a throat or scuttled a ship" . . .'.[47]

In 1893 rumours of loyalist drilling attracted less attention in
Britain, for wild threats of resistance appeared less plausible, with
the anti-climax of 1886 still large in the public memory. But as the
reality of bloodshed became (or appeared to become) more remote,
its acceptability as an argument against the Bill was acknowledged
among a broader range of Irish Unionist opinion: rhetorical use of
the threat was a less blatant incitment, and could be used with
impunity by the more circumspect loyalist representatives. Within
the Irish Unionist parliamentary party, therefore, warmongering was

[42] *Pall Mall Gazette*, 1 June 1886, quoted in *IT*, 2 June 1886, 5.
[43] *Pall Mall Gazette*, 2 June 1886, quoted in *IT*, 3 June 1886, 6.
[44] Hansard, 3rd ser. (1886), ccciv. 1088.   [45] Ibid. 1094.
[46] Ibid. 1231.   [47] Ibid. cccvi. 1057.

no longer confined to the most bitter Orange representatives. Saunderson and Johnston reworked their threats of 1886, but otherwise moderate members, like Richard Dane, who sat for North Fermanagh, and D. P. Barton (Mid-Armagh), were no less minatory. Dane foresaw Home Rule as precipitating civil war, and the expulsion of the 'English garrison'.[48] Barton, on the other hand, could offer the House evidence of an unequivocal personal commitment to resistance. During the Second Reading, he revealed that he had enrolled 'as one of the organisation that now existed in Ulster . . . he did not know what that act might lead to—[but] it might lead to his spending his life in penal servitude'.[49] As with Johnston's warnings, this pious expression of political devotion merely provoked ironical laughter: the House remained unconvinced— even by the sudden and impassioned rhetoric of a comparative moderate.

Indeed Liberals and Nationalists reacted to the foreboding of loyalist members with mockery. Henry Labouchere, during the Second Reading of the 1886 Bill, dismissed the pretensions of the Orangemen, and of William Johnston, 'their chosen representative': 'if', he quipped, not inaccurately, 'they judged the intelligence, or the loyalty, or the patriotism of these Orangemen by their chosen representative, they should have an exceedingly poor opinion of them'.[50] Johnston's threats of civil war were so many 'cock and bull stories'. T. D. Sullivan, a Nationalist, taking his cue from 'Labby', directed ridicule at the uneasy mixture of prim respectability and heroic conviction which characterized much loyalist rhetoric. In a barely concealed reference, again, to Johnston, Sullivan caricatured an anonymous Ulster member who dreamt at night of King William III, the Orange hero of the Boyne: 'he imagined himself mounted on a great white horse with his sword in hand, charging by the side of King William, smiting the unfortunate Papists hip and thigh'.[51] Loyalist sabre-rattling was characterized witheringly as 'silly speeches'. Later in the same debate William Harcourt derided references to Ulster resistance by feigning anxiety at the prospect of the 'very formidable combination' of Johnston, Saunderson, and Randolph Churchill in military alliance. Goschen's contribution was

---

[48] Hansard, 4th ser. (1893), viii. 1297.   [49] Ibid. x. 1705.
[50] Hansard, 3rd ser. (1886), cccv. 1342. Arthur Griffith, for one, had a higher opinion of 'Ballykilbeg': Davis, 'Sinn Fein Press', 65.
[51] Ibid. cccv. 1355.

not forgotten: 'we must invoke the melodramatic valour of my right hon. Friend, the Member for East Edinburgh—we must send for our family solicitor, make our wills and do our duty . . .'.[52]

Effective Liberal and Nationalist ridicule was a measure of the failure, in debating terms, of these doom-laden prophesies and threats. Indeed, such threats enabled Liberal speakers to side-step the more problematic aspects of the Ulster Party's arguments, and to concentrate on the weaker and more disreputable element of their case. Irish Unionist politicians were possibly sincere in directing the attention of the House to their supporters' fears of repression, and interest in resistance; they were certainly convinced that the House would respond sympathetically to their evidence of local alarm—an alarm so intense that respectable citizens contemplated taking violent defensive action. Allusions to armed resistance were not wholly rhetorical, therefore. But, given the lack of evidence to substantiate loyalist claims, and the frequent inconsistency of such claims, these may be judged as at least partly tactical: as a means of swaying parliamentary opinion.

This was a profound miscalculation, the consequences of which alarmed both British Conservatives and some, more circumspect, Irish loyalists. Successive loyalist speakers, in both the debates of 1886 and 1893, sought to dissociate themselves from their more extreme colleagues in the Ulster Party, stressing that Orangeism had only a minority following in the Protestant community, and repudiating threats of armed resistance. Several (Edward Macnaghten, J. P. Corry) prefaced their remarks with a declaration that they were not members of the Orange Order.[53] During the Second Reading debate on the 1893 Bill, Sir Thomas Lea, Liberal Unionist member for South Londonderry, offered an apologetic defence of Orangeism, claiming that the movement was 'not understood in the House': Orangemen, far from being the thugs of Liberal rhetoric, were 'law-abiding subjects [who] desired to obey the Queen, and parliament'.[54] But the emphasis of Lea's speech fell ultimately on the overwhelmingly non-Orange opposition to the Bill.

Disavowing Orangeism in 1886, moderate loyalists disavowed, too, its threats of violence. The member for North Tyrone, Lord

---

[52] Ibid. cccvi. 769. In 1892 Harcourt renewed his jibes: Lucas, *Saunderson*, 179–81.

[53] Ibid. ccciv. 1090.   [54] Hansard, 4th ser. (1893), xi. 503.

Ernest Hamilton, joined Liberals in dismissing the idea of civil war—
this was 'absurd and childish nonsense'.[55] Later in the Second
Reading Colonel Edward King-Harman, an Irish Unionist who sat
for the Isle of Thanet, was interrupted by an outraged William
Johnston, when he suggested that oppressed loyalists would be likely
to emigrate rather than fight. Johnston looked forward to manning
the last ditch, where King-Harman claimed that 'there was no serious
intention of civil war, or of fighting on the part of the loyal
population'.[56]

Firebrands like Johnston were a serious embarrassment when their
bluster was greatest—as in 1886. Bluster won as much mockery as
acceptance in England, and brought comparatively moderate
loyalists, seeking to portray a considered Unionism, into direct
conflict with their extreme colleagues. In endeavouring to salvage
some parliamentary credibility, moderates found themselves lending
credence to Liberal and Nationalist taunts. Only when the reality
of an Ulster army and popular passion became indisputable could
Irish Unionist MPs unite, and plausibly warn parliament of the threat
of civil war; and this would not happen until 1912 (and perhaps
not even then).

But, extremism also anguished and embarrassed Conservative
parliamentary opinion. Many Tories were instinctively out of
sympathy with Orangeism, dismayed by its narrowness, and (rightly)
suspicious of its ultimate loyalty to the British connection. George
Wyndham, as Chief Secretary, deplored 'Orange uncouthness', and
found 'the parochialism of the Ulster right-wing . . . beyond
belief'.[57] But even a less eccentric Tory, the Earl of Cadogan, was
moved by his experience as Irish Viceroy to ask of Walter Long: 'are
you sure all Ulstermen are *loyal* in the best and most unselfish sense
of the word? I will not write what I think . . .'.[58] Conservative
governments continually struggled to restrain Orange extremists from
acts of provocation or retaliation. Successive Chief Secretaries sought
ineffectually to curb Orange militancy through contact and influence
with its more amenable leaders—Lord Arthur Hill, the Earl of Erne.
But such influence exposed these relative moderates to the criticism

[55] Hansard, 3rd ser. (1886), ccciv. 1498.   [56] Ibid. cccvi. 1050.
[57] J. W. Mackail and Guy Wyndham (edd.), *Life and Letters of George
Wyndham*, (2 vols.; London, [1924]) ii. 436, 459. Though see below, ch. 3.1, for
the context of such remarks.
[58] WLP, Add. MS 62411, Cadogan to Long, 29 Sept. 1907.

of those Orange elements unwilling to be seen as creatures of British Conservatism.[59] Restraining influence, even when exercised through friendly personal contact, had consequently little effect.

Orange bluster in the Home Rule debates was thus no less an embarrassment for many British Conservatives than for moderate Irish Unionists. Few Conservatives dwelt on the loyalists' threats and predictions, and those few were defensive and apologetic in tone. Walter Long thought in 1886 'that the great majority of English members . . . would be inclined to use as strong, if not stronger, language if they had been subjected to the same troubles and trials as the Ulstermen had experienced'.[60] But the force of Long's comment was dismissive: Ulster militancy *was* merely 'strong' language. Salisbury's comments at the Crystal Palace (4 March 1886) and at St James's Hall (15 May) were equally apologetic, urging a sympathetic English response to unattractive Ulster rhetoric.[61] In the second reading of the 1893 Bill, Joseph Chamberlain referred to Ulster members' threats of resistance, but merely in the context of an abusive speech from the Chancellor of the Duchy, James Bryce.[62] Chamberlain's concern was repudiation of Bryce, and not positive encouragement for loyalist resistance plans: he argued, not in defence of their right to armed defiance, but rather (like Salisbury) merely in defence of their right to be taken seriously as representatives of Ulster opinion. Of all the Conservative leaders participating in the debates of 1886 and 1893, Lord Randolph alone offered unequivocal support for Ulster militancy—and by 1893 he was too ill and insignificant for his endorsement to matter.[63]

The two Home Rule debates are important in the context of British and Irish Unionist relations because it is here that the partnership is likely to be closest. There are two reasons for this. Firstly, in 1886 and 1893 the Conservative Party was in opposition, and had, therefore, no responsibility for Irish government. Thus, it might be expected that in these years the Conservatives' acceptance of even

---

[59] HLRO, Papers of Edward Gibson, First Baron Ashbourne B 22/40, Cadogan to Ashbourne, 7 July 1902. Quoted in A. B. Cooke and A. P. W. Malcomson, *The Ashbourne Papers, 1869–1913: A Calendar of the Papers of Edward Gibson, First Lord Ashbourne* (Belfast, 1974), 87. See also ABP, Add. MS 49828, fo. 326, Balfour to West Ridgeway, 1 Sept. 1889. For Saunderson's reaction to Erne and the Rostrevor affair, see ESP, T 2996/4/33, Erne to Saunderson, 14 July 1902.
[60] Hansard, 3rd ser. (1886), cciv. 1102.   [61] See above, nn. 6, 7.
[62] Hansard, 4th ser. (1893), viii. 1741.   [63] Ibid. 1609.

an extreme loyalist case would be less restrained than at any other time. A second reason for presupposing agreement lies in the mutual political advantage created by Irish Unionist and British Conservative co-operation against Home Rule. The cause of Union appeared to win a sympathetic popular audience in both Britain and Protestant Ireland, and Tory and loyalist shared an interest in cultivating this sympathy. Both also shared a parliamentary political interest in the Union—Conservatives through the accession of dissident Liberals, Irish Unionists through their enhanced significance for the Conservative leadership. Political success for one party was, however, contingent on the co-operation of the other against Home Rule: the Conservative Party could not capitalize on the popularity of the Ulster cause without the public sympathy of its representatives; and the plausibility of the Ulster Party's constitutional defence against Home Rule depended in turn on Conservative patronage.

Given this dependence, it might be expected that the parties' alignment on this issue, above all others, would be complete. The first section of this chapter has sought, not to dispute that the relationship was closest during the Home Rule debates, but rather to show how, despite the pressures for unity, the parties still contrived to remain significantly independent. Subsequent sections of the chapter will explore the development of the parties' bond, in relation to several features of Tory policy in Ireland. In general this amounts to a saga of distrust and estrangement, but it will be clear already that the seeds for this lay less in the evolution of Tory policy than in a more fundamental chasm between British and Irish politics. The history of the parties' relationship in these years has little to do with the conventional Liberal historiographical picture of amity and collusion, or indeed with more recent and sceptical analyses.[64] The constructive Unionists, and in particular George Wyndham, did not destroy the unity of the parties, and not simply because such unity had never existed: it will be shown here that constructive unionist reform inspired a much more complex response from Ulster Unionist representatives than is generally assumed. When the Ulster Party revolted against Wyndham in 1905, they were merely exposing problems in the parties' bond which had been perceptible in 1886.

[64] See e.g. J. L. Hammond, *Gladstone and the Irish Nation* (London, 1938); A. B. Cooke and John Vincent, *The Governing Passion: Cabinet Government and Party Politics in Britain, 1885-1886* (Brighton, 1974).

For the Home Rule debate, no less than the indictment of Wyndham, had revealed that Ulster Unionist behaviour in parliament was conditioned by a range of local electoral considerations far removed from the British preoccupations of the Tory elders.

3. *Land*

By far the most important area of Conservative legislation for Ireland, judged whether by permanence of result or the amount of parliamentary time occupied, was land. The structure of Irish society, and indeed the physical landscape of Ireland, were deeply marked by Tory reform, while narrowly constitutional initiatives often created no more than a temporary electoral stir. And yet the political repercussions of reform were immense, both within Irish Unionism, and in its relations with the British Unionist movement. Land ownership had been a conspicuous feature of loyalist leadership in Ireland, and the extension of purchase, combined with the increasing unpopularity of landlordism, placed the effective survival of this command in jeopardy. Moreover, landownership had been a vital bond linking British and Irish Unionism, and the vulnerability of the Irish landed classes threatened this alliance. Thus, while some sanguine Unionists predicted that land reform, and especially purchase, would remould Irish Nationalism, a more complete change came first within their own movement.

Land affected the interests of most Unionists in Ireland, and consequently land legislation had also more immediate political implications. Long-term phenomena like the decline of landlordism were partly the cumulative result of successive laws, but individual reforms also had an impact upon the Irish Unionist movement, and upon its bond with British Unionism. In the following pages analysis of the loyalist reception to Tory legislation is largely confined to the parliamentary party. However, even within this comparatively small band of men there was a bewildering variety of attitudes and influences. If land was central to the process of drift between British and Irish Unionism, then this was not because reform generated any permanent animosity, or affection, between the whole Ulster Party and its government. Individual measures inspired different reactions, and a complex variety of influences governed the shifting attitudes of the Ulster Party. If land reform and Unionist drift were linked, then the roots of this relationship lay rather in the assumptions underlying reform than in the immediate impact of individual measures.

Unionist land legislation, from the Act of 1887 to Wyndham's reform of 1903, built upon the achievements of two pioneering measures: Gladstone's Land Act of 1881, and the Land Purchase ('Ashbourne') Act of 1885. Gladstone's reform granted the three 'Fs' of tenant agitation (fixity of tenure, free sale, and fair rent), but it was the new mechanisms for rent assessment which contained the seeds of future controversy.[65] Salisbury abhorred the measure ('a threat to the very foundations of civilisation'), and much of his defence of subsequent Unionist reform was based upon the need to mitigate the contractual quagmire created by its provisions.[66] The Ashbourne Land Purchase Act, passed under his own first government, was accordingly a more modest measure, seeking to refine and expand the unsatisfactory purchase clauses of Gladstone's reform. Through the Ashbourne Act, a Treasury grant of £5 million was provided, allowing a tenant to borrow the full money value of his landlord's share in a holding. Many proponents of the landed interest, including Salisbury, favoured the principle of land purchase, and the cautious practice of the Ashbourne Act, and the encouragement of peasant proprietorship developed into a firm tenet of Conservative thought on Ireland.[67]

But the paradox inherent in this policy—creating peasant landowners meant expelling an existing landed class—threatened to convey the Unionist ship of state from the Scylla of tenant rebellion to the Charybdis of landlord dissent. The careful diplomacy needed to steer an even course between these rival claimants proved extremely difficult and expensive to sustain, and it was only after years of experiment, and at some cost to the British Treasury, that a *via media* was located in 1903. Until then, Tory governments were moved rather by the fear of Presbyterian or Nationalist farmer agitation than by the squeals of landlordism; yet since it rapidly became obvious that concession was dependent on dissent neither farmers nor landlords could be publicly content with Tory reform. Before the accession of Wyndham, it seemed that the principal achievement of the Tories' policy on land was to offend, with studied impartiality, all the combatants within the Irish land war.

---

[65] See Barbara Solow, *The Land Question and the Irish Economy (1870-1903)* (Cambridge, Mass., 1971), 156 ff.

[66] Hansard, 3rd ser. (1887), cccxiii. 1604.   [67] Solow, *Land Question*, 188.

The first significant Conservative experiment with the conditions of land tenure occurred in the Irish Land Law Act of 1887. This extended the benefits of the measure of 1881 to 100,000 leaseholders, and provided for the revision of all judicially settled rents affected by the fall in prices between 1881 and 1886. Salisbury heartily disliked this Bill, furthering, as it did, the interference by government in private contract between landowner and tenant.[68] Privately he admitted its true purpose: the Bill, he wrote some years later, contained 'some very bad provisions—but they were the price of obtaining the votes of the Liberal Unionists, and of the left wing of our own party, for the Crimes Act'.[69]

Irish landlords were initially unenthusiastic about the content of the bill, but this reflected a comparative lack of interest, rather than any restrained hostility. The measure had been launched with a Crimes Bill, as a response to the Plan of Campaign, and it was the issue of law and order, and the threat of a spreading Plan, which dominated the platform speeches of landlord leaders like Saunderson at this time. Indeed Saunderson contributed comparatively little to discussion on the Bill, and J. C. Flynn, member for North Cork, was moved to complain that the Colonel had not sat through a whole debate on any of the amendments.[70] W. G. Ellison-Macartney, member for South Antrim, was a rather more active proponent of the landed case, but even he swathed his suspicions in ambiguity, balancing a general acceptance of the measure with the rejection of detail.[71] The *Belfast News Letter*, which rarely strayed from landed orthodoxy, offered a clearer reflection of landlord priorities in applauding the measure, and echoing Balfour's arguments in its defence.[72]

Why, then, did landlords accept an unfavourable measure with comparative equanimity? Like Salisbury they were prepared to regard the measure as the price of sustained Liberal Unionist support— though their willingness to accommodate new allies had definite bounds. Thus, at a meeting of Tory MPs and peers on 20 July 1887 Saunderson argued strongly that the amended Land Bill was too great

---

[68] Ibid. 177. L. P. Curtis, *Coercion and Conciliation in Ireland, 1880-1892: A Study in Conservative Unionism* (Oxford and Princeton, 1963), 333.

[69] HLRO, Papers of George Henry, Fifth Earl Cadogan, CAD 756, Salisbury to Cadogan, 22 Nov. 1895. Quoted partly in Marsh, *Popular Government*, 249.

[70] Hansard, 3rd ser. (1887), cccxviii. 855.   [71] Ibid. 848.

[72] *BNL*, 5 Apr. 1887.

a sop to Liberal Unionist opinion.[73] However, this was a rare outburst, for landlord representatives were generally wary at this time of appearing intolerant towards reform, and fearful of exciting Protestant liberal opposition. They had supported the Land Bill of 1881, in the context of the Land League's comparative success among Protestant farmers; and though in 1886-7 the Plan of Campaign won very little approval in North-East Ulster, landed Toryism still treated the threat of farmer dissent with extreme caution. Rumours, and the isolated acceptance of the Plan on several estates within the heartland of Protestant Ulster embellished this threat, while the radical Unionist representatives, Lea and Russell, were only too eager to present further evidence of farmer militancy.[74]

Thus, though northern Irish landlords were still well represented within the House of Commons, they were more vulnerable at a local level. The coincidence of reform and redistribution in 1884-5 with the growth of the Home Rule threat had temporarily sheltered them from some of the effects of a greatly increased electorate, but political pliability was the price that they had to pay for continuing to enjoy a disproportionate share of parliamentary power. Many landlords at this time were grimly reconciled both to the instability of the Unionist alliance, and to the electoral pragmatism of Protestant farmers: some, indeed, like Saunderson, were apparently convinced of the ultimate inevitability of Home Rule.[75] This fatalism further undermined any obstinacy, and encouraged a more cautious reception to the Land Bill of 1887. After the death of Parnell, and the defeat of Home Rule in 1893, landlords grew more confident and assertive; but by then their numerical representation within the Ulster Party was more closely in line with their local position, and the passion of their self-defence reflected this weakness.

In 1887, however, Irish landlordism was still a force to be reckoned with in the Commons, and the government treated its grievances with

[73] For Saunderson and the Earl of Kilmorey's complaints at the Carlton meeting of 19 July see Peter Davis, 'The Liberal Unionist Party and the Irish Policy of Lord Salisbury's Government, 1886-1892', *Historical Journal*, xviii. i (Mar. 1975), 94. Also Alfred E. Pease, *Elections and Recollections* (London, 1932), 185. Chatsworth House, Papers of Spencer Compton, Eighth Duke of Devonshire, 340/2147, Randolph Churchill to Hartington, 22 Aug. 1887.

[74] *BNL*, 9 July 1887. Lawrence M. Geary, *The Plan of Campaign, 1886-1891* (Cork, 1986), 49-53.

[75] Montgomery Papers, D 627/428/50, R. Bagwell to Montgomery, 12 Aug. 1888.

sympathy. Government tact, particularly in the matter of ministerial appointments, helps to explain the comparatively restrained response of Irish landed MPs to Balfour's Land Bill. Though at the beginning of the year, Edward Saunderson and other Tory landowners were growing uneasy at the spread of the Plan and at the inactivity of the government, the supersession of Hicks-Beach as Chief Secretary, and the appointment of Edward King-Harman as Parliamentary Under-Secretary for Ireland offered the prospect of improvement.[76] King-Harman, member for the Isle of Thanet, owned 73,000 acres in the Irish midlands and possessed ties both with Irish landlordism and the English party command. A close acquaintance of Aretas Akers-Douglas, he was associated with the 'Kentish Gang' so influential within late-nineteenth-century Toryism.[77] His appointment, roundly condemned by radical Unionists like Russell, was clearly a public expression of the limitations, and the ultimately conservative function of Irish land reform—and Irish landed representatives responded with appropriate enthusiasm.[78]

The limitations of reform were more explicitly stated later, in August 1887, when the government accepted a number of restrictive amendments to the Land Bill, introduced in the House of Lords. Randolph Churchill observed that 'the old Tories for the most part have got the upper hand quite damnably', and attributed the government's action to the impression made upon Salisbury by Saunderson's taunting allusion to Liberal Unionist ascendancy.[79] While it is possible that Churchill was fanning the flames of Liberal Unionist outrage (these comments were addressed to Chamberlain and Devonshire respectively), there is little doubt that Irish landed opinion in parliament was reasonably satisfied with the final shape of the Bill. Saunderson continued to dwell on the unrest within Ireland in his public utterances of August 1887—but his few allusions to the Land Bill were wholly positive. The *Belfast News Letter* was

[76] *BNL*, 9 Apr. and 16 Apr. 1887. Balfour's record as Secretary of State for Scotland ought to have offered encouragement: Blanche Dugdale, *Arthur James Balfour, First Earl of Balfour, KG, OM, FRS &c* (2 vols., London, 1936), i. 83–90.
[77] Aretas Akers-Douglas Papers, U564/13, Diary for 1885. Eric, Viscount Chilston, *Chief Whip: The Political Life and Times of Aretas Akers-Douglas, First Viscount Chilston* (London, 1961), 4–5.
[78] See n. 76.
[79] JCP, JC 5/14/36, Churchill to Chamberlain, 22 Aug. 1887. Devonshire Papers, 340/2147, Churchill to Hartington, 22 Aug. 1887. For the context of these letters see Foster, *Lord Randolph Churchill*, 340.

equally enthusiastic, although its magnanimity was somewhat taxed by the acrimonious stand made by northern radical Unionism in the aftermath of the Bill's passage.[80]

But if Irish landlords grimly accepted the measure in outline as the price of local vulnerability, and exploited their parliamentary strength to alter unacceptable details, then Irish Liberal Unionists, threatened both in the Commons and in the constituency, responded more bluntly and aggressively. T. W. Russell, speaking at Ballymoney on 30 May 1887, described the Bill as 'an admirable complement to the Act of 1881', but proceeded to condemn its treatment of three crucial questions: tenant bankruptcy, townparks, and the provision of reform for long leaseholders.[81] This balance between general approval and rasping, detailed indictment was sustained during a local Liberal Unionist campaign in early June, and, again, when Russell and Lea met Joseph Chamberlain at Devonshire House on 8 July.[82] But by then, in the light of government immobility, Russell's observations were growing icier in tone; and the later threat of a rupture on the issue of amendments confirmed this drift from polite ambiguity. With the success of the Lords' revisions Russell's invective was fully unleashed, and on 18 August he complained that the government had 'allowed a most valuable bill . . . to be whittled down'.[83] Though he voted for the government, and reaffirmed his Liberal Unionist faith at Dungannon on 1 September, he had temporarily resigned his party whip around 20 August.[84] And this action, in the context of landlord contentment, was eloquent testimony to the nature of ministerial priorities, and to the distribution of parliamentary strength at the time.

For Irish, no less than English Unionists, the 1887 Land Bill debates were a serious test of the viability of their alliance. This aspect of the Bill's significance was widely recognized at the time and Hartington, for example, felt compelled to write to Joseph Chamberlain, warning him against undue pressure on the government.[85] Irish Conservative members also accepted the broader political significance of the Bill, moderating their private anger, and avoiding extreme language likely to alienate their Liberal Unionist

[80] *BNL*, 20 July 1887.   [81] *BNL*, 31 May 1887.
[82] *BNL*, 1, 2, 3 June 1887, 9 July 1887.
[83] Hansard, 3rd ser. (1887), cccxix. 1036.
[84] Davis, 'Liberal Unionist Party', 95. *BNL*, 20 Aug. 1887.
[85] JCP, JC 5/22/29, Hartington to Chamberlain, 13 July 1887.

partners. The *Belfast News Letter* in particular treated the opinions and complaints of Chamberlain with great gravity, though—as has been noted—T. W. Russell inspired much less sympathy.[86] All elements of Irish Unionism harboured doubts about the measure, and their economic interests diverged; but concern, both for the safety of the government, and for their own unity of support, limited the extent to which they permitted lack of enthusiasm to develop into outright opposition. In this way the government was able to pass, without serious internal repercussion, a measure which a broad section of Unionist opinion regarded as unsatisfactory.

The Tory commitment to land purchase and peasant proprietorship was stronger than their desire to meddle in the contractual problems associated with rent assessment (even though the perceived anomalies in the Act of 1881 were a recurrent source of anxiety). Interest in purchase derived not only from a belief that it would aid the pacification of Ireland, and counteract Home Rule, but also from immediate electoral pressures. The desire for purchase was particularly strong in Ulster, and it was recognized that, unless Conservative governments continually worked to meet this demand, several constituencies might be lost to Unionism. The threat of Presbyterian tenant desertion was perennial, and was urged for virtually every measure of land reform, but in the late 1880s it was particularly associated with purchase. 'I believe', wrote Lord Castletown to Chamberlain in April 1888, 'that if the Arrears Question were settled, and the Purchase System helped on . . . that every seat in the North, except two or three in Cavan and Monaghan, would be safe'.[87] Balfour, too, was aware of the specific association of Ulster with the demand for purchase when, in 1888, he pushed through parliament a bill which provided £5 million additional funding for the Ashbourne Act: 'I attach the greatest importance to the measure', he claimed, '[for] to throw it out would give real grounds of complaint to the Ulster leaseholders'.[88]

However, landed Tories within the parliamentary Ulster Party were bitterly divided on the merits of purchase, and even individual opinions developed with time. Saunderson greeted Balfour's Bill with the approving observation that only through an extension of the

[86] *BNL*, 20 July 1887.
[87] JCP, JC 8/6/3A/10, Castletown to Chamberlain, 8 Apr. 1888.
[88] MSPH, E/Balfour/256, Balfour to Salisbury, [Aug. 1888].

Ashbourne Act was 'to be found the real, final and just solution of the Irish land question'; other of his landed colleagues, particularly Thomas Waring, member for North Down, were privately more suspicious of the policy.[89] Nevertheless, the Bill of 1888 was sufficiently modest in its ambitions to attract little criticism, and it passed swiftly into law. A comprehensive reform would have to await a freer parliamentary timetable.

The evolution of Balfour's Purchase of Land (Ireland) Act of 1891, as with its predecessors, involved delicate treatment of landlord susceptibilities. The measure was privately cast as a pragmatic defence of Irish landlordism, and each stage of its protracted development was accomplished after full (if not always mutually satisfactory) communication between the government and landlord representatives, especially those in the Commons.[90] As early as June 1889, only months after the passage of the measure of 1888, Balfour had sketched a radical scheme of purchase for the edification of the cabinet. The draft made provision for compulsion—the principle by which the property of peculiarly recalcitrant landlords might be forcibly sold—and Balfour defended this on the grounds that it best served the interests of Irish property.[91] When T. W. Russell independently published a not dissimilar proposal in October 1889 the government was handed a useful opportunity to canvas landed opinion, and W. H. Smith subsequently corresponded with the MPs, R. U. Penrose-Fitzgerald, Ellison-Macartney, and Mulholland.[92] Impressed by the ferocity of their disapproval, Smith reluctantly concluded that compulsory purchase was beyond the capacity of a Tory ministry—even though, like Balfour, he had been originally favourable to the proposal, and was unsympathetic to landed obstinacy.[93]

Like Balfour, Smith was appalled that Irish landlords had so inadequate an understanding of their self-interest; like Balfour he affected a pedagogic and despairing tone towards his Irish charges

[89] *BNL*, 6 Nov. 1888. MSPH, E/Waring/; Waring to Salisbury, 30 Apr. 1890. Salisbury's reply is partly quoted in Curtis, *Coercion and Conciliation*, 352.
[90] CAB 37/25/31, suggestions towards a scheme for land purchase in Ireland, 4 June 1889.
[91] Ibid.
[92] T. W. Russell, 'A Resumé of the Irish Land Problem', *The Nineteenth Century*, xxvi (Oct. 1889), 608–21. ABP, Add. MS 49846, fo. 108, Smith to Balfour, 10 Oct. 1889. Akers-Douglas Papers, C 25/93, Smith to Akers-Douglas, 16 Oct. 1889.
[93] ABP, Add MS 49846, fo. 102, Smith to Balfour, 8 Oct. 1889.

('How is it possible to help them—and I sometimes think—is it worthwhile to try?).[94] Nevertheless, whatever their impatience and distrust, Balfour took account of Smith's intelligence, omitting any reference to compulsion in the final draft of his measure. Before the introduction of the Bill this substantive concession had to be complemented by a more superficial gesture—by counselling landed opinion, and by mollifying the anxious landed magnates of the Landowners' Convention. Promises were given by Balfour to the landed MPs, Saunderson and Ellison-Macartney, that they should find no difficulty in giving the measure 'a hearty support in the House of Commons'.[95] The Irish Attorney-General, D. H. Madden, was recruited to allay any residual and 'exaggerated ideas of the nature of the forthcoming Bill', harboured by the parliamentary spokesmen of Irish landlordism; and he was able to report back to Balfour on 7 November 1889 that his object had been accomplished.[96] Such, then, were the lengths to which Balfour and the Tory government were prepared to go in order to retain the loyalty of their landed MPs; and such was their perceived importance.

Madden's optimistic prognosis of the tenor of landed opinion was not wholly fulfilled. When, on 24 March 1890, the Bill was introduced before the House of Commons, the *Belfast News Letter* responded ecstatically ('one of the most splendid pieces of legislative workmanship ever presented to parliament'), and the lobby correspondent of the Press Association reported unanimous acceptance among the Ulster members.[97] Yet this consensus seems to have been rooted more firmly in perplexity than in informed approval, for the bill was difficult, and mature consideration of its proposals led to considerable division of opinion both among landlord MPs and even within the Landowners' Convention. While Lord Waterford confidently forecast that he could obtain a hearty acceptance of the Bill from his local branch of the Convention, the landowners of Fermanagh rejected 'this violent and complicated measure'.[98] Within parliament, landed dissent was led by Ellison-

[94] ABP, Add. MS 49846, fo. 116, Smith to Balfour, 7 Nov. 1889.
[95] PRONI, William Ellison-Macartney Papers, D 3649/20/33, Balfour to Macartney, n.d., enclosing a copy of letter to Saunderson; ABP, Add. MS 49828, fo. 431, Balfour to Saunderson, 4 Nov. 1889.
[96] ABP, Add. MS 49815, fo. 105, D. H. Madden to Balfour, 7 Dec. 1889.
[97] BNL, 7 Apr. 1890.
[98] ABP, Add. MS 49846, fo. 219, Lord Waterford to Balfour, 17 Apr. 1890. BNL, 7 Apr. 1890.

Macartney, who condemned the Bill as one-sided, and drafted merely for the soothing of tenant opinion.[99] However neither he nor C. E. Lewis and Thomas Waring, who shared this view, were prepared to reject the measure—and other leading landed MPs were actively willing to vote for the Second Reading. The *News Letter* merely replicated this confusion, descending from joyful paean in March and April to a feline indictment of peasant proprietorship on 12 July, after Balfour had announced the postponement of the Bill.[100]

Though there were other influences—Parnellite obstruction, the impending close of the parliamentary session—landlord disquiet clearly had a role in the temporary shelving of the Bill, and dissidents like Waring publicly approved this denouement.[101] Moreover, discussions between Balfour and the Landowners' Convention were resumed while the Bill lay in limbo, and the fruits of this diplomacy were eventually incorporated into a modified measure which was laid before the House in December 1890.[102] Predictably, given its parentage, this measure was greeted with greater enthusiasm by the representatives of Irish landlordism than they had been able to summon for the original reform, and even Macartney grudgingly pledged his support.[103] Edward Saunderson, more thoroughly representative of Irish Toryism, predicted that 'the passing of the Bill would sound the death knell of demagogues and agitators', though by explaining his support ('for the good of the Empire'), he highlighted a lingering disquiet.[104]

Indeed, a new clause to the Bill, introduced by Balfour in May 1891, which would have limited its provisions to holdings worth less than £30, attracted universal condemnation among Irish Unionists, who feared that 'many of the most deserving farmers of the north would be excluded from the benefits of the Act'.[105]. The Belfast Conservative Association condemned Balfour's proposal, and Ellison-Macartney acted as teller when the House divided on the

[99] Hansard, 3rd ser. (1890), cccxliii. 1894.
[100] *BNL*, 12 July 1890; cf. *BNL*, 1 Apr. 1890.   [101] *BNL*, 5 July 1890.
[102] ABP, Add. MS 49847, fo. 150, Waterford to Balfour, 15 Oct. 1890. Add. MS 49847, fo. 153, memo from the Irish Landowners' Convention, 13 Oct. 1890. Add. MS 49847, fo. 181, Waterford to Balfour, 29 Oct. 1890. Add. MS 49847, fo. 227, Villiers-Stuart to Balfour, 20 Nov. 1890. Add. MS 49847, fo. 230, Lea to Balfour, 22 Nov. 1890.
[103] Hansard, 3rd ser. (1890), cccxlix. 442.
[104] Ibid. ccclii. 813. *BNL*, 18 Apr. 1891.
[105] *BNL*, 21 May 1891.

issue.[106] Russell, for the Liberal Unionists, wrote from his sick-bed on 13 May 1891, pleading with Balfour to retract his amendment on the grounds that 'the blackguards who have kept the country in hot water these ten years shall have the freehold of their farms, and that the sober thrifty loyal Ulstermen who have resisted the most overwhelming attempts to corrupt them should be punished for their loyalty and honesty'.[107] Despite this last-minute stand (which was, after all, an attempt to extend the measure), the Bill passed into law with the, albeit qualified, blessing of Unionist Ireland. But if both landlords and radicals had private doubts about the measure, then these became irrelevant in the light of its unpopularity with the tenantry, who were suspicious of its complexity, and who looked forward to a more generous settlement under a Liberal government.[108]

The purchase act of 1891 brought to an end a period of innovatory legislation which Russell dubbed 'the era of experiment'.[109] This was also, perhaps consequently, a period when the landed representatives of Irish Toryism enjoyed significant influence, and demonstrated flexibility in their response to legislation. Within the House of Commons landlords were still well represented among Irish Tory MPs, and among the dominant northern element this political strength was complemented by a relative financial security.[110] Of course, there was no absolute distinction between northern landed wealth and southern indebtedness, and it would be hard to uncover any irrevocable law linking the political behaviour of northern and southern landowners with their respective financial positions. Still, it may be suggested that the comparative wealth of northern landowners permitted a more pragmatic response within parliament to reform legislation than was financially possible for their southern counterparts. Admittedly, southern landlordism had no monopoly over intransigence, and the most outspoken representative of the landed interest was probably W. G. Ellison-Macartney, whose father held a small estate in County Tyrone. But many other northern landowners—Saunderson, Arthur Hill, R. T. O'Neill, J. M.

---

[106] *BNL*, 26 May 1891.

[107] ABP, Add. MS 49848, fo. 170, Russell to Balfour, 13 May 1891.

[108] Curtis, *Coercion and Conciliation*, 354–5.

[109] T. W. Russell, *Ireland and the Empire: A Review* (London and New York, 1901), 184.

[110] L. P. Curtis, 'Incumbered Wealth: Landed Indebtedness in Post-Famine Ireland', *American Historical Review*, lxxxv. 2 (Apr. 1980), 366.

McCalmont—flexed and swayed at this time with ministerial opinion, while the few southern magnates within the 'Ulster' Party— Arthur Smith-Barry, Penrose-Fitzgerald—were invariably associated with the hard-line stand. Some southern landowners had financial assets other than Irish estates: Smith-Barry, for example, held extensive property in Cheshire and Huntingdonshire. But it is as representatives of a generally impoverished southern class, rather than as solvent individuals, that these men should be judged; and their bitterness reflected the insecurity of their class rather than their personal circumstances.

The pattern of landed opinion was by no means fixed, was developing within this period, and would develop later, when the Unionists returned to power in 1895. Flexibility, thus, was not simply a matter of geography or liquidity, but was also related to the perceived merits of an individual measure, and to the prevailing political condition of Ireland. The reasonably tolerant attitude of landed MPs towards the Act of 1887 may be explained by the still insecure condition of the Unionist alliance, and by the progress of the Plan of Campaign, where the franker criticism of the purchase measure of 1891 perhaps reflected greater political confidence. In 1887 landlords were arguing from a position of comparative strength within Irish Toryism, conscious all the while of Liberal Unionist opinion in the aftermath of the Round Table Conference. Outside parliament, however, the Plan of Campaign was spreading, and northern farmers were demanding reform of the 1881 Land Act.

This balance between the parliamentary strength of landed Toryism and local weakness had altered by 1891, and would continue to alter through the rest of the decade. Landed representation within the Irish Tory parliamentary party of course remained virtually the same as in 1887—but the O'Shea divorce had weakened the opposition, and local conditions had altered dramatically. Prominent radical Unionists were now considerably more certain allies, particularly when, as with Russell, they had remained at the forefront of the battle against Home Rule. There were certainly bitter local disputes between Tory and Liberal Unionist, usually over constituency representation: but this very bitterness reflected the strength of their joint commitment to Unionism, as compared with the more circumspect conduct after 1886.[111] Moreover, the threat of farmer

---

[111] For some of the difficulties see Macknight, *Ulster as it is Twenty Eight Years' Experience as an Irish Editor* (2 vols.; London, 1896), ii. 157.

defections weakened with the gradual demise of the Plan of Campaign—from the success of the Ponsonby Syndicate, through to the collapse of the agitation on the De Freyne and Delmege estates in February and April 1891.[112] Landed Tories within the parliamentary Ulster Party were probably therefore at the height of their powers at this time—comparatively free from external political restraints, numerically strong, and placated by the government. The combined effects of two general elections, in 1892 and 1895, and renewed farmer agitation, would bring an abrupt end to this period of relative strength and confidence.

If landed Tories were becoming more assertive, then by contrast the two Liberal Unionist MPs, Lea and Russell, were appreciably more restrained in 1891 than in 1887. This was partly because in 1887 the government was both vulnerable, and had not yet fully demonstrated that its Irish policy was anything other than narrowly coercive. But there were other factors. Russell, by far the more outspoken of the two MPs, was gradually, if temporarily, distracted from combative reformism into militant Unionism. After 1887 he was a familiar figure on British public platforms as a critic of Home Rule, and even during the closing stage of debate on the Land Bill of that year he had been called away to provide support for the Unionist candidate at the Northwick by-election.[113] He was an aggressive opponent of the Plan of Campaign, and a tireless member of the Irish Loyal and Patriotic Union. Throughout the period he remained committed to a radical programme of land purchase, and though the government's achievements in this respect fell short of his ideals, ministers were still responding constructively to Liberal Unionist pressure. Thus by the last years of the second Salisbury government the need, and the political opportunities for radical stridency had temporarily diminished, and Russell had little difficulty in demonstrating the fruitfulness of his association with Toryism.

For Irish Unionists the nature of the land debate developed after 1891 with alarming rapidity. The defeat of Home Rule in 1893, and of the Rosebery government in 1895, ought to have provided a boost to morale, particularly among landowners, but new pressures and a new framework of alliance offset these nominal triumphs. For the

---

[112] Geary, *Plan of Campaign*, 136-7.
[113] *BNL*, 2 Sept. 1887, Russell in Dungannon.

success of Unionism in 1893 occurred only with the aid of the House of Lords, and after an electoral rebuff in 1892; while the fall of the Liberal government meant that John Morley's initiatives on the land question—his Evicted Tenants Bill, Select Committee and Land Bill—fell into the Tory lap. Furthermore, for Irish landlords the elections of 1892 and 1895 had considerably diminished their representation within the Irish Unionist parliamentary party, while the defeat of Home Rule threatened a weakening of internal Unionist arbitration. This threat was partially realized when in 1894–5, Russell spearheaded a popular campaign in Ulster to focus support for Morley's Land Bill.[114]

One of the most striking features of the land debate within the Ulster of 1895 was the way in which its focus was gradually shifting out of the House of Commons. Hitherto, apart from the constitutional question, the Nationalists had had the monopoly of extra-parliamentary agitation. Radical Unionists had certainly conducted miniature campaigns before 1894, such as that in South Derry in the spring of 1887—but they had eschewed mass agitation. Russell's campaign of 1894–5 was therefore a significant departure from precedent, and particularly in that he aimed specifically to pressure recalcitrant Ulster MPs into a more flexible stand on Morley's reform proposals.[115] Such brazen coercion of those who were nominally political allies was counter-productive, and the consequences of Russell's campaign reverberated throughout landlord–tenant relations for the rest of the decade.

But if Russell was extending his interest in extra-parliamentary politics at this time, then Tory landowners were also now relatively less concerned with direct contribution to parliamentary debate than with the lobby politics of the Irish Landowners' Convention. In part this shift reflected the greater vulnerability of Tory landlordism in 1895, in comparison with the period before 1892. Landowners were weaker, both politically and financially, and their militancy grew in proportion to the strength of the threats which they faced. Land purchase was beginning to take a toll of their estates, and though it has been argued that the political repercussions of this were negligible, the electoral evidence of landed retreat within Ulster

---

[114] Alvin Jackson, 'The Irish Unionist Parliamentary Party, 1885–1906', D.Phil. thesis (Oxford, 1986), 350–3.
[115] See e.g. *Northern Whig*, 13 Oct. 1894, 18 Oct. 1894.

suggests otherwise.[116] Those landlords who remained in the Ulster Party, and who sat for county constituencies, were made vulnerable by the local farmer pressure orchestrated by Russell, first in 1894, but also subsequently and with greater ferocity. Landlords sitting for English or urban seats were comparatively free from the effects of such campaigns, as were their colleagues in the House of Lords. But the general threat posed by Russell's demands on landed incomes remained, and by 1896 there was an additional financial pressure created through the expiry of the fifteen-year judicial term of the 1881 Land Act (and the likely reduction of rents as a consequence).[117]

Some features of this weakness—tension, political division among landlords—will subsequently be discussed in greater detail, but one of its most significant implications demands a brief preliminary treatment. Because southern Irish Unionism was disproportionately landed in nature, and because Ulster Unionism had a much more complex class base, the threat of schism over non-constitutional issues was always present.[118] Thus, the vitality of northern landlordism was crucial to Unionist unity, and, in so far as it came under threat, so the integrity of the whole party was imperilled. Given the challenge posed by Russell, and their falling parliamentary representation, landlords were a progressively less significant feature of the northern movement; and accordingly the late 1890s witnessed a drift between the political concerns of the two Unionisms. The obsession of southern Unionists with the misdeeds of Horace Plunkett, and the exclusively northern battle between Russell and official Unionism, illustrated the chasm between the parties which had opened by 1900.[119]

Arthur Balfour had continually complained of the political and emotional vulnerability of Irish landlordism in the late 1880s, but it was only when Gerald Balfour held the Irish Office (between 1895 and 1900) that the parliamentary implications of this weakness

---

[116] Curtis, 'Incumbered Wealth', 366–7.

[117] Andrew Gailey, *Ireland and the Death of Kindness: The Experience of Constructive Unionism, 1890–1905* (Cork, 1987), 35–7.

[118] For the landed nature of southern Unionism see Patrick Buckland, *Irish Unionism, i. The Anglo-Irish and the New Ireland, 1885–1922* (Dublin and New York, 1972), pp. xiv–xv.

[119] Gailey, *Death of Kindness*, 157–8.

became fully apparent.[120] The first and major reform of Gerald's tenure, the Land Act of 1896, brought swiftly to the fore the extent to which the Unionist consensus of the second Salisbury government had collapsed. Russell's campaign in support of John Morley had signalled that Protestant tenants were freeing themselves from the political constraints imposed by their support for Unionism; and Irish landlords responded in 1896 with a degree of economic self-assertion which (in view of their earlier pliability) took the government by surprise.

Yet the political origins of Gerald Balfour's Bill were scarcely calculated to mollify embattled landlordism.[121] When Salisbury had formed his third administration in 1895, Russell's hold over northern farming opinion had singled him out for appointment to junior office. But Russell had demanded a commitment to specific reform proposals as the price of his acquiescence. Salisbury and Balfour conceded the substance of Russell's demands, and the radical took office as Parliamentary Secretary to the Local Government Board on the basis of their pledge.[122] When, in April 1896, Gerald Balfour presented a Land Bill before the House of Commons, its details mirrored exactly Russell's earlier programme of reform. In July 1895 Russell had publicly asserted at Fintona that the government had committed itself to a further extension of the Act of 1881, and to the protection of farmer improvements. Sub-let land was to be brought under the Gladstonian act, and the government had allegedly promised the expansion of purchase facilities, and a revision of the mechanisms for rent assessment. In April 1896 Gerald Balfour's Land Bill proposed reforms within these same terms, and Russell's earlier claims were thus wholly vindicated.[123]

The landed members of the Ulster Party were angrily aware of Russell's influence. But, while this generated a certain amount of

---

[120] Balfour's memoranda for the cabinet contain possibly the fullest and frankest statements of his views. PRO, CAB 37/20/42, suggestions for a bill to enable tenants to purchase their holdings, 4 Oct. 1887; CAB 37/22/3, problems on the Clanricarde Property, 7 Nov. 1888; CAB 37/25/31 suggestions towards a scheme for land purchase in Ireland, 4 June 1888.

[121] Andrew Gailey perhaps underestimates Balfour's commitment to a comprehensive reform early in 1895: Gailey, 'Unionist rhetoric and Irish Local Government Reform, 1895–1899', *IHS*, xxiv. 93 (May 1984), 55.

[122] *BNL*, 17 July 1895. Whittingehame, Arthur Balfour Papers, TD 83/133/71, Salisbury to Balfour, 28 June 1895. Salisbury Papers, E/Russell, Russell to Salisbury, 2, 4 July 1895.

[123] Hansard, 4th ser. (1896), xxxix. 781. Gailey, *Death of Kindness*, 38–9. *BNL*, 17 July 1896.

anguish in the Tory press, it was also true that the Bill of 1896 was only the latest in a line of legislative sops to Liberal Unionism. Thus, although much had changed between 1887 and 1896 in terms of political context, there were strong similarities between the landed responses to the reforms of these years. Just as he had done earlier, Saunderson complained of the influence of Liberal Unionists in 1896, bemoaning the government's susceptibility to the pressure of Russell. If he was now more rancorous, then both Saunderson and the other landlord spokesmen, as in 1887, grudgingly accepted the outlines of the reform, while stressing the desirability of amendment.[124] Outside parliament, the Landowners' Convention and the Tory press condoned and echoed the policy of hesitant approval; it was not until later in the summer of 1896 that the forces of landlordism began to agitate for the rejection of the measure. Landed MPs were, therefore, initially prepared to work towards an appropriate compromise, and their willingness to bargain was encouraged by the government.

For, just as in 1889–90 the political representatives of landlordism had been actively placated by ministers, so, too, in 1896, Arthur Balfour offered private assurances that the government was anxiously following the development of landlord opinion, and was prepared to enter into negotiation.[125] The diplomacy of the winter of 1889–90 had a further parallel in a series of discussions between leading landowners and the Balfour brothers from the end of May to the beginning of July 1896. Already, by the middle of June, it was clear to T. M. Healy that some provisional agreement had been reached between the government and its wavering landed support on the basis of an amended Bill.[126] Just as the Land Bill of 1887 had been redeemed by a series of successful amendments, so in June 1896 it seemed that Irish landlordism would be appeased through an anodyne reform.

In 1887, according to Randolph Churchill, Salisbury had accepted limitations on the scope of the Land Bill in order to pacify militant

---

[124] Ibid. xli. 651–9. *BNL*, 5 June 1896.

[125] ESP, uncatalogued, Balfour to Edward Saunderson, 11 June 1896 ('I am firmly convinced that it is as much in the interests of the landlords as of the tenants'). Lucas, *Saunderson*, 251–2.

[126] Salisbury Papers, E/Londonderry/170, Londonderry to Salisbury, 14 May 1896. Hansard, 4th ser. (1896), xli. 1031. F. S. L. Lyons, *The Irish Parliamentary Party, 1890–1910* (London, 1951), 229.

landlordism.[127] But in 1896, despite early tokens of ministerial goodwill, there was no final surrender to landlord pressure. Instead, the government resisted the attempts by landowners to amend the measure, favouring the alternative suggestions made by T. M. Healy. And the government remained·obdurate—even though by 27 July a meeting of landed MPs had decided to move for the rejection of the Bill.[128] This apparent shift in ministerial sympathies reflected the pressure of Russell, supported in cabinet by Chamberlain, and that of Healy, each of whom had been alarmed by the early symptoms of landed ascendancy.[129] But this is certainly not the full explanation for the volte face. The opinion of Russell, and of the Liberal Unionists, had not moved the government in 1887, even though Salisbury and Tory Unionism had then been more susceptible to such pressure. And Healy's support over the Bill, while certainly valuable, can only realistically have been a temporary phenomenon. Why, then, did the government, faced by rival Irish suitors, plump so resolutely for a combination of the Nonconformist radical and the Catholic conservative?

In part the explanation must rest with the nature of landed strength, and with the government's perception of landlord opinion. The experience of the second Salisbury government had been that the landlord lobby, though formidable, was ultimately tractable, and that, though landlords might complain, their commitment to the Union restrained them from rebellion. Thus, when the Bill was originally proposed, Salisbury signified his commitment to northern landed opinion, while predicting that its objections would be 'not loud but deep'.[130] There is also some evidence to suggest that Carson, who emerged as one of the chief landlord spokesmen, reacted favourably to an early draft of the measure, and thereby misled the government for the future. Certainly Arthur Balfour was surprised and offended by the aggressive nature of Carson's subsequent opposition: 'he had not a right to forget that we belonged to the same party, and that as colleagues under most difficult and anxious circumstances we had fought side by side in many a doubtful battle'.[131]

---

[127] See n. 79.   [128] Lucas, *Saunderson*, 252–3. BNL, 28 July 1896.
[129] Gailey, *Death of Kindness*, 95.
[130] Cadogan Papers, CAD 731, Salisbury to Cadogan, 2 Oct. 1895.
[131] ABP, Add. MS 49831, fo. 227, Arthur Balfour to Lady Frances Balfour, 23 May 1899. Balfour blamed Carson for the landlord agitation of 1896. See Curtis, *Coercion and Conciliation*, 417; ABP, Add. MS 49831, fo. 69, Arthur Balfour to Lady Betty Balfour, 27 Apr. 1900; MSPH, E/Balfour/88, Balfour to Salisbury, 7 May 1900.

But, if ministers were gambling on the strength of the landowners' party commitment, then the risks of failure seemed to be minimized by the divisions within landed opinion which were betrayed by the debates. Past experience had revealed not merely that landlords were fundamentally loyal, if cantankerous, Tories; more recent evidence suggested that landowners were both loyal and, now, vulnerable.

Where in the debates on the Bills of 1887, 1890, and 1891 few Irish Unionists participated, and their opinion divided along party lines, debate on the bill of 1896 attracted a greater number of Irish Unionist contributions, while exposing a smaller and more isolated body of landed opinion. If there had been divisions within the Ulster Party over earlier measures, then these had been largely masked by silence, and the integrity of the Party had been preserved. But in 1896 the Party was not only divided, but now publicly and explicitly divided. And the nature of the schism had changed, as well as the degree of its exposure. In 1887 the confrontation between Tory and Liberal Unionist had been essentially a confrontation of classes, landlord and tenant. By 1896 this equation no longer existed, and Tories who had strong landed connections emerged as proponents of the Bill and of the tenant interest. On the other hand, where in 1887 the parliamentary representatives of Irish Liberal Unionism were both radical, the Irish Liberal Unionists of 1896 were more restrained and Whiggish. Thus, if some of the Tories were voting for the tenants in 1896, then prominent Liberal Unionists emerged as landlords' men.

The paradoxical nature of division on the bill did not produce, however, a stronger landlord lobby. For not only were landlord numbers within the parliamentary Ulster Party diminished, those remaining in the Commons were often subject to intense political pressure from their constituencies. For example, D. P. Barton, who (though a lawyer) was from a landowning family, represented the strongly farmer constituency of Mid Armagh, and was necessarily conscious of the vagaries of local tenant opinion.[132] Urban members, and those sitting for Trinity College, could be more flexible in their response, as could the Unionists who represented English constituencies. But though H. O. Arnold-Forster, Liberal Unionist member for West Belfast, was able to sympathize with much of the

---

[132] Hansard, 4th ser. (1896), xli. 640. John Bateman, *The Great Landowners of Great Britain and Ireland* (4th edn., London, 1883), 361.

landlord case, other Belfast representatives assumed a lower profile, fearing the consequences of associating themselves with an anti-populist line.[133] For while Russell exploited the threat of rural revolt, Labour and independent Unionists in Belfast were wielding the charge of élitism against their urban Tory opponents.[134] Thus by the closing stages of debate on the Bill, propertied Toryism was effectively confined within an electoral laager, and only a very few MPs—Saunderson, Smith-Barry, Carson—could express a fervent landlordism with total impunity. These men, with two or three colleagues, constituted a distinct landlord lobby, viewed warily by the rest of the parliamentary Ulster Party. Lacking effective support within the Commons, the landlord MPs turned to the Lords, and to the Irish Landowners' Convention for political assistance.

It is occasionally argued that constructive Unionist measures like the Land Bill of 1896 exacerbated the divisions within Irish Unionism. It is also sometimes argued that such measures propelled Irish Unionism towards extinction.[135] But the evidence of the debates in 1896 suggests that it is possible to turn these arguments on their head. The outcome of this conflict—ministerial resistance to landlord amendments—was not so much the cause of a political revolution, as the reflection of a shifting distribution of power within Irish Unionism. Thus the government did not create the local pressure on MPs like Barton, who might otherwise have been consistent landlord sympathizers. Such pressure emerged from the local strength of the farmer lobby, and from the activities of Russell as leader of farmer militancy. In theory the tensions which existed within Irish Unionism might have been resolved more favourably for landlordism, had it not been for Unionist measures like the Act of 1896. But this is merely speculation, and it is to ignore the fact that landed vulnerability was as acute in 1894-5, under a Liberal government, as in 1896, under a Unionist ministry. Indeed, part of the motivation behind Unionist land reform was the desire to rescue landed property on the best terms possible, and it was occasionally argued by Unionists like Balfour that to abandon reform would represent a surrender of initiative to an aggressive and expropriating Home Rule

[133] Hansard, 4th ser. (1896), xliii. 948 (Rentoul) and 959 (Arnold-Forster).
[134] Henry Patterson, *Class Conflict and Sectarianism: The Protestant Working Class and the Belfast Labour Movement 1868-1920* (Belfast, 1980), 37-41.
[135] Gailey, *Death of Kindness*, 137.

administration.[136] Given the weakness of landlordism in the Commons, a phenomenon over which the government had little control, and given the strength of Russell, the Act of 1896 probably did represent the best terms which could have been achieved in the interests of property. Anything less would have been to court the anger of Liberal Unionism, to increase the likelihood of farmer unrest in Ulster, and thereby heighten the risk of a later and more swingeing assault on landlordism.

On the other hand, it is all too easy to underestimate the political resources of landlordism in the later 1890s. Here the emphasis has been on the Commons, and on the increasing vulnerability of Irish landed MPs. But while there can be little doubt that Irish landlordism was increasingly unsuited to a popular political forum, it possessed alternative vehicles for its interests. The Irish Landowners' Convention had been in existence since 1887, and had been foreshadowed by earlier landed groupings.[137] But it was only in the late 1890s that the Convention came into its own as the most important political resource open to landlordism. Hitherto a landed leader like Saunderson had been able to threaten the government with the displeasure of a united Irish Tory parliamentary party.[138] After 1896, and the evidence of landed isolation, this was an unrealistic stratagem, and landed MPs had to fall back on other, extra-parliamentary resources. In a sense, therefore, landlordism was being squeezed from the Commons in this period. Indeed, it may be suggested that the mid-1890s saw a more general readjustment within landlordism from the politics of parliamentary strength to the politics of marginalization. The venom of landed MPs in 1896, and the increasing importance of the Convention, reflected this descent.

The later 1890s was thus a period of realignment, a time of relative parliamentary weakness, and residual political strength for landlordism. After 1896 Irish landed MPs, and other landowners, sought compensation for their vulnerability in the Commons, and they experimented with a variety of strategies before accepting the cushioned oblivion offered by the Land Act of 1903. The last years

---

[136] CAB 37/25/31, suggestions towards a scheme for land purchase in Ireland, 4 June 1889.
[137] Geary, *Plan of Campaign*, 101–7. See *The Irish Land Question: Proceedings and Speeches of the Landowners' Convention held on September 14th and 15th at the Leinster Hall, Molesworth Street, Dublin* (Dublin, 1887).
[138] ABP, Add. MS 49845, fo. 156, Saunderson to Balfour, 2 Nov. 1889.

of the decade were made conspicuous by the frenzied nature of landed political activity, where under George Wyndham there was greater resignation, and a more constructive attitude towards ministerial suggestion. It seems that in these final years of the nineteenth century landed MPs were exploring the measure of their political irrelevance, and were only belatedly reconciled to an unfavourable result.

Leading proponents of landlordism in the Commons, offended by the offhand attitude of the government, and agitated by their own lack of support in 1896, sought to recoup their influence, and primarily through the exploitation of alternative Irish issues. The plight of a vulnerable landlord class had had limited appeal, but in the months following the passage of the Land Act, other, more marketable causes emerged. Landed leaders like Saunderson, confronted by an Irish administration in crisis, seized the opportunity to broaden their indictment, and thereby to demonstrate their capacity for troublemaking. If the Land Act of 1896 reflected the government's choice of the lines of least resistance in Ireland, then landlords were anxious to ensure that such a decision would not be made so easily in the future.

In the immediate aftermath of the Land Act, two issues held out political possibilities for landlordism. The first of these arose from the findings of a Royal Commission, which had been constituted in 1894 by the late Liberal government in order to investigate the financial relations between England and Ireland. The Commission reported in 1896, before anger over the Land Act had subsided, and argued that, in terms of its capacity to pay, Ireland was overtaxed.[139] Salisbury and the government reacted dismissively to the report, and prominent Irish Unionists like Lord Dufferin and Ava endorsed this scepticism.[140] But within the House of Commons those landlord MPs who had been the principal opponents of the government in 1896 seized on the Report of the Royal Commission as an issue which was both popular in Ireland, and offered no threat to their own financial standing. Edward Saunderson was probably

[139] Cailey, Death of Kindness, 101. See also Alice E. Murray, A History of the Financial and Commercial Relations between England and Ireland from the Time of the Restoration (London, 1903), 394 ff; Thomas Lough, England's Wealth: Ireland's Poverty (3rd edn., London, 1897); Thomas Kennedy, A History of the Irish Protest against Overtaxation from 1852 to 1897 (Dublin, 1897).
[140] Cadogan Papers, CAD 974, Dufferin to Cadogan, 23 Dec. 1896.

the most vociferous advocate of the Commission Report among Irish Unionist MPs, working with the Nationalists to promote a controversy throughout 1897 and 1898.[141] Other landed veterans of 1896 identified themselves with the cause, to the chagrin of more circumspect loyalist colleagues. When Irish Unionists and Nationalists held a joint meeting in March 1897 in order to agitate for a reduction in Irish taxation, four Irish Unionists attended, and of these three had been associated with the stand against the Land Bill. The attitude of the remaining Irish Unionist members was hinted at by the fourth participant, Horace Plunkett, who observed that 'Saunderson, Carson, Lecky and myself were the only Unionists who would consent to dirty themselves by attending'.[142]

The tactical alliance with Nationalists over financial relations was a dramatic but unconvincing development, given that landlords sustained their threnody on the state of the land law. The taxation grievance was arguably symptomatic rather than substantive, and the government could therefore afford to defy the apparent unity of Orange and Green. More typical of landowning concerns, but no less a medium for their bile, was the issue of law and order, and particularly the activities of William O'Brien in County Mayo. A Unionist government was more vulnerable on this than on the problem of overtaxation in Ireland, and the landed lobby in parliament was proportionately more eager to exploit the possibilities of advantage.

When O'Brien delivered a violent speech at Cahir, County Mayo, in January 1897, Gerald Balfour chose to ignore the incitement, and the landed lobby was thereby provided with further evidence of ministerial infamy. As over financial relations, those Irish Unionists who were now the most bitter critics of government had also been numbered among the landlord recusants of 1896. The Marquess of Londonderry, for example, had been one of the chief spokesmen in the Lords for the landed defence, and emerged in February 1897 as the peer most agitated by the Cahir incident. In the Commons, Edward Saunderson sustained the criticisms which he had first voiced over the Land Bill, pressing home Londonderry's case in a parliamentary question delivered to Gerald Balfour on 9 March.[143]

---

[141] Lucas, *Saunderson*, 258-60.

[142] Plunkett Foundation, Oxford, Horace Plunkett Diaries, 9 Mar. 1987.

[143] Hansard, 4th ser. (1897), xlvi. 253 (Londonderry); Hansard, 4th ser. (1897), xlvii. 287 (Saunderson).

The tenor and scope of Londonderry's 'malicious performance' were sufficient evidence that the Marquess was more interested in a general indictment than a specific complaint; but both Gerald Balfour and Cadogan, the Irish viceroy, had little doubt that Saunderson's terse contributions on the subject also 'were not conceived in a spirit of loyalty to the government or any real anxiety for law and order'.[144] The Cahir debate, for the landed lobby, was as intimately connected with the humiliation of 1896 as with a minor offence committed in a Mayo village.

While the exploitation of issues like financial relations and law and order provided publicity for the landed opponents of the Irish administration, their chief parliamentary resource lay in the sympathetic attitude of the Prime Minister. Salisbury had been ill during the evolution of Gerald Balfour's land reform, and he had evidently only the weakest grasp of its implications. Caught unaware by the depth of landed animosity, Salisbury came to resent 'the disastrous land act . . . which adds so much to our difficulties now, and which almost disables me for the future from defending the rights of property in Ireland'.[145] He was by no means uncritical of Irish landlordism, and he had been angered in particular by the stand on financial relations.[146] But, while scathing of individual miscreants, and enraged by occasional collective lapses, Salisbury was a determined patron of Irish landlords.

Few of the landed critics of his government escaped unadorned by office or title. Of the sharpest spokesmen between 1886 and 1892, Lord Kilmorey was invested with the Order of St Patrick in 1890, while Ellison-Macartney was appointed Financial Secretary to the Admiralty in 1895. Of the rebels in 1896, Saunderson was given a British Privy Counsellorship (1898), and Arthur Smith-Barry was honoured with an Irish Privy Counsellorship (1896) and a British peerage (1902). Penrose-Fitzgerald was created a baronet in 1896. Carson the 'big bad boy' of F. C. Gould's cartoon found himself Solicitor-General in 1900, while Londonderry was appointed to the cabinet as Postmaster-General.[147]

[144] Cadogan Papers, CAD 1055, Gerald Balfour to Cadogan, 9 Mar. 1897.
[145] Cadogan Papers, CAD 971, Salisbury to Cadogan, 22 Dec. 1896.
[146] Gailey, *Death of Kindness*, 95.
[147] Ibid., n. 86. This perhaps exaggerates Salisbury's disdain for Irish landlordism. Salisbury's reference to Belmore illustrates not so much his general attitude to the landed class as his—wholly justified—assessment of one undistinguished Irish magnate. Gould's cartoon of Carson is reproduced in H. Montgomery Hyde, *Carson: The Life of Sir Edward Carson, Lord Carson of Duncairn* (London, 1953), 185.

The favour shown by Salisbury in the distribution of patronage was eventually reflected in his handling of landed dissent. When, in March 1897, the landowners of the Convention began to call for an inquiry into the operation of the Land Act of 1881, Salisbury encouraged this stand, and urged them to publicize the inadequacies of the Land Commision Courts.[148] In April 1897 the Convention processed a batch of resolutions repeating the calls for a committee of inquiry into the Gladstonian Act, and demanding compensation for its inequities. Again, Salisbury responded sympathetically, and in the teeth of Gerald Balfour's objections, persuaded the cabinet to accede to the landowners' request.[149] A Royal Commission was constituted under Sir Edward Fry, and after this corroborated much of the landowners' case against the administration of the land law in Ireland, Salisbury offered further tokens of his loyalty.[150] When, on 18 January 1899, representatives of the Landowners' Convention interviewed Cadogan demanding the enactment of the Fry Report, the viceroy was cagey; but on 20 January Salisbury granted an audience to the duke of Abercorn, representing the Convention, and offered much more support than Cadogan had been able to muster.[151] The immediate outcome of this eccentric diplomacy was that the Irish viceroy, outflanked by a combination of the Prime Minister and militant landlordism, was brought close to resignation. And it was only at the prompting of the Irish Lord Chancellor that Salisbury was moved to offer a vague account of the Abercorn meeting by way of placating Cadogan.[152] Cadogan remained, and Salisbury was thereby spared an embarrassing revelation of his preference for landed opinion over that of his own Irish ministers.

The bond between Salisbury and Irish landlordism possessed two varieties of implication for government policy in Ireland. After mid-1897 the government was generally more willing to tailor

---

[148] Cadogan Papers, CAD 1068, Lecky to Cadogan, 20 Mar. 1897. MSPH, E/Abercorn/61, Abercorn to Salisbury, 12 Mar. 1897.

[149] Gailey, *Death of Kindness*, 117.

[150] Agnes Fry, *A Memoir of the Rt. Hon. Sir Edward Fry, GCB* (Oxford, 1921), 109-13.

[151] MSPH, E/Cadogan/159, Cadogan to Salisbury, 25 Jan. 1899. Cadogan Papers, CAD 1464, Abercorn to Cadogan, 17 Jan. 1899; CAD 1466, Cadogan to Clonbrock, 18 Jan. 1899; CAD 1475, Cadogan to Salisbury, 25 Jan. 1899.

[152] Cadogan Papers, CAD 1472, Salisbury to Cadogan, 24 Jan. 1899. MSPH, E/Ashbourne/58, Ashbourne to Salisbury, 22 Jan. 1899.

legislation to landlord requirements. There was no systematically partial policy, but grievances were now seriously assessed, and the snubs which had been offered in 1896 were scrupulously avoided. When, in the spring of 1897, landowners demanded an extension of the agricultural rating grant to Ireland, they were offered compensation within the terms of the local government reform[153] They secured a refined Department of Agriculture Act in 1899, and the rectification of a long-standing grievance through the promulgation of the Tithe Rent Charge Act in 1900.[154] Though they did not achieve the full enactment of the Fry Report—fresh legislation was out of the question after the experience of 1896—their support for the Commission was condoned by Salisbury, and inspired some painful calculations in the Irish Office.

Much of this legislative success was achieved in spite of the attitudes of the Irish administration, and through the agency of the Prime Minister. It was thus a logical progression for landlord ambition that the composition of the government should be matched to the type of legislation which they wanted enacted. Salisbury's plans to remove both Gerald Balfour and Cadogan from their respective Irish posts in 1900 were seen as a collapse before landlord pressure.[155] Certainly, the dismissal of T. W. Russell from the Local Government Board in November 1900 was precipitated by demands from Saunderson, Abercorn, and the landed faction.[156] And, though W. G. Ellison-Macartney, a prominent landed sympathizer in junior office was also dropped in 1900 (probably at the insistence of Chamberlain), he was compensated with a British Privy Counsellorship, where Russell entered the back-benches without similar reward. Cadogan remained in Viceregal Lodge until 1902, thanks to the combined support of Devonshire and Arthur Balfour; but Gerald Balfour was replaced by George Wyndham who, whatever his subsequent record, seemed to be a candidate satisfactory

[153] Gailey, *Death of Kindness*, 44–6.   [154] Ibid. 119.
[155] Devonshire Papers, 340/2842, Devonshire to Cadogan, 30 Oct. 1900. Horace Plunkett Diaries 27 Oct. 1900. MSPH, E/Balfour/133, Chamberlain to Balfour, 21 Oct. 1900 (copy), E/Balfour/127, Balfour to Salisbury, 17 Oct. 1900.
[156] ESP, uncatalogued, Salisbury to Saunderson, 26 Sept. 1900. MSPH, E/Abercorn/76, Abercorn to Salisbury, 9 Oct. 1900; E/Abercorn/79, Abercorn to Salisbury, 31 Oct. 1900. PRONI, Abercorn Papers, D 623/A/331/98, Salisbury to Abercorn, 11 Oct. 1900; D 623/A/331/99, Salisbury to Abercorn, 29 Oct. 1900; D 623/A/331/101, Salisbury to Abercorn, 20 Oct. 1900.

to landlord sentiment.[157] His promotion, allied with the more extensive purging of the government, seemed to signify a renaissance in the political power of Irish landlordism.[158] While this lacked all semblance of popular endorsement, the resources of landlordism appeared to offer, in 1900, a secure political future, regardless of the state of local Unionism or of the spread of land purchase.

Superficially, then, the position of landlords in 1900 was strong. They had ministerial influence, expressed both in terms of patronage and of legislation. They had a number of vocal and dedicated parliamentary spokesmen, particularly in the House of Lords, who enjoyed direct access to Salisbury. Moreover, their dyspeptic attitude towards the Cadogan–Balfour regime won significant support within Dublin Unionism—support which directly contributed to the defeat of two Unionist MPs who were associated with the constructive policy (Campbell and Plunkett).[159] Yet, there was no alteration in political fundamentals, no real recovery from the vulnerability which has been identified for the middle of the decade. Instead, paradoxically, the parliamentary achievement of landlordism in the late 1890s reflected merely its growing weakness at all levels of the parliamentary hierarchy. Much of their evident success hinged on the intervention of one key sympathizer, the Prime Minister; and much of the pressure which was brought to bear on Salisbury came from the extra-parliamentary agencies of landlordism, a source which reflected the faltering position within the Commons.

Thus, the landed renaissance rested precariously upon a number of favourable circumstances, which temporarily masked, but did not reverse, the decline into parliamentary oblivion. The local political conditions of 1894–5 had determined the government's priorities in 1896, and these were renewed after the autumn of 1900, when Russell launched a popular agitation in Ulster for compulsory purchase.[160] The relative quiescence of northern farmers between 1895 and 1900, and the silencing of Russell through office, had allowed landlords a measure of influence which would have been otherwise unthinkable. Russell's campaign of 1900 restored the political balance of the mid-1890s, and landlordism was accordingly

[157] Devonshire Papers, 340/2842, Devonshire to Cadogan, 30 Oct. 1900; 340/2844, Balfour to Devonshire, 2 Nov. 1900; 340/2846, Salisbury to Devonshire, 6 Nov. 1900. MSPH, E/Cadogan/199, Salisbury to Cadogan, 6 Nov. 1900.
[158] See ch. 6.   [159] Gailey, *Death of Kindness*, 158.
[160] Jackson, 'Irish Unionist Parliamentary Party', 366.

eclipsed. Furthermore, the comparative success of Russell's efforts reflected the unpopularity of hardline landed Unionism in the north, for the endorsement which had been won among Dublin Tories at the general election was not repeated within Ulster. Rather, Belfast Toryism remained cautiously sympathetic towards figures like Plunkett, who had incurred the wrath of landed Toryism and its Dublin allies; and the northern Unionist press reacted with anger when Plunkett and Campbell were defeated through the intervention of hardline opponents.[161] These developments, allied with the weakening landed lobby among Ulster MPs, indicated that unreconstructed landlordism was increasingly a southern phenomenon, no longer politically viable within the heartland of Irish Unionism.

The insubstantial nature of the landed recovery was revealed in the final years of Unionist supremacy. For if, between 1895 and 1900, the government's favours had been bestowed haphazardly among landed and tenant loyalists, then this indecisive flirtation was resolved after George Wyndham's appointment. The last phase of constructive Unionism was marked by the virtual supersession of blatant landlordism as an effective force within Irish Unionist parliamentary representation. There was no repetition of the anger and rhetorical violence of 1896, and while this new calm was partly related to the favourable nature of Wyndham's successive reform proposals, it was also now apparent that landlords had very little room for manœuvre. Russell's sustained campaign for compulsory sale and purchase, allied with the activities of William O'Brien and the United Irish League, compelled the Unionist governments towards pliability. Lacking any foxhole in popular politics, loyalist landlords were at the same time pathetically reliant on the government for some means of financial and political survival.

Working through the Ulster Farmers' and Labourers' Union, and a network of local tenant associations, Russell had developed a campaign for compulsion which threatened the electoral supremacy of conventional Unionism in rural Ulster. Urban Unionists were comparatively unmoved by Russell's call (as the result

<hr>

[161] *BNL*, 5 Oct. 1900, 27 Sept. 1900, 22 Sept. 1900: 'It is to be hoped that his Lordship [Ardilaun] and those acting with him will see the wisdom of withdrawing their candidature and thus allowing Mr. Plunkett an easy victory.'

of the South Antrim by-election in February 1903 indicated); but a combination of Unionist and Nationalist farmer votes secured victory for Russellism in two farming constituencies, East Down and North Fermanagh.[162] Most other landed MPs, inspired by this threat, pledged themselves to support compulsion, while avoiding the ultimate humiliation of pledging allegiance to 'the political pervert', as the *News Letter* dubbed Russell.[163] Landed representatives like W. G. Ellison-Macartney sought to counter the agitation by creating a rival popular issue in law and order, but neither this nor the widespread personal abuse of Russell achieved any significant short-term impact. Indeed, given the utter inability of official Unionism to cope, it was left to the government to quell the farmers' rebellion.

But the tottering parliamentary position of Irish landlordism was not simply the result of a local assault, even though Russell's agitation had reduced several landed MPs to abject complaisance. There had been no significant fall in landlords returned to the Commons in 1900, but a combination of factors, including Russell's campaign, had the effect of diminishing the impact of those landowners who remained in the parliamentary Ulster Party. Of the MPs for Irish constituencies who had been prominent opponents of the 1896 Land Bill, only Saunderson, increasingly dogged by ill-health, remained to challenge Wyndham. Carson had been effectively silenced through office. Of the landlords representing English seats, Smith-Barry had been removed from the Commons in 1902 by a peerage. W. G. Ellison-Macartney, who looked set to become the focus of opposition to Wyndham, left parliament in 1903 to become Deputy Master of the Royal Mint.[164]

But even more significant than these back-bench casualties was the fate of Irish landlordism within the cabinet. It has been stressed that the comparative success of landed assertiveness in 1899–1900 depended largely on the patronage of Salisbury—a precarious foundation for political achievement, given the Prime Minister's age and infirmity. Once Salisbury retired, in June 1902, landlordism was

[162] Private Possession, William Moore Papers, Joseph Wilson to Moore, 9 Feb. 1903: 'my experience is that all the urban voters without exception are bitterly opposed to Russellism.' Jackson, 'Irish Unionist Parliamentary Party', 381–2.
[163] *BNL*, 17 Apr. 1903.
[164] Macartney was a particular thorn in Wyndham's side: ABP, Add. MS 49804, fos. 18–20, Wyndham to Balfour, 3 Mar. 1902.

more fully exposed to ministerial whim. And the subsequent resignation of Lord George Hamilton from the cabinet represented a further, if less significant, setback.[165] It was thus a greatly weakened landlord party which confronted the challenge of Russellism and Wyndhamite reform. And, just as the vulnerability of parliamentary landlordism had been a phenomenon identifiable in the 1880s and before, so the exclusively southern character of the landed party in 1902-3 represented the culmination of a much older trend.

Given the precarious state of landed opinion, it was not surprising that George Wyndham's cautious Land Bill of 1902 won virtually the unanimous support of the parliamentary Ulster Party. There were few tactical qualms, though the irreconcilable Ellison-Macartney chose in public statements to dwell on the law and order and the labourer questions, rather than actively support the Chief Secretary or his initiative.[166] But other Ulster Party speakers in the spring of 1902 were more sympathetic, and even the amiably unenlightened J. M. McCalmont was able to bless the bill at two loyalist gatherings in May.[167] Indeed the irony of this reception lay in the fact that a bill consciously formulated to satisfy tenant opinion should have been so warmly endorsed by the landlords—and so firmly rejected by the rural agitators.

Balfour had argued frankly to Sir Michael Hicks-Beach that 'we can hardly hope to keep [Ulster] . . . if a purchase bill holds out to them no prospect of relief'.[168] Yet, despite this priority, both Russell and his Ulster Farmers' Union greeted Wyndham's Bill with deep scepticism. Though Russell struggled to avoid any outright condemnation from the farmers, a faction within his Union clung to the principle of compulsion, and repudiated the whole measure, which was based upon a scheme of voluntary purchase.[169] The Chief Secretary eventually succumbed to Russell's criticism, and Russell in turn grew more supportive, but these seeds of reconciliation

[165] Hamilton's account of the circumstances of his resignation is in Lord George Hamilton, *Parliamentary Reminiscences and Reflections, 1886-1906* (London, 1922), 318-27.
[166] e.g. Macartney at the annual meeting of the IUA, 10 Apr. 1902, *BNL*, 11 Apr. 1902.
[167] Others joined in *BNL*, 1 Apr. 1902 (Moore); 16 May 1902 (McCalmont); 21 May 1902 (McCalmont); 19 June 1902 (Ulster Party).
[168] ABP, Add. MS 49695, fo. 135, Balfour to Beach, 15 Feb. 1902 (copy).
[169] *BNL*, 5 Apr. 1903, 23 Apr. 1902.

were never given a chance to mature. For both Redmond and the Ulster Tories, from their respective vantage points, remained opposed to any compromise, and Wyndham's offer of talks, though lauded by Russell, was spurned by the Nationalist leader and treated as a humiliation by the editor of the *News Letter*.[170] But, despite the grumblings of the Tory press, its repudiation of Wyndham's trimming contained no alternative strategy for victory over tenant agitation. It was left, therefore, to the Chief Secretary's tactical gymnastics to inspire a reform satisfactory to farmer opinion, and thereby to offer Ulster Unionism a future of unity and strength. Indeed, if they were appalled by his promiscuous diplomacy, then Ulster Unionists were still too vulnerable to reject out of hand the Chief Secretary's proposals—whatever the grubbiness of their origins.

Wyndham's first Land Bill had been a gamble, in that he had risked humiliation in order to mollify his Russellite and Nationalist opponents. And though the Bill itself failed, Wyndham had gone some way towards patching a compromise between Russell and northern landlordism. At any rate, he had coaxed Russell into declaring publicly what the agitator had hitherto confided only to intimates—that he would agree to a measure which fell far short of compulsory sale and purchase.[171] The Chief Secretary's subsequent land reform was thus launched onto a better charted political channel, and not only because Russell's flexibility had been fully exposed. For the Land Bill of 1903 appeared in the aftermath of an agreement reached between a number of representative farmers and landowners, sitting in Dublin in the winter of 1902–3 as the Land Conference. Their report, which embodied a scheme of Treasury-funded, voluntary purchase, won extensive approval, even from those, who like Saunderson, had been sceptical of the viability of the Conference. Exploiting this unexpected consensus, Wyndham introduced his second Land Bill into the Commons on 25 March 1903.[172]

As over the Bill of 1902, the parliamentary Ulster Party was virtually unanimous in support of this measure, though inevitably personal and political circumstances dictated degrees of enthusiasm.

[170] *BNL*, 20 June 1902, 25 June 1902, 30 June 1902.
[171] Horace Plunkett Diaries, 14 Mar. 1902.
[172] Earl of Dunraven, *Past Times and Pastimes*, (2 vols.; London [1922]), ii. 3–25, 179. Gailey, *Death of Kindness*, 189–91. The approval of the Landowners' Convention impressed Wyndham: Mackail and Wyndham (edd.), *Letters*, ii. 453.

Just as in 1896, an MP's temper was partly related to the nature of his constituency, those sitting for English, urban and university seats lacking the restraints imposed upon the county members. Thus, the Irish Unionist MPs who were most grudging about the Bill included Carson, representing Trinity College, C. C. Craig, representing the largely urban South Antrim seat, and G. W. Wolff, member for East Belfast.[173] Landlords naturally featured large among the sceptics, but professional and middle-class representatives were also prepared to be critical—and not merely because they were reflecting local opinion. Some had private qualms about extended purchase, while there were others who perhaps were more unhappy about Wyndham's methods than about the Bill. Certainly John Atkinson, member for North Antrim and Attorney General for Ireland, was increasingly alarmed by what he perceived as political chicanery in Dublin Castle.[174]

However, despite a wide range of doubts, only a handful of Ulster members identified themselves with the landlords' cause and with an attitude of sustained disapproval. The parliamentary Ulster Party formed a sub-committee to monitor the progress of the Bill through the Committee stage, but the amendments which it devised were largely constructive, and related to the treatment of farm labourers.[175] The focus of landowning unrest lay, not within the structures of the Ulster Party, but in the Landowners' Convention, and in a distinct parliamentary committee representing the landed interest. This last was chaired by Sir John Colomb (who sat for an English constituency), and, when the Bill was under debate, it met daily to formulate strategy.[176] However, the committee attracted the participation of only two or three Ulster members, and seems to have been composed largely of peers and representatives of English seats. When the London correspondent of the *News Letter* identified the seven principal champions of the landed interest in the Commons, only three of these (Saunderson, Craig, and Lonsdale) were Ulster members.[177] Even so, the designation of both Craig and Lonsdale was hardly warranted by their parliamentary conduct, and Lonsdale's electoral agent was both surprised and shocked by the label.[178] On

---

[173] *BNL*, 4 May 1903 (Carson at Oxford). ABP, Add. MS 49709, fo. 117, Carson to Balfour, 4 May 1903. *BNL*, 27 Mar. 1903 (Wolff at landlords' meeting).
[174] TCD, W. E. H. Lecky Papers, 1835/2357, Atkinson to Lecky, 2 July 1903.
[175] *BNL*, 15 May 1903.   [176] *BNL*, 19, 24, 25 June 1903.
[177] *BNL*, 8 July 1903.
[178] PRONI, Joshua Peel Papers, D 889/4C/2, 950, Peel to Lonsdale, 9 July 1903. Peel urged Lonsdale to 'wire a contradiction'.

the other hand, even those who were unequivocal landlord
spokesmen were, in the light of 1896, comparatively mild in their
observations. Edward Saunderson, the only Ulster MP to have
refused a commitment to compulsion, proclaimed a general blessing
on the measure, both at public engagements and in the House of
Commons. And C. C. Craig, one of Wyndham's most indefatigible
opponents on virtually every issue, offered similar approval for 'the
main features of the bill'.[179]

This complaisance had extensive roots. Given the weakness and
isolation of landlordism, an attitude of reasonableness was perhaps
simply a recognition of realities. Moreover, the measure itself offered
landlords highly favourable opportunities for sale, created by
subventions from the Treasury. But there were other, more narrowly
political influences on the attitude of loyalist MPs. Pre-eminently,
the Bill looked set to separate T. W. Russell from his electoral base,
for Russell's sanction of the measure had been repudiated by his
Ulster Farmers' and Labourers' Union. The Union adhered to
compulsion; and while Russell lamely described the Bill as
'compulsion by inducement' this exercise in semantics carried little
weight with hardline farmer opinion.[180] Confronted with a
potential schism, Ulster Unionists could afford neither any sustained
resistance to the Bill, nor the chance that Russell might exploit their
stand to reconstruct his own support.

The Party's attitude was also determined by the intelligence at their
disposal. With previous reform bills a significant feature of loyalist
frustration had been their ignorance of the government's intentions:
this had influenced unrest about Balfour's reform proposals in 1889,
and Cadogan's legislative programme for 1899.[181] In 1903, by way
of contrast, Wyndham not only negotiated extensively with
Redmond, he also consulted leading loyalists during the progress of
his Bill.[182] And where in 1896 Ulster Unionist sensitivities had been
wholly sacrificed to the task of mollifying the Nationalists, Wyndham

[179] BNL, 19 June 1903 (Saunderson at the United Club). Hansard, 4th ser.
(1903), cxxv. 1329-30. BNL, 17 April 1903 (Craig at the Orange Hall, Lisburn).
[180] BNL, 16 April 1903 (UFLU demands compulsion). BNL, 10 Mar. 1903
(Russell at Aughnacloy: 'if there was not to be compulsion by coercion, there had
to be compulsion by inducement').
[181] Cadogan Papers, CAD 1472, Salisbury to Cadogan, 24 Jan. 1899. ABP, Add.
MS 49845, fo. 156, Saunderson to Balfour, 2 Nov. 1889; Add. MS 49828, fo. 431,
Balfour to Saunderson, 4 Nov. 1889 (copy).
[182] BNL, 24 June 1903.

reacted more constructively in 1903. Thus when loyalists repeatedly pointed to the plight of the labouring population, Wyndham responded by committing the government to a reform bill.[183] Amendments to the Land Bill were treated more even-handedly than in 1896. Indeed, even if Wyndham had kept the Ulster Party wholly in the dark about his intentions, then at least one leading Irish Unionist MP was privy to leaks from the Irish Land Commission concerning the evolution of the Bill.[184]

All this information and communication meant that the scope for panic which had existed in earlier years was not a feature of the debates in 1903. That Wyndham sustained a complex array of support owed more perhaps to the eloquence of British cash than any profound measure of personal trust. Nevertheless, his treatment of loyalism in 1903 was deemed to be satisfactory, and if well-placed Unionists like Atkinson were suspicious of the Chief Secretary's relations with Nationalism, then these qualms had not yet gained popular currency.[185] Given this communication between the Ulster Party and Wyndham, there seemed little justification for Russell's disturbing premonition of March 1903 that loyalism would soon be 'rudely disillusioned' with its government.[186]

Wyndham's great reform effectively ended twenty years of Unionist legislation on Irish land. Yet, despite this tradition, the Act of 1903 was unique, and not least because it inspired an unprecedented unity within the Ulster Party. For, hitherto, the chief characteristic of the government's relations with the loyalist back-bench had been their complexity, and the absence of any sustained alliance or antagonism. Rather, land reform inspired a network of divisions among Ulster Unionist MPs as intricate and extensive as hairline cracking on old china. The complex of support and opposition inspired by the measures before 1903 contained a large measure of unpredictability, and the government was frequently taken by surprise as attitudes evolved. For there was no simple determinant of an Ulster Unionist MP's stand

[183] *BNL*, 9 July 1903.
[184] PRONI, Edward Carson Papers, D 1507/1/1903/1, Rathmore to Carson, 15 Mar. 1903. J. H. Franks was the mole, and Rathmore promised 'more material of the same kind'.
[185] See above, n. 174. Saunderson lauded Wyndham's handling of the Bill, Hansard, 4th ser. (1903), cxxv. 1329-30.
[186] *BNL*, 10 Mar. 1903, Russell at Aughnacloy.

on reform, much depending instead on a puzzlingly broad range of personal and political circumstances and pressures.

Many of these influences have already been identified in the analysis of individual reforms, but a brief recapitulation may be offered. An MP's occupation clearly helped to condition his response to a measure, although, for example, there was no necessary relationship between landownership and landlord sympathies. Similarly, the professional classes offered no predictable attitude to land reform, and a radical Tory lawyer like R. M. Dane could emerge as a tenant advocate, while a self-made entrepreneur like G. W. Wolff clung to landlordism. The retreat of the lower gentry into the professions explains the pro-landlord sympathies of W. G. Ellison-Macartney and William Moore, two sons of the manor and barristers who relied upon legal and other earned income. However, the attitude of lawyers generally reveals no obvious pattern, since the profession embraced a wide variety of opinion on landed matters.

The location of a member's constituency was more important. As tenant fervour in North-East Ulster developed, landlords who represented farmer constituencies were increasingly vulnerable, and therefore increasingly pliable. Southern Irish Unionists, who were concentrated in the greater Dublin area, imposed no such restrictions on their representatives, and indeed the interests of one constituency (Trinity College) demanded the active expression of landlord sympathies. Irish landlords representing English constituencies enjoyed a similar freedom of action, and had emerged by 1903 as the effective leaders of the landed cause in the Commons. Thus, the parliamentary retreat of landlordism had a distinctive spatial form; and the growing divide between landownership and popular loyalist politics was highlighted by this new, physical separation.

On the other hand, party allegiance seems to have played an insignificant role in the determination of sympathies on land reform. Admittedly, the fiercest advocates of tenant right, Russell and Lea, were Liberal Unionists, while the staunchest landlords were Tories, but this did not reflect any more general relationship between class commitment and party membership. Irish Toryism in the Commons numbered among its ranks committed reformers like Dane and J. A. Rentoul, while the Liberal Unionist members included Lecky and William Kenny, both of whom identified with the landowning cause. Before 1892, when Russell and Lea were the only Irish Liberal Unionist members, there was certainly the risk that opposition to

tenant claims might be construed as opposition to Liberal
Unionism, but with the recruitment of more Whiggish MPs the threat
of cleavage between the Unionist parties over land considerably
diminished. The retirement of Lea in 1900, and the apostasy of
Russell, reduced this threat further; and though some tensions
remained, the drift of Toryism and Liberal Unionism in Ireland,
as in England, was towards fusion. Thus, while the potential
for division existed in the early years of the alliance, this
was never realized, and the differences between the parties
were contained within manageable local clashes, and within a
rigidly Unionist arena.

Attitudes were, however, influenced by a variety of political factors
external to the Unionist alliance. The threat represented by
opponents, whether the Russellites or, earlier, the Land League, had
proved decisive in the evolution of Ulster Unionist opinion, and
undoubtedly influenced the Ulster Party's response to land legislation
under the second Salisbury government and in 1902-3. Both
Russellism and the Land League shared the same facility for recruiting
Protestant votes, and neither movement was wholly susceptible to
the simple repetition of loyalist pieties. More was demanded from
the Ulster Party by way of political response, and this often took
the dual form of calls to loyalty and a commitment to remedial
legislation. At times of farmer quiescence or constitutional security,
hardline landlords were less willing to compromise, but generally
the trend within the Ulster Party was towards the public acceptance
of farmer grievance, suitably laced with qualifications. Thus by 1901
all but one of the Ulster members were committed to compulsory
purchase—a consensus unimaginable in 1885—although these
pledges were invariably more complicated than they seemed, and
certainly did not imply support for the ambitions of T. W.
Russell.[187]

But, if the influences on Ulster Party opinion formation were many
and varied, then other aspects of the relationship between the Party
and Toryism displayed greater stability. Not all English ministerial
patrons remained loyal to their Irish clients, and Joseph Chamberlain,
for example, dropped both Russell and his own enthusiasm for Irish
land after 1900; but a more durable bond lay in the respective

---

[187] BNL, 16 May 1902. McCalmont at Larne defends himself against the charge
of breaking his pledge to support compulsion.

commitments of Salisbury and Arthur Balfour.[188] Balfour displayed
a sustained interest in the state of Ulster farmer opinion throughout
the period, and he was acutely sensitive to the possibility of tenant
defections from the Union. Salisbury on the other hand, true to his
broader commitments to the rights of property, was patron to the
landlords of the Ulster Party, a role which was only reinforced by
the aberrant act of 1896. Indeed, after 1896, Salisbury's willingness
to appease landlordism was diluted only by British party
considerations and by his relative ignorance of Irish land law.
Certainly his sympathies bore little relation to political realities in
Ulster, and it is likely that many of the difficulties which Ulster
Unionism faced after 1900 were rooted in the Prime Minister's glib
partiality of earlier years.

Chief among the political realities of Ulster, and a conspicuous
feature of the parties' relationship, was the relative decline of
landlordism as a parliamentary force. Successive general elections
saw a reduction in the number of landlords returned for Ulster
constituencies, and the development of constraints upon those who
remained in the Commons. Landowners remained influential, both
through their strength in the Lords, and through the power of the
Landowners' Convention, but it is to this period that their decline
within popular loyalist politics may be traced. A fuller investigation
of this phenomenon is reserved for a later section of the book, but
it may be noted that one of the consequences of decline was the
marginalization and eradication of hardline landlordism within the
House of Commons.[189] The landed reaction to the Bill of 1896 was
a testimony to vulnerability, and though, thanks to Salisbury,
some concessions were subsequently wrenched from the Castle
administration, by 1900 Lecky was commenting upon the isolation
of Irish landlordism within parliament.[190] Russell's campaign for
compulsory purchase, and the fear which it inspired among Ulster
members, revealed the precarious position of the remaining landed
MPs. And the reception of Wyndham's Land Bills in 1902 and 1903,
though carefully planned and managed, was faint-hearted in
comparison with earlier critiques. By these years much of the
responsibility for the defence of Irish landlordism had devolved upon

[188] Joseph Chamberlain was unenthusiastic about Wyndham's Land Bills: Gailey,
Death of Kindness, 193.   [189] See below, ch. 5.6.
[190] Montgomery Papers, T 1089/298, Lecky to Montgomery, 3 Dec. 1900.

a small number of southern Unionist and English members, in alliance with peers. And this in itself indicated the weakness of the landed position within Ulster politics.

These varied developments contributed more generally to the moulding of the relationship between Toryism and the loyalist movement. The unity of these parties was always more readily assumed in years of opposition, when administrative and financial realities could not sully the shared commitment to Union, Queen, and Empire. On the other hand, Unionist government, and particularly its Irish policy, continually generated grievance among one or other faction within loyalism, with the result that, by 1906, most varieties of loyalist could display scars inflicted by their English co-partisans. This was certainly true of the landlords, but even Unionist farmers who had profited more obviously from Tory legislation, had only made progress through a relatively sustained conflict with government. The main political by-product of constructive Unionism was thus not so much the weakening of Irish Unionism, as the weakening of some of the ties between Irish Unionism and the British party. Constructive Unionism converted the intimacy of 1886 and 1893 into a more commercial relationship. Constructive Unionism threatened to make all Irishmen the clients of a paternal administration, and to treat loyalism as merely one of several contenders for British patronage. Thus Unionist land reform did not create the divisions between loyalist landlord and tenant, but it did provide these tensions with a much wider significance. Indeed constructive Unionism generally offered the chance of internal loyalist unity, providing as it did both legislation to heal rural class wounds, and the conciliation of Nationalism as an appropriate rallying point.

But it was not simply the machinery of government which was forcing apart British and Irish Unionism. The weakening of parliamentary landlordism contributed to this drift, for it was among the Irish landed MPs that some of the closest personal and political connections with Britain were to be found. *Arriviste* lawyers and businessmen had generally slighter personal bonds with Britain, and their heightened presence in the Commons made for a more functional relationship between the Unionist parties. A landlord like Saunderson was much more fully integrated into the social life of the House of Commons than many of his middle-class successors, and he enjoyed good and close relations with leaders like Salisbury.

Indeed, Salisbury played an important part in binding loyalists, particularly landowners, to the national party, taking the trouble to reply at length not only to magnates like Abercorn, but also to an eccentric like William Johnston.[191] The disappearance from politics of Salisbury, Saunderson, and genial squires like J. M. McCalmont altered this intimacy, and the reorganization of Ulster Unionism after 1904 confirmed the strength of middle-class particularism.

Landlords and land legislation were thus central both to the development of Tory–loyalist relations, and to the evolution of Ulster Unionism itself. Landlord-MPs were at once a threat and an aid to good relations, and their influence could be used both as a political cement and as a solvent. Calling themselves Irish or Anglo-Irish, they had, nevertheless, a firmer grasp of the British social and political landscape than their successors; and their departure from parliament foreshadowed the drift of Ireland and loyal Ulster from the Union.

4. *Irish Local Government*

Loyalist representatives, contrary to past assertions, were on the whole not unsympathetic to the principle of Irish local government.[192] It is true that some landlords, the chief beneficiaries from the system of Grand Juries, were suspicious of abdicating power to elected councils, but this feeling was naturally especially prevalent among southern loyalists. Moreover, the die-hard minority was small and comparatively mute—if only because the corollary of their argument involved depriving Unionist cess-payers of democratic local government, in those northern areas where they constituted the majority of the population.

The Conservative Party had been committed to a measure of local government for Ireland since Salisbury's Caretaker Ministry of 1885.[193] The state of lawlessness had provided them, when returned

---

[191] See the correspondence of Saunderson with Salisbury in the Salisbury Papers. Numerous letters from Salisbury to the Colonel have recently come to light in the possession of Saunderson's grandson. WJD, D 880/2/47, Salisbury to Johnston, 19, 23 Dec. 1895. See also MSPH, E/Johnston/12, Johnston to Salisbury, 20 Dec. 1895.

[192] Cf. Curtis, *Coercion and Conciliation*, 381.

[193] Ibid.; see also Catherine Shannon, 'The Ulster Liberal Unionists and Local Government Reform, 1885–1898', *IHS*, xviii. 71 (Mar. 1973), 408–9.

to power, with a pretext for pigeon-holing the issue, but in 1888 two circumstances contrived to resuscitate interest. In that year the government passed a measure of local government reform for England and Scotland, though the claims of Ireland were not considered in the bill. These received a more substantial airing when, in May 1888, the first of Joseph Chamberlain's *Birmingham Daily Post* articles appeared, later published in pamphlet form as *A Unionist Policy for Ireland*. Chamberlain advocated a comprehensive scheme of local government for Ireland, with provincial and county councils exercising wide powers over local administration, and his initiative highlighted the problems of Irish county administration.[194]

No Irish Conservative was publicly enthusiastic about the *Birmingham Daily Post* programme, and leading Irish Liberal Unionists were similarly disturbed, even though they could not openly repudiate the scheme without being seen to threaten Chamberlain. Their preferred alternative was the extension of British-style local government to Ireland, and to some degree this was a conscious tactical ploy to counteract Chamberlain's 'awful scheme of provincial councils'.[195] Indeed the demands for local government were echoed by some Irish Tories, again apparently as a diversionary tactic. For example, in October 1889 William Ellison-Macartney tried to direct Unionist reforming zeal into the comparatively safe area of local government, and away from the more contentious land question.[196]

Thus, Arthur Balfour's Local Government Bill, introduced in February 1892, won wide support within the Ulster Party.[197]

---

[194] Curtis, *Coercion and Conciliation*, 381; for the long-term influence of Chamberlain's programme see Davis, 'Liberal Unionist Party', 98. In the interests of alliance Chamberlain felt compelled to drop his federal and council schemes— 'one of the chief forfeits in all his political career' claimed Garvin: J. L. Garvin and J. Amery, *The Life of Joseph Chamberlain*, (6 vols.; London, 1932-69), ii. 424. For the Chamberlain proposals see Joseph Chamberlain, *Speeches on the Irish Question: A Collection of Speeches delivered between 1887 and 1890* (London, 1890), 104-5.

[195] Montgomery Papers, D 627/428/97, William Kenny to Montgomery, 21 Apr. 1889 (quoted in Patrick Buckland, *Irish Unionism: A Documentary History 1885-1923* (Belfast, 1973) 268). Shannon, 'Ulster Liberal Unionists', 413-14.

[196] Akers-Douglas Papers, C 25/93, W. H. Smith to Akers-Douglas, 16 Oct. 1889.

[197] Shannon overestimates opposition to the Bill. Ulster members had registered their opinions before its appearance, but even the most anxious accepted its necessity. ABP, Add. MS 49849, fo. 99, Thomas Waring to Balfour, 22 Sept. 1891. Whittingehame, Arthur Balfour Papers, TD 83/133/67, Russell to Balfour, 6 Nov. 1891. ABP, Add. MS 49830, fo. 229, Balfour to Abercorn, 9 Sept. 1891.

Landed grumbles were certainly sustained, but the chief feature of the measure was less the concession of county government than the battery of restraints planned for the new councils. The bill proposed to create county and district councils, which were to be elected by a franchise of all cess-payers. Minority interests were to be protected by a system of cumulative voting, designed to secure wide and popular representation—whether of loyalists in southern counties, or of Nationalists in northern.[198] Checks were proposed on the spending powers of the new councils: any body of twenty or more cess-payers had the right to impeach a council for mismanagement before two judges.

These safeguards, designed for the satisfaction of loyalists, did on the whole win their approval. Some members, notably J. A. Rentoul, equivocated—not because they thought the safeguards insufficient, but rather because they saw them as an unnecessary encumbrance to the Bill.[199] On the other hand, Orange Conservatives like Saunderson and Johnston welcomed the Bill unreservedly, and T. W. Russell, the only Liberal Unionist to contribute to debate, was scarcely less enthusiastic. In an able defence of the measure against an assault by William O'Brien, Russell on 24 May 1892 itemized its contents—and pronounced warm approval of all but two features. Like William Ellison-Macartney, he was doubtful about the need for judicial appeal, but, like Ellison-Macartney, his final verdict was positive: it was a 'substantially good Bill in principle'.[200]

The 'substantially good Bill' was read a second time on 24 May 1892—and unceremoniously dropped on 13 June. The truth was *not* as George Wyndham suggested, that 'nobody cared a damn' about its fate: Ellison-Macartney and Rentoul, for the Ulster members, had each refuted this suggestion, demonstrating interest and enthusiasm, on several occasions during the debates.[201] Rather, the government found itself approaching the end of the session with a Bill which, though in substance attractive to its loyalist support, was the target for effective and obstructive criticism from the Opposition benches.[202] In any case, merely by introducing the

[198] Curtis, *Coercion and Conciliation*, 384–5.
[199] Hansard, 4th ser. (1892), i. 768 (Rentoul).
[200] Ibid. iii. 1691 (Russell).
[201] Curtis, *Coercion and Conciliation*, 386, quoting John Biggs-Davison; *George Wyndham: A Study in Toryism* (London, 1951), 63.
[202] Hansard, 4th ser. (1892), iv. 1600.

measure the government had fulfilled both a long-standing party commitment, and an obligation to Liberal Unionist—more particularly Irish Liberal Unionist—opinion. Given the limits created by a departing and crowded parliamentary session, abandonment of the Bill was really the only option open to ministers.

The hesitancy of loyalist support for local government, perceptible among some landed elements in 1892, was much more pronounced when, in February 1898, Gerald Balfour introduced another, substantially revised Bill.[203] Thus, while loyalists in both houses of parliament maintained a shaky solidarity in welcoming the measure, there was a noticeable variation in the strength of enthusiasm. Several local Unionist associations and Orange lodges openly declared their distrust and lobbied Ulster Party members accordingly.[204] But the latter, with one exception (W. E. H. Lecky), united in support of the Chief Secretary.[205]

Learning by the tactical errors committed on the Land Bill of 1896, ministers were anxious to obtain a private expression of views from the Irish landowner interest. The chief opponents of the government in 1896 were named in cabinet as potentially valuable intermediaries—Arthur Smith-Barry from the Commons Ulster Party, and Abercorn, Clonbrock, and De Vesci from the Lords.[206] On 11 December 1897 Arthur Balfour interviewed Abercorn, who, as in 1892, was fearful for the interests of the large cess-payer, and for the loyal minority in general, under Nationalist-controlled local government: fearful of 'the danger of giving too much power, without proper safeguards, which might hereafter be used in any strong outburst of passion against those whom it might most injuriously affect . . .'.[207] Balfour temporized over Abercorn's complaints, avoiding any commitment—but even in canvassing the duke's opinion, he had mitigated one important source of loyalist grievance. Abercorn was flattered by Balfour's politeness ('he was very nice to

[203] For the origins of the Bill see Gailey, 'Unionist rhetoric', 61–2; Gailey, *Death of Kindness*, 40–50.

[204] W. E. H. Lecky Papers, 1832/1687, 1700b, 1704, 1711, various Orange lodges to Lecky, Mar.–Apr. 1898.

[205] Elizabeth Lecky, *A Memoir of the Rt. Hon. W. E. H. Lecky* (London, 1910), 314. WJD, D 880/2/50, 21 Feb. 1898. Shannon identifies Lecky as a supporter of the proposal, 'Ulster Liberal Unionists', 421.

[206] Cadogan Papers, CAD 1258, Ashbourne to Cadogan, 10 Dec. 1897.

[207] Ibid., CAD 1261, Abercorn to Cadogan, 12 Dec. 1897.

me'), and left satisfied—if not by the substance of the meeting, then at least by its confidentiality.[208]

Abercorn's interview was a formal acknowledgement by government of landlord rights to consultation, rather than a negotiation over substantive issues: when Gerald Balfour met Smith-Barry and Richard Bagwell, a Liberal Unionist historian and amateur politician, their discussion focused on more practicable opportunities for progress. 'Both', reported Balfour, '[are] sound on the subject of fancy franchises and artificial safeguards [for the protection of loyalist representation]'; both, however, demanded the exclusion of 'priests'—by this they effectively meant Catholic priests—fearing that the hierarchy would otherwise dominate the proposed councils.[209] Sharing Abercorn's fear of recklessly extravagant councils, Smith-Barry and Bagwell urged on Gerald Balfour the desirability of imposing a statutory limit on the amount of road rate which district councils might levy. Anxious to conciliate these potential leaders of opposition, Balfour conceded the legitimacy of their two chief demands, and incorporated specific remedies into his proposals.[210]

Consideration of loyalist qualms helped to provide a satisfactory response from the Ulster Party when, on 21 February, the Bill was introduced into parliament; indeed William Johnston confided to his diary that the reform had been 'approved all round'.[211] It offered a range of checks, deliberately designed to relieve loyalist concern. It provided for constraints on district council expenditure: county councils possessed powers of veto over a district council's budget. Moreover, without the consent of the Local Government Board, no district council could exceed by more than 25 per cent in any one year the average of the three previous years expenditure on roads. A large agricultural grant was provided for the purpose of reducing rates on land; this was seen as a sop to the large landowners.[212] Other sops included the desired exclusion of priests through a blanket ban on all ministers of religion from membership of the councils. A focus of loyalist approval in the 1892 Bill—exclusion of police from local government control—reappeared in the Bill of 1898. And

[208] Ibid.
[209] Cadogan Papers, CAD 1265, Gerald Balfour to Cadogan, 16 Dec. 1897.
[210] The cabinet was less enthusiastic than Gerald Balfour: Gailey, *Death of Kindness*, 47-8.
[211] WJD, D 880/2/50, 21 Feb. 1898.
[212] Horace Plunkett Diaries, 21 Feb. 1898. Russell, *Ireland and the Empire*, 197.

the landlord-dominated Grand Juries, still responsible for county administration, were given a transitory power of self-perpetuation: rather than suffer immediate abolition, they had the right of nomination to three seats on the first County Councils.[213]

The more extreme Irish Unionist members declared themselves to be under pressure to resist the Bill.[214] Representation of this pressure was, however, a useful warning to government in a tradition of similar warnings of the state of public opinion—given, for example, by T. W. Russell in the land debates: popular pressure on the local government issue evidently did not particularly influence the Ulster Party itself. W. E. H. Lecky, who had spoken against the Bill in its early stages, but who had been ultimately converted to half-hearted approval, shrugged off local agitation to maintain resistance.[215] Edward Saunderson variously characterized Irish Unionist opinion as being at first wholly indifferent, and then a little later largely opposed to the Bill.[216] Such inconsistency did little for the Irish Unionist case, which was really designed to restrain the government from radical excess.

In general Saunderson gave a qualified acceptance to the measure, though he hinted at the need for amendment. Here he was refuted by the populist Conservative member for East Down, James Rentoul, who condemned any suggested 'mutilation': if change had to be made, it should, he argued, serve to widen the scope of the Bill rather than otherwise.[217] Saunderson's coolness survived the Second Reading, but he confessed his support for the Bill as 'the inevitable sequitur to the policy of the Unionist Party', now that Ireland appeared peaceful; and he disavowed, for himself and for his party, 'factious opposition'.[218]

It was left to an Irish Liberal Unionist, W. E. H. Lecky, junior member for Trinity College, Dublin, to offer the most critical reception.[219] Like other speakers from the Irish Unionist party, Lecky pledged his support for the measure—but his approval ended with this pledge. The remainder of his speech, on 21 March, during the Second Reading, was a detailed and testy critique of the principles

[213] Hansard, 4th ser. (1898), liii. 1246.
[214] Ibid. lxii. 162 (Saunderson) and 553 (Londonderry).
[215] W. E. H. Lecky Papers, 1832/1704, Lecky to Greer (copy), 5 Apr. 1898.
[216] Hansard 4th ser. (1898), lv. 492; Ibid. lxii. 162.   [217] Ibid. 438.
[218] Ibid. 497–8.   [219] Ibid. 455. Lecky, Memoir, 317.

and practice of the Bill. Ireland, he argued, judged by any criterion, was 'as little suited for democracy as any country in Europe'.[220] But all this constituted a maverick response, the plea of an idiosyncratic conservative intellectual, rather than that of a practical, constituency-bound, Irish Unionist member. To a section of landed Unionists Lecky undoubtedly represented their innate fears at their most uncompromising; but this group, itself a small, albeit noisy, minority, had already been largely won over to the government by the negotiations of December 1897. With Saunderson, Londonderry, and Abercorn all offering more or less warm support, Lecky was isolated, and his call to reaction could safely be ignored by the government. And, by April, even he had had second thoughts.[221]

By July the ambivalence of the Ulster Party had evaporated, for the Bill had survived the Committee Stage with its checks and sops largely unimpaired. Saunderson could now laud it as a source for sectarian and class conciliation.[222] In February a *Westminster Gazette* cartoon had portrayed the Balfour brothers as two monks preaching to 'Saundersonus' and 'Johnstonus' in 'Orangeland': Saunderson's final conversion to the Local Government Bill suggests the greater subtlety of government proselytizing in 1898, than over the Land Bill in 1896.[223]

Ulster constituency opinion had shown comparatively little interest in local government reform, whereas it followed, and pre-empted the course of land politics with unabated enthusiasm. Constituency apathy allowed Ulster members a greater freedom of action on local government than they ever possessed on rural questions. The government could not rely on sympathetic Ulster opinion to quell loyalist dissent in parliament—and nor could it show the same disregard for loyalist parliamentary opinion over local government as it had occasionally shown to such opposition on land questions. Both local government bills, in 1892 and (to a lesser extent) 1898, embodied restrictions which had been tailored to accommodate Irish Unionist wishes. Potentially dissident Unionist opinion had been carefully canvassed before the introduction of the 1898 Bill, and its particular concerns were deliberately treated. Government solicitude, both in principle and in substance, disarmed die-hard Unionist

[220] Lecky, *Memoir,* 317.   [221] Ibid.
[222] Hansard, 4th ser. (1898), lxii. 163.
[223] William Johnston noted the cartoon: WJD, D 880/2/50, 21 Feb. 1898.

opinion, and ensured that the radical Bill of 1898 won an almost uniformly favourable response from both reactionary and liberal elements of the Ulster Party.

Thus, the introduction of democratic local government brought no obvious or immediate change in the relationship between the parties. Yet the broader implications of reform for Ulster Unionism were very great, in that the Act of 1898 represented a further broadside against landed political authority. Unionist squires who had been well represented on the Grand Juries, all but disappeared from the new councils in the southern counties, and even within Ulster their position seems to have been undermined. Detailed analysis of the composition of the Ulster county councils remains to be undertaken, but there is substantial, if isolated, evidence which suggests that landlords were suffering a relative decline in political strength.[224].

In so far as local government reform promoted the retreat of the squires, it helped to alter the stability of the Unionist partnership. The act provoked neither a sense of outrage nor cancerous suspicion among the government's supporters in Ireland—but it would mould both the strength and, indirectly, the forms of Ulster Unionism. There was certainly little outcry; but the equanimity of northern loyalists obscured the extent of the revolution which had been enacted.

5. Catholic Higher Education

The successive efforts of Arthur Balfour and George Wyndham to provide a Catholic University in Ireland created for the Irish Unionists new external alliances and internal polarities. The debates on land legislation had generally left a small and isolated group of landed Unionists relying on sympathetic support from the Lords; discussion of the two local government bills had established considerable sympathy between a comparatively united Ulster Party and the cabinet. But the issue of Catholic university education exposed more

---

[224] For the fate of the landed chairman of the new Antrim County Council see PRONI, W. R. Young Papers, D 3027/7/8-11, 'Recollections of 75 Years in Ulster', 248-9. For the southern position see Gailey, *Death of Kindness*, 138-9; Ian d'Alton, 'Cork Unionism: Its Role in Parliamentary and Local Elections, 1885-1914', *Studia Hibernica*, xv (1975), 155-7.

fully than before the division between the liberal and Orange elements within the Ulster Party; and it revealed, too, the bond of anti-Catholicism which united the Party's Orange faction with English sectarian feeling. Over other issues, dissident elements of the Ulster Party relied for English support on class sympathizers (like Salisbury and Londonderry), or on those on the make within Conservatism (like Randolph Churchill and Walter Long). With the question of Catholic University education, however, a faction of the Ulster Party found itself in sympathy with a popular element of English Unionist opinion; and thus an issue which might have divided British and Irish Unionism never became practical politics.

At the end of the nineteenth century Irish Catholics possessed no university which combined the spiritual benefits provided by the blessing of their Church with the material benefits of government funding. The Queen's Colleges at Belfast, Cork, and Galway, grouped in 1850 into the Queen's University in Ireland, had been condemned as 'godless' by the formidable combination of Pius IX, O'Connell, and the Irish bishops; and subsequent efforts to provide a more tolerable institution had either foundered, as in 1873, or proved wholly inadequate.[225] In 1854 the Catholic University of Ireland was established under the rectorship of Newman but, although this offered opportunities of higher education to the faithful, it served in the long term to exacerbate the Catholic grievance. For, while Newman's College struggled for funds, the Queen's Colleges enjoyed an annual subvention of around £30,000 from the public purse; and, consequently, from the perspective of the hierarchy, it seemed that impiety was being subsidized at the expense of Catholic fidelity.[226] Disraeli's creation of an examining institution, the Royal University of Ireland, mitigated some of this bitterness through providing fellowships to the Catholic University; but the real grievance remained intact by the late 1880s.[227]

Yet, even the most well-disposed or pragmatic of governments was severely restricted in what it could offer to Irish Catholic opinion. In general, ministers paid lip service to the principle that no form of denominational education should enjoy state funding, but in practice the operation of the Royal University had already violated

[225] T. W. Moody, 'The Irish University Question in the Nineteenth Century', *History*, xliii (1958), 97-9, 101.   [226] Ibid. 100.
[227] Ibid. 102.

this.[228] Moreover, all reforms still faced close scrutiny from each element of the Irish political and religious scene, and the identification of a broadly satisfactory proposal was thus tantamount to reconciling Orange with Green. Balancing the claims of Catholics with the fears and principles of Trinity College, the Presbyterians, and with Ulster Unionism in general, was the basic task of any ministerial reformer; yet successive Unionist Chief Secretaries responded to this challenge with an alacrity which bore little relation to the political dangers that they faced.

Though Arthur Balfour had been considering different proposals for a Catholic University as early as mid-1887, it was only in August 1889 that he declared to parliament his intention of dealing with the question in the near future.[229] Orange members of the Ulster Party were taken by surprise, and dismayed, but the reaction of the most extreme was swift and discouraging: William Johnston, secretary to the Party, and a member of the ruling Orange body in Ireland, immediately penned an angry letter to the *News Letter*.[230] By mid-September he was preparing resolutions for submission to a loyalist meeting—one declaring against Home Rule, and a second denouncing Balfour's proposed 'ultra-montane' university.[231] However, Ulster Party colleagues also fell victim to Johnston's unrestrained suspicion: William Ellison-Macartney, more moderate than Johnston, jocularly reported to Balfour that 'Ballykilbeg looks upon me as hopelessly entangled in the embraces of the scarlet lady'.[232] And this gradation of opinion, even among Orange MPs, heralded later and more comprehensive divisions within the Ulster Party.

If the potential opponents of Balfour's scheme were divided, then his supporters within loyalism were no more easily identifiable. One recurrent theme within the otherwise tortuous history of the university issue was the uncertainty of Balfour's Presbyterian backing. Presbyterian academics, though an obvious source of advice for government, frequently, if unintentionally, misrepresented the

---

[228] Moody, 'University Question', 102.
[229] Curtis, *Coercion and Conciliation*, 389. Moody, 'University Question', 104.
[230] WJD, D 880/2/42, 29 Aug. 1889.
[231] Ibid., 18–19 Sept. 1889.
[232] ABP, Add. MS 49845, fo. 38, W. G. Ellison-Macartney to Balfour, 23 Nov. 1889.

broader views of their church, while the opinions of the Presbyterian moderators, who held office for one year only, developed
with each successive incumbent. In 1885 and 1888, J. L.
Porter, President of Queen's College, Belfast, had argued for
the creation of a Catholic teaching university, and the expansion
of Queen's College, Belfast, into a University of Ulster.[233] This,
as Balfour subsequently pleaded, had provided the basis for
his ideas in 1889, and yet the Presbyterians of the Ulster
Party, and in the General Assembly of the Church, remained
highly sceptical.[234] The uncertainty within the ranks of the Presbyterian command, in combination with the firmer opposition
of leading members of the Church of Ireland, represented a
major obstacle to Balfour's ambitions.[235] For so long as he failed
to engage Presbyterian sympathies, Balfour could not possess
a broad enough consensus in Ireland to float any specific
proposal.

Also, the nervous reaction of Irish Orangeism to Balfour's overtures
was echoed within sections of English Unionism. Many Tories were,
as Balfour himself was aware, 'outraged' by what was regarded as
a government commitment to endowed denominational higher
education.[236] H. J. Atkinson, a Nonconformist Conservative
member, warned of the electoral consequences if the scheme were
pushed; and his foreboding was corroborated by the predictions of
R. W. E. Middleton, the Party's Principal Agent.[237] Salisbury joined
the swell of Unionist misgiving.[238] First-hand expressions of local
Unionist opinion percolated through to Balfour in Orange and
Protestant Association resolutions: Lancashire Orangeism was
mobilized in support of its Irish parent-movement. Lodges in
Manchester, Preston, Liverpool, Toxteth, and Salford petitioned
Balfour in condemnation of his university statement; and they were
joined by the Baptist Union of Great Britain, the Bristol Protestant

---

[233] Moody, 'University Question', 104.
[234] ABP, Add. MS 49846, fo. 59, William Clarke, Moderator of the General
Assembly, to Balfour, 11 Feb. 1890; fo. 108, Balfour to Clarke, 27 Feb. 1890
(copy).
[235] WJD, D 880/2/42, 6 Nov. 1889. The Church of Ireland primate approved
Johnston's line.
[236] Curtis, *Coercion and Conciliation*, 390.
[237] MSPH, H. J. Atkinson to Salisbury, 18 Oct. 1889 (quoted in Curtis, *Coercion
and Conciliation*, 390).
[238] Curtis, *Coercion and Conciliation*, 390.

League, and the Scottish Protestant Alliance.[239] Even beyond the heartland of English Orangeism, Ulster extremism wielded influence. Evelyn Hubbard, Unionist candidate in the North Buckinghamshire by-election reported that he was likely to lose the support of 'one of the staunchest and most influential Unionists in the division'—a Buckinghamshire landowner and Irish Protestant—unless he pledged that he 'would not oppose the Irish loyalist party' on the university question; Hubbard, in turn, looked to Balfour for reassurance.[240]

Among Liberal Unionists Balfour found little compensating support. Joseph Chamberlain had offered a tentative and preliminary approval for Balfour's plans, but Hartington had swiftly intervened to urge restraint.[241] Promising his silence, Chamberlain suggested that English Liberal Unionists would take their cue from expressions of opinion in Ulster—and, unless 'the Ulstermen' reacted in anger, 'I do not think that any considerable proportion of the Liberal Unionists will object'.[242] However, Chamberlain was evidently extrapolating from his own lack of interest. In reality, the bonds between English and Irish anti-Catholicism were even more vital than he had observed; and the most dangerous complaint, as Balfour was acknowledging by mid-September, came 'rather from the no-popery middle class in England than from the Orangemen in Ireland'.[243] Chamberlain himself came to agree: writing to Balfour on 26 September, he recognized that he had misjudged the 'great vigour' of the 'old prejudices'—and he now actively counselled that the university proposals should be dropped.[244]

Those less excitable Ulster members were soothed by a declaration given by Balfour in a letter of 24 September addressed to William Ellison-Macartney. Seeking to conciliate Irish Nonconformists (whose importance he now clearly recognized), Balfour repudiated the idea of reforming Catholic higher education 'without doing

[239] ABP, Add. MS 49845, fo. 40, Secretary LOL 476 (Salford) to Balfour, 23 Sept. 1889; fo. 48, Secretary LOL 35 (Toxteth) to Balfour, 30 Sept. 1889; fo. 52, Secretary LOL 56 (Manchester) to Balfour, 30 Sept. 1889; fo. 56, Secretary LOL 182 (Liverpool) to Balfour, 1 Oct. 1889; fo. 87, Secretary, Bristol Protestant League, to Balfour; fo. 93, Secretary, Baptist Union of Great Britain, to Balfour, fo. 99, Secretary, Scottish Protestant Alliance to Balfour.
[240] ABP, Add. MS 49845, fo. 29, Hubbard to Balfour, 13 Sept. 1889.
[241] JCP, JC 5/22/44, Hartington to Chamberlain, 1 Sept. 1889.
[242] JCP, JC 5/22/144, Joseph Chamberlain to Hartington, 3 Sept. 1889 (copy). See the fragmentary quotation in Garvin and Amery, Life, ii. 426.
[243] MSPH, E/Balfour/290, Balfour to Salisbury, 17 Sept. 1889.
[244] ABP, Add. MS 49773, fo. 18, Chamberlain to Balfour, 26 Sept. 1889.

something for the presbyterians as well'.[245] He confessed the strength of opposition to his proposals, and hinted, reluctantly, at their probable abandonment: 'if we cannot carry the Party, there is no point in making the attempt'. Confirmation that the university scheme had been dropped did not reach the Ulster Party until the beginning of November, but it had long been evident that the proposal involved too many risks to be worthwhile.[246]

This would remain true for later Unionist efforts at tackling the Irish university dilemma. The issue was thrashed out within the Commons in January 1897, and again in February 1898, but division and embarrassment inside the Party were the only obvious outcome. Each debate revealed a considerable cleavage within the Ulster Party between hardline Orange elements led by Saunderson and William Johnston, and more liberal members, who broadly supported Balfour and the concept of a national Catholic university: these included W. E. H. Lecky and Edward Carson.[247] But such divisions did not leave the die-hards isolated, as had occurred over other issues like land; rather they retained sympathy with an important body of parliamentary and ministerial feeling, and so helped to maintain a veto on Balfour's efforts towards progress on the university issue.

In the debate of January 1897, Balfour dissociated himself from William Johnston's vitriolic condemnation of Catholic claims.[248] The other main Ulster Party contributor at this time was W. E. H. Lecky, who, predictably more moderate on the university question than on local government, found himself in general agreement with Balfour. Lecky's main concern as member for Trinity College was its preservation from interference—the maintenance of its 'national and unsectarian character'. But even he registered his approval of non-denominational education (and, by inference, his suspicion of any endowed Catholic institution).[249] Given the warmth of the opposition, and the qualms of moderates like Lecky, Balfour was forced to concede that a settlement could not yet be attempted.

---

[245] ABP, Add. MS 49828, fo. 355, Balfour to Ellison-Macartney, 24 Sept. 1889. Macartney Papers, D 3649/20/32, Balfour to Macartney, 24 Sept. 1889.
[246] WJD, D 880/2/41, 6 Nov. 1889. Lord Arthur Hill privately informed Johnston that the university scheme had been dropped.
[247] Marjoribanks and Colvin, Lord Carson, i. 273. Lecky, Memoir, 314.
[248] WJD, D 880/2/49, 22 Jan. 1897.
[249] Lecky, Memoir, 291.

Orange and other expressions of disapproval may have temporarily
pre-empted the launching of any proposal, but Balfour's commitment
to a government-funded, predominantly Catholic university remained
intact. Despite the discouragement of January, he subsequently
commissioned the Catholic William Kenny, Irish Unionist member
for St Stephen's Green, Dublin, and Solicitor-General for Ireland,
to compile a memorandum on alternative schemes of denominational
higher education.[250] Kenny, however, stressed the very dangerous
political consequences of pushing the issue—not only for Unionist
support in the north of Ireland, but also, as Balfour already knew
from his experience in 1889, for support in England. Furthermore,
the government's hopes of a deal with the Catholic hierarchy
were, Kenny reported, quite unfounded: the desired barter of
a university settlement for a public commitment from the hierarchy
to law and order would never be accepted, and could never be
effective.[251] Kenny's report merely confirmed the magnitude of the
difficulties which Balfour faced, and the extent of the latter's
isolation. Kenny's personal circumstances gave his opinion special
significance, but his forecast of northern Unionist opinion
contributed to the confusion of advice which Balfour was receiving
on this score. And his report was set aside as soon as an opportunity
emerged to reopen the university question.

When Catholic education was again debated in February 1898,
Balfour confirmed his approval of the Irish demands. Orange Ulster
members were enraged at their leader's persistence, William Johnston
confiding with dark piety to his diary that Balfour had again 'given
utterance to unsound sentiment'.[252] Such unrest was given point by
the more material threats of Ellison-Macartney, the Financial
Secretary to the Admiralty, who privately warned the First Lord,
Goschen, that he would resign if the government committed
itself to establishing a Catholic University.[253] And resignation
scaremongering now emerged at a cabinet level: Walter Long,
President of the Board of Agriculture, and an Orange ally, reported
to Cadogan the cabinet conviction that 'any attempt to legislate on
the university question would break up the party'.[254]

[250] Whittingehame, Arthur Balfour Papers, TD 83/113/32/41, memorandum on
a Catholic university by William Kenny, 3 May 1897.
[251] Ibid.   [252] WJD, D 880/2/50, 16 Feb. 1898.
[253] Ibid., 9 Feb. 1898.
[254] Cadogan Papers, CAD 1309, Long to Cadogan, 18 Feb. 1898.

By the spring of 1898, Balfour found that he had been isolated by a combination of government ministers, Orangemen, and the anti-papist middle-classes. He deplored, and was repelled by Orange bigotry, but now he could not afford to forget that such narrowness was also the characteristic of elements of the English party. Thus, in terms of the broader relationship between loyalism and English Unionism, Balfour's tenacity had as yet brought little change. If there was schism, then it was as much between Balfour and his own support, as between English and Irish Unionist.

Balfour, however, clung to his belief that a consensus of approval in Ireland would nullify all opposition from within the English party to his proposals.[255] Before the spring of 1898, despite the deceiving indications of Presbyterian pleasure, such a consensus had proved elusive, but significant shifts within the hierarchy and the General Assembly soon suggested that it was not unattainable. In June 1897 the Catholic bishops had published a statement moderating their stand on the university question; and in March 1898 the Presbyterian General Assembly responded by indicating that, while it still rejected the preferential endowment of one form of denominational education, support for all the main forms would be more tolerable.[256] This last had been the principle behind Balfour's plans in 1889, and he remained committed to balancing Catholic and Presbyterian claims. The redefinition of these claims in 1897–8 appeared to bring the university question into the realms of practical politics; and accordingly Balfour sought to investigate the extent of the agreement which was emerging in Ireland.

In October 1898 R. B. Haldane, who had been associated with reform of the University of London, travelled to Ireland on behalf of Balfour in order to canvass opinion on the university question.[257] Haldane placed the outlines of a scheme before several ecclesiastical and political leaders, and discussed the possible creation of two Irish universities out of the existing Queen's College Belfast and University

---

[255] CAB 37/48/82, memorandum on Irish University Education by A. J. Balfour, 12 Nov. 1898.

[256] Moody, 'University Question', 104. CAB 37/48/77, 'The Irish University Question: Memorandum written by Mr. Haldane at the request of Mr. Arthur Balfour', 20 Oct. 1898.

[257] CAB 37/48/77, 'The Irish University Question'. Dudley Sommer, *Haldane of Cloan: His Life and Times, 1856–1928* (London, 1960), 98–100.

College Dublin (the former Catholic University). The highlight of
the visit, to judge by the evidence of Haldane's autobiography, was
a pilgrimage to the Ara Coeli and Cardinal Logue, but in the long
term Haldane's negotiations in Belfast were no less revealing and
influential.[258] For Haldane left the north convinced that 'the leading
men in Ulster would probably turn out to be supporters of the
scheme', and he conveyed this judgement to Balfour.[259] When the
reform proposal was published, in January 1899, it became clear
that Haldane's optimism, like earlier assessments of Ulster opinion,
had been an over-simplification; and that, accordingly, Balfour was
attempting to build upon a consensus which did not exist.[260]

Haldane had accurately identified the divisions within the
parliamentary Ulster Party over the university scheme, and Balfour in
turn had emphasized to the cabinet the fact that seven Irish Unionist
MPs were committed to a reform.[261] But divisions between the
loyalist leadership and its support, and gradations of opinion within
Presbyterianism, were less clearly observed, with the consequence that
Balfour's scheme won a cooler reception in Ulster than might have
been predicted from Haldane's intelligence. Orange opposition to a
Catholic university remained a vital political phenomenon, which MPs
like Horace Plunkett defied at their peril.[262] Furthermore, Haldane
and Balfour had also exaggerated the importance of Thomas Hamilton,
president of Queen's College Belfast, as a representative of Presbyterian
feeling; and Haldane had allowed Hamilton's enthusiasm to infect the
report which he submitted to Balfour and the cabinet.[263] In reality,
Hamilton spoke only for the Queen's Presbyterians, a minority who
were prepared to tolerate both an effectively Catholic university and
the status of Trinity College, in return for the aggrandisement of their
own institution. However, the limitations of Hamilton's advice only
became clear much later, and even subsequent Unionist
administrations continued to seek his opinion, and be misled.[264]

[258] R. B. Haldane, *An Autobiography* (London, 1929), 124–34.
[259] CAB 37/48/77, 'The Irish University Question'.
[260] Gailey, *Death of Kindness*, 129–30.
[261] CAB 37/48/77, 'The Irish University Question'. CAB 37/48/82, 'The Irish
University Question', 12 Nov. 1898.
[262] Trevor West, *Horace Plunkett, Cooperation and Politics: An Irish Biography*
(Gerrard's Cross, 1986), 57.
[263] CAB 37/48/77, 'The Irish University Question', CAB 37/48/82, 'The Irish
University Question'.
[264] See n. 291.

In immediate practical terms these misjudgements were of less importance than the opinion of the cabinet. On 18 November 1898 Balfour submitted a draft bill, together with Haldane's memorandum, to his ministerial colleagues. He based his defence of the proposals both upon their intrinsic merit, and the thread bare cry of the constructive Unionists that 'a failure to pass such a measure would be a plain admission that, on some subjects at least, a Unionist parliament could not legislate for Ireland'.[265] But defending the credibility of Unionism proved less of an anxiety than maintaining the unity of the party, and the cabinet greeted the proposal with polite scepticism. Even Balfour's supporters felt—with some justification— that he had glossed over the extent of opposition; while opponents like Walter Long, though piously lauding the ingenuity of Balfour's plan, firmly recommended that it should be shelved.[266] Already under pressure from extreme Protestants in his Liverpool West Derby constituency, Long warned against the agitation 'which would develop when it becomes known that a Catholic university is to be established, and nothing is to be done about ritualism'.[267] Practical politics told against the bill, and ministers, swayed rather by electoral realities than by Balfour's ideals, vetoed his proposal.

Balfour made public his opinions in January 1899, but the response, especially in Ireland, was scarcely more encouraging than that offered in the cabinet. Russell and Carson each provided a qualified welcome, while warning that the proposed Belfast university would excite considerable Presbyterian opposition.[268] The extent to which Hamilton was out of touch with popular sentiment was only now gradually exposed; and it was repeatedly emphasized both to Balfour, and in the press, that the majority of Presbyterians sought the affiliation of their Queen's College to the University of Dublin, and would be dissatisfied with any scheme which did not touch Trinity College.[269] Presbyterian resentment of the Anglican

---

[265] CAB 37/48/82, 12 Nov. 1898.

[266] ABP, Add. MS 49831, fo. 5, Cadogan to Gerald Balfour, 18 Nov. 1898; Add. MS 49776, fos. 10, Long to Balfour, 27 Nov. 1898.

[267] ABP, Add. MS 49776, fo. 10, Long to Balfour, 27 Nov. 1898. Stanley Salvidge, *Salvidge of Liverpool: Behind the Political Scene, 1890–1928* (London, 1934), 33.

[268] ABP, Add. MS 49709, fo. 97, Carson to Balfour, 28 Jan. 1899; Add. MS 49853, fo. 31, Russell to Balfour, 27 Jan. 1899.

[269] ABP, Add. MS 49709, fo. 100, Carson to Balfour, 21 Feb. 1899, enclosing (fo. 102) a memorandum by George Salmon, Provost of Trinity. See also Cadogan Papers, CAD 1492, Lecky to Cadogan, 16 Feb. 1899.

domination within Trinity was thus a more active political force than their ambitions for the Queen's College, even though isolated academics like Hamilton might be swayed by delusions of collegiate grandeur.[270] The additional contribution of anxious representatives of Trinity, like Provost Salmon, ensured that Balfour's plans were finally and effectively scuppered.[271]

Where Gerald Balfour as Chief Secretary had displayed little personal interest in the university question, his successor, George Wyndham, took up the cause with an almost reckless zeal. Various breezy definitions of his objectives in office featured a Catholic university. To his brother he confided in December 1901: 'I want to smash the agitation, introduce a Land Bill, get money for a harbour-fishing policy in the West, and float a Catholic University'.[272] In January 1902 he wrote to his father, expressing similar goals, with equally breath-taking confidence. And, in November 1902, in a memorandum written for Balfour (*A Policy for Ireland*), he reiterated his commitment to Catholic higher education.[273]

Yet Wyndham's confidence did not reflect any lessening of the difficulties with university reform. For, as under his predecessors, the fate of any scheme still rested with the construction of an intricate consensus between the Catholic church and English and Irish Unionists. And, as in the past, the key to this consensus was judged to lie in a reconciliation of Presbyterian and Catholic aspirations. Wyndham affirmed that he 'would do nothing' without Irish Unionist assent, but in practice, given the solidity of Orange opposition, this meant mollifying Presbyterianism.[274] There remained the related problem of the attitude of Trinity College, but in the past its position had been defined more readily than that of popular opinion in the

---

[270] ABP, Add. MS 49853, fo. 34, Balfour to Hamilton, 30 Jan. 1899 (copy). These animosities should be seen in a broader context of Presbyterian anti-Anglican feeling: J. R. B. McMinn, 'The Myth of "Route" Liberalism in County Antrim, 1869-1900', *Eire-Ireland*, xvii. 1 (Spring 1982), 102. McMinn, 'The Reverend James Brown Armour and Liberal Politics in North Antrim, 1869-1914', Ph.D. thesis (Belfast, 1979), 333.

[271] ABP, Add. MS 49709, fo. 102, memorandum by George Salmon, [Feb. 1899].

[272] Mackail and Wyndham (edd.), *Letters*, ii. 434, 436.

[273] ABP, Add. MS 49804, fo. 96, memorandum, 'A Unionist Policy for Ireland', by George Wyndham. The best dissection of Wyndham's interest in Catholic higher education is in Patricia McCaffrey, 'The Wyndham University Scheme, 1903-1904', *Irish Ecclesiastical Review*, cx. 6 (Dec. 1968). Gailey, *Death of Kindness*, 198-201.

[274] Mackail and Wyndham (edd.), *Letters*, ii. 471.

north. Thus, like his mentor, Arthur Balfour, Wyndham started from the assumption that no Catholic reform could be countenanced 'without doing something for the Presbyterians as well'.[275] In terms of political strategy this meant disrupting any united loyalist opposition, by isolating irreconcilable Orange elements. Moreover, by securing Presbyterian allegiance to any scheme of reform there was a greater chance that English opinion might prove favourable. Lastly, the centrality of Presbyterianism within Wyndham's calculations was made necessary through the development of its anti-Anglican sentiment, and through its more active animosity towards Trinity.[276]

The impossibility of achieving complete Irish Unionist approval for any reform was underlined when Lord Robertson's Royal Commission on University Education reported in the spring of 1903.[277] Much of the force of the Report was lost through the many disagreements which its findings encompassed; but the majority recommendation that a Catholic College be created in Dublin, linked with the Queen's Colleges into the Royal University, provoked uproar among Irish Unionist MPs.[278] Opposition was led by the younger, hardline generation—yet even parliamentary veterans like R. T. O'Neill, while proclaiming moderation, were no less discouraging than their junior colleagues.[279] However, apart from the bile of a C. C. Craig, there was little that was novel in this reaction, and there can have been little surprise or disappointment in the Irish Office. More intriguing, given the fervent adherence of advisors like Hamilton to the Haldane scheme, was a report submitted by the Presbyterian church to the Commission in which Anglican control of Trinity College Dublin was held up as an affront to Catholic and dissenting opinion.[280] The brief of the Robertson Commission had not embraced Trinity, but it was clear that any scheme which left the College untouched would be unlikely to engage Presbyterian support.

The publication of the Commission's Report occurred when Wyndham was preoccupied with his Land Bill, and consideration

---

[275] See n. 245.

[276] A. J. Megahey, 'The Irish Protestant Churches and Social and Political Issues, 1870–1914', Ph.D. thesis (Belfast, 1969), 200.

[277] Moody, 'University Question', 105.

[278] *BNL*, 14 Apr. 1903 (O'Neill at Ballymena; R. H. Wallace at Spa); *BNL*, 17 Apr. 1903 (Craig at Lisburn).

[279] *BNL*, 17 Apr. 1903 (O'Neill).

[280] Megahey, 'Protestant Churches', 197–9. CAB 1483, 1903, report of the Royal Commission on University Education in Ireland.

of its implications was deferred to the autumn of 1903. He set down his ambitions within the sphere of Catholic higher education only in September 1903, when he outlined a variant of the Robertson recommendation.[281] But in the discreet negotiations which subsequently took place between the Castle and representatives of the Irish churches, the Robertson scheme was swiftly dropped in favour of a plan to amalgamate Queen's College Belfast, Trinity College, and a new Catholic College into the University of Dublin.[282] In this dramatic shift of purpose two problems have been identified: firstly, why did Wyndham change his mind, adopting a solution which he knew that spokesmen for Trinity found objectionable? Secondly, why given his repeated concern for Trinity, did he ultimately treat its sensitivities so brutally?[283]

Clearly the Irish government's priorities in seeking a settlement were partly determined by Sir Antony MacDonnell, Wyndham's Under-Secretary, who favoured the University of Dublin scheme. It has also been suggested that Wyndham cared less about the final shape of reform than about the need to weaken the claims of the hierarchy over any new Catholic college.[284] But this priority raises the issue of the Presbyterian influence over Wyndham's attitude, an influence which has been rarely considered, but which may help to elucidate some of the complexities of the negotiations in late 1903. For at the heart of Presbyterian doubts about university reform was the fear that the government would create a college, whose denominational status would be acknowledged through its constitution.[285] Thus, only by forcing the bishops to surrender their claims to *de jure* representation on the governing body of any new College, could Wyndham set Presbyterian, and English, qualms to rest.

The importance of winning all varieties of Protestant assent was frequently acknowledged by Wyndham, but the opinion of Presbyterians was a major preoccupation in the autumn of

ABP, Add. MS 49804, fo. 181, Wyndham to Balfour, 17 Sept. 1903 (quoted in Mackail and Wyndham (edd.), *Letters*, ii. 467).

[282] McCaffrey, 'Wyndham University Scheme', 330.

[283] Ibid., and Gailey, *Death of Kindness*, 201.

[284] McCaffrey, 'Wyndham University Scheme', 348.

[285] Bodleian Library, Antony MacDonnell Papers, MS Eng. Hist. c351, fo. 49, J. MacDermott to MacDonnell, 16 Jan. 1904.

1903.[286] This was all the more true because of the attitude of influential and extreme loyalists like Lord Londonderry and Saunderson, the latter of whom threatened to reject the Tory whip in the event of any proposal for a denominational college.[287] Prominent Presbyterians dismissed 'the bluster of the Orangemen', and Wyndham was equally unimpressed, yet without the active support of any alternative body of northern opinion, it was likely that such bluster would assume disproportionate significance.[288] Wyndham was thus anxious to conciliate the Presbyterian church, and to extract a definite commitment of support; and it can scarcely have been coincidental that the scheme which was eventually floated followed recent Presbyterian demands.

If Wyndham's efforts were partly designed to win the active allegiance of the Presbyterians, then he was swiftly disillusioned. Although Thomas Hamilton offered consistently encouraging reports of likely support, this enthusiasm was never reflected in the attitude of the General Assembly.[289] Opinion there remained bitterly divided, and while a shaky unanimity might emerge around certain gut attitudes— fears of denominationalism, fears of Trinity—it was more difficult to build these beliefs into a coherent policy on education.[290] It seems clear that Wyndham was seriously misled by Hamilton's optimism, and indeed one of the Chief Secretary's aides, Murray Hornibrook, subsequently lamented that they had taken 'Hamilton as representing presbyterian opinion in 1904, but apparently he did not, and does not . . .'[291]

Thus, when on 14 January 1904 the reform proposal was publicly floated under the name of Lord Dunraven, there was no significant demonstration of Presbyterian support.[292] Instead, extreme loyalism in the shape of Lord Londonderry was able to gain the initiative, and to lay Wyndham's efforts swiftly to rest. On 22 January 1904 Londonderry chaired a Unionist meeting in Dublin, and publicly

---

[286] Mackail and Wyndham (edd.), *Letters*, ii. 471. MacDonnell Papers, MS Eng. Hist. c351, fo. 15, Hamilton to MacDonnell, 12 Nov. 1903; fo. 17, Hamilton to MacDonnell, 17 Nov. 1903, fo. 113, Sinclair to MacDonnell, 15 Jan. 1904.

[287] McCaffrey, 'Wyndham University Scheme', 334.

[288] MacDonnell Papers, MS Eng. Hist. c351, fo. 15, T. Hamilton to MacDonnell, 12 Nov. 1903.

[289] Ibid., fo. 113, Thomas Sinclair to MacDonnell, 15 Jan. 1904.

[290] Ibid., also fo. 49, J. MacDermott to MacDonnell, 16 Jan. 1904.

[291] Private Possession, Papers of George Wyndham, Hornibrook to Wyndham, 17 Feb. 1907.

[292] McCaffrey, 'Wyndham University Scheme', 342.

proclaimed that the government had no intention of reforming university education.[293] This placed Wyndham in an impossible position. He had no cabinet authority to repudiate Londonderry's assertion; and in any case to reveal publicly the nature of his recent diplomacy would have been to create a political uproar. On the other hand, to confirm the government's lack of interest was to destroy all credibility among those with whom he had been secretly negotiating. Faced with this unenviable choice, Wyndham opted to confirm Londonderry's declaration, and thus to surrender his ambitions.[294]

The Balfourian commitment to a Catholic university received a final public airing in April 1905. In the Unionist parliament's last debate on the subject, the Irish loyalist case was represented by John Gordon, the Presbyterian Liberal Unionist member for South Londonderry: Gordon reiterated his Church's hostility to the principle of endowed denominational education, claiming that greater sectarian segregation would be the inevitable by-product of any college designed for Catholics.[295] This unequivocal repudiation from a representative Presbyterian emphasized the extent of the government's failure to mobilize potential support within Irish Unionism. In 'a speech of impotence and despair', Balfour conceded this failure, admitting that he had been unable to convert the cabinet, the Commons, or the Unionist public to the reform.[296] He reaffirmed his commitment to a Catholic University—but admitted that, given the strength of opposition, there was little likelihood of more material achievement. His evident distress was a fitting epitaph to fifteen years of abortive negotiation.

Walter Long and Londonderry had represented cabinet opposition to Balfour at its most extreme; the Orange members from Ulster, especially Saunderson and Johnston, demonstrated the limits of bitterness in the Commons. But Balfour's real failure lay, not in the continued opposition of these traditional exponents of the Conservative right, but rather in the scepticism of potentially more susceptible and moderate elements. The equivocation of Irish Presbyterians thwarted efforts to isolate extreme Orange opinion,

[293] ABP, MS 49804, fo. 203, Wyndham to Balfour, 18 Jan. 1904. *BNL*, 23 Jan. 1904.
[294] Hansard, 4th ser. (1904), cxxix. 233.
[295] Hansard, 4th ser. (1905), cxlv. 117.
[296] Ibid. 133. See also *The Annual Register for 1905*, 131.

and helped to provide continued justification for the sectarian doubts of English sympathizers.

Balfour was only half correct, therefore, in identifying the true obstacles to progress as British, rather than Ulster Unionism—for the two blocs of opinion were not wholly separate.[297] British Unionist feeling, especially in Orange Lancashire, looked for guidance on Irish questions to Ulster, just as Lord Londonderry looked to Ulster Orangeism to provide one element of his political testament and support. English militant Protestantism and Orangeism looked with favour on the opinions of their Irish brethren; British Nonconformist Unionists were thought by leading cabinet members to be influenced by their Irish co-religionists. English sympathy for Ulster opinion could never be an independent obstacle for government, since it was not, by definition, an independent phenomenon. That there was division in the English party over Catholic university education merely reflected the confusion among Ulster Unionist representatives; and this in turn meant that the issue never really threatened the integrity of the relationship between the parties.

It was left to Augustine Birrell to square the sectarian circle by carrying a reform of university education. Yet though, in the context of Tory failure, the Irish Universities Act of 1908 seemed a startling achievement, the reality was more conventional.[298] Tories like Balfour and Wyndham had failed because they had sought the chimera of political consensus. Birrell, on the other hand, harboured fewer political sensitivities, and he was free from the constraints which encumbered his Unionist predecessors. For Ulster loyalists the substance of Birrell's reform was of less importance than its origins within the Home Rule ministry. But, if their uproar was partly a tactical phenomenon, then Birrell was no less devoted to the spirit of party, baiting and mocking his loyalist opponents with relish. By the time of the third Home Rule Bill, Irish Unionist MPs could look back upon a period of Liberal government which, in contrast to the

[297] Ibid. 143.
[298] Cf. Patricia Jalland, 'A Liberal Chief Secretary and the Irish Question: Augustine Birrell, 1907-1914', *HJ*, xix. 2 (1976), 431. Leon O'Broin, *The Chief Secretary: Augustine Birrell in Ireland* (London, 1969), 21-4. For the Irish Unionist reaction see *BNL*, 22 Feb. 1908 (C. C. Craig at Glenavy); 17 Apr. 1908 (Moore and Craig at Antrim); 21 Apr. 1908 (Moore at Portadown); 15 May 1908 (London letter); 1 June 1908 (London letter); 14 July 1908 (James Craig at Comber).

trimming administrations of Gerald Balfour and George Wyndham, was characterized by rigid partisanship. The debate on the Irish Universities Bill, while temporarily firing the zeal of Orange extremists, ultimately helped to convince a broad body of Unionist opinion that their presence in parliament was of little consequence.[299]

6. *Summary*

The essential problem in the parties' relationship lay with their mutual inability to sustain a consistent programme for Ireland which attracted the approval of all their support. Thus, the partnership could never be simple, or easily definable, because neither British nor Irish Unionism was a homogeneous bloc of opinion. As electoral alliances, each spanned a broad range of thought (or lack of it) on the problems of Irish government. Neither could, or did, offer a single, systematic definition of what they expected from government.

British Conservative leaders—even before Liberal Unionists were fully incorporated into government—sought to create a consensus on Irish affairs between the most 'advanced' radical and the most crusty Tory. Arthur Balfour's 'kicks and ha'pence' policy of Irish government was thus less a consistent programme than a pragmatic effort to balance a series of divergent party political commitments.[300] His achievement in Ireland was his success with this balance—persuading British radicals and Irish Presbyterians that Westminster rule could achieve as much as any Parnellite or Gladstonian alternative; persuading Tory landowners and Orangemen that the cause of Union was more important than the concessions made on its behalf. Later Conservative Chief Secretaries were less dexterous than Balfour, partly because they were less sensitive to the implications of internal opposition. Indeed, with the bogey of Home Rule in the background, the particular need for such sensitivity had apparently disappeared. Problems of Irish administration, and the temptations of millenarian reform, assumed greater significance than the parochial worries of Irish Unionist MPs.

However, like Balfour, the Conservative front-bench in general recognized the need to keep faith with its Irish colleagues, and

[299] See ch. 7.
[300] This is Peter Davis's conclusion in his 'Liberal Unionist Party', 103.

especially when Home Rule seemed imminent. Indeed, much of the force of the Conservative defence of the Union sprang from the prospective plight of the 'loyal minority' under a Home Rule government, and much of the self-justification of Liberal Unionism centred, too, on the problem of Ulster—in Chamberlain's assessment, 'a terrible nut for the G.O.M. to crack'.[301] The significance of Ulster in British Unionist rhetoric provided loyalist representatives with influence; and the support of some or all Ulster MPs was important for British party credibility.

But Ulster's political significance, and therefore British Conservative sympathy, were partly contingent on the immediacy of the Home Rule threat. The reasonable, though still incomplete, solidarity between loyalist and Conservative in the years 1886–93 gradually disintegrated after the seemingly conclusive defeat of the second Home Rule Bill. When the first real test of the partnership appeared, in 1896, with the Irish Land Bill, two areas of fracture emerged: internally, between fellow Irish Unionist members, and externally between some Irish Unionists and the Conservative command. Partial unity within Unionism was restored only by the apparent reappearance of the Home Rule threat in 1904. But in 1904, for the first time since 1884, the Conservative leadership (or, at any rate, part of it) was held to be the source of the threat; and the Ulster Party showed that it was prepared to ditch these leaders in order to promote internal unity.[302] As always, the failure of the partnership, and of a parliamentary policy, was reflected in the redirection of loyalist energies into the constituencies of Ulster.

A commitment to the Union was not the only, though it was certainly the most obvious, bond between the British and Irish parties. In the 1880s, within the House of Commons, each was distinguished by the strength of its landed lobby, and thus landownership—specifically landownership in Ireland—constituted a further link in the chain of alliance. But, as with Home Rule, the significance of landed parliamentary representation was on the wane, and this in turn affected relations between the parties. Where the Unionist party had once been virtually a forum for the propertied élite, this was no longer so apparent by 1900; and the growing ascendancy of local political pressures within the Irish movement

---

[301] Devonshire Papers, 340/2152, Joseph Chamberlain to Hartington, 27 Oct. 1887.   [302] See ch. 6.

further helped to imperil the consensus of privilege. Middle-class representatives of Ulster Unionism, while sharing many of the opinions of their English counterparts, do not seem to have been so fully at ease within British politics as their landed predecessors, and they were in any case more completely restrained by local party organization.

Two other circumstances combined to weaken the Ulster Unionist influence within British Conservatism. British Conservatives, and Liberal Unionists, alone paid lip service to the loyalist cause, and this meant that loyalists could only realistically expect political redress from these colleagues.[303] A second factor thwarting Ulster ascendancy lay in the unstable nature of the alliance between Irish Conservatives and Liberal Unionists. Presbyterian tenant farmers joined with Anglican landowners in an electoral marriage whose only successful function was defence of the Union; over many other issues, the putative allies followed their own sectarian or economic interests. The landlord-leader of the Ulster Party, Edward Saunderson, conceded its limitations by stressing the single area of unity: 'that is that we should never permit hon. Gentlemen opposite [the Nationalists] to rule over us'.[304] Thus, Conservative policy, in particular constructive Unionist measures, seldom inspired a single coherent response from loyalist Ireland, and the government was spared the agitation of a continuously united Ulster bloc. This ultimately induced a false sense of security among Tory leaders, and their complacency, in turn, promoted a dangerous disregard for certain elements within loyalism, particularly the landowners.

This disunity did not mean, however, that Ulster members focused their energies exclusively on internal feuding, for loyalist factions looked beyond their Party to the Conservative leadership for allies. Different Conservative leaders adopted and defended different points of view on Irish loyalism: Salisbury, by conviction a proponent of the rights of property, was 'the champion of the Ulster landowner interest'; Arthur Balfour, more pragmatic, was impressed by the implications for Unionism of Protestant tenant agitation.[305] From either side of the Unionist alliance came rival pressures: strong personal support for the radical Presbyterian T. W. Russell came from Chamberlain, the radical Unitarian; Walter Long and Lord Londonderry championed the landlord and Orange causes. Sectarian

---

[303] See ch. 2.   [304] Hansard, 4th ser. (1892), iv. 1610.
[305] MSPH, E/Cadogan/185, Cadogan to Salisbury, 22 Apr. 1900.

and economic sympathies governed some of these alliances, but ambitious right-wing Conservatives like Long and Londonderry did not fail to observe the political muscle represented by the Ulster Party die-hards. The politics of loyalism were indeed 'a traditional place of resort for Tory politicians temporarily needing to make a figure'— but Ulster, and the Ulster Party, offered more: rising politicians like Long were able to strengthen their position permanently by moulding Ulster Party concerns into their platform.[306]

Disunity did not, therefore, wholly negate loyalist influence within Conservatism, since the Ulster Party, even in unity, never offered any comprehensive political programme. On the contrary, the polarization of Party opinion replaced an amorphous solidarity; and this permitted leading Conservatives, who had been able to offer only general sympathy for the limited, constitutional concerns of a unified loyalism, to promote and profit from a well-defined section within the movement. Thus, Irish Unionist influence rested on personal and factional ties, parliamentary ability, and other intangibles, rather than on consistently regimented parliamentary action, or any all-embracing affection for the British party. In this way, a united Ulster Party secured the fall of Wyndham in 1905, when relations between the British and Irish Unionist commands were at their worst; and even a divided Party could contribute materially to Gerald Balfour's departure from Ireland in 1900.

[306] Foster, *Lord Randolph Churchill*, 246.

5

MP and Constituency, 1885–1911

> These were our supermen. When one of them was elected to
> Parliament we gathered around the big house to cheer, and
> perhaps get a mug of tea and a bun, but we were socially
> connected with them by a rope of sand, and industrially linked
> to their interests by a cash nexus. We drank wine from the
> common chalice on the Communion Table, but our communion
> began and ended there.
>
> Alexander Irvine[1]

1. *Introduction*

Conservatism in Ireland, no less than in Britain, responded to the
challenge of franchise reform through the reorganization of its
constituency base. The Irish Franchise Act of 1850 had encouraged
the creation of a Central Conservative Society in Dublin, which,
manned by zealous young lawyers, sent help to the northern heartland
of Toryism; the Irish Reform Act of 1868 inspired the formation of
a Central Conservative Association in Belfast. County Toryism followed
this lead with the development of registration societies, and the
discovery of a new interest in the annual revision session.[2] The
election defeat of 1880, and the prospect of a further grant of
parliamentary reform, focused attention on the remaining inadequacies
of organization—and the Ulster Constitutional Union (1880), replaced
by the Ulster Constitutional Club (1883), were each developed as a
response to the absence of a central co-ordinating body.[3]

---

[1] Alexander Irvine, *The Souls of Poor Folk* (London, 1921), 40.
[2] K. T. Hoppen, *Elections, Politics and Society in Ireland, 1832–1885* (Oxford,
1984), 33, 284. Brian M. Walker, 'Party Organisation in Ulster, 1865–1892', in Peter
Roebuck (ed.), *Plantation to Partition: Essays in Ulster History in honour of J. L.
McCracken* (Belfast, 1981), 191–210. See also Brian M. Walker, 'Parliamentary
Representation in Ulster, 1868–1886', Ph.D. thesis (Dublin, 1976).
[3] Walker, 'Parliamentary Representation', 156.

The collapse in the early 1870s of the Dublin-based Central Conservative Society had highlighted both the pressing need for co-ordination, and also the retreat of Irish Conservatism to what K. T. Hoppen has called its 'northern laager'.[4] Organizational initiative devolved from the increasingly isolated Tories of the national capital to the Protestant northern province. Southern Conservatism certainly retained parliamentary influence, as was revealed during the course of the land debates: but this was not achieved through sustained success at the polls. At the general election of 1885 no Tory was returned for any constituency outside Ulster (except Trinity)—indeed, no popular seat was captured further south than Mid-Armagh. Strong Conservative organization existed only in eastern and central Ulster, and in a very few winnable southern seats (South County Dublin, St Stephen's Green, Dublin).[5] In the majority of southern constituencies Irish Tories were resigned to permanent electoral supersession.

On the other hand, the concentration in Ulster of local Tory organization has obscured the rather limited nature of popular participation within the party structure. Where the hierarchy of committees in a constituency was fully manned (and not just paper creations for the benefit of English sponsors), political initiative came from either a local propertied élite, or, occasionally, from Belfast or London. Even—probably especially—at the times of greatest popular political awareness (the Home Rule Bill crises), Unionist constituents rarely assumed effective control of their local party organization. Between elections, and in the aftermath of the defeat of the second Home Rule Bill, even docile political participation vanished, and electoral organization in many Unionist constituencies became merely a polite fiction.

While these phenomena might have been predicted from the contemporary English experience (and, in particular, from the work of Lowell, Ostrogorski, and A. H. Birch), they appear less conventional when judged within the context of loyalist rhetoric.[6] This naturally stressed the unanimity and fervour of Unionism,

[4] Walker, 'Party Organisation', 197; Hoppen, *Elections*, 290.
[5] Walker, 'Party Organisation', 208.
[6] A. L. Lowell, *The Government of England* (rev. edn., New York, 1924), i. 498-504. A. H. Birch, *Small-Town Politics: A Study of Political Life in Glossop* (Oxford, 1959), 45-53. M. Ostrogorski, *Democracy and the Organisation of Political Parties*, (2 vols.; London, 1902), *passim*.

repudiating Nationalist insinuations that the movement was less of a popular reaction than a landed conspiracy. The reality lay, inevitably, between the extremes of interpretation; but it was ironic that Irish Unionists, who had sanctified the bond with Britain, should have been so eager to obscure the limited, and thus very British, nature of their party organization.

By the beginning of the twentieth century, the political and economic environment which had sustained this apathy gradually disintegrated; and the Irish Unionist political élite began to experience the full impact of the democratizing reforms of 1884-5.[7] This was an era of flux for the relationship between MP and constituent. In the mid- and late 1880s each was separated, not only by the effects of a shared constitutional faith (which freed a Unionist member from too close a popular interest in his beliefs or actions); but also by external agencies of control (the British Conservative Party, influential provincial leaders), and by local economic relationships (especially that of landlord and tenant). By 1900 these three barriers had altered sufficiently to allow the emergence of a movement for greater popular control of parliamentary representation. Here it is suggested that the social and political unity which characterized the mass movement against the third Home Rule Bill originated partly in a redefinition of local political relations dating back to the turn of the century.

2. Local Funding

Where constituency organization existed, whether real or nominal, it comprised a divisional committee elected by representatives from the polling districts. Each district (North Fermanagh, for example, boasted seven) contained a committee constituted probably by the voluntary attendance of electors rather than through formal election.[8] Poor social standing seems to have been no barrier to

---

[7] For the parallel English experience, see e.g. Janet Howarth, 'The Liberal Revival in Northamptonshire, 1880-1895: A Case-Study in Late Nineteenth-Century Elections', *Historical Journal*, xii. 1 (1969); 86; Peter Stansky, *Ambitions and Strategies: The Struggle for the Leadership of the Liberal Party in the 1890s* (Oxford, 1964), 295. For details of the electoral changes see B. M. Walker, 'The Irish Electorate, 1868-1915', *Irish Historical Studies*, xviii. 71 (Mar. 1973).

[8] Cf. Ostrogorski, *Democracy and Organisation*, i. 332-3.

participation at this level. As within contemporary Conservatism, most associations had a minimum annual subscription of one shilling, and thus an outlay of a penny a month allowed any Unionist to participate in local politics.[9] Mary Arnold-Forster found, in March 1891, that her husband's West Belfast Committee consisted of 'working men, living mostly in the very poor quarters of the town'.[10] Semi-literates could hold office: one such, Thomas Little of Clabby, in North Fermanagh, acted as an incoherent but prolific district secretary in 1885.[11]

In November 1885 Thomas Little's committee organized local meetings to follow the weekday services of the 'preacher' (probably the Presbyterian minister).[12] However, many other local party managers encountered greater difficulties, often because of the size of constituencies, and a disparate electorate. R. B. Phillips of the North Tyrone Unionist Association found in April 1891 that it was impossible to fix a regular day for divisional meetings because of the differing workloads of the farmers who comprised its membership.[13] T. J. Atkinson of the East Donegal Association could not organize a Unionist meeting even with the unique threat of Lord Salisbury's visit to the North West: it was, he pleaded in 1893, 'a very difficult matter in this large county to arrange a successful meeting'.[14] Frequently between elections no constituency meetings were held as the organizational hierarchy fell into abeyance. By 1900 in both North Fermanagh and Mid Armagh committees had to be reactivated by the Unionist agent; while in South Antrim the secretary of the Constitutional Association complained about the 'apathy' of a number of the local branches—'some of them being practically in a dormant condition'.[15] In these circumstances, the constituency machinery came to serve merely as a means of registering decisions taken by others: parliamentary candidates, for example,

[9] PRONI, South Antrim Constitutional Association Papers, D 2165/1/5, Constitution and Rules, 19 Feb. 1886, clause 5. Lowell, *Government*, i. 500.

[10] Trinity College Dublin, Papers of H. O. Arnold-Forster, TCD 5000/163a, Mary Arnold-Forster to Jane Forster, 31 Mar. 1891.

[11] PRONI, Falls and Hanna Papers, D 1390/26/1/1/104, Thomas Little to J. W. Dane, 13 Nov. 1885.   [12] Ibid.

[13] PRONI, In-Correspondence of the Irish Unionist Alliance, D 989 (unclassified), R. B. Phillips to Cox, 30 Apr. 1890.

[14] Private Possession, Cochrane Papers, T. J. Atkinson to Ernest Cochrane, 12 May 1893.

[15] SACA Papers, D 2165/1/5, minutes for 14 Sept. 1900. Cf. Birch, *Small-Town Politics*, 46.

were frequently confirmed in their status by divisional committees, having been chosen by an influential individual or clique.[16]

Given that in many divisions, until the late 1890s, an MP was free from organized pressure, he could neglect local representative duties with impunity. Certain practical difficulties encouraged this: oscillating between Westminster and Ulster gave an MP little time to nurse his constituency. T. L. Corbett, a popular and efficient MP for North Down, was 'very seldom' in the constituency.[17] Even the highly committed H. O. Arnold-Forster complained of the wearisome journeys from London to Belfast. These inevitably had an effect on his constituency work; though, while canvassing for his first election, and in 1893, he attended many meetings in West Belfast, this activity subsequently declined.[18] Arnold-Forster compensated for this neglect through intense activity at Westminster, but many other MPs offered neither parliamentary nor constituency service to the electorate. For most MPs contact with the constituency came, not through the committee hierarchy, but through their agent.[19] For most, in the absence of an active local political body, the nature of this contact was limited to an annual speech, handling patronage, and supplying cash.

The three nominal functions of constituency organization were to supervise and finance the registration of voters, to select the parliamentary candidates for the constituency, and to work for their election. In divided northern, and in many southern, constituencies, registration and revision work represented the chief occupation of the local party.[20] Association secretaries (Joshua Peel in Mid-Armagh, C. F. Falls in North Fermanagh) fought tenaciously for the Unionist cause at the revision sessions held in each constituency during the autumn. Success—securing the registration of party

[16] Ostrogorski, *Democracy and Organisation*, i. 447–8; Lowell, *Government*, i. 505–6; ii. 51–2.

[17] PRONI, Ronald McNeill Papers, MIC 63/2, R. G. Sharman-Crawford to McNeill, 7 Apr. 1910.

[18] Arnold-Forster Papers, TCD 5000/188, H. O. Arnold-Forster to Florence O'Brien, 22 Oct. 1893. Cf. Birch, *Small-town Politics*, 51.

[19] For the importance of the agent see Birch, *Small-Town Politics*, 47; Lowell, *Government*, i. 495–7; H. J. Hanham, *Elections and Party Management: Politics in the Time of Disraeli and Gladstone* (2nd edn., Hassocks, 1978), 233–48; Peter Marsh, *The Discipline of Popular Government: Lord Salisbury's Domestic Statecraft, 1881–1903* (Hassocks, 1978), 194. For a modern study see G. O. Comfort, *Professional Politicians: A Study of British Party Agents* (Washington, 1958).

[20] Walker, 'Party Organisation', 198–200; SACA Papers, D 2165/1/5, Constitution, clause 3.

supporters or sustaining objections against the entitlement of opponents—hinged largely on gathering detailed information about the constituency; and this, in turn, was largely a matter of local enthusiasm and the availability of funds. Success at the revision courts could pave the way to victory at the polls. Brilliant work by the South County Dublin Registration Association, funded by the ILPU, formed the basis of Horace Plunkett's victory in 1892. Careful sifting of information on West Belfast voters helped Arnold-Forster win the seat at the same general election: well-prepared electoral registers also helped his voters to weed out Nationalist personation.[21] In East Tyrone, where there was a thin Nationalist majority, a comparatively small Unionist association was brought close to insolvency by 1910 through the cost of frenzied registration work.[22]

However, in the 'no hope' constituencies the inevitability of defeat, allied with an often intense insecurity, engendered Unionist atrophy: registration work was abandoned, and a beleaguered Unionist community avoided a high political profile, fearful of Nationalist backlash.[23] The party agent in East Cavan, Thomas Chambers, found in December 1891 that Protestants who had at first greeted his registration work enthusiastically, and with offers of help, proved to be wary of any public political commitment. A bailiff called Acheson, having originally agreed to supply Chambers with information on his district, confessed three days before the revision session that his 'friends objected to him having anything to do with the matter'.[24] Another bailiff, who had given a similar promise of help, developed a strategic illness which prevented him fulfilling his commitment.[25]

In the South Donegal constituency the Unionist agent, M. C. Sinclair, was more sympathetic to his community's vulnerability. In arguing for a defensive registration policy—pursuing objections to 'bad' Nationalist votes rather than promoting Unionist claims—Sinclair offered his personal solution to the dilemma encountered

[21] Arnold-Forster Papers, TCD 5000/173, H. O. Arnold-Forster to Florence O'Brien, 18 July 1892; Walker, 'Party Organisation', 193.
[22] ETUA, D 1132/5/1, fund-raising circular, signed by Gunning-Moore, Glasgow, and Lowry of the Association, July 1910.
[23] Cork, an area of comparative strength, witnessed greater Unionist activity, though there were still problems: Ian d'Alton, 'Cork Unionism: Its Role in Parliamentary and Local Elections, 1885-1914', *Studia Hibernica*, xv (1975), 143-61.
[24] IUA Letters, D 989, T. Chambers to Cox, 8 Dec. 1891.   [25] Ibid.

by many southern Unionists: how to reconcile political principle with social survival.[26] Since Nationalist agents rarely bothered to fight the revision in largely Catholic constituencies, all names added to the register at the session would be known to be Unionists, and this would have been most unwelcome publicity for a small, minority community. At the East Cavan session of 1891, for example, the Unionists won only twenty-three claims—but on the other hand, by concentrating their resources, they sustained over 400 objections to 'bad' Nationalist votes.[27]

Fear had a northern counterpart in apathy. In some vigorously Orange constituencies there was little need for formal organization; but neglect was not simply a concomitant of strength.[28] As in the south, Ulster registration work was hampered, not by insufficient organizational verve (agents throughout Unionist Ireland were enthusiastic politicians *manqués*), but by neglect and inefficiency at a lower level of the political hierarchy. A. J. Dudgeon, a Clones solicitor with knowledge and experience of northern marginals, complained in 1892 of slapdash preparation for the revision courts. There was 'in the case of revision in the country districts . . . no such thing as a proper house to house inspection' by agents who would afterwards attend the court. 'I am personally aware', he wrote to F. E. Ball of the Irish Loyal and Patriotic Union, 'that at the last revision session for East Donegal we lost many objections which were well founded by reason of our . . . not being able to identify properly the particular house or holding against which the objection was levelled . . .'.[29] In a crucial marginal, Londonderry City, the president of the Unionist Association complained to T. W. Russell of the scarcity of volunteers to gather funds for revision expenses.[30] R. B. Phillips, in charge of registration in another marginal (East Tyrone), pointed to similar apathy in 1890, bemoaning the 'impossibility of getting assistance' for his work.[31]

Much more frustrating for election agents was a widespread and persistent refusal among even comparatively wealthy northern

[26] IUA Letters, D 989, M. C. Sinclair to Cox, 29 July 1890.

[27] Ibid., T. Chambers to Cox, 8 Dec. 1891.

[28] Ostrogorski, *Democracy and Organisation*, i. 345-6, 584; Patrick Buckland, *Irish Unionism* i. *The Anglo-Irish and the New Ireland, 1885-1922* (Dublin and New York, 1972), 18; Marsh, *Popular Government*, 206-7.

[29] IUA Letters, D 989, A. J. Dudgeon to F. E. Ball, 18 July 1892.

[30] Ibid., William Tillie to T. W. Russell, 31 Mar. 1894.

[31] Ibid., C. Litton Falkiner to Cox, 11 Sept. 1890.

Unionists to subscribe to the party's funds. This may have been partly a reaction to the sustained and aggressive demands made upon individual pockets by the numerous loyalist campaign organizations. Such demands were certainly successful at times of crisis, and the IUA, for example, could command impressive sums of money; but the financial muscle of the Alliance and similar bodies has wholly overshadowed the severe problems faced by local Unionist organizations. As in England, voters expected a rich candidate or constituency landowner to assume responsibility for most of the election and revision expenses.[32] But the parsimony of some Irish Protestants exceeded this expectation, as the Duke of Abercorn complained in a letter of September 1886; 'the people up here are not like those in England, and it is with the greatest difficulty that we can get them to subscribe anything'.[33] This indication of popular priorities is particularly suggestive, given that the Home Rule scare was still pervading the Irish Unionist community at the time.

Abercorn's complaint was borne out in the experience of election agents throughout northern Ireland. Sometimes prospective donors affected disgust at the nature of the fund-raising enterprises, even though association treasurers were often local squires and brought decorum to the exercise of their duties. Nevertheless, when, in October 1885, the Finance Committee of J. C. Bloomfield's North Fermanagh campaign attempted to raise £1,000 from the party faithful, it met with, at best, a lukewarm response; at worst, some of the more sensitive Tories were horrified by the spectacle of a mendicant party. One crusty gentleman farmer scribbled on his subscription circular, 'I think it most discreditable to the county to send round the hat in this form, and must decline to be any part of it'.[34] An attempt in 1910 by the East Tyrone Unionists to raise much needed cash provoked similar outrage.[35]

But the fundamental problem was less a matter of sensitivity about methods than the unpopularity of sacrifice. In 1888 Hugh de Fellenberg Montgomery of the South Tyrone Unionist Association, recorded a drop in fund-raising, confessing that 'we cannot count on increased local subscriptions, even though every effort will be

[32] Birch, *Small-Town Politics*, 46; Lowell, *Government*, ii. 48-9.
[33] KRO, Aretas Akers-Douglas Papers, C 28/1, Abercorn to Akers-Douglas, 18 Sept. 1886.
[34] Falls and Hanna Papers, D 1390/26/1/1/26, printed circular, 23 Oct. 1885.
[35] ETUA Papers, D 1132/5/2, Hugh Adair to Lowry, 12 Sept. 1910.

made to obtain them'.[36] His colleague in North Tyrone, E. T. Herdman, echoed Abercorn in doubting whether 'the money for election expenses could ever be raised here . . . the general impression is to get someone with ample funds, but it is difficult to say what may turn up . . .'.[37] In North Fermanagh a constituency meeting cheerfully promised £180 to help wipe out the £500 debt of the 1887 revision session—but only £80 was actually paid.[38] In West Belfast the Joint Registration Committee had amassed, by the end of 1889, debts nearing £500; the secretary of the ILPU received complaints about the niggardliness of Belfast Unionists towards all but 'their own churches and charities . . . perhaps that is one reason why they are well off'.[39]

Reluctance to contribute to Unionist funds was not in practice incompatible either with fierce party loyalty, or with willingness to work for the cause. But the most uncompromising partisans (in terms, at any rate, of verbal commitment) often expected repayment for even minor election or registration work, whether conveying voters to the poll, or giving evidence at revision courts.[40] Accepting these claims would have infringed the Corrupt Practices Act of 1883, and solicitors like Dane and Falls in North Fermanagh, or Peel in Mid Armagh, had to fight running battles with 'loyal' election workers presenting wildly exorbitant or flagrantly illegal demands for reimbursement.

Irish Protestants, cushioned by widespread English sympathy, and by the House of Lords veto, were often insufficiently bound to Unionism to consider it worth even trivial pecuniary sacrifice. The industrial and commercial magnates of Belfast, reliant upon external investment and responsible to shareholders, were certainly alarmed by the likely depreciation of their capital under Home Rule—and subscribed accordingly; but their concerns had little direct relevance to the mass of rural Unionists upon whom county organization rested.[41] For them Home Rule was more obviously a cultural and

[36] IUA Letters, D 989, H. De F. Montgomery to Houston, 24 Aug. 1888.

[37] PRONI, Hugh De Fellenberg Montgomery Papers, D 627/428/40, E. T. Herdman to Montgomery, 20 Mar. 1888.

[38] IUA Letters, D 989, Dane to Houston, 8 Aug. 1888.

[39] Ibid., Montgomery to Cox, 2 Sept. 1888.

[40] PRONI, Joshua Peel Papers, D 889/4c/5A, letter book for 1885–6.

[41] Buckland, *Anglo-Irish*, 18–19; Patrick Buckland, Irish Unionism, ii *Ulster Unionism and the Origins of Northern Ireland* (Dublin and New York, 1973), 11; Buckland, *Irish Unionism 1885–1923: A Documentary History* (Belfast, 1973), 59–72; JCP, JC 8/5/3/26, Edward Harland to Chamberlain, 24 May 1886.

sectarian than a financial threat, which could be effectively combated through aggressive Orangeism or Protestantism rather than the donation of cash. Writing in 1900, Hugh Montgomery focused years of local political experience in assessing Ulster tenant farmers: 'if I know anything about the northern farmer, he will shout and vote . . . and write letters to the *Northern Whig*—but he will not subscribe . . . he will not commit outrages'.[42] On this bedrock of insouciance, Irish Unionist activists—MPs and agents—had to create the semblance of a committed popular movement.

What local money was subscribed came largely from the great property owners of the constituency, and from its parliamentary representative; in the late 1880s these categories overlapped considerably.[43] Abercorn complained to the Conservative whip, Aretas Akers-Douglas, that the popular attitude to fund-raising was: 'we have a rich man amongst us—he must pay'.[44] In North Tyrone, Abercorn virtually single-handedly financed the Unionist association. The constituency's revision expenses for 1890 came to £750, of which over £400 was subscribed by the Duke.[45] Helping to finance three brothers' parliamentary careers (including that of the Tory cabinet minister, Lord George Hamilton) strained Abercorn's £53,000 rental and already, by 1888, his enthusiasm for politics was evaporating: 'the Duke', E. T. Herdman confided to Montgomery, 'thinks the amusement too costly'.[46] Other landed magnates adopted a similar attitude, and Lord Antrim, for example, had to apologize for not subscribing to the Ulster Loyal Union—since 'I pay large taxes to the government, and have had my rents reduced to a minimum'.[47] Three major landowners in North Fermanagh together contributed virtually half the total sum raised for Unionist registration expenses in 1886–7. Like Abercorn, however, the Fermanagh landowners' generosity had definite bounds—and by July

[42] TCD, W. E. H. Lecky Papers, TCD 1832/1997, H. De F. Montgomery to Lecky, 21 Nov. 1900.
[43] See below, ch. 5.6. The three chief contributors to the County Antrim Constitutional Association in 1884 were Macnaghten MP (£50), Wallace MP (£30), and Lord O'Neill (£50): Young Papers, D 3027/6/3, scrapbook containing political ephemera.
[44] Akers-Douglas Papers, C 28/1, Abercorn to Akers-Douglas, 18 Sept. 1886.
[45] IUA Letters, D 989, R. B. Phillips to Cox, 25 Nov. 1890.
[46] Montgomery Papers, D 627/428/40, Herdman to Montgomery, 20 Mar. 1886.
[47] Young Papers, D 3027/5/6/2, Lord Antrim to Young, 13 May 1889.

1887 an appeal for additional funds produced no response, despite 'frequent applications' to the most wealthy by the agent, J. Whiteside Dane.[48]

Throughout the period 1885–1906 and before it was generally expected that the Unionist candidate, or his patron, should subscribe lavishly to election and registration costs. Thus the absence of a candidate frequently threatened financial disaster, and insolvency was a permanent threat in some northern marginals, and seats with strong Nationalist majorities.[49] Elsewhere formal agreements were sometimes concluded between a member and his constituency, allocating the responsibility for expenditure. John Ross, MP for Derry City between 1892 and 1895, engaged with his local Unionist association to pay the whole of his election expenses, provided that the association, in return, paid all registration and revision costs.[50] Other candidates and MPs sustained a heavier burden. D. P. Barton and John Lonsdale, successive MPs for Mid Armagh, each paid their own election costs, while maintaining a flow of cash for registration work and local charities: this chimes with the experience of wealthy English members like W. H. Hornby and Max Aitken.[51] A Mr Browne, prospective candidate for North Fermanagh in 1889 was told by constituency managers that 'if he gave 300 or 250 [pounds] a year, the county would give about £150, and that would put us on a first class footing'.[52] E. M. Archdale, MP for North Fermanagh between 1898 and 1903, contributed £100 annually to the local party; his successor, Godfrey Fetherstonhaugh, received a pained rebuke when he ventured to offer £25.[53] Horace Plunkett was allegedly rejected as candidate for the constituency in 1903 'because his purse was not long enough': certainly his successful rival for the Unionist nomination, James Craig, was the stockbroking son of a millionaire distiller.[54]

---

[48] Walker, 'Parliamentary Representation', 164; IUA Letters, D 989, J. W. Dane to Houston, 29 July 1887.   [49] See n. 22.

[50] IUA Letters, D 989, Tillie to T. W. Russell, 31 Mar. 1894.

[51] P. F. Clarke, 'British Politics and Blackburn Politics, 1900–1910', HJ, xii. 2 (1969), 304–5; P. F. Clarke, Lancashire and the New Liberalism (Cambridge, 1971), 23–4.

[52] Montgomery Papers, D 627/428/84, E. M. Archdale to Montgomery, 17 Mar. 1889.

[53] Falls and Hanna Papers, D 1390/26/6/90, various to G. Fetherstonhaugh, 11 Apr. 1907.

[54] BNL, 11 Mar. 1903.

External funding was provided by the Dublin-based Irish Loyal and Patriotic Union, and by the London Unionist Joint Committee. Direct contributions from Belfast were rare before the mid-1890s, and only assumed vital significance during the growth of public reaction against the third Home Rule Bill. The comparative insignificance of Belfast as a source of cash for provincial, let alone national, Unionist organization is significant, since this probably retarded the development of the narrowly Ulster Unionism which was dominating Irish loyalist politics by 1912. In the 1880s and 1890s indebted Unionist associations in western Ulster, and in other marginal constituencies, turned gladly to the Dublin organization for financial assistance. In many of these constituencies, influential Unionists harboured an instinctive distrust for Belfast, repudiating interference in local affairs (even in the form of the Ulster Convention League), and resenting Belfast Unionism's hard-headed line on funding.[55] In particular, provincial Liberal Unionists were offended by the aggressively Tory aspect of Belfast Unionism. For all these Dublin offered a more congenial source of alliance and support.

At an early general meeting of the ILPU priority was attached to extending the movement's organization into Ulster—and this remained an ambition at least until 1893.[56] Ulster constituency associations were encouraged to affiliate to the ILPU, and their applications for grant assistance were treated sympathetically. The South Tyrone association received between £150 and £200 annually in the late 1880s. North Fermanagh regularly received grants of £50.[57] Careful sifting of the ILPU and Irish Unionist Alliance records for the period brought to light only one Ulster constituency—East Tyrone—which had been wholly refused assistance.[58]

In September 1890 an ILPU agent, the historian and amateur politician, Caesar Litton Falkiner, was sent to western Ulster to establish links with local constituency associations. Litton Falkiner won the immediate affiliation of East Donegal and North Tyrone:

[55] Montgomery Papers, D 627/428/193, Adam Duffin to Montgomery, 27 Aug. 1892. Printed in Buckland, *Documentary History*, 196. Buckland, 'The Unity of Ulster Unionism, 1886–1939', *History*, lx (1975), 211.

[56] Buckland, *Anglo-Irish*, 17.

[57] IUA Letters, D 989, Montgomery to Cox, 24 Aug., 2 Sept. 1888; J. W. Dane to Houston, 29 July, 29 Oct. 1887.

[58] PRONI, Minute Book of the ILPU General Council, D 989/A/1/4, 30 Aug. 1889.

'Mr. Phillips [of the North Tyrone Association]', he reported to headquarters, 'has actually paid to me the gratifying fee of £1'.[59] By November 1893, eleven Ulster constituencies were represented on the General Council of what had become the Irish Unionist Alliance, several of them recipients of grants.[60] And in December 1893 a resolution was passed by the Council, inviting the affiliation of the remaining Ulster associations.[61]

However, with the foundation in 1892 of the Ulster Convention League, the Irish Unionist Alliance grew more wary of sending aid north. The Alliance's long-term goal was the establishment of a central system of funding for Irish registration societies, with joint contributions from the two Unionist Parties, the Convention League, and the IUA itself. Failing this (and an effort to establish such an agency appears to have foundered in 1896), the IUA was prepared to confine its funding activity to the three southern provinces, allowing the Convention League primary responsibility for Ulster.[62] The broad determinant of both strategies seems to have been a fear that the League might evade its proper responsibility for funding, leaving the IUA, with the British Unionist Party, to support the registration activity of the whole island. Thus, when indebted northern Unionist associations (those, for example, in Derry City, North Tyrone, and North Fermanagh) applied to the IUA for assistance, its executive committee was prepared to respond with an increase in aid, but only if the Ulster Convention League offered an equivalent increase.[63] An informal parity of contribution from Dublin and Belfast seems to have developed in the mid-1890s and lasted into the new century.

Suspicion remained the dominant feature of the relationship between the IUA and the Ulster organizations, and full-blooded co-operation only really occurred within the neutral electoral arena supplied by English contests. In the exceptional circumstances of early 1895—with a Liberal government in power, and an impending general election—representatives of northern Unionism combined

[59] IUA Letters, D 989, C. Litton Falkiner to Cox, 11 Sept. 1890.
[60] PRONI, Minute Book of the IUA Executive Committee, D 989/A/1/5, 24 Nov. 1893.
[61] Minute Book of the IUA General Council, D 989/A/1/4, 5 Dec. 1893.
[62] PRONI, Minute Book of the IUA Parliamentary Consultative Committee, D 989/A/1/5, 17 June 1896. See also Minute Book of the IUA Executive Committee, D 989/A/1/5, 30 May 1894.
[63] Minute Book of the IUA Executive Committee, D 989/A/1/5, 13 June 1894.

with the IUA to create a fund for loyalist campaign work in Britain.[64] But, although it was boasted that the Ulstermen had the 'direct co-operation' of the Alliance, northern fund-raising was, in reality, a quite separate endeavour: indeed a sense of rivalry permeated some of the publicizing literature.[65] A more permanent agency for shared funding emerged in 1908 with the Joint Committee of the Unionist Associations of Ireland; but again, this had little to do with the solvency of local party associations in Ulster, and in any case it developed at a time of drift between northern and southern Unionism.[66]

Representatives from Conservative Central Office and from the Liberal Unionist Association combined in the Unionist Joint Committee to create a second external source of income for Ulster constituencies. The Joint Committee maintained an Irish Registration Department, captained by the formidable Chamberlainite, John Boraston; and this channelled cash into loyalist constituency associations with an enthusiasm which varied according to the perceived importance of Irish electoral affairs. Like the IUA, the UJC displaced the potential dominance of Belfast in the late 1880s and 1890s; and, for a time, its largesse helped make tolerable political interference by the central party in local Ulster affairs.

The Joint Committee was distinguished both by its munificence, and by the powers of intervention which it claimed—for, rather more than the IUA, its managers were keen to ensure that value for money was obtained. Where the Alliance was generally content to receive an informal written report from the secretaries of client associations, UJC officials were prepared to carry out on-the-ground inspections. In May 1889 Boraston visited various Ulster constituencies in order to audit the books of local associations, and to check the adequacy of their registration work.[67] Later in the year, representatives of the Committee threw the South Tyrone Association into a state of nervous excitement with the threat of a tour of inspection: half the

[64] PRONI, UUC Papers, D 1327/1/11, minutes of the Joint Committee held in London, 11 Mar. 1895.

[65] Private Possession, Fortwilliam Unionist Club Papers, minutes of meeting held on 2 Aug. 1895 and accompanying literature for the 'United Ulster Unionist Fund', Mar. 1895.

[66] See ch. 7.

[67] Montgomery Papers D 627/428/101, John Boraston to Montgomery, 12 May 1889, printed in Buckland, *Documentary History*, 180.

association's grant of £150 rested on the representatives' assessment of local party achievement.[68]

After 1893, with the development of the Ulster Convention League, the UJC retreated from northern constituency work; but Boraston, professing himself sceptical about the Convention League's prospects, continued to claim a watching brief over Irish electoral affairs.[69] Given that, in the short term, neither the League nor any other northern body proved capable of supplying the financial needs of Ulster associations, his attitude was well founded. Even by the end of the Edwardian period the UJC remained an essential source of support for the weaker local parties. In 1904 William Teele, Treasurer of the North Fermanagh Loyalist Registration Association, was applying to Boraston for help: 'we would not have embarked', he pleaded, 'on the work for the above years [1903–4], but for the belief that we would receive the usual assistance from your association'.[70] And as late as 1907–10 Boraston was sending between £50 and £75 to the indebted Unionists of East Tyrone.[71]

However, in the long term, the significance for the Ulster constituency budget of external cash, whether from London or Dublin, was diminishing from a peak of dependence reached in the late 1880s and early 1890s. This shift was partly a function of the slow development of northern Unionism's institutional framework, but it was also connected with a general dampening of Unionist activity after the election of 1892, and the second Home Rule Bill. The major financing agencies had welcomed the dissolution of June 1892 as an opportunity to test the value of their registration investment. Thus, the Joint Committee, with the assent of the party leaders, had declared that every constituency should be supplied with a Unionist candidate in order to exploit fully the Parnellite split.[72] But the massive Unionist effort of 1892 produced a gain of only five seats, and trifling party polls in the southern and western counties

[68] Montgomery Papers, D 627/428/106–7, Boraston to Montgomery, 17 July, 29 Aug. 1889.

[69] Ibid., D 627/428/192, Boraston to Montgomery, 11 Aug. 1892.

[70] Falls and Hanna Papers, D 1390/26/6/55, Teele to Boraston, 7 Nov. 1904; Walker, 'Parliamentary Representation', 164; Falls and Hanna Papers, D 1390/26/6/59, Teele to Boraston, 24 Nov. 1904.

[71] ETUA Papers, D 1132/5/2, Boraston to Lowry, 21 Dec. 1907, 18 Dec. 1909, 28 Nov. 1910.

[72] Minute Book of the IUA General Council, D 989/A/1/4, 23 Apr. 1891.

of Ireland. IUA propaganda hailed the election as a demonstration that 'Irish Unionism was a growing and conquering cause'; but more dispassionate observers—like Edward Saunderson and Horace Plunkett—fully realized the true and limited nature of the advance.[73]

The election, followed by the rejection of the Home Rule Bill, sapped both local and central enthusiasm: key marginals like Derry City and North Tyrone suffered relative neglect (and ultimate loss) in the face of determined Nationalist activity. Subsequent elections, in 1895 and 1900, were fought with Ireland low among the priorities presented to the electorate.[74] Ireland had been snatched from the centre of the British political stage, and no future Chief Secretary would claim, as Balfour had done in 1889, that 'the battle for Irish seats will be by far the most important at the next general election'.[75] Deprived of national relevance, constituency associations were increasingly thrown onto their own resources, turning to their MP or to popular reorganization for aid. The flow of cash from Dublin and London to Irish constituencies was checked. In a very real institutional sense, the electoral success of British Unionism in the late 1890s—because it was not directly founded on Irish issues—tended to weaken the link between the central party and its local Ulster base.

3. External Influence and Selection

The emergence of Ulster Unionism involved, therefore, throwing off some of the shackles imposed by external funding. But the development of a northern movement affected a much wider range of political activities, and soon other forms of external involvement in loyalist politics underwent a decline. As over funding, this was frequently as much a matter of external neglect as local challenge,

---

[73] IUA *Annual Report for 1893* (Dublin 1894). Also Plunkett Foundation, Oxford, Diaries of Horace Plunkett, 21 Feb. 1898 ('the national spirit only sleeps'). Also Whittingehame, Arthur Balfour Papers TD 83/133/70/8, Horace Plunkett to Alice Balfour, 4 Nov. 1894.

[74] IUA *Annual Report for 1900* (Dublin, 1901), 6; Marsh, *Popular Government*, 245.

[75] ABP, Add. MS 49827, fo. 553, Balfour to Akers-Douglas, 18 Jan. 1889. A. V. Dicey held a similar view: Montgomery Papers, D 627/428/150, Dicey to Montgomery, 22 Dec. 1890.

but the overall effect—the growing isolation or self-reliance of the north—was the same in both cases. This evolution was reflected within a second function of the constituency association: the selection and running of parliamentary candidates.

'I have laid down a rule, from which I have never departed', Arthur Balfour wrote with characteristic disingenuousness, 'that the suggestion or selection of candidates for Irish seats is altogether outside my province'.[76] Balfour's two immediate successors as Chief Secretary, his brother Gerald, and George Wyndham, each adhered to this principle (though with some lapses). But Balfour himself, despite conventional and pious rhetoric, was an unrepentant meddler in the politics of local selection contests.

To some extent, this distinction between Balfour and his successors reflects a broader redefinition of the relationship between Irish and British Unionism. Relations were generally much cooler by 1906 than in the late 1880s. The Plan of Campaign demanded a mobilization of the government's Irish allies which neither Gerald Balfour nor Wyndham ever had to effect. Balfour's coercive policy, and its apparent success, gave him a popular Irish Protestant following which neither of his successors enjoyed: 'They will do anything they think would please you', John Ross told Balfour in discussing the electors of North Antrim, '[but] any dictation or even suggestion from any other person they would resent'.[77] Moreover, success and popularity had wider implications, bringing to the office of Chief Secretary a credibility among Irish Unionists which it subsequently lost. Balfour could issue advice on the selection of candidates, confident that it would carry weight. Local Unionist associations invited Balfour's services as arbiter in constituency disputes over selection; in some cases local associations asked Balfour to *undertake* the selection of candidates.

His influence spanned Unionist Ireland. In Ulster he was polite and discreet, qualifying recommendations by disavowing any intent to exceed his rightful authority. When, in May 1891, James Henderson, an influential East Belfast Conservative, approached Balfour for advice on selection, his reply was modest and hesitant—but contained, nevertheless, an unequivocal statement of preference.[78] In the neighbouring northern division of the City, the

---

[76] ABP, Add. MS 49829, fo. 980, Balfour to James Henderson, 13 May 1891.
[77] ABP, Add. MS 49848, fo. 69, Ross to Balfour, 21 Feb. 1891.
[78] See n. 76.

Unionist candidature was quietly negotiated by Balfour, the sitting member (Sir William Ewart), and the Conservative Chief Whip (Akers-Douglas). The final decision on selection appears to have been taken in London, without the presence of any local party representative.[79]

In southern constituencies, where the selection process was often devoid of any practical significance, Balfour could interfere with a more brazen assertion of the government's interests. At the Cork by-election of 1891, following the death of Parnell, he canvassed widely against a Unionist candidature: 'I went to the very limits of interference', he admitted to Goschen.[80] In South County Dublin he came out strongly in favour of Horace Plunkett, berating those Unionists who doubted Plunkett's suitability.[81] Even the electors of Trinity College accepted his advice without cavil. Early in Balfour's Chief Secretaryship, Lord Ashbourne warned against Trinity's intolerance of outside interference; but by May 1890, Balfour had no need of such caution, and could promote the candidature of Edward Carson quite openly.[82]

Certain constituencies not only accepted Balfour's interference, but also encouraged it: some were prepared to exploit him as a broker, through whom representations could be made more effectively to desirable potential candidates. North Antrim Unionists approached the Chief Secretary in order to determine whether his cousin, C. B. Balfour, would accept nomination for their constituency.[83] The Unionists of South County Dublin were similarly anxious to recruit one of Balfour's relations—such was the standing, and prospective electoral value of the family name.[84] But South Dublin's trust went further: failing one of the Balfour clan, the constituency was virtually prepared to grant the Chief Secretary freedom to select whom he liked.[85]

[79] See n. 75.
[80] ABP, Add. MS 49830, fo. 428, Balfour to Goschen, 12 Dec. 1891.
[81] ABP, Add. MS 49830, fo. 609, Balfour to H. L. Barnardo, 12 May 1892. Balfour had been worried, though, by accusations that Plunkett was using his membership of the Congested Districts Board for advantage: Trevor West, *Horace Plunkett, Cooperation and Politics: An Irish Biography* (Gerrard's Cross, 1986), 38–9.
[82] ABP, Add. MS 49815, fo. 12, Lord Ashbourne to Balfour, 19 June 1887; Add. MS 49709, fo. 93, Balfour to Carson, 12 May 1890 (copy).
[83] ABP, Add. MS 49829, fo. 637, Balfour to C. B. Balfour, 15 Jan. 1891; Add. MS 49829, fo. 681, Balfour to Montgomery, 27 Jan. 1891.
[84] ABP, Add. MS 49829, fo. 902, Balfour to Eustace Balfour, 27 Apr. 1891.
[85] ABP, Add. MS 49829, fo. 909, Balfour to I. T. Hamilton, 29 Apr. 1891. ABP, Add. MS 49830, fo. 265, Balfour to Middleton, 6 Oct. 1891.

None of Balfour's successors (except, possibly, Walter Long) enjoyed this breadth of popular acceptance within loyalism. The reaction against unpalatable policies on law and order, land, and education found one form of expression in the chilling of relations between Irish constituency associations and the Unionist Castle administration. Neither Gerald Balfour nor Wyndham was ever invited to arbitrate in local selection procedures, as Arthur Balfour had been. Neither, on the other hand, showed much desire to intervene in local politics: grass-roots loyalism had a comparatively slight role in the calculations of both ministers.[86]

Where once Arthur Balfour had given priority to Irish election contests and internal Unionist relations, now such contests had a purely local significance. By the late 1890s central party interest in Irish constituency politics was confined to the condition of those seats whose members were being considered for promotion to one of the law offices, or to the Bench.[87] Trinity had reverted to the wary independence described by Ashbourne in 1887. When, in 1902, Wyndham wanted to secure one of the Trinity seats for his Solicitor-General, James Campbell, he tried first to win over Salisbury, through Schomberg McDonnell, rather than attempt direct personal communication with the College hierarchy.[88] The approaches made to Balfour on local initiative—like those by Henderson and Ewart in Belfast, and Hamilton in Dublin—had characterized a broader unity between loyalist feeling and Unionist government: such trust would have been unthinkable as loyalist disillusion developed, and particularly after 1902-3.

Until the mid-1890s, national leaders like Arthur Balfour also intervened to cool the frequent inter-party quarrels of the Irish alliance. Thereafter, as with other forms of central interference, this solicitude failed—and Irish Unionists were left to provide their own solutions for their own problems.

British Liberal Unionists and Conservatives had forged an electoral pact in July 1886 in order to curtail the number of petty constituency disputes. In Ulster, however, the Liberal Unionist Association had

[86] Andrew Gailey, 'The Unionist Government's Policy towards Ireland, 1895-1905', Ph.D. thesis (Cambridge, 1983), 66-7 and passim.

[87] See e.g. Akers-Douglas Papers, C Lp.5/66, Akers-Douglas to Middleton, 20 Feb. 1896. Also HLRO, Cadogan Papers, CAD 979, Middleton to Cadogan, 28 Dec. 1896. MSPH, E/Cadogan/145, Cadogan to Salisbury, 14 Dec. 1897.

[88] MSPH, George Wyndham to McDonnell, 15 Apr. 1902.

nothing to lose by internal wrangling after their disastrous performance at the general election of 1885; and it chose to avoid any constraining commitment. As a consequence of this, and of overweening Tory pride, several Ulster constituencies were racked by Unionist feuding, each party to the alliance seeking ascendancy over the other.[89]

The process of arbitration between these embittered allies often involved an appeal to the British leadership. Local party functionaries were keen to undertake such requests, partly because London represented an appropriately awesome final court of judgement; also because corresponding with celebrated figures provided the vicarious thrill of participation in high politics. For their part, the leadership was not unwilling to respond, since they, too, had narrow party commitments; and they understood the publicity value of Irish Unionist unity.

Thus, when a representative of the North Derry Constitutional Association wrote to Arthur Balfour in December 1893 concerning a local intra-party squabble, he won a lengthy and circumspect reply. Balfour wrote:

I have had the advantage of talking the matter over very fully with Mr. Chamberlain; and while we are agreed in our recognition of the invaluable services of the Liberal Unionist Party in Ulster, and in our earnest hope that their desire for a somewhat increased share of the Unionist representation . . . will receive careful consideration . . . we think that the interests of the cause would be best served by leaving the representation of N. Derry with that section of the Unionist Party which has held it since 1886 [the Conservatives].[90]

Anxious for harmony, without conceding his sectional case, Balfour attempted to shift some responsibility onto Joseph Chamberlain—associating him in an endorsement of the Conservative candidate.

But where local Conservatives had appealed to Balfour, Thomas Sinclair, chairman of the Ulster Liberal Unionist Association, placed his party's case before Chamberlain.[91] Forced to choose between

[89] Thomas Macknight, *Ulster as it is, or Twenty Eight Years' Experience as an Irish Editor* (2 vols.; London, 1896), ii. 157. See also Akers-Douglas Papers, C 169/3, Devonshire to Akers-Douglas, 29 July 1889 for central intervention in the West Belfast selection contest.

[90] Bodleian Library, Oxford, J. S. Sandars Papers, MS Eng. Hist. c725, fo. 92, Balfour to McCausland, 8 Dec. 1893 (copy).

[91] ABP, Add. MS 49773, fo. 63, Chamberlain to Balfour, 28 Apr. 1894.

Balfour's platitudes and local Liberal Unionist self-interest, Chamberlain wrote to Balfour in May 1894, avoiding any reference to the joint commitment of December; instead, echoing Sinclair, he preached the need to extend the parliamentary representation of Irish Liberal Unionism, throwing Balfour's vacuous magnanimity in his face. 'You have always joined in the hope', he reminded Balfour, 'that Ulster Tories would give consideration to the claims of the Liberal Unionists for increased representation. Is this not an opportunity for a peace offering?'[92] Division at constituency level, thus, reverberated through the hierarchy of the alliance, each Unionist leader adopting the narrow cause of their constituency support.

The episode illustrates how seriously British politicians viewed factional division in the Irish party. There is little evidence to suggest that, except in atypical cases like Austen Chamberlain and East Worcestershire, the highest level of leadership was so thoroughly ensnared within similar, local British difficulties.[93]

There were both structural and tactical reasons for the attention which loyalist Ireland had enjoyed. More mediation was needed because there seem to have been proportionately more quarrels. And national leaders responded to local appeals because, in the aftermath of Home Rule, they needed to sustain a semblance of unanimity among the Ulstermen whose virtues they had so recently extolled. When that need diminished—when the prospect of a renewed Home Rule agitation grew more remote—loyalist bickering no longer possessed British implications. Because Ireland had ceased to be an important electoral issue, British leaders did not have to risk committing themselves in petty Ulster conflicts: there was no longer any special British advantage to be had in winning consensus. Russellism was certainly viewed by Balfour and Wyndham as a serious threat, but their response took the form of legislation rather than direct electoral interference.[94] Otherwise Ireland slipped into the background of high politics, and the broader significance of the ferocious local quarrels vanished.

In the absence of firm organizational ties binding British and Irish Unionism, informal ministerial interference had taken on a

---

[92] ABP, Add. MS 49773 fo. 63, Chamberlain to Balfour, 28 Apr. 1894.

[93] David Dutton, *Austen Chamberlain: Gentleman in Politics* (Bolton, 1985), 19–20.

[94] Andrew Gailey, *Ireland and the Death of Kindness: The Experience of Constructive Unionism, 1890–1905* (Cork, 1987), 176–7.

disproportionate importance. Ulster Unionism did not embrace English Unionist movements like the Primrose League with any enthusiasm for Orangeism provided a more meaningful form of popular political ceremonial and theatre; and northern constituencies lay beyond the sceptical gaze of Captain Middleton and the Conservative Central Office.[95] Moreover, the reduction of such interference in Ireland provided a further contrast with the position in England, where the trend was towards a consolidation of the central role in local affairs. Ulster Unionist constituencies were certainly undergoing realignment, like their English Tory counterparts; but the connection which was ultimately forged bound them to Belfast, rather than to London.[96]

The decline of central interference, whether in arbitration or over selection, contributed in at least two ways to the growth of Ulster insularity, and to the growth of a specifically Ulster political movement. Firstly, the ending of interference represented a collapse in communication between government and local support. Irish Unionists were deprived of one more form of contact with the Castle administration. Indeed, under Gerald Balfour and George Wyndham, other forms of communication suffered which had had significance under Arthur Balfour, and would briefly return to significance under Walter Long (patronage ties, for example, and the participation— however inconsequential—of senior Irish Unionists in the formulation of government policy).[97]

The second significant area of contribution to the development of Ulster insularity lies in the fact that government interference was not only a bond between constituency and minister, but also a bond between constituency and Dublin. The distancing of Castle and popular Unionism was part, therefore, of a broader movement away from a Dublin-oriented movement. With the increasing weakness of any organizational link to the island's capital, northern Unionists' political activity became increasingly centred on a provincial network, based in Belfast.

[95] Martin Pugh, *The Tories and the People, 1880–1935* (Oxford, 1985), 168, 215–16 for membership figures; Ian d'Alton, 'Southern Irish Unionism: A Study of Cork Unionists 1884–1914', *Transactions of the Royal Historical Society*, xxiii. 3 (Jan. 1973), 84–6.

[96] Marsh, *Popular Government*, 183–209; Jane Ridley, 'Leadership and Management in the Conservative Party in Parliament, 1906–1914', D.Phil. thesis (Oxford, 1985), 21, 44.

[97] See ch. 6.

4. Lord Arthur Hill and Selection, 1880-1908

The demise of central interference, and the growth of local political autonomy, were each accelerated by the fading influence over selection of Lord Arthur Hill, the Conservative Irish Whip. The Irish Tory party was historically a law unto itself; but, in so far as there existed a formal command structure binding it to the British party, then Hill stood at its heart. British pressure was traditionally exercised through casual personal contact, especially between magnates like Salisbury and Abercorn or Erne; and, an albeit steely, informality was the chief characteristic of Arthur Hill's period of dominance. Hill represented the British leadership in the province between 1885 and 1898, but well before the end of his reign his style of electoral management was under threat.[98]

Though Hill's importance has been recognized, the full scope of his activity has remained impenetrable.[99] It is certainly clear that, even more than an interested and meddling Chief Secretary like Balfour, Hill interfered in local electoral affairs, acting as constituency broker to likely parliamentary candidates. But, where Balfour's brokerage was generally in response to constituency initiative, and was often linked specifically to members of the Cecil clan, Hill interfered more widely, particularly in seats where representative organization was weak, or where his family's £97,000 rent roll carried an influence of its own.[100]

Hill defended the Conservative landed and propertied establishment, promoting its representatives, and conniving against more independent and populist politicians. In October 1885 he attempted to rescue the Irish Solicitor-General from Orange opposition in the North Armagh constituency; and he felt able to offer the minister nomination for the neighbouring Mid Armagh seat.[101] In June 1886 he worked to defend the linen magnate,

[98] ABP, Add. MS 49773, fo. 99, Balfour to Chamberlain, 29 Feb. 1896 (copy).

[99] Walker, 'Parliamentary Representation', 526; A. B. Cooke, 'A Conservative Party Leader in Ulster: Sir Stafford Northcote's Diary of a Visit to the Province, October 1883', *Proceedings of the Royal Irish Academy*, lxxv, sect. C. 4 (1975), 72, n. 49.

[100] John Bateman, *The Great Landowners of Great Britain and Ireland* (4th edn., London, 1883), 137.

[101] PRONI, Carleton, Atkinson, and Sloan Papers, D 1252/42/3/40, Lord Arthur Hill to John Monroe, 26 Sept. 1885; Frank Thompson, 'The Armagh Elections of 1885-1886', *Seanchas Ardmhacha: Journal of the Armagh Diocesan Historical Society*, viii (1977), 367.

William Ewart, from independent opposition in North Belfast.[102] Ten years later he was promising to use his influence to secure the West Down seat for the son of Lord Dufferin and Ava.[103]

Erratic independents like William Johnston of Ballykilbeg were, on the other hand, prospective victims of Hill's string-pulling. It seems clear, for example, that Hill quietly opposed Johnston's attempt to win South Belfast in 1885. On two occasions in 1885, Hill attempted to wrest 'Ballykilbeg' from South Belfast, through the offers, first of East Down, and later that year, of West Belfast.[104] This may well have been regarded as a means of detaching Johnston from his popular electoral base: East Down was strongly under the influence of the Hill family, and Johnston could have been dismissed from the representation with ease. West Belfast contained a strong Nationalist poll, and a severely divided Protestant community: Conservative failure was therefore virtually assured.

The Hill family owned a total of over 120,000 acres, some 78,000 of which were in County Down. This provided particular political weight in two constituencies—East and West Down. Just as Lord Arthur had felt able to offer the eastern division to Johnston in June 1885, so in 1890 he successfully nominated a Presbyterian lawyer, James A. Rentoul, to the same seat. The sitting member, R. W. B. Ker, himself a wealthy landowner, was removed without difficulty.[105] Some years later, Rentoul would be the intended victim of a second attempted deposition, also possibly masterminded by Arthur Hill.[106]

West Down was held by Hill on behalf of his family for thirteen years, during which time he was offered one contest (in 1886, by a Nationalist, who won only 15 per cent of the poll); and, in May 1898 when he retired, his son succeeded him in the representation of the division.[107] Hill had earlier reached a bizarre arrangement

[102] PRONI, Abercorn Papers, D 623/A/331/29, Salisbury to Abercorn, 30 June 1886. Salisbury Papers, E/Hill/10, Hill to Salisbury, 25 June 1886.

[103] PRONI, Dufferin and Ava Papers, D 1701/H/B/F, Hill to Dufferin, 19 July 1897.

[104] WJD, D 880/2/37, 10 June, 21 Nov. 1885. See also Aiken McClelland, 'Johnston of Ballykilbeg', M.Phil. thesis (Coleraine, 1978), 99.

[105] WJD, 880/2/243, 7 Mar. 1890. Also J. A. Rentoul, *Stray Thoughts and Memories* (Dublin, 1921), 130-2.

[106] Rentoul, *Stray Thoughts*, 26.

[107] Brian M. Walker, *Parliamentary Election Results in Ireland, 1801-1922* (Dublin, 1978), 138. WJD, D 880/2/50, 20 May 1898.

with the Marquess of Dufferin and Ava, whereby the ex-viceroy pledged his support for Hill's claims upon a colonial governorship; for his part, Hill, upon appointment, promised to work for the succession of Dufferin's son to the representation of West Down. However, because of Joseph Chamberlain's truculence, Hill's proconsular ambitions were never realized, and his own son suddenly discovered an interest in parliament and in the constituency. Dufferin was therefore politely rebuffed, and Captain A. W. Hill was elected unopposed—as indeed his father had predicted.[108] The Captain sat, a largely silent member, until 1905, his career being distinguished only by the censure of his Ulster colleagues.[109]

Outside the family fief, Arthur Hill's political influence had already peaked in the mid-1880s, and was thereafter on the decline. His personal standing was weakened by financial difficulties, partly a consequence of bad relations with the sixth Marquess of Downshire, and partly a result of his having fallen victim to a fraudulent solicitor.[110] His position in the party suffered. The die-hard Conservatism which had been appropriate to the early years of Balfour's Irish administration ceased to be so, after the Party returned to office in 1895, in coalition with Chamberlainite radicals like T. W. Russell. Indeed it was well known that the Colonial Secretary disliked Hill; and the Irish Conservative press was considerably ruffled when news leaked in 1896 that Chamberlain would not appoint the veteran Tory to a governorship.[111]

Within Ulster Hill's one-dimensional Unionism, imposed by the leadership upon a compliant public, was being superseded; and a more diverse movement, rooted in popular economic and sectarian concerns, was taking its place. Hill represented an age when the elders of Irish loyalism enjoyed an exaggerated importance.[112] An anti-Home Rule consensus shaped the broader politics of Irish Protestant society—and popular opinion, held in awe by the threat of Nationalist revolution, was prepared to be marshalled by its 'natural'

[108] Dufferin Papers, D 1701/H/B/F, Hill to Dufferin, 28 May 1896, 10 July 1896, 12 July 1896, 27 Nov. 1896, 3 Dec. 1896, 19 July 1897, 26 July 1897.
[109] BNL, 15 May 1903.
[110] ABP, Add. MS 49773, fo. 99, Balfour to Joseph Chamberlain, 29 Feb. 1896 (copy)
[111] BNL, 12 May 1896.
[112] Cf. Ostrogorski, Democracy and Organisation, i. 590-1.

social leadership.[113] By the end of the century, several forms of economic-based unrest had gained sufficient strength to be able to challenge the pretensions of the existing leaders. Hill's style of management (discreet overtures to Orange and Masonic colleagues, economic pressure on social 'inferiors') was no longer so easily accomplished. Even in the family seat of East Down an attempt to remove the sitting MP foundered, when the victim threatened an appeal to the electorate.[114] Hill himself lost heavily to the populist sectarian, T. H. Sloan, when he contested South Belfast in January 1906. He was returned for West Down in 1907, but with the smallest majority ever secured in the constituency (784 votes); and his high-handed treatment of the new constituency association created a bitterness which remained until his final retirement, only eight months after the election.[115]

Hill's interference had exploited a popular neglect of constituency organization, and this, in turn, was born of Unionist solidarity. For so long as the Union dominated Irish politics, then service in the constituency hierarchy seemed a peculiarly inadequate form of political expression: Ulster Unionists were evidently more ready to man the last ditch than a selection committee. By implication, the identity of parliamentary representatives often lacked significance: so long as an MP was a loyal Unionist, had money and moral respectability, and was prepared to register his vote in a minimum number of critical divisions, then his name or manner of selection appeared immaterial.[116] The chief exceptions to this consensus in the era of Home Rule politics sprang from party rivalries between Conservatives and Liberal Unionists; and, though recurrent and sometimes fierce, these were confined to a very few constituencies.[117] The individuality of candidates began to possess a political significance only when their prospective electors developed an interest in a wider range of economic and sectarian questions.

[113] Cf. Henry Patterson, *Class Conflict and Sectarianism: The Protestant Working Class and the Belfast Labour Movement, 1868-1920* (Belfast, 1980), 23.

[114] Rentoul, *Stray Thoughts*, 26.

[115] DRO, Theresa Londonderry Papers, D/Lo/C/666/23, Long to Lady Londonderry, 21 Nov. 1907. BL, Walter Long Papers, Add. MS 62412, J. M. McCalmont to Long, 19 Dec. 1907.

[116] Cf. Ostrogorski, *Democracy and Organisation*, i. 345-6; Peter Richards, *Honourable Members: A Study of the British Backbencher* (London, 1959, 37.

[117] Macknight, *Ulster as it is*, ii. 157.

The attainment of 'normal' politics (even within the limited context
of the Protestant community) would only occur after the seemingly
conclusive defeat of Home Rule in 1893.

5. Internal Threats, 1885–1910

Opposition to old-style constituency management, and to the
indifferent quality of parliamentary representation which it
promoted, grew in the mid-1890s, and was voiced by three economic
or sectarian pressure groups: farmers, Presbyterians, and Protestant
labour in Belfast. These groups lobbied as Unionists, but ultimately
they aimed less for reform than for the end of the existing structures
of Protestant parliamentary representation. Each movement had its
specific grievances, and its growth was governed by separate factors.
Each, on the other hand, focused its opposition through election
campaigns, and shared a particular view of the failings of organized
Unionism. Though formally distinct, the three movements can
therefore be treated as part of one broad reaction to the inadequate
nature of Ulster parliamentary representation.[118]

The opposition of Protestant workers to the élitist Belfast
Conservative Association, and its MPs, dated from as early as 1868,
when William Johnston, in collusion with the Orange and Protestant
Working Men's Association, was elected to Westminster through the
votes of Protestant artisans.[119] The OPWA, as Henry Patterson has
shown, particularly condemned the middle-class monopoly of parliamentary representation in Belfast, foreshadowing subsequent independent Unionist criticism. Johnston himself indicted the incapacity of
Ulster Conservative MPs, proclaiming with brutal directness that 'for
all the good some of the Ulster members do the Orange cause, they might
as well have been selected from the Deaf and Dumb Institute'.[120]

However, the Johnstonian rebellion was comparatively short-lived,
for the Conservative Association's reorganization of 1880 incorporated Orangeism within its structure, and took the wind from
independent sails.[121] Though Johnston and a fellow populist,

[118] See Patterson, *Class Conflict* for labour dissent and, for Presbyterian and
farmer unrest, J. R. B. McMinn, 'The Reverend James Brown Armour and Liberal
Politics in North Antrim, 1869–1914', Ph.D. thesis (Belfast, 1979).
[119] Patterson, *Class Conflict*, 3.   [120] Ibid.
[121] Ibid. 11.

E. S. W. de Cobain, were returned as working men's representatives in 1885, Home Rule ushered in a period of relative quiescence for Belfast Conservatism. The 'two nations' theme of Unionist rhetoric (prosperous, developed Ulster as distinct from a backward south) provided an effective integrationist ideology to curb Protestant class antagonisms. Wealth and prosperity had become central to the Ulster Unionist's self perception, and the propertied élite within the Conservative Association could now be represented as central to the leadership of Ulster's resistance.[122]

After the defeat of Home Rule in 1893, and of the Rosebery government in 1895, independent populist candidatures returned as a feature of Belfast parliamentary politics (Table 5.1). None of the Unionist seats in Belfast was free from threat, and even in vulnerable West Belfast, where there was only one, disastrous, independent candidature, H. O. Arnold-Forster was under continuous pressure from 'that brutal, pig-headed, section of your Belfast constituents'.[123] Indeed, Mary Arnold-Forster, his wife, rejoiced in 1898 that revision work in West Belfast had fallen behind, for she reasoned that a small majority on the books diminished the likelihood of opposition from a Unionist labour candidate.[124]

Though the populist candidatures varied in form and causation, most shared common ground in criticizing the limited base of Unionist constituency organization. Adam Turner justified his candidature for North Belfast in January 1896 by claiming that the selection of his Conservative rival, Sir James Haslett, had taken place without proper consultation of the constituency.[125] Thomas Harrison's abortive rival candidature stressed a similar argument— that existing political organization had failed to produce candidates 'who would look at working class questions from the working class point of view'.[126] Fighting the same constituency in 1900, Harrison returned to the theme: '"the working classes of Belfast", he told a

[122] Ibid. 21–3.
[123] Arnold-Forster Papers, TCD 5000/277, Florence O'Brien to H. O. Arnold-Forster, 19 Oct. 1901.
[124] Arnold-Forster Papers, TCD 5000/237, Mary Arnold-Forster to Florence O'Brien, 22 Oct. 1898.
[125] *BNL*, 10 Jan. 1896. Patterson discusses Turner's candidature in *Class Conflict*, 39.
[126] *BNL*, 11 Jan. 1896.

TABLE 5.1. *Non-Nationalist Opposition to Belfast Unionism, 1890–1910*

Year	Candidate	Belfast Seat	Party	Opponent's Party	Independent Poll (%)
1892	W. T. Charley	East	Ind. U.	Unionist	35
1896	A. Turner	North	Ind. U.	Unionist	49
1900	T. Harrison	North	Ind. LU.	Unionist	31
1902	T. H. Sloan	South	Ind. U.	Unionist	56
1905	W. Walker	North	Labour	Unionist	47
1906	W. Walker	North	Labour	Unionist	48
1906	T. H. Sloan	South	Ind. U.	Unionist	55
1906	A. M. Carlisle	West	Ind. LU	U & Nat.	2
1907	W. Walker	North	Labour	Unionist	41
1910 (J)	R. Gageby	North	Labour	Unionist	39
1910 (D)	T. H. Sloan	South	Ind. U.	Unionist	38
1910 (D)	T. H. Sloan	South	Ind. U.	Unionist	33

Source: Brian Walker, *Parliamentary Election Results in Ireland, 1801–1922* (Dublin, 1978).

a sympathetic audience, "have never been represented in parliament". (A Voice: "Not by Haslett, anyway")'.[127]

Such complaints were echoed within militant Protestant politics. Robert Lindsay Crawford's paper, *The Irish Protestant*, helped pave the way for T. H. Sloan's South Belfast victory of August 1902 by relating the shortcomings of the Irish Unionist parliamentary party to what has been called the 'oligarchic structure of [local] Unionist politics'.[128] In March 1902 the paper announced that 'the control of Irish parliamentary seats lies, so far as Irish protestants are concerned, in the hands of a small minority, whose political instincts have been moulded in the Carlton Club . . .'.[129] Patterson has demonstrated that this report was the earliest expression of what subsequently developed into a theme of Independent Orange rhetoric.[130] Certainly Sloan himself, until his short-lived incorporation within the Ulster Party, highlighted the oligarchic failings of loyalist electoral organization.

---

[127] *BNL*, 1 Oct. 1900. Harrison's candidature is discussed by Patterson in *Class Conflict*, 43.

[128] Henry Patterson, 'Independent Orangeism and Class Conflict in Edwardian Belfast: A Reinterpretation', *PRIA*, lxxx, sect. c (1980), 11.

[129] Patterson, 'Independent Orangeism', 13.   [130] Ibid.

Presbyterian sectarian candidates employed a similar complaint against the narrowness of clique-ridden constituency organization. Fuelled by a sectarian dispute over the candidature for North Down in 1898, a Presbyterian Unionist Voters' Association was formed at Belfast in November of that year; among the aims which this embraced was that of promoting Presbyterian representation in the Commons.[131] The County Council elections of April 1899 suggested that this platform enjoyed wide support, and at the general election of 1900 several candidates emerged, backed by the resources of local Presbyterianism.[132] Mid and East Antrim, together with South Belfast, were thought to be particularly under threat from the Presbyterians, but at least one informed Unionist observer—Thomas Sinclair—recognized that the rebels themselves were more vulnerable than their theoretical electoral strength implied.[133]

T. L. Corbett was the standard-bearer of the PUVA in North Down. 'I am fighting the battle of the electors', he told a Portavogie audience on 2 September 1900, 'in order that the clique in Belfast might in future be debarred from putting in any candidate they liked.'[134] Fuller details of the 'clique's' infamy were offered at a Ballyblack meeting on 12 September, The undemocratic nature of the Conservative candidate's selection was stressed: the premature appearance of Colonel Crawford's election posters 'showed that the little clique had chosen the colonel before he was even waited on . . .'.[135] Corbett's manifesto underlined these arguments, while repudiating—as he had done throughout the campaign—any intention of dividing the Unionist party. He gave prominence to his effort to form 'a really representative Unionist Association'—an effort which had been thwarted by a landed Conservative cadre that 'in the past has claimed to dictate to the electors [and which] considers its continued domination of more consequence than the rights of the people, or the peace of the party'.[136]

His candidature, though formally sectarian, appealed to a broader constituency alienated by the limitations of official party organization. He embraced Presbyterian grievances, without repelling Anglicans; he embraced tenant grievances, without compromising his Unionism. He was a populist, therefore, who maintained a firm

[131] McMinn, 'Armour', 139.   [132] Ibid. 142.
[133] Dufferin Papers, D 1701/H/B/F, T. Sinclair to Dufferin, 18 June 1900.
[134] BNL, 3 Sept. 1900.   [135] BNL, 13 Sept. 1900.
[136] BNL, 27 Sept. 1900.

connection with orthodoxy—and, when elected, he was speedily incorporated into the official Ulster parliamentary party. By 1910, his politics had become so conventional that he earned the accolade of 'a very good, true fellow' from Walter Long, then chairman of the Irish Unionist members, and a strict party disciplinarian.[137]

Corbett's Presbyterian colleagues included Dr King-Kerr in East Antrim, and R. J. McMordie, invited by the Ballymena branch of the PUVA to stand for Mid Antrim.[138] King-Kerr, while not formally a PUVA candidate, had its support, and embraced its aims and rhetoric: 'no one needs to be told', commented a sceptical *Belfast News Letter*, 'that this gentleman is to be its [the PUVA] standard-bearer'.[139] King-Kerr echoed Corbett's grievances concerning the failings of local party organization: 'there was in East Antrim a Constitutional Association', he commented ironically to a meeting on 4 October, '. . . the greater part of . . . [which] had since died off'.[140] Like Corbett's opponents in North Down, the East Antrim Association had allegedly 'managed' the selection of the official candidate, Colonel McCalmont, having invited only a carefully vetted selection of its membership to a nomination meeting held at Ballyclare.[141] 'There were 8900 electors in East Antrim', King-Kerr challenged a meeting on 7 October, '. . . would they allow 50 or 60 men who met in Ballyclare to select their representative? Was that fair?.[142]

Of these challengers, only Corbett triumphed over his official opponent. Moreover, although his victory was greeted by province-wide Presbyterian euphoria, and (most unusually for a local election) by the production of various items of commemorative ware, the PUVA subsequently 'faded away'.[143] Militant Presbyterian energies, were directed into T. W. Russell's campaign for compulsory land purchase, which, as Sinclair predicted, 'threatened to inflict a much more serious rift upon the Ulster Unionist Party than the PUVA'.[144] Large numbers of Presbyterians voted in February 1902 for

[137] Theresa Londonderry Papers, D/Lo/C/666/112, Walter Long to Lady Londonderry, 7 Apr. 1910.   [138] *BNL*, 27 Sept. 1900.
[139] Ibid.   [140] *BNL*, 5 Oct. 1900.
[141] Ibid.   [142] *BNL*, 8 Oct. 1900.
[143] Crockery jar with Corbett's portrait in author's possession; McMinn, 'Armour', 142.
[144] McMinn, 'Armour', 142. Dufferin Papers, D 1701/H/B/F, Sinclair to Dufferin, 12 Nov. 1900.

James Wood, the successful Russellite candidate for East Down
(Arthur Hill's former fiefdom). Nonconformist votes swept Edward
Mitchell to victory in the North Fermanagh contest of March
1903.[145]

Presbyterianism was traditionally associated with farmer
radicalism, but the PUVA had propagated a more self-consciously
sectarian dissent, focusing its concerns on the identity of Ulster
representatives—their religion, their occupation—as much as on their
parliamentary action. T. W. Russell, on the other hand, combined
sectarian, farmer, and general political unrest into a movement which
rocked the foundations of Ulster representation between 1900 and
1906. He inherited the PUVA's grievances against oligarchic local
organization, and he incorporated them into a broader anti-
establishment platform.

Even before Russellism had enveloped the PUVA platform, farmer
rhetoric had exploited the inadequacy of existing political structures.
The ubiquitous Thomas Harrison, standing for North Derry as a
tenant candidate in 1895, complained that the selection of his official
opponent, John Atkinson, had taken place 'without the farmers and
the working-men of the constituency'.[146] In 1898 E. C. Thompson,
an independent Unionist standing for North Fermanagh, boldly
repudiated his landowning opponent, E. M. Archdale: 'a Committee', he complained, 'self-selected, or rather nominated, and
in no sense representative of the electors of North Tyrone, has
arbitrarily selected a candidate . . . I dispute their right to act in this
manner'.[147] James Orr, standing against Edward Saunderson in
North Armagh, stressed that he was a local man, 'living in the heart
of the constituency, and accessible at all times to the voters', where
his opponent, evidently, could claim none of these attributes.[148]
Russell's candidates took up the theme, pointing to their own
democratic selection, and making play of corrupt official procedures.
Edward Mitchell's North Fermanagh success was founded on a
campaign which highlighted the inadequacies of official local

[145] *BNL*, 7 Feb. 1902; St John Ervine, *Craigavon: Ulsterman* (London, 1949),
95-9. Carson called Nonconformist and Catholic co-operation 'an unholy
alliance': Private Possession, William Moore Papers, Carson to Moore, 28 Jan.
1906.

[146] *BNL*, 9 July 1895.

[147] Falls and Hanna Papers, D 1390/26/9, election poster, Oct. 1898.

[148] *BNL*, 27 Sept. 1900.

organization; and subsequent Russellite candidates echoed Mitchell's line of attack.[149]

This consensus between labour, farmers, and Presbyterians sometimes embraced Unionists otherwise loyal to their party, and to existing forms of representation. Official doubts about local organizational adequacy seldom emerged in public, at any rate before the growth of Russellism: complacency such as that radiated by the *Belfast News Letter* predominated. But, particularly after election failure, weak party organization might be highlighted as a means of avoiding more personal recrimination. And even loyal Unionists, like their opponents, were sometimes driven to question the acceptability of an MP's parliamentary conduct. King-Kerr, the East Antrim Presbyterian rebel, had complained in October 1900 that 'Colonel McCalmont's sin during his parliamentary career had been the sin of omission. In the 15 years during which he had represented East Antrim he would like to know what part Colonel McCalmont had taken in the debates affecting agricultural interests . . .'.[150] The *News Letter* voiced a similar objection to Captain A. W. Hill, the persistently silent member for East Down.[151] A Conservative supporter of the South Antrim MP, W. G. Ellison-Macartney, complained that 'the feelings of Ulster constituencies could be safely ignored because there was no cohesion among Ulster Unionist representatives'.[152] Independent Orange criticism focused similarly on the Ulster Party's failure to influence government policy (and in particular to wean the Castle from conciliation).[153] Conservatives complained that the party had failed to provide government patronage; independents complained that Ulster members 'were only using the electors as the stepping stones to some profitable job'.[154] Occasionally the Conservative press went so far as to express limited sympathy for worthy independents (Corbett in North Down; Lawther in South Antrim).[155]

By the end of the century, thus, there had developed a broadly-based distrust both of Unionist constituency organization, and of the poor quality of representation which it promoted. External influence on selection procedures was condemned; corrupt clique-management was exposed. The financial dependence of official

[149] Buckland, *Ulster Unionism*, 24.

[150] *BNL*, 4 Oct. 1900.

[151] *BNL*, 29 Sept. 1900.

[152] *BNL*, 27 Sept. 1900.

[153] Patterson, 'Independent Orangeism', 10.

[154] *BNL*, 16 Jan. 1906.

[155] *BNL*, 27 Sept. 1900.

organization escaped criticism, but then any call for a popular foundation to political funding was scarcely likely to win votes. In any case, Russellism itself depended upon subventions from a very few wealthy patrons: a William Gibson was identified by Horace Plunkett as Russell's financial backer, while a prospective Russellite candidate in North Down donated £1000 to his master's campaign fund.[156]

This reaction had a more general significance, for it was symptomatic of a profound shift in electoral relations. In the Home Rule era, popular political participation was generally limited to theatrical gestures at times of particular crisis (Lord Randolph Churchill's Ulster Hall meeting of February 1886, the Ulster Convention of 1892). Between 1886 and 1893, while there is every indication of a sustained, if sometimes superficial, Unionist fervour, there is also evidence which indicates a widespread reluctance to contribute to local party organization. In some constituencies, there was no contribution because there was no organization. In some constituencies, both in Belfast and in the counties, effective management of electoral affairs was confined to a small, propertied clique: this could exercise authority and command deference so long as decisive Unionist leadership was a community priority. With the rejection of Home Rule this priority vanished and popular political activity increased, a renewed interest in local organization forming part of a broader critique of the quality of Ulster representation.

Irish Unionist MPs experienced, therefore, a dramatic change in their relationship with the constituency. From a period when popular opinion offered little restraint, MPs found after 1893 that they were subject to a closer, or at any rate a different, form of scrutiny. From a period when certain MPs were wholly dependent on the whim of individuals, or influential local élites, most found themselves liberated from all but the constraints of popular exposure. The character of the parliamentary Ulster Party was now more likely to be determined by representative opinion within the constituency. In this sense, Ulster MPs and their electors were more fully at one.

---

[156] Plunkett Diaries, 2 Aug. 1901. National Maritime Museum, Arnold White Papers, WH1/80, Russell to White, 11 Aug. 1906. I am grateful to Dr R. H. Williams for this reference.

TABLE 5.2. *The Spread of Land Purchase in Ulster, 1870-1909*

Land Sold and Vested in the Purchasing Tenant (Acres)		Proceedings Instituted and Pending by 1912 (Acres)	Area Unsold (Acres)
Acts of 1870-1896	Acts of 1903-1909		
772,904	850,435	1,044,896	2,256,370

Source: Parliamentary Papers 1912-13, lxxi. 764, [Cd. 6130].

6. Landowners and Local Politics, 1885-1910

This alignment of MP and constituency developed partly as a consequence of the Ulster Party's reaction to its unpopularity, and partly, too, because of the decline of landed political influence.[157] The party's response to its unpopularity involved improving political organization in the north; and thus the closer relationship between MP and voter was bought at the cost of a progressively Ulsterized Unionism. On the other hand, the weakening of the landed position in the Commons was also related to this new alignment, at once both a symptom and a cause. Landed MPs were the particular victims of popular disquiet, but their departure from parliament also created scope for new developments within loyalist representation.

Table 5.2 traces the growth of land purchase between 1870 and 1909, and indicates how far a farmer proprietorship had been created by the terminal date. Table 5.3 reveals that, though over 2.5 million acres in Ulster had been sold, this figure was proportionately less than in the rest of Ireland. By the Edwardian period it is clear both that landlordism was on the decline in Ulster, and that there yet remained considerable scope for farmer agitation. Moreover, the

---

[157] There is a considerable literature on this phenomenon, and on its implications for late nineteenth-century British politics. Of particular relevance are W. L. Guttsman, *The British Political Elite* (London, 1963), 125-37; J. P. Cornford, 'The Parliamentary Foundations of the Hotel Cecil', in R. Robson (ed.), *Ideas and Institutions of Victorian Britain: Essays in Honour of George Kitson Clark* (London, 1967), 281-3; Howarth, 'Liberal Revival', 85-92; Ridley, 'Leadership and Management', *passim*.

TABLE 5.3. *Land Purchase in Ulster and the Rest of Ireland, 1870-1909*

Province	Sales and Pending Sales (in Acres)	Unsold (Acres)	Proportion Sold : Unsold
Leinster	2,664,994	1,887,206	1 : 0.71
Connaught	2,567,372	1,061,897	1 : 0.41
Munster	3,540,847	2,122,723	1 : 0.6
Ulster	2,668,235	2,256,370	1 : 0.85

Source: Parliamentary Papers, 1912-13, lxxi. 764 [Cd. 6130].

disposal of estates in England, as in Ireland, was occurring only after several decades of reduced rental income.[158]

One effect of the progress of purchase, particularly in the context of falling rents, lay in the further weakening of landed social and political influence. The roots of these phenomena predated the Land War; but purchase, because it meant the physical destruction of the great estates, brought the crisis of landlordism to a head. Estates contracted, and local political relationships suffered readjustment. Formerly at the head of rural society, landowners found themselves increasingly displaced, and released from many of their former responsibilities of leadership.

Deprived of a social role, their political status suffered.[159] Northern squires, though still more wealthy than those in the south and west, were affected by the broader unpopularity of landlordism; and while their political position was stronger than that of their southern counterparts—it could scarcely have been weaker—this very strength was an object of popular indictment.[160] Consequently they were less likely to sit in parliament for northern constituencies than formerly: lawyers and businessmen increasingly dominated the Ulster Party in the Commons.[161] They were less likely to exercise complete control over selection procedures. The expense of fighting North Tyrone prevented members of the Hamilton family standing for the seat after 1895; previously the Unionist nomination had been wholly

[158] Barbara Solow, *The Land Question and the Irish Economy, 1870-1903* (Cambridge, Mass., 1971), 175. Guttsman, *Political Elite*, 127-33.

[159] See Guttsman, *Political Elite*, 137.

[160] L. P. Curtis, 'Incumbered Wealth: Landed Indebtedness in Post-Famine Ireland', *American Historical Review*, lxxxv. 2 (Apr. 1980), 366-7.

[161] See ch. 3.1.

controlled by them.[162] As has been noted, East Down, and ultimately West Down, fell from the control of the Hill family.

On the other hand, Lord Deramore was perhaps overstating his case in remarking that by 1889 'territorial influence is gone, and gone for ever': some influence remained, albeit in a bastardized form, well into the new century.[163] In 1910, for example, Viscount Castlereagh, whose father, the sixth Marquess of Londonderry, had sold off much family land in Down, could still command the refusal of one of the county divisions—though only with the connivance of Walter Long and the linen magnate, Thomas Andrews.[164] Furthermore, this influence may now have had more to do with the Marquess's stature as a Unionist statesman than with his son's social credentials. Significantly, Ronald McNeill, despite the patronage of Londonderry, could not carry the nomination for the same division, partly because of his family 'connection with the land agency'.[165] On the other hand, Arthur Hill could command a residual loyalty as late as 1907, even among the relatives of his independent Unionist opponent, Andrew Beattie.[166] And squires continued to thrive within the representative institutions of the Northern Ireland state.[167] Thus, the retreat of landed influence was by no means dramatic; and the restrictions which came to be imposed upon the county grandees perhaps seem severe only when judged in the light of their former ascendancy. Popular respect certainly survived the collapsing economic role of the great estates, even though such respect was not now automatically carried into politics.

No longer so well represented in parliament, landlords' contributions to local party funds began to decline. This would be expected from the evidence of falling rentals, and indeed some magnates, like Lord Antrim, admitted the connection.[168] Lawyers, like Godfrey Fetherstonhaugh in North Fermanagh, often acquired both a constituency and its financial burden from landlord

---

[162] See e.g. Lord Ernest Hamilton, *Forty Years On* (London, [1922]), 203.

[163] Rentoul, *Stray Thoughts*, 26. Curtis, 'Incumbered Wealth', 366-7.

[164] Theresa, Lady Londonderry Papers, D/Lo/C/666/107, Long to Lady Londonderry, 1 Feb. 1910; D/Lo/C/633/1, T. Andrews to Lady Londonderry, 12 Apr. 1910.

[165] McNeill Papers, MIC 63/2, J. B. Lonsdale to McNeill, 21 Apr. 1910.

[166] Edith M. Clarke, *Round About Rathfriland* (Rathfriland, 1981), 146.

[167] John Harbinson, *The Ulster Unionist Party, 1882-1973: Its Development and Organisation* (Belfast 1973), 110, 125-6.

[168] Young Papers, D 3027/5/6/2, Antrim to Young, 13 May 1889.

predecessors.[169] In North Down T. L. Corbett inherited annual expenses of some £300 from the squire R. G. Sharman-Crawford.[170] And in East Tyrone financial survival was only assured through recurrent fund-raising: local landed magnates like Lord Ranfurly and Lord Castlestuart could provide only comparatively small sums for their association by the end of the Edwardian period.[171]

The retreat of the landlords was related to the developing relationship between Unionist representative and elector. As has been observed, this retreat was also a feature of British politics, but here the nature of British and Irish electoral experience should be distinguished perhaps by its contrasts rather than the reverse.[172] For, with the development in Britain of modern party organization, some of the more obvious parallels between the quality of parliamentary representation in the two islands ceased to exist. The rise and fall of caucus control in late-nineteenth-century Britain, as noted by Lowell and others, has no direct relevance to the contemporary Irish experience (even though some subsequent developments in Irish Unionist organization might be related to British Tory precedents). Thus, in Britain MPs were gradually freeing themselves from caucus control, and able to perceive themselves as 'representative of the nation at large, rather than as a delegate of a borough'.[173] But in Ireland, by the end of the century, while massive personal expenditure was still expected, there was greater local pressure on a loyalist MP for political accountability. This affected all varieties of representative, but it seems that the new generation of professional and business MPs was more threatened, and more susceptible to threat than their landed colleagues.

Certainly with the departure from politics of MPs like Edward Saunderson and R. T. O'Neill a long tradition of landed indifference to electoral opinion was interrupted. Where a wealthy banker and merchant like J. B. Lonsdale, or a solicitor and rentier like C. C. Craig, fussed and fretted about the state of their constituencies,

---

[169] Falls and Hanna Papers, D 1390/26/6/90, various to Godfrey Fetherstonhaugh, 11 Apr. 1907.
[170] McNeill Papers, MIC 63/2, R. G. Sharman-Crawford to McNeill, 7 Apr. 1910.
[171] ETUA Papers, D 1132/5/2, Ranfurly to Lowry, 24 Sept. 1910; Castlestuart to Lowry, 19 Sept. 1910.
[172] See n. 157.   [173] Lowell, *Government*, i. 513-14, 549-84.

Saunderson stood firmly on his landed principles, heedless of local pressure. He was the only loyalist member who had refused a commitment to compulsory purchase by 1901; and, more generally, he was but a sporadic patron to his constituents.[174] Similarly, Captain A. W. Hill and Lord Ernest Hamilton each failed to defend their constituents' interests in the Commons, attending only occasionally, and contributing little; R. T. O'Neill was no more voluble.[175] Occasionally this blithe disregard for local feeling was bluntly presented to the electorate, as O'Neill confided to his mother in July 1892:

I think it is very silly for so many Conservative candidates to try to give enigmatic answers on important questions. I took the line of telling them [the electors of Mid Antrim] my views, and if they did not like them, they might get someone else to represent them, and it has certainly paid . . . I put it very plainly that I would not be tied by any promises.[176]

Such bravado recalled the tone of eighteenth-century political debate, and it was surely rooted in the exercise of parliamentary power by the landed gentry over many decades.[177] Indeed, the forebears of Saunderson, O'Neill, Hamilton, and Hill had sat as MPs, where a C. C. Craig or a Lonsdale possessed a less distinguished political pedigree. The familiarity of the role bred landed confidence and, occasionally, contempt; and, when a challenge did occur, it was treated as a culpable breach of trust. Saunderson was appalled when an independent Unionist candidate emerged in 1900 in his North Armagh seat: on the other hand, James Craig and Lonsdale, products of a different social and electoral milieu, treated such opponents as an occupational hazard.[178] When the barrister William Moore, who had an ancient family bond with North Antrim and with the squirearchy, was defeated for that constituency in 1906, his family regarded the outcome as 'almost a personal affront'. According to Moore's daughter, North Antrim had been treated as the family's 'home town', and defeat had destroyed 'a happy relationship we all had with many people'.[179]

---

[174] See my *Edward Saunderson and the Evolution of Ulster Unionism 1865–1906* (Belfast, forthcoming); Reginald Lucas, *Colonel Saunderson, M.P.: A Memoir* (London, 1908), 310.

[175] See above, ch. 3.2.

[176] Private Possession, R. T. O'Neill Papers, O'Neill to Lady Anne O'Neill, 9 July 1892.

[177] See e.g. Richards, *Honourable Members*, 157.

[178] Macartney Papers, D 3649/20/51, Saunderson to Macartney, 1 Oct. 1900.

[179] Private Possession, Nina Patrick Diaries, 27 Jan. 1906.

Thus, the departure of the landlords helped to free Ulster constituencies from representatives isolated by, and reliant upon, deference. Lawyers and businessmen had no 'natural', or dynastic, right to any rural parliamentary seat—and their money helped to secure electoral success and local goodwill rather than freedom from local political control. Many constituencies by 1906 were as dependent on the wealth of their MP as in 1885; but they were now prepared both to accept cash, *and* impose terms. In this way, the survival of old financial arrangements obscured a new relationship between an MP and his constituency.

7. The Ulster Unionist Council

This relationship was buttressed by structural reform within Unionism. Unionist organization had been overhauled in the 1880s and again in 1892, following the Ulster Convention.[180] A Convention League was founded, and at the same time a movement to establish local Unionist clubs developed under the leadership of Viscount Templetown: this achieved some success before dissolving in 1895, and after its re-emergence in 1911.[181] But the 'original basic unit in the structure of Ulster Unionism' was not, as has been suggested, the Unionist club, which had a merely ancillary political role, but rather the constituency association, whose emergence in the mid-1880s has been described by Brian Walker—and whose condition at the end of the decade has been analysed earlier in the chapter.[182] The revitalization of these associations in 1905–6 reforged the bond between an MP and his constituency, where hitherto this relationship had only rarely been anchored to any stable political structure.

The reorganization of local Unionist associations and the creation of an Ulster Unionist Council in the years after 1904 have been recognized as crucial developments in the history of modern Unionism.[183] It has been demonstrated how the emergence of the Council helped to undermine Independent Orange attacks on the Ulster Party; and indeed, independent opinion was sceptical of the

[180] Harbinson, *Ulster Unionist Party*, 20.   [181] Ibid. 21–2.
[182] Ibid. 73; Walker, 'Parliamentary Representation', 385–405.
[183] F. S. L. Lyons, 'The Irish Unionist Party and the Devolution Crisis of 1904–1905', *IHS*, vi. 21 (Mar. 1948), 1–22; Harbinson, *Ulster Unionist Party*, 23–4.

function of reorganization, ascribing it to the 'fear of losing seats' rather than 'any honest desire to evolve a sound and constructive policy for the benefit of the country'.[184] Fear of the Independent Orange threat, as represented by Sloan and R. G. Glendinning, may have been influential; but, as is argued in the next chapter, reorganization ought also to be judged in the context of a second constituency threat—that presented by Russellism.[185]

These reforms may be linked in a more general sense to local political developments. It has been shown how, by 1900, a popular consensus had developed, conscious of the inadequacies of party organization and leadership. This consensus embraced both supporters of Unionism, and those whose grievances took them outside the official movement. Loyal party members combined with Presbyterian, farmer, and labour dissent to create a formidable lobby, resentful of the Ulster Party's freedom, and of local political impotence. Thus, a vital part of the context within which reorganization occurred was a popular indictment of the existing structures of Unionism.

The motivation of the Council's founders has been traditionally explained in terms of the devolution affair of 1904-5. Yet, there is a variety of evidence to suggest that Unionist MPs, made vulnerable by local electoral threats rather than by the scare of devolution, wished to cast off the antique forms of political organization which had been forged under their landed predecessors. Local opinion was demanding, and in some cases achieving, a redefinition of the relationship with its Unionist representative; and the responsibility for reform was being thrust upon the MPs of the Ulster Party. The UUC may be seen as their response to this challenge.

William Moore, the North Antrim MP, organized an important preliminary meeting for the Council on 2 December 1904. Past accounts have generally related this action to his crucial role in the devolution debates—but not, however, to the condition of his constituency, where he was under severe pressure from the farmer lobby.[186] Furthermore, the literature publicizing this meeting was issued by T. H. Gibson specifically 'at the direction of the Ulster

---

[184] *Irish Protestant*, 3 Feb. 1905. Quoted in Patterson, *Class Conflict*, 65.
[185] See ch. 6.
[186] An exception is Richard McMinn, 'Liberalism in North Antrim, 1900-1914', *IHS*, xxiii. 89 (May 1982), 20-5.

Unionist Parliamentary Party', and contained no reference to the threat of devolved government: delegates were asked only to 'consider the formation of a Central Unionist organisation'.[187] Other invitations were issued in the name of J. B. Lonsdale, secretary to the parliamentary Ulster Party.[188] The resolutions placed before the meeting were concerned substantially with the general relationship between Unionist opinion and Ulster Party parliamentary policy—exactly the issue which had been attracting widespread criticism before the devolution affair had broken in October 1904.[189] Only at the first public meeting of the new body, in the Ulster Hall, Belfast, on 3 March 1905, was the affair given prominence—and this could hardly have been otherwise while the sensational Commons debates on the subject were still fresh in the public mind.[190]

The Ulster Unionist Council, and the reorganization of local Unionist associations, may be treated, therefore, partly as an effort to redefine the relationship between constituency and representative. The initiative was taken by members of the Ulster Parliamentary Party—since it was they who were suffering at the polls, and from populist accusations. If the apparent involvement of the Irish administration in a scheme for devolution precipitated this initiative, then it was also a response to long-term weaknesses, which had attracted popular condemnation since the mid-1890s.

Whether streamlined Unionism achieved its paper aims is debatable. The Ulster Party had envisaged that the UUC should represent a further connecting link between Ulster Unionists and their parliamentary representation, which would 'settle in consultation . . . the parliamentary policy'.[191] To this end, ten nominees of the parliamentary party met with twenty elected representatives of popular Unionism to form the Council's Standing Executive Committee.[192] In theory, therefore, the UUC provided a mechanism, by which Ulster Party MPs might be brought under greater public scrutiny. But with the closing of Unionist ranks in the wake of the devolution episode, the effectiveness of this mechanism was never rigorously tested.

---

[187] Buckland, *Documentary History*, 203.
[188] UUC Papers, D 1327/7/6A, UUC Cuttings Book; 'Ulster Council and Ulster Union of Constitutional Associations' invitation, 2 Dec. 1904.
[189] Lyons, 'Irish Unionist Party', 13; Harbinson, *Ulster Unionist Party*, 35.
[190] Buckland, *Documentary History*, 204.   [191] Ibid.
[192] Harbinson, *Ulster Unionist Party*, 24.

TABLE 5.4. *Occupational Composition of the UUC Standing Committee,*
1910

Category[a]	Landed		Middle Class					Unidentified
	1	2	3	4	5	6	7	8
Number	9	13	21	5	10	4	2	2

[a] 1. Peerage, sons of peers. 2. Landed gentry. 3. Merchants and
Manufacturers. 4. Newspaper proprietors and editors. 5. Lawyers. 6. Other
professionals (doctors, civil engineers, army officers). 7. Lower professionals
(factory managers, retail agents).

Sources: *Belfast Street Directory for 1910; Burkes Landed Gentry of Ireland*
(1904 and 1958 edns.); R. M. Young, *Belfast and the Province of Ulster*
(Brighton, 1909); E. Gaskell, *Ulster Leaders, Social and Political* (London,
1914); *Who's Who for 1910.*

The value of the UUC in immediate electoral terms was equally
doubtful. The lack-lustre nature of the organizational revolution which
had occurred certainly generated some disappointment: 'it is to be
regretted' the *Northern Whig* commented primly, 'that since its formation the Council has not at all times displayed quite as much vitality
and initiative as was expected by its founders'.[193] But the very fact of
reorganization, and the existence of an institutional vehicle for liaison,
deflated criticism, and restored the parliamentary party's popular credibility. Moreover, the spread and development of divisional organization
after 1905, while scarcely a rigorous popularization, did permit local
Unionist opinion to wield greater control over their MP.[194]

Who was represented on the Council? Clause six of its constitution
awarded substantial powers to the Standing Committee. Assuming
that the re-emergence of the Home Rule threat in 1906 mitigated
class tensions within Unionism, it might have been expected that this
Standing Committee would have facilitated a restoration of the old
governing classes of the movement. In fact this assumption was not
fully borne out: a breakdown of its membership in 1910 reveals
instead that the Committee mirrored the state of parliamentary
representation in the predominance of middle-class elements, and
particularly of manufacturers associated with the linen industry. Indeed,

[193] *Northern Whig*, 31 Jan. 1907.
[194] For a different perspective on the UUC see Buckland, *Ulster Unionism*, 21.

in 1910 the three honorary secretaries of the UUC were linen magnates. The landed classes claimed only twenty-two out of sixty-six Committee members, a substantial but fading representation which reflected their position within constituency politics. Thus there is some basis for the suggestion that the UUC merely recast the existing balance of power within Unionism into a new form. But if the UUC did not embody any democratic transformation, then it was scarcely a nursery for the renaissance of landed politics: rather it confirmed the bourgeois predominance which had been developing within Unionism from the 1880s.

From a different perspective, the creation of the UUC was a northern Unionist achievement, and bound local constituency associations more closely to leadership from Belfast. Indeed, in the context of ancient animosities between Belfast and the Ulster hinterland, the Council was a useful forum for urban and rural unity within the north. The *Northern Whig* reflected in 1907:

To act as a small Ulster parliament was from the first our ideal of the work of the Unionist Council, . . . we have too few opportunities of taking counsel together and our county members . . . complain with justice that they have no regular method of pressing their opinions on the central authorities. The UUC affords a means of remedying that evil.[195]

Thus the UUC—the prototype of a loyalist parliament—may be seen as a natural climax in a long process of Ulsterization, originating with provincial reorganization in the 1880s, and confirmed by the gradual retreat of the Irish Unionist Alliance and the Unionist Joint Committee from northern constituency work.

This is not to exaggerate the immediate and practical significance of these developments for the emergence of a brash Ulster Unionism. For, so long as Unionism was primarily dependent upon parliamentary activity, then it could maintain a fuller Irish character. Only when constitutional opposition to Home Rule had failed, and Unionist endeavours had come to rely upon popular organization, and on a credible military threat, did the process of Ulsterization attain its full significance. Only at this late stage did the actions of northern parliamentary representatives, educated or resident in the south, become less important than the prospect of a northern civil war.

With the removal of the Lords' power of absolute veto in 1911, parliament was no longer an adequate vehicle for the Unionist case.[196]

---

[195] *Northern Whig*, 31 Jan. 1907.   [196] See ch. 7.

But, by staking their future on military strength, Ulster Unionists were also effectively abandoning their isolated and vulnerable southern allies. The true importance of organizational revision was, therefore, only fully demonstrated by the paramilitary activity of 1912-14. Only then was a Belfast-based organization mobilized to exclude effective southern participation.

8. *Summary*

Unionism combined comparative political apathy with lavish political organization—conforming to certain aspects of Ostrogorski's classic model of British party organization. Democratic structures in Ostrogorski's Britain, no less than in Unionist Ireland, veiled limited popular participation.[197] The newly-formed Conservative and Unionist associations of the mid-1880s, in alliance with movements like the ILPU, fulfilled a function similar to Ostrogorski's caucus, shaping a party orthodoxy out of the diversity of Protestant political opinion.[198] Party government was conducted by wire-pullers—in the Irish Unionist example by constituency agents, and, at a provincial level, by functionaries like E. S. Finnegan and Dawson Bates.[199] Indifference, whether in Britain or in Ireland, was countered by the expansion of formal organization, and by presenting the public with political theatre: mass meetings, wild oratory, bands, marches.[200]

This conformity is significant, for it reveals that, while Irish Unionism developed from a unique social and religious polarity, the forms of its political expression and structure were little different from those in contemporary Britain. Thus, by concentrating on the climaxes of Unionist activity (1886, 1892-3, and 1912-14) historians have located a unique political zeal and obscured a more prosaic reality. Apathy often prevailed among both British and Irish Unionists in the intervening periods, only occasionally relieved by carefully regimented expressions of the popular will.

Indeed, even at the times of greatest popular political activity, Ostorgorski's reservations ring true. 'Thinking in battalions', the manufacture of public opinion by mass meeting, the cult of party

---

[197] Ostrogorski, *Democracy and Organisation*, i. 582.   [198] Ibid. 586.
[199] Ibid. 352-62, 581.   [200] Ibid. 584, 588.

and the obliteration of individuality: all typified Unionist popular politics.[201] In this way, Irish Unionists attending the Ulster Convention, or the UUC, were no more unique in their choice of political medium than the Liberals of the National Liberal Federation, or the Tories of the National Union.

The growth of farmer and Presbyterian organization, representing a further source of caucus-style pressure, countered the outmoded deference politics of Unionists like Arthur Hill and helped to forge a closer link between the popular will and parliamentary representation. MPs began to function more fully as delegates of local opinion, responding closely to organized constituency pressure— where formerly they had enjoyed greater freedom, acting as delegates only in so far as they had been returned to uphold Unionism.[202] With the growth of local organization, and the gradual parliamentary supersession of landlords, the bond of deference between representative and elector weakened. Carpet-bagging lawyer MPs— the type is familiar in a contemporary British context—fulfilled a similar role to landowning MPs, dispensing cash and patronage; but they enjoyed neither the same social standing, nor the same parliamentary freedom.

What had changed, therefore, between 1885 and 1911 was not primarily the geographical scope of Unionism—since, in parliamentary terms, Ulsterization only attained significance in 1912. What had changed was rather the internal structure of the movement—the relationship between leader and led. As in Britain there was what Peter Clarke has called 'a qualitative change in the style of politics'.[203] In an English constituency like Blackburn the passage of dynastic MPs like the Hornbys was helping to broaden the scope of electoral debate, so that by 1910 the borough had 'ceased to be local in its politics'.[204] But in Ireland, precisely the reverse process was occurring: until the crisis of 1912, Unionism was being localized, developing from the very broad terms of the Home Rule debate towards a more complicated, and often locally devised, political agenda. MPs lost some of their parliamentary freedom: for many rural members—men like Lonsdale in Mid Armagh, or Moore in North Antrim—local organization and local concerns came to infringe upon what had previously been an unencumbered

[201] Ibid. 585, 590.
[203] Clarke, 'Blackburn Politics', 326.
[202] Ibid. 493–501.
[204] Ibid.

parliamentary freedom. As in the Nationalist party hierarchy, some of the burden of Unionist policy formulation was shifting from Westminster to the constituency.[205] In this sense, therefore, the extra-parliamentary activity of Unionists in 1912–14 was merely a logical conclusion to an older redefinition of the MP's function.

[205] F. S. L. Lyons, *The Irish Parliamentary Party, 1890–1910* (London, 1951), 198–9.

6

Ulster Members and Wyndham, 1900–1905

. . . they found him in Ireland rather an intriguer. If he *is* an intriguer I should say it was of a very suburban kind—I don't know this side of him. I feel myself that George Wyndham is too good a fellow to dabble in sciences over which he has no mastery—and the only two faults I should find in him are want of judgement and want of nerve. He is seldom right except in literary matters.

Margot Asquith[1]

1. *Introduction*

Promenaders, strolling through Hyde Park in May 1905, were struck by the bowed and listless figure of George Wyndham. Whether in the Park, or in the lobbies of the House of Commons, it was agreed that Wyndham, painfully readjusting to a workless and unstructured routine, presented a miserable spectacle: 'it is pathetic to see him', remarked St John Brodrick sadly, '. . . with no work to do and only the sense of defeat'.[2] Former opponents, 'even among the loud-mouthed denouncers of his policy and methods', were cowed by Wyndham's personal misery; friends, like Henry Bellingham, and Lord Edmund Talbot, were upset and outraged by his fate.[3] Only a few irretrievably embittered Ulstermen were unimpressed—holding that Wyndham's fall had offered a timely political salvation. Beyond Ulster pubs and Orange halls, however, it was said that squalid suspicions had blighted a brilliant parliamentary career; and that in

[1] Private Possession, Margot Asquith Diaries, 28 Oct. 1905.
[2] Bodleian Library, Oxford, Papers of William Waldegrave Palmer, Second Earl of Selborne, ii, fo. 41, St John Brodrick to Selborne, 12 May 1905.
[3] GWP, Henry Bellingham to Sibell Grosvenor, 15 Mar. 1905; Lord Edmund Talbot to Sibell Grosvenor, 15 Mar. 1905 ('Even the Orangemen didn't shout as loud as they might . . .'); W. H. Fisher to Sibell Grosvenor, 6 Mar. 1905.

the aftermath of the devolution scandal, Wyndham had sacrificed himself—or had been sacrificed—to soothe the primal anxieties of loyalist backwoodsmen.

Wyndham was accused by Irish loyalists of conniving in a scheme of devolution which had appeared in September 1904, ostensibly from the pens of Lord Dunraven and the Irish Reform Association. Ulster members had reacted hysterically to rumours of ministerial chicanery; and the revelations offered by a parliamentary debate held in February 1905 allowed them to extort the Chief Secretary's resignation. But the devolution débâcle represented much more than an ephemeral parliamentary *coup* for loyalism. The local consequences of Wyndham's humiliation were of greater significance, embracing a remarkable reversal in the electoral fortunes of the Ulster Party. In the aftermath of the affair, the machinery of the Party was permanently altered: MPs were gradually superseded as the spearhead of loyalist political action by a more locally based organization. Edward Saunderson's conception of an essentially parliamentary movement was abandoned; and the party which embodied his ideal—the first Irish Unionist party—was dissected and restructured in the wake of its failure.

2. Ulster MPs, Wyndham, and MacDonnell, 1900-1904

The repudiation of the Chief Secretary by Ulster Unionism was by no means inevitable; and Wyndham's resignation occurred, not as the climax to a linear progression of unrest, but rather at the termination of a much more fluid relationship. Ulster members greeted Wyndham's appointment as Chief Secretary with pleasure. They remembered him as Arthur Balfour's courageous side-kick at the Irish Office during the Plan of Campaign; they remembered him, too, as the uncompromising advocate of the British case against the Boers, while Under Secretary at the War Office.[4] Carson, William Ellison-Macartney, William Johnston, John Lonsdale, and a former Ulster member, John Ross, all wrote to Wyndham, expressing their pleasure, and assuring him of the confidence of the Irish Unionist community: indeed Ellison-Macartney had canvassed opinion at the bastion of Irish Toryism, the Kildare Street Club, and found that

---

[4] Hansard, 4th ser. (1904), cxxxix. 736-7.

the appointment was 'most favourably received'.[5] 'I am certain that you have the good wishes of every Irish Unionist member, and that you may rely upon their cordial support', affirmed J. B. Lonsdale.[6] Only T. W. Russell, of the Ulster leaders, dissented from this consensus of approval.[7]

Wyndham at first did much to justify this attitude. When soi-disant Ulster Unionist farmers rose in agitation, he responded with the Land Bill of 1902.[8] He never lost sight of loyalist opinion during the evolution of the Land Act of 1903 (corresponding with northerners like Hugh de Fellenberg Montgomery); and though he misjudged Ulster opinion on the university question, this was partly because he had been misled by his Belfast contacts.[9] He appointed one of the most uncompromising of the 'Orange bigots', William Moore, as his parliamentary private secretary; and in February 1903, when Moore contracted typhoid, one of the most anxious visitors to his bedside was the Chief Secretary.[10] He maintained friendly contact with Orange leaders like the Earl of Erne, and impressed even crusty landed Tories like the Earl of Gosford.[11] He appeared occasionally at the Kildare Street Club: he hunted and socialized with southern Protestant squires.[12]

Until 1902, therefore, Wyndham (for all his disdainful posing in private) had forged a reasonably amicable relationship with Irish Unionists and their parliamentary representatives. William Johnston

[5] GWP, William Ellison-Macartney to Wyndham, 9 Nov. 1900; John Lonsdale to Wyndham, 8 Nov. 1900; Carson to Wyndham, 5 Nov. 1900; John Ross to Wyndham, 8 Nov. 1900. PRONI, William Johnston Diary, D 880/2/52, 14 Nov. 1900. Lord Balcarres did, however, foresee Wyndham's likely fate among Irish loyalists. See John Vincent (ed.), The Crawford Papers: The Journals of David Lindsay, Twenty-Seventh Earl of Crawford and Tenth Earl of Balcarres 1871–1940 during the Years 1892 to 1940 (Manchester, 1984), 63.

[6] GWP, Lonsdale to Wyndham, 8 Nov. 1900.

[7] See e.g. T. W. Russell, Ireland and the Empire: A Review (London and New York, 1901), 131.

[8] Andrew Gailey, 'The Unionist Government's Policy Towards Ireland, 1895–1905', Ph.D. thesis (Cambridge, 1983), 165–8.

[9] PRONI, Hugh De Fellenberg Montgomery Papers, T 1089/308, Wyndham to Montgomery, 7 Nov. 1902; T 1089/311, Wyndham to Montgomery, 25 Aug. 1903.

[10] Private Possession, Nina Patrick Diary, iii. 43–4.

[11] GWP, George to Sibell Grosvenor, 14 July 1901. Erne's association with Wyndham was the subject of a ruffled letter to Saunderson: PRONI, Saunderson Papers, T 2996/4/33, Lord Erne to Saunderson, 14 July 1902. PRONI, Erne Papers, D 1939/21/10/42, Wyndham to Erne, 9 Feb. 1902.

[12] J. W. Mackail and Guy Wyndham (edd.), The Life and Letters of George Wyndham (2 vols.; London, [1924]) ii. 439–40.

offered persistent support until his death in July 1902; Edward
Saunderson, an acquaintance of several years standing, declared that
Wyndham had 'backbone'—high commendation from a militia colonel
with pretensions to the military virtues.[13] There had certainly been
occasional frosty exchanges: in June 1901, for example, Saunderson
had tabled a motion, calling for a nominal reduction in Wyndham's
salary; but he had intended merely to draw attention to a particular
grievance (which had originated under Gerald Balfour's regime) and
he swathed his proposing speech in apology.[14] It was only after
1902 that the party bond which existed between Wyndham and even
the most fiery loyalist began to weaken. In terms of parliamentary
contact, estrangement developed in three phases, Irish Unionist anger
graduating from law and order, through the case of Constable
Anderson, to the devolution affair. Each grievance was a substantive
concern, but behind each lay the pressure of popular opinion on
Ulster MPs.

The growth of William O'Brien's United Irish League was
accompanied by a proliferation of agrarian crime. While law and
order policy was traditionally a loyalist interest, the politics of their
concern in 1902 were more complex than usual. For the most
articulate spokesman of loyalist rage, William Ellison-Macartney,
UIL lawlessness offered an important opportunity to resuscitate a
waning political career. Between 1900 and 1901, Ellison-Macartney
had suffered a number of reverses: his South Antrim constituency
had been angered by his reluctance, as an important junior minister,
to dispense government patronage; and as a consequence he had
narrowly escaped defeat at the general election of 1900, when even
the *Belfast News Letter* had expressed doubts about his local
effectiveness.[15] Yet, for all his official integrity, Ellison-Macartney
was dismissed from the government in 1901, in order to make way
for a Liberal Unionist, H. O. Arnold-Forster.[16] Excluded from
office, isolated from local politics, Ellison-Macartney desperately
needed to reassert his position within the loyalist hierarchy.

Unionist reaction against the violence of the United Irish League
was promoted and led by Ellison-Macartney—in an attempt to
recover his constituency position by proving that he was not the

---

[13] Hansard, 4th ser. (1901), xcvi. 327.   [14] Ibid.
[15] *BNL*, 27 Sept. 1900, 4.
[16] MSPH, E/Balfour/141, Balfour to Salisbury, 23 Oct. 1900.

ministerial lackey of popular complaint. This campaign was all the more profitable for having the support of ministers like Ashbourne and Cadogan, and the louder approval of the Tory press, particularly the *Times*, the *Morning Post*, and *Globe*.[17] In January 1902 he alleged that the 'general attitude of the government in Ireland . . . had created an atmosphere which clothed with the garb of approval all those who were opposed to Unionist principles', while placing Irish Unionists in a position of 'comparative inferiority'; he involved himself in an embarrassing parliamentary exchange with John Atkinson, Irish Attorney-General and a nominal Ulster Unionist colleague.[18] As yet, however, this stridency found little favour with the majority of the Ulster Party, and members like William Johnston and William Moore dissociated themselves from the more violent bluster of their partners.[19] Wyndham suspected that no security policy would permanently mollify Ellison-Macartney and his followers; and for the moment he refused to concede the only act which would buy their short-term approval, namely the proclamation of the United Irish League. In the event, Ellison-Macartney was silenced rather more efficiently—by being appointed Deputy Master of the Royal Mint.[20]

Ellison-Macartney's law and order campaign was the first prolonged assault by an Irish Unionist on the Wyndham regime. Others, more circumspect, held back; but though Ellison-Macartney's bile was equalled only in the loyalist campaign of 1904, the substance of his criticism came to be accepted and reiterated, in milder form, by colleagues like William Moore. Nevertheless, such disquiet was given little immediate opportunity to develop, for, where loyalist animosity had been fully engaged by T. W. Russell in 1901, Wyndham's Land Bill largely consumed their parliamentary energies in 1903. The Bill has been discussed elsewhere; it attracted considerable Irish Unionist approval, leaders like Saunderson and John Lonsdale complimenting Wyndham on his achievement.[21] Thus, good feeling between the Chief Secretary and Ulster Unionists

---

[17] Andrew Gailey, *Ireland and the Death of Kindness: The Experience of Constructive Unionism, 1890–1905* (Cork, 1987), 180.

[18] Hansard, 4th ser. (1902), ci. 877–8.

[19] Ibid. civ. 82 (Johnston); Ibid. cxi. 1057 (William Moore).

[20] ABP, Add. MS 49804, fo. 18, George Wyndham to Balfour, 3 Mar. 1902. KRO, Akers-Douglas Papers, C 354/1, Ellison-Macartney to Akers-Douglas, 13 Jan. 1903.

[21] See ch. 4.3.

was temporarily revived, in spite of the symptoms of strain evident in 1902.

Indeed even long after 1902 it was Sir Antony MacDonnell, and not Wyndham, who was the focus of loyalist suspicion, and this remained the case until the final revelations of the devolution debates. Ellison-Macartney and Moore had achieved comparatively little popular impact in Ulster by hectoring Wyndham on the inadequacies of law enforcement. But when, in September 1902, a Catholic Irishman—MacDonnell—was appointed to head the Castle bureaucracy, the Ulster Party gained a more powerful cause, for they could now capitalize on the sectarian fears of their support by tracing every petty act of maladministration to the 'crypto-Nationalist' at the Chief Secretary's side. Wyndham continued to escape the burden of loyalist abuse: he found himself portrayed, rather, as a man of honour, bedevilled by the 'sinister influence' of his Permanent Under-Secretary.[22]

Irish Unionist MPs raised three issues in 1904 to illustrate the partiality of MacDonnell's administration. Their first grievance featured two police constables of Roundstone, County Galway, who had been reprimanded at the behest, allegedly, of MacDonnell and a local Catholic priest. The second allegation concerned the discrimination practised supposedly against a Protestant doctor by the predominantly Catholic Board of Guardians of Ballinasloe, also in County Galway. In this Antony MacDonnell featured as a sectarian conspirator, condoning and abetting the discrimination committed by the Ballinasloe Guardians.

T. H. Sloan was deputed to raise the Ballinasloe case in the Commons, and on 7 July 1904 he tabled a motion on the Civil Service Estimates.[23] Again it may be emphasized that Ulster Unionists, as yet, presented no coherent condemnation of the Chief Secretary: Wyndham, Sloan conceded, was 'not responsible in this matter'; Edward Saunderson similarly avoided any direct indictment of the Chief Secretary.[24] C. C. Craig, MP for South Antrim, hinted at Wyndham's culpability, but the significance of his contribution lay rather in anticipating the themes of loyalist rhetoric in the Anderson and devolution debates. Craig referred darkly to Ulster constituency anger; and he was in no doubt that the burden of responsibility 'for

---

[22] Hansard, 4th ser. (1904), cxxxix. 776.   [23] Ibid. cxxxvii. 1026.
[24] Ibid. 1028, 1030.

so much of what they considered bad and unfair government' lay with Antony MacDonnell.[25]

The Ballinasloe debate revealed the depth of loyalist concern with the MacDonnell regime: northern siege-fears were enlivened; suspicions of a discriminatory appointments policy were given free rein. Two aspects of the case, however, have particular significance in the context of loyalists' stand on devolution. Loyalist MPs were alienated, not from Wyndham, but from his appointee, MacDonnell: the residue of an earlier, happier relationship with the Chief Secretary remained. This distinction between minister and civil servant was continually implied because loyalists were not primarily worried by general government policy, but rather by the particular issue of alleged discrimination over patronage.

However, it is also significant that the protagonists of the Ballinasloe debate (as in the other loyalist assaults) were not the 'more reactionary' of the Ulster members.[26] Those Ulster MPs most readily associated with reaction or fiery sectarianism—Edward Saunderson and Tom Sloan—were conspicuously more moderate than later Ulster speakers. Sloan and Saunderson did open the loyalist case; but Saunderson owed this pre-eminence to his seniority, while Sloan, elected as an independent, was demonstrating his newly-won integration among 'official' Ulster colleagues (Saunderson referred pointedly to Sloan as 'a very valuable member of the Party to which he belonged').[27] It was rather C. C. Craig and William Moore who resuscitated Ellison-Macartney's bitterness—and converted what might otherwise have been a predictable loyalist harangue against Nationalist 'corruption' into an indictment of Wyndham: earlier speakers had concentrated merely on the culpability of the benighted local Guardians. And Moore and Craig also, unexpectedly, represented the extremity of Ulster Party opinion during debate on its third, and chief, grievance of 1904: the case of Police Constable Anderson.

Anderson was an officer of the Royal Irish Constabulary, stationed at Kiltimagh, County Kilkenny.[28] Though a Protestant, he was

[25] Ibid. 1040.
[26] Cf. F. S. L. Lyons, 'Irish Parliamentary Representation, 1891–1910', Ph.D. thesis (Dublin, 1947), 211.
[27] Hansard, 4th ser. (1904), cxxxvii. 1031.
[28] Details in Wiltshire Record Office, Trowbridge, Walter Long Papers, 947/69, MacDonnell to Wyndham (copy), 17 July 1904; Lyons, 'Parliamentary Representation', 211–12. E. O'Halpin, *The Decline of the Union: British Government in Ireland, 1892–1920* (Dublin, 1987), 42–3.

engaged to a Catholic girl, Bridget Sweeney. During their courtship it was alleged by several townspeople that Anderson had been guilty of 'improper' conduct, but a police tribunal subsequently declared the complaints unfounded. Ulster MPs, who took up Anderson's case, claimed that his chief accuser among the residents of Kiltimagh, Father Denis O'Hara, had sought out Antony MacDonnell in order to contest the verdict; MacDonnell had, at the priest's instruction, reconstituted the inquiry into the affair. The witnesses at the new inquiry, it was alleged, had been marshalled by O'Hara—with the result that Anderson was convicted of misconduct, and dismissed. Though the hapless constable was eventually reinstated and transferred, Ulster members were enraged by what they claimed had been 'a nefarious conspiracy' between MacDonnell and O'Hara, designed to thwart a mixed marriage, and to pervert justice.[29]

The Anderson case had been given considerable publicity in both England and Ireland, especially by C. C. Craig, and consequently the secretary of the Ulster parliamentary party found little difficulty in extracting a promise of parliamentary time for the issue.[30] The intimacy between Anderson and Bridget Sweeney was paraded, in brutal detail, before the Commons on 3 August 1904. This debate, and its prelude, revealed once again, not so much the uniformly bad feeling between Ulster members and Wyndham, as a more fluid relationship. Saunderson played a comparatively moderate and pacific role, while Moore and Craig again attempted to force the pace of criticism.

Despite past assertions that Wyndham casually dismissed loyalist opinion, there is evidence to suggest that he did much to avert the confrontation which was developing in August 1904.[31] In February Saunderson had approached him representing the depth of loyalist concern over Anderson's plight. Wyndham reacted immediately, complaining to MacDonnell that Anderson's dismissal had been 'a severe penalty' and that he ought to be reinstated.[32] Though Wyndham disavowed any intention of collapsing before sectarian

[29] Hansard, 4th ser. (1904), cxxxix. 741.

[30] J. B. Lonsdale, the Ulster Party secretary, and Sir Alexander Acland-Hood, Unionist Chief Whip, arranged to provide a day for discussion of the Anderson case—apparently without the knowledge of Wyndham: Hansard, 4th ser. (1904), cxxxvii. 1040.

[31] Gailey, Death of Kindness, 201, and passim.

[32] Trowbridge, Walter Long Papers, 947/69 George Wyndham to MacDonnell (copy), 20 Feb. 1904. Hansard, 4th ser. (1904), cxxxix. 738.

pressure, he argued that appeasing Ulster Party opinion on this issue would promote a calmer party atmosphere for discussion of the larger question of education.[33] Without informing MacDonnell, Wyndham browbeat Neville Chamberlain, Inspector General of the Royal Irish Constabulary, into agreeing to reinstate Anderson 'with full back pay'. 'The truth is', MacDonnell later complained, 'that his [Wyndham's] subsequent *volte face* was due to the pressure of Ulster MPs, who believed that, in connection with the case, they had me in jeopardy'.[34]

Saunderson sustained his comparatively moderate tone during the debate on the Anderson case. As party chairman, he led the Ulster attack, but he was restrained and apologetic, referring gracefully to Wyndham's 'great ability' and 'chivalrous character': his account of the affair cast MacDonnell unequivocally in the role of villain.[35] But where Saunderson had concentrated largely on providing the House with the facts of Anderson's defence, William Moore, characteristically, launched into a more direct assault on Wyndham— aided again by C. C. Craig. Where Saunderson had confined himself specifically to the details of the constable's plight, and to a related case, Moore and Craig expanded on the broader iniquities of the administration: both alluded to the prospect of a parliamentary revolt.[36]

Despite the variations in stridency which were emerging within the Ulster Party, many Irish Unionists members agreed that the Anderson case, like that of the Ballinasloe doctor, illustrated an offensive trend in government. Most argued that the Anderson and Ballinasloe affairs formed part of a general anti-Protestant and Unionist policy, superintended by Antony MacDonnell. Moore suggested that while MacDonnell held sway in Dublin Castle, 'there was no chance of justice for a Protestant'.[37] T. H. Sloan placed the Anderson case in the context of other alleged acts of oppression committed on Protestants. C. C. Craig claimed that 'altogether apart from the merits of the [Anderson] case . . . there could be little doubt that Sir Antony MacDonnell's sympathies lay entirely with his fellow-religionists and were as entirely against the interests of the Loyalists in the North'.[38] The Party secretary, John Lonsdale, pointed to

[33] Ibid.
[34] Trowbridge, Walter Long Papers, 947/69, memorandum by Sir Antony MacDonnell, 2 May 1905.
[35] Hansard, 4th ser. (1904), cxxxix. 736, 738.
[36] Ibid. 758–9, 773, 776.   [37] Ibid. 758.   [38] Ibid. 771, 772.

systematic discrimination against the Protestant counties of Ulster in the matter of police tax.[39]

Related to the increasingly general and bitter nature of their indictment was the Party's preoccupation with the state of constituency opinion. Most Irish Unionist speakers pointed to the effects of alleged maladministration on their political support. Moore betrayed a fundamental concern in looking forward with trepidation to the general election: 'before matters went too far', he pleaded, 'something should be done to avoid the danger of the Ulster members being returned by their constituents as an independent Party, absolutely out of touch with the English Unionist Party'.[40] Corroboration for this dismal outlook came from an unlikely source: Joseph Devlin, uncannily prescient, referred to Moore's own likely electoral defeat.[41] John Lonsdale, for the loyalists, claimed that the Wyndham administration was 'estranging those whose loyalty to the Constitution had been the main barrier against separation'—the Ulster farmers.[42] Irish Unionist members were frightened at developments within their constituencies, and they unhesitatingly blamed an unsympathetic Unionist government.

The Ulster Party was therefore highly agitated on the eve of the devolution revelations. Party members were worried by their unpopularity and, led by William Moore and Charles Craig, they sought a scapegoat in Antony MacDonnell. They linked the gradual defection of their support to what they deemed a systematic policy of discrimination, perpetrated in the name of a Unionist administration. Their once amicable relationship with George Wyndham crumbled. While an acquaintance of long standing like Saunderson sought to side-step the Chief Secretary's personal culpability, Party young-bloods were not prepared to moderate their criticism at the cost of constituency disapproval.

It becomes clear, thus, that loyalist anger against the Wyndham regime in 1904 was deeply rooted, and complex in origin: their repudiation of MacDonnell over the Anderson and Ballinasloe cases was not only a reflex sectarian response—though it may have been partly an expression of outraged Protestantism. F. S. L. Lyons, writing in 1948, suspected that the Irish Unionist challenge over devolution demonstrated a more fundamental malaise, yet he

[39] Hansard, 4th ser. (1904), cxxxix. 779.   [40] Ibid. 758-9.
[41] Ibid. 745.   [42] Ibid. 780.

ultimately accepted Orange rhetoric at a conventional valuation, assuming that Ulster members had merely graduated from grubby sectarianism over Anderson to grubby siege-fears over devolution. If he regarded the devolution debate as a progression from the Anderson affair, Lyons did not attempt to identify the ways in which Ulster Party fears had survived unaltered, and were as firmly rooted in electoral calculation as in Protestant conviction.[43]

3. The Loyalist Case against Wyndham

The social web which supported Arthur Balfour's byzantine leadership has also enmeshed the historiography of devolution. With one contemporary exception—Lord Dunraven—the 'facts' of the scandal were established either by the friends and relations of Balfour or of George Wyndham, his client. Discounting various more shameless apologetics published immediately following Wyndham's death in 1913, the first chronicle of devolution was provided by J. W. Mackail and Guy Wyndham in their 1924 tombstone 'Life and Letters' of George Wyndham: Mackail was Wyndham's literary confidant; Guy was his brother.[44] In 1932 Blanche Dugdale published an article on the 'MacDonnell–Wyndham Imbroglio' in the *Quarterly Review*: this was a by-product of her biography of Arthur Balfour, her uncle, and embodied the same personal fidelity.[45] F. S. L. Lyons, the first outsider to approach devolution, synthesized these sources for his article of 1948, and this has survived virtually unchallenged as the definitive statement.[46]

Lyons confirmed the following narrative framework: Antony MacDonnell, despite strong Nationalist connections, and the qualms of Balfour, had been imported by George Wyndham as Permanent Under-Secretary for Ireland. But he had appended one difficult condition to accepting office: that he should possess what he loosely defined as 'adequate opportunities of influencing the action and policy

---

[43] F. S. L. Lyons, 'The Irish Unionist Party and the Devolution Crisis of 1904–1905', *IHS*, vi. 21 (Mar. 1948), 1–22.

[44] Correspondence between Wyndham and Mackail on literary matters is preserved among George Wyndham's surviving papers.

[45] Blanche E. C. Dugdale, 'The Wyndham-MacDonnell Imbroglio, 1902–06', *Quarterly Review*, cclviii. 511 (Jan. 1932), 15–39.

[46] See n. 43. Andrew Gailey's *Death of Kindness* is an important revision from the high-political perspective.

of the Irish government', and that he should be permitted to exercise 'freedom of action within the law'.[47]

Having arrived at Dublin Castle, MacDonnell exploited his 'freedom of action' in cultivating a professional connection with the Earl of Dunraven, whose work through the Irish Reform Association had inspired Wyndham's Land Act of 1903. Dunraven subsequently invited MacDonnell to help thrash out a more sweeping constitutional reform: assuming Wyndham's approval, together with that of Lord Dudley (the Irish viceroy), MacDonnell collaborated with Dunraven in composing two reports, published on 31 August and 26 September 1904. The second report was an elaboration of the first—but each recommended the creation of an Irish legislative and financial council. When, in February 1905, it became known that MacDonnell, as the civil servant of a Unionist government, had, with the approval of a Unionist viceroy, co-written a scheme of devolution, Irish Unionist MPs rebelled. It was impossible, given the evidence of MacDonnell and Dudley's action, to accept that the Chief Secretary had avoided involvement; and thus Wyndham, protesting his innocence, but stripped of political credibility by the insurgent loyalists, had been forced to resign.

In the Lyons hypothesis, the driving force behind Irish Unionist rage was their suspicion that Wyndham had sanctioned Antony MacDonnell's work for the Reform Association. Lyons acquitted Wyndham from any direct knowledge of his Under-Secretary's involvement, arguing that a foolish administrative error had created a breach in communication.[48] In this, he expressly followed the conclusions of one of Wyndham's private secretaries, Murray Hornibrook, published as an appendix to the Life and Letters of 1924.[49]

Many of Wyndham's contemporaries—from social contacts like Margot Asquith and Betty Balfour to political underlings like John Atkinson—assumed, however, that Ulster Party suspicions were better founded than Hornibrook and Lyons claimed: Margot Asquith snootily dismissed him as 'an intriguer, albeit of a very suburban kind'.[50]

---

[47] Lyons, 'Irish Unionist Party', 4; Mackail and Wyndham (edd.), Letters, ii. 760-1.

[48] Lyons, 'Irish Unionist Party', 8-9.

[49] Mackail and Wyndham (edd.), Letters, ii. 764, 796-7.

[50] Diaries of Margot Asquith, 28 Oct. 1905. I am grateful to Mrs Eleanor Brock for this reference. Trowbridge, Walter Long Papers, 947/131, John Atkinson to Walter Long, 3 Oct. (no year), quoted in extenso by Gailey, Death of Kindness, 233. Gailey, following the Trowbridge archivist dates this letter to 1911—but internal evidence indicates 1906 as a more likely year of composition, thus making Atkinson's testimony all the more telling.

But, of all the historians who have discussed devolution, only Andrew Gailey has accepted that such contemporary gossip may have had substance. Gailey has argued convincingly that what Wyndham opposed in August–September 1904 was not so much the Reform Association proposals as their inopportune appearance: 'what he really objected to was public pronouncement on questions that he had yet to decide on'.[51] Wyndham, 'whether intentionally, or not', had encouraged his political and civil service acquaintances to hold faith in a perpetual process of reform; when this hit obstacles, and Wyndham backtracked, his confidants were left 'bitter over their betrayal'.[52]

That the misunderstanding between MacDonnell and Wyndham ran deeper than an administrative error is probable; but there is little evidence to prove beyond reasonable doubt either the Lyons–Hornibrook orthodoxy, or the Gailey–Ulster Party allegation. What *is* indisputable is that some of the principal difficulties with Hornibrook's account have either been glossed over, or have only recently emerged. These are set out below.

Central to the loyalist indictment was the contact between MacDonnell and Wyndham in August and September 1904, and by implication the extent to which Wyndham knew, or approved of, his subordinate's involvement with devolution. Clearly related to this is the further issue of the contact between MacDonnell and Wyndham and between Dunraven and Wyndham in these same months. Lyons, following Hornibrook, omitted all reference to contact between the Chief Secretary and Dunraven. Hornibrook's memoir, however, contradicts the evidence of Dunraven himself, given in parliamentary speeches, his *The Crisis in Ireland* (1905), and in his autobiography of 1922.[53] In the latter Dunraven mentioned that 'during August I had several conversations with the Chief Secretary and Sir Antony MacDonnell': indeed, at one interview with Wyndham, on 27 September 1904, he claimed that the Reform Association report was debated.[54]

[51] Gailey, 'Policy Towards Ireland', 230.   [52] Ibid. 218.
[53] Mackail and Wyndham, (edd.), *Letters*, ii. 791–3, referring to The Earl of Dunraven, KP, *The Crisis in Ireland: An Account of the Present Condition of Ireland and Suggestions Towards Reform* (London and Dublin, 1905); and to Hansard, 4th ser. (1905), cxli. 437.
[54] The Earl of Dunraven, KP, CMG, *Past Times and Pastimes*, (2 vols.; London, [1922]), ii. 26–7.

Hornibrook derided this evidence, suggesting that Dunraven had confused discussions on an earlier, abortive, but wholly innocuous, reform plan, with those on the contentious manifesto of 1904.[55] This argument did not mention Dunraven's testimony in his autobiography, for Hornibrook's memoir, though published in 1924, had been written as far back as 1913; and it could not take account of Dunraven's detailed and specific allegation. Given that the Earl had been able to quote an exact date for one of his meetings with Wyndham, it seems improbable that he should have forgotten the year in which they took place.

Wyndham, in his principal parliamentary apologia, stated that he had seen Dunraven on the subject of a 'third', moderate Irish party in 1903, after the success of the Land Purchase Act.[56] He did not, however, mention *when* any later contact had occurred—or that he had seen Dunraven immediately before the launching of a far-reaching reform manifesto. Hornibrook did not pursue the subject, referring only allusively to Wyndham's habit of discussing all manner of topics—without, of course, any serious intent.[57]

But two fragments of evidence among the papers of Arthur Balfour tend to confirm Dunraven's case. On 5 March 1905, when Wyndham was at his wits' end, he wrote in despair to Balfour, referring to 'gossip which makes me think that Dunraven is talking'; 'nothing which occurred in September [1904] led me to expect any manifesto', he claimed—inferring, perhaps, that 'something' *did* occur.[58] Given the juxtaposition of this odd disclaimer with the reference to 'talking', Wyndham may have been alluding to the substantive conversations which Dunraven, in 1921, suggested had taken place. It is otherwise difficult to perceive what Dunraven could 'talk' about, given that, according to Hornibrook and Wyndham, there had been no conversations on devolution in 1904.

MacDonnell, writing in a confidential memorandum on the devolution scheme (later printed in the Mackail and Wyndham volume), stated that when, in August 1904, he had been first approached by Dunraven, he immediately informed Wyndham, 'and asked him [Wyndham] if he had seen Lord Dunraven': 'I have seen Lord Dunraven', was Wyndham's reply according to MacDonnell's

[55] Mackail and Wyndham (edd.), *Letters*, ii. 792.
[56] Hansard, 4th ser. (1905), cxli. 653.
[57] Mackail and Wyndham, (edd.), *Letters*, ii. 792-3.
[58] ABP, Add. MS 49805, fo. 42, Wyndham to Balfour, 5 Mar. 1905.

testimony, 'and hope to see him again'.[59] The substance of this interview was evidently not conveyed to MacDonnell—and it is possible that discussion was limited, as Wyndham and Hornibrook subsequently implied, to the notional advantages of a third, centrist party in Ireland. However, it is hard to believe that Dunraven, on the brink of launching a radical reform manifesto, should have waived the opportunity of debating his principal proposals— especially as he claimed to have seen Wyndham on the day following the publication of the second report.

In fact it is quite clear that Wyndham, despite subsequent denials, knew of MacDonnell's work over devolution in August 1904, and that he had given both MacDonnell and Dunraven evidence of his sympathy. Certainly at a crucial meeting of devolutionists held in mid-September Wyndham's approval of the first Reform Association scheme was taken for granted. This general proposal, published on 31 August, had created a demand for extrapolation, and when MacDonnell and Dunraven met with Dudley and 'two friends'— both Unionist MPs—to hammer out further details 'they expressed a doubt whether from Wyndham's approval of the August general scheme, they were justified in assuming that he would approve of this particular scheme'.[60] On Dunraven's prompting, the 'express authority' of the Chief Secretary was not sought, and the scheme was published, apparently without Wyndham's knowledge, on 26 September.[61]

Yet on 10 September MacDonnell had written to Wyndham in Germany, referring to the August manifesto and to his continued co-operation with Dunraven. This was a crucial letter, since it indicated clearly the extent of the Under-Secretary's connection with the Irish Reform Association; and it indirectly threw onto Wyndham the responsibility for approving or censuring his subordinate's conduct.[62] During the controversy which subsequently arose over these issues, Wyndham denied that he had seen the letter, and Hornibrook claimed that it had been mislaid within the pages of a

[59] ABP, Add. MS 49857, fo. 47, memorandum by MacDonnell concerning his part in the devolution negotiations, 8 Feb. 1905.

[60] WLP, Add. MS 62409, John Atkinson to Long, 16 Aug. 1905. The attendance of two Unionist MPs is an intriguing and, hitherto, unremarked aspect of this meeting. One of these was Sir John Dickson-Poynder, ABP, Add. MS 49802, fo. 202, Dudley to Balfour, 26 Feb. 1905.

[61] Ibid.

[62] Lyons, 'Irish Unionist Party', 9.

neglected Congested Districts Board report.[63] Yet it now seems clear both that Wyndham had seen this letter, and had actually replied to it. In a private memorandum written for Balfour by Lord Dudley, the viceroy reported:

I understood from MacDonnell that his letter not only mentioned what he was doing for Dunraven, but also gave news about the Dunsandle estate, and that Wyndham replied as regards the estate, but did not mention the Reform Programme. I do not wish to shift any responsibility that I should bear upon Wyndham, but should like you to know the facts.[64]

Wyndham later privately remarked to MacDonnell that he had not attached the same importance to the letter that the Under-Secretary had; and indeed it was only in February 1905 that he acknowledged to Balfour that he had seen it.[65]

   That Wyndham avoided written commitment, taking refuge in silence or intricate denials, seems clear, and may partly explain the confusion surrounding the various accounts of the devolution negotiations. Wilfrid Scawen Blunt noted the significance of the careful wording in Wyndham's public repudiation of the September scheme, and even Lord Dunraven drew a clear distinction between 'conversations with the Chief Secretary or Under Secretary as such' and 'perfectly informal conversations with Mr Wyndham and Sir Antony MacDonnell'.[66] This differentiation between private and official roles seems to inform most of Wyndham's comments on his knowledge of the events of August and September 1904—for otherwise statements such as 'I do not know and I do not wish to know whether, or to what extent, Lord Dunraven has ever discussed Irish policy with Sir A[ntony] M[acDonnell]' are palpably false.[67] It is now indisputable that Wyndham did know of MacDonnell's work with Dunraven and devolution in the late summer of 1904, even if a fuller explanation for the Chief Secretary's

---

[63] Mackail and Wyndham (edd.), *Letters*, ii. 764.
[64] ABP, Add. MS 49802, fo. 203, Dudley to Balfour, 26 Feb. 1905.
[65] Mackail and Wyndham (edd.), *Letters*, ii. 788. Contrast Wyndham's official memorandum on this meeting, Mackail and Wyndham (edd.), *Letters*, ii. 766. Gailey, *Death of Kindness*, 249, n. 53.
[66] Dunraven, *Crisis in Ireland*, 35. W. S. Blunt, *My Diaries* (London, 1919–20), ii. 110.
[67] Mackail and Wyndham (edd.), *Letters*, ii. 766.

tolerance must be left to a biography or a history of constructive Unionism.[68]

A further doubt concerning Hornibrook's evidence emerges from the hitherto neglected papers of Denis Hyde, Wyndham's last private secretary. These suggest that, after Wyndham's death, a debate raged among his friends and family concerning the fate of his own political archive—controversy focusing on the material relating to Wyndham's career in Ireland. Charles Gatty, one of Wyndham's closest friends, and author of a memoir (*George Wyndham: Recognita* (1917)), wrote to Denis Hyde in anticipation of the destruction of the archive—by, it would seem, Wyndham's supporters, in order to 'rescue' him: though why destroying his political papers should represent any form of salvation is left unclear. Gatty continued:

It has gradually become plain to me that there is a difference of opinion as to what should be done about the Chief's papers . . . Now you [Hyde] have, or had, the Chief's [Wyndham's] full statement of his Irish debacle, and I was going to advise you, if you still had it, to type a copy, and above all to sign it as a true copy . . . then let come what come may.[69]

Here there are three difficulties: what this private statement might have been; why Wyndham felt it necessary to write such a statement, given his laboured parliamentary testimony; and why Gatty feared its destruction (as it is clear he did).

A second letter, written by Gatty in October 1915, makes it clear that the fate of the Wyndham papers was still unresolved; but, in mentioning the archive, Gatty alludes tantalizing to T. M. Healy: 'I can see you [Hyde] pumping Tim up tight! He will probably burst in the House [of Commons], cover everyone with filth, and do your cause infinite harm'.[70] Why Hyde should need Healy's silence regarding the Wyndham papers is again unclear.

But, placing these references in the context of Wyndham's intimacy with Healy, it may be that the destruction of his papers—for it seems that they *were* largely destroyed shortly after his death—occurred because they contained evidence of political indiscretion, probably with Healy, among others. Guy Wyndham's privately printed edition

[68] See Max Egremont, *The Cousins: The Friendships, Opinions and Activities of Wilfrid Scawen Blunt and George Wyndham* (London, 1977), 244–52. Gailey, *Death of Kindness*, 235–54.
[69] Private Possession, Denis Hyde Papers, Charles T. Gatty to Hyde, Christmas Day 1913.
[70] Hyde Papers, Charles T. Gatty to Hyde, 25 Oct. 1915.

of George's letters contains a note by Moreton Frewen, in which he described plans for a meeting between Healy and Wyndham—to discuss devolution. Wyndham, Frewen claimed, had sent his apologies: 'George would not have it at any price'.[71] But, perhaps 'George' and 'Tim' did not need an intermediary to arrange a discussion on the future of Irish government any more than they had needed an intermediary to discuss the Irish Land Bill of 1903.[72]

4. Fighting Devolution

Interpretations of the reaction to devolution have generally placed the events of 1904-5 within the context of traditional loyalist fears. Irish loyalists were, of course, dedicated opponents of Home Rule; moreover, their distrust of British Conservative leaders predated even the emergence of a conciliatory Irish policy. But two aspects of the parliamentary debates on the MacDonnell affair suggest that Home Rule neuroses were not loyalists' sole motivation in hounding Wyndham: first, their strategy of alliance; second, the specific nature of their concerns, as brought forward in debate.

If Irish Unionists had been genuinely and predominantly worried by the threat of Home Rule in February 1905, then they chose an oddly self-defeating means of expression. Pressure on the Irish administration was created by, in effect, a parliamentary alliance of Irish Nationalist and Irish Unionist, although mavericks like Tim Healy sustained conventional party sniping. Nationalist contributors were generally careful not to soften their antagonism towards Dublin Castle—but they characterized Antony MacDonnell as a heroic reformer, constantly under threat of betrayal from a vacillating and ambiguous Chief Secretary.[73] Irish Unionists increasingly moderated their criticism of MacDonnell, and they fully confirmed the Nationalist caricature of Wyndham. Members like William Moore corroborated Nationalist claims that every section of the population was alienated from the Irish administration.[74]

---

[71] Guy Wyndham (ed.), Letters of George Wyndham, 1877-1913, (2 vols.; Edinburgh and London, 1915), ii. 197-8.

[72] For Healy's view of their close friendship, see T. M. Healy, Letters and Leaders of My Day, (2 vols.; London, [1928]), ii. 463-4. For Wyndham's view, see Mackail and Wyndham (edd.), Letters, ii. 198.

[73] Hansard, 4th ser. (1905), cxli. 628.   [74] Ibid. 634.

Furthermore, the parliamentary debates, which provided loyalists with an opportunity to air their suspicions, were initiated by Nationalists. On 20 February 1905 Ulster members converted John Redmond's customary Home Rule amendment into a long jeremiad on the appointment of Antony MacDonnell; and Nationalists joined with Unionists when the focus of attack shifted to Wyndham. In the division on this amendment only six loyalists voted with the government; of the six, five were office holders—and two of these (Atkinson and Campbell) held hopes of imminent promotion.[75] Most Irish Unionists abstained though two independent Unionists (Russell and Edward Mitchell) were sufficiently incensed to vote with Redmond and the Irish party. On 21 February, Redmond tabled an adjournment motion to call attention to 'the present conditions under which Sir Antony MacDonnell holds the office of Under-Secretary'; and again Irish Unionists spoke in support of a Nationalist lead, voting virtually as they had done in the earlier division.[76]

By uniting with Nationalists in censuring a Unionist government, Ulster Party members revealed that Home Rule had comparatively little to do with their fears. They opposed government over the devolution scare, partly because they desperately needed an issue on which to make a popular stand—and not only because they wanted to reaffirm their political faith. What gripped Irish Unionists was thus the urgent need for opposition—and not necessarily opposition to Home Rule.

This was further reflected in the emphasis of their complaints. In the debates of February 1905 loyalist members broadened the front of their attack away from the specific issue of devolution and onto the government's long-term record. They revived themes from earlier discussions on the Anderson and Ballinasloe affairs, directing attention to the material effects of the MacDonnell regime on Irish Unionists. Popular British interest in the plight of Wyndham gave loyalists a uniquely large audience for these fundamental concerns, and devolution swiftly lost pre-eminence to more prosaic problems of constituency management. As one Irish Unionist MP candidly informed the Commons: 'they did not get many opportunities of bringing these things forward in the House, except on an occasion like this—and they would dwell . . . on them'.[77]

[75] Ibid. 875; *pace* Lyons, 'Irish Unionist Party', 18, n. 59.
[76] Hansard, 4th ser. (1905), cxli. 910, 964.   [77] Ibid. 635.

William Moore, the North Antrim MP, perceived a direct link between Antony MacDonnell and what he described as 'the systematic boycotting of counties, because they were Unionist, from participation in public funds'.[78] It was this, 'the persistent unfairness of the policy of the Irish government', he claimed, and not the particular scandal of Wyndham's association with devolution, which had done more than anything else to goad Irish Unionists into revolt.[79] Home Rule, he admitted, was not central to their present concerns: 'it was not a question of approval or objection to Home Rule . . . but a question of confidence in the Irish government'.[80] His colleagues embroidered this characteristic theme. Through the Nationalist ascendancy over a spineless Chief Secretary, Unionist aspirations and interests were sacrificed: fundamental civic rights came under threat. There was no redress for Unionist victims of agrarian violence, no confidence in the willingness and capacity of the government to afford protection. A shadowy conspiracy between Wyndham, MacDonnell, and the Catholic hierarchy loomed large over the Orange imagination.

Sound electoral calculation dictated the direction of this attack. Arthur Balfour was fond of complaining that there were two aspects of Irish administration which he loathed—the sea journey to Dublin, and demands for government office and favour: 'the passage and the patronage'.[81] Perhaps more than in England, the ability of an MP to gain office and grants for his constituency was an important part of his representative function. It had obvious benefits: the ability to move government created an elevated local status. The MP, or, more often, an astute electoral agent, might heal local political antagonisms through the careful distribution of funds. Joshua Peel, agent for John Lonsdale, was quick to see the specific value of winning places for dissident Presbyterian electors in the Mid-Armagh constituency.[82] The corollary of this was the risk of alienating influential areas of the electorate by failing to promote individual or sectional claims. This, again, was particularly true for the Presbyterians, who were occasionally inclined to put forward their own sectarian candidate

---

[78] Hansard, 4th ser. (1905), cxli. 635. [79] Ibid. 636.
[80] Ibid. 641-2.
[81] HLRO, Cadogan Papers, CAD 1398, Gerald Balfour to Cadogan, 19 Oct. 1898.
[82] PRONI, Joshua Peel Papers, D 989/4C, letter books for the period 1885-1916.

in opposition to the 'official' nominee. As an efficient agent, Peel identified this risk, and was prepared to use it against any 'official' candidate or MP whose efforts on behalf of the constituency were judged to be inadequate.[83]

Irish Unionists expected Conservative government to respond to their requests as tokens of good faith between political allies. Under Wyndham, the demands of even-handed administration tended to loosen this feudal link, and thus the Irish Unionist MP's ability to secure government money, never strong—if only because of competing Unionist claims—was drastically curtailed. Irish Unionist supplicants believed that there was active discrimination against them, and that their representative was powerless to counter this. In Edwardian Mid-Armagh, Joshua Peel took it for granted that Lonsdale's support for the government would be materially repaid: when it became clear that lobby support did not translate easily into government cash, Peel was indignant: '*You* have been treated scandalously', he told Lonsdale, 'It seems as if you were, after all your support for the government, to receive no consideration . . .'.[84]

Balfour once condemned St John Brodrick for believing that government should be organized so as to provide a system of rewards and punishments, in preference to undisturbed administrative efficiency.[85] Irish Unionists talked about jobs and money in February 1905, partly because they shared Brodrick's 'stick and carrot' conception of government, but also because the failure to satisfy their constituents was endangering local status and support. Since the MP was the main channel of communication between his constituency and central government, his value to the former was inevitably linked to tangible evidence over the latter—whether through winning the appointment of a Sub-Postmaster, or the resignation of a Chief Secretary. Thus, the threat to Irish Unionist MPs' political survival came, not from Sir Antony the devolutionist but from Sir Antony the Permanent Under-Secretary, who held influence over allocation of government resources. Local thirst for place and pension therefore forced Irish Unionists to recast the terms of their February assault on government, away from a clean-cut denunciation of Home Rule, and onto a more pressing constituency concern.

[83] Ibid.
[84] Peel Papers, D 989/4C/2, 1000, Peel to Lonsdale, 1 Oct. 1903.
[85] ABP, Add. MS 49764, fo. 31, Balfour to J. S. Sandars, 10 Oct. 1905.

Just as in the debates of 1904, therefore, local worries fuelled Irish Unionist rage. Given grass-roots unrest at seemingly ineffectual representation, Ulster members needed to offer a distraction. They needed to prove why Ulster constituencies apparently suffered financial discrimination despite their own endeavours; and because of a more serious electoral threat—that presented by T. W. Russell—they badly needed an issue on which to reconstruct their popular support. In short, they needed a Home Rule scare.

Thus, contrary to a recent suggestion, Irish Unionist members did not seek a graceful means of escape from their February campaign; the devolution scandal, like the prospect of Balfour's defeat, offered too many opportunities.[86] Ulster members like C. C. Craig were not merely indulging in wild rhetoric by welcoming a general election, and the return of a Liberal government.[87] In the interests of unity and survival the Ulster Party needed Liberal success, just as they needed MacDonnell and devolution.

Three Irish Unionists corresponded with Arthur Balfour in February 1905—and two of these have been cited in support of the contention that the Ulster Party was struggling to avoid a major confrontation. On 17 February Edward Saunderson wrote to Balfour, describing the relationship between Irish loyalists and the government as having 'been strained almost to breaking point'— and demanding an assurance that 'in the immediate future Sir A. MacDonnell shall cease to remain in his present post'.[88] It has been suggested that, given the parliamentary revelations of 16 February— revelations by Wyndham concerning MacDonnell's involvement with Dunraven—Saunderson's demand was comparatively moderate, and was representative of a general willingness to compromise.

But there are difficulties with this argument. First, Wyndham's statement had not been volunteered, but was in response to the interrogation of a loyalist MP, C. C. Craig, in the House of Commons. Second, the tactic which has been imputed to loyalists— private flexibility and public obstinacy—implies that they were cultivating greater public expectations than they were prepared to

---

[86] Gailey, *Death of Kindness*, 255–60.

[87] *IT*, 19 Jan. 1905, 1, (Craig, speaking at Glenavy, County Antrim: 'would the interests of the loyalists of Ireland be in any worse hands under a Liberal government than under the present system?').

[88] ABP, Add. MS 49857, fo. 161, Edward Saunderson to Balfour, 17 Feb. 1905. Cf. Gailey, *Death of Kindness*, 258.

satisfy: that is to say, they were inviting public humiliation and electoral disaster. Moreover, Saunderson's moderation has to be seen in the context of his personal circumstances. As has been shown, he had been consistently more reasonable with Wyndham than MPs like Craig and Moore; and in any case on 17 February he was lying gravely ill at Strangford, County Down, wholly out of touch with parliamentary developments.[89] He was therefore merely echoing a loyalist demand first raised in 1904—and not offering an emollient. The tone of the letter in itself suggests that conciliation was far from Saunderson's mind.

The second contact between Balfour and the loyalists came in a letter written by Carson in the aftermath of the debate on Monday, 20 February: 'I am told by [William] Moore', he wrote, 'that if you are in a position to state that McD[onnell] will occupy the ordinary position of Under Secretary, they will be satisfied, and vote with us . . .'.[90] This offer reflected a growing opinion in Ulster that MacDonnell, though holding unpalatable views, had merely acted within the terms granted him by Wyndham. Ulster members and the Conservative press had become much more sympathetic towards MacDonnell in the aftermath of the debate's revelations, and they were becoming correspondingly more hostile towards Wyndham: Carson's letter merely documents this transition in the Ulster mood.[91] Furthermore, terminating MacDonnell's special terms of appointment, represented an indictment of Wyndham, who had granted the terms, rather than of MacDonnell. Neither Balfour, nor Wyndham, could have accepted this seemingly innocuous suggestion.

The third loyalist letter, written to Balfour on the following day (21 February) has not been fully cited in recent work. This came from J. H. M. Campbell, MP for Dublin University, who dramatically stepped up Carson's demands, suggesting that Ulster Party loyalty

[89] Hansard, 4th ser. (1905), cxli. 633, Moore refers to Saunderson's illness and convalescence. See also Reginald Lucas, *Colonel Saunderson, M.P.: A Memoir* (London, 1908), 357–9. Gailey, *Death of Kindness*, 258.

[90] ABP, Add. MS 49709, fo. 125, Edward Carson to Balfour, 20 Feb. 1905. Gailey, *Death of Kindness*, 258.

[91] ABP, Add. MS 49709, fo. 14, Carson to Balfour, 18 Feb. 1905. Edward Carson himself, in the aftermath of Lansdowne's revelations, regretted having defamed MacDonnell. This development of thought is also reflected in the editorials of the *IT*: cf. *IT*, 3 Mar. 1905, 4, with the editions of 20 and 23 Feb. 1905. The *IT* on 3 Mar. 1905, 4, stated bluntly that it was too late for Wyndham to save his position— for the letters which he had read to the Commons had indicated his weakness and MacDonnell's strength.

might be restored 'if you could see your way in the course of debate to intimate, first, the probable retirement of Lord Dudley, and second, the termination of the special conditions under which Sir A. MacDonnell holds office'.[92] Sacking the viceroy, demoting MacDonnell, and thereby indirectly censuring Wyndham, scarcely represented a gesture of conciliation. Yet, this overture came from one of the more moderate (or, at any rate, more promotion-conscious) Irish Unionist members. Hard-line loyalist opinion, represented in the *Irish Times*, was already baying for Wyndham's resignation; so that, even had Campbell's drastic diplomacy been accepted by Balfour, there was little likelihood of wholehearted loyalist acquiescence.

Irish Unionists, developing themes from earlier criticism, pioneered the parliamentary and constituency attack on George Wyndham. Loyalist ministers—John Atkinson, Edward Carson—had been among the first to register their suspicions on public platforms; loyalist back-benchers were among Wyndham's most vituperative critics, William Moore and C. C. Craig being the first to raise the issue of MacDonnell's involvement with devolution in parliament.[93] Ulster opposition was bitter, and sustained: though they were prepared to avoid abstaining during the crucial votes on 21 and 22 February, they offered no easy compromise. They recruited substantial press and back-bench sympathy; and, when Wyndham resigned office, most contemporaries had no doubt that his fall was an achievement of Ulster stridency.[94] Though the governments may have been hamstrung by the administrative precedents created through the Younghusband Affair (as Gailey has suggested), there seems little reason to suppose that the devolution scare was anything other than an Ulster Party creation for Ulster constituency consumption.[95]

5. *Russell and the Ulster Unionists*

Lyons and his successors ascribed a broader impact to the loyalist campaign than merely the destruction of one ministerial career.

[92] ABP, Add. MS 49857, fo. 109, J. H. M. Campbell to Balfour, 21 Feb. 1905. Gailey, *Death of Kindness*, 258, n. 9.

[93] Lyons, 'Irish Unionist Party', 12, 15–16.

[94] Plunkett Foundation, Oxford, Horace Plunkett Diaries, 9 Mar. 1905. GWP, Henry Bellingham to Sibell Grosvenor, 15 Mar. 1905.

[95] Gailey, 'Policy Towards Ireland', 247; Gailey, *Death of Kindness*, 255–91.

Patrick Buckland, for example, shared Lyons's belief that the shock administered by MacDonnellism goaded Irish Unionists into the creation of a mass electoral organization.[96] The MacDonnell affair explained the foundation of the Ulster Unionist Council in March 1905, which, in turn, co-ordinated loyalist resistance in 1912. In the long term, therefore, the MacDonnell affair decisively affected local Irish politics, galvanizing a community which had grown complacent under ten years of Unionist government.

There are, however, a number of problems with the argument of direct causal connection. It has been suggested in greater detail in chapter 5 that the preliminary meetings held to promote the Council emphasized a long-term need for organization, rather than the need for immediate response to MacDonnell and Wyndham.[97] Second, the response of the loyalist community to a Home Rule scare had often involved a call to militancy, rather than to electoral organization. If the creation of the Ulster Unionist Council was, as Lyons had argued, directly and solely linked to the devolution scandal, loyalist resort to military threats, and isolated displays of armed resistance might equally have been expected in 1904–5. Last, any theory of simple causal connection ought at least to consider alternative potential motives for organization—to consider what other real or imagined threats were faced by the Irish Unionist political leadership when the devolution scare broke in October 1904.

Between 1900 and 1906 the most serious political challenge to the leadership came, not from Castle devolutionists, or Home Rulers, but from within Ulster constituencies, from independent Unionists. Before 1900, independent candidates rarely emerged from traditionally Unionist constituencies; and few were ever successful. Those who were relied heavily on personal popularity, rather than on any exceptional platform; and, once elected, they were often speedily assimilated into the official Irish Unionist parliamentary party. After 1900, this stability was shaken. Between 1900 and 1906, of eight by-election contests in Unionist constituencies, six were caused by independent candidates. And, for the first time, the force

---

[96] Lyons, 'Irish Unionist Party', 12–13; Lyons, *Ireland Since the Famine* (2nd edn., London, 1972), 295; Patrick Buckland, *Irish Unionism* ii. *Ulster Unionism and the Origins of Northern Ireland* (Dublin and New York, 1973), 20–1. An expanded version of the arguments in this section may be found in my 'Irish Unionism and the Russellite Threat, 1894–1906' *I.H.S.*, xxv. 100 (Nov. 1987).

[97] See above, ch. 5.7.

of this challenge came from a well-organized body of opinion, with a distinctive manifesto, and an able leader—the maverick member for South Tyrone, T. W. Russell.[98]

When the devolution scandal emerged, Russell had created a very serious electoral challenge: his candidates had fought against official Unionists in three by-elections, and had won two seats in constituencies with unbroken records of Unionist success. So in 1905 Irish Unionists needed a review of their electoral machinery, not because they were losing seats to Home Rulers, but because they were losing seats to Russellites. Russellism was populist and angry; and the Ulster Party looked to secure its constituency roots.

This defensive reflex took two forms. Revitalized election machinery, ostensibly a response to the Home Rule bogey, helped win back ground lost to Russell. In North Fermanagh the Constitutional Association, which had languished for years, was virtually extinguished in the aftermath of a Russellite by-election victory in March 1903.[99] Morale was restored by the creation of the bond with the Ulster Unionist Council, and by an injection of cash from central Unionist funds. At the 1906 general election, the sitting Russellite member was ousted by an official candidate and thereafter Unionist ascendancy was uninterrupted. In Mid Armagh, machinery which normally ground to a halt between elections, was revived with the emergence of Russellite militancy.[100] Strong promotion of the Unionist candidate in January 1906 deterred all opposition—this in a constituency with a long tradition of real, or threatened, independent candidatures.

But the Ulster Party's reaction to Russell also involved exploiting the MacDonnell affair, both as a useful counter-issue to the land debate, and as a means of winning constituency confidence through creating a political initiative. The Land Question was too contentious and dangerous for prolonged debate; Home Rule in the abstract was an old, and increasingly tedious rhetorical straw man. Sir Antony, and Wyndham, on the other hand, were safe and novel targets—

[98] Alvin Jackson, 'The Irish Unionist Parliamentary Party, 1885–1906', D.Phil. thesis (Oxford, 1986), 362–88.

[99] PRONI, Falls and Hanna Papers, Solicitors, D 1390/26/6. Cf. C. F. Falls to W. G. Henderson, 27 Mar. 1903, with the activity and enthusiasm generated by the prospective 'Central Ulster Unionist Association', Falls to E. M. Archdale, 15 Nov. 1904; Falls to T. H. Gibson, 15 Nov. 1904; Falls to Gibson, 14 Jan. 1905.

[100] Peel Papers, D 889/4C/3, Peel to J. B. Lonsdale, 24 Nov. 1904; Peel to J. B. Lonsdale, 29 Nov. 1904.

and they had immediate relevance for every Irish Unionist who had had an unfavourable encounter with government.

Suspicions of the Unionist government competed with suspicions of Ulster Party landlordism as the dominant local political emotion. Like Moore in North Antrim, John Lonsdale recognized that his personal political interest lay in the primacy of the MacDonnell affair; and both members sought to relegate the land debate by thrashing out the intricacies of devolution in the Commons and locally, where parliamentary debates were widely reported and avidly read.[101] Joshua Peel, Lonsdale's agent, was convinced of the electoral value of this strategy: in the aftermath of Wyndham's resignation, he was able to report to Lonsdale that 'the Ulster members have risen immensely in public esteem and confidence . . . [and] none stands higher than yourself'.[102] In other Ulster constituencies resolutions of support were passed by once sullen Unionist bodies—such as the Antrim Workingmen's Constitutional Association, which voted its 'best thanks' to the Ulster Party, singling out C. C. Craig and William Moore for special commendation.[103]

By creating the MacDonnell crisis, and then appealing to voters as the party of Protestantism and patriotism, Unionists were able to score a significant electoral victory over Russellism in 1906. The Russellite vote fell from an average of 51 per cent (of the total poll), during the by-election successes of 1902–3, to 44 per cent at the General Election.[104] Russell never recovered from this popular rebuff—and he subsequently abandoned the politics of agitation in order to take office under the Liberals.

In 1902–3 Russellite candidates polled well because large numbers of Nationalists (who did not normally get an opportunity to vote safe Conservative seats) combined with small numbers of Nonconformist dissidents. Russell was dependent, therefore, on what Carson called an 'unholy alliance' of Catholic and Protestant.[105] In East Down, in 1902, Methodist and Presbyterian defection from

[101] See e.g. J. R. B. McMinn, 'The Reverend James Brown Armour and Liberal Politics in North Antrim, 1869-1914', Ph.D. thesis (Belfast, 1979), 353.

[102] Peel Papers, D 889/4C/3, Peel to J. B. Lonsdale, 10 Mar. 1905.

[103] IT, 4 Mar. 1905, 8.

[104] Brian M. Walker, Parliamentary Election Results in Ireland, 1801-1922 (Dublin, 1978).

[105] Private Possession, William Moore Papers, Carson to Moore, 28 Jan. 1906.

Unionism ensured the victory of James Wood.[106] Joshua Peel, Unionist agent for Mid Armagh, wrote of the poll that 'it makes one indignant to think that those presbyterians, for the sake of getting a presbyterian into parliament, would join hands with the enemies of the Union and their country'.[107] In North Fermanagh between 400 and 750 Nonconformist Unionists (depending on rival party estimates) voted with Nationalists for the Russellite candidate.[108]

These combinations were successful only in rural constituencies, since Russell's appeal was primarily to farmers: 'in my experience', wrote Joseph Wilson, a South Antrim Unionist manager, 'all the urban voters, without exception, are bitterly opposed to Russellism'.[109] Russell recognized this: in the mixed rural/urban constituency of South Antrim, he discounted the possibility of winning votes in the four large towns of the area, and warned those living in country districts 'how much depended upon their action on polling day'.[110] Even in East Down, where his candidate had been successful, Russell privately admitted that the contest had been 'very much closer than I expected . . . the farmers, bar the Orange lot, stuck to their guns well [but] it was Lisburn and Ballynahinch that weighed so heavily against us'.[111] In general, Russell tried to avoid heavily urban constituencies, and may have been tempted into South Antrim because the outgoing MP was William Ellison-Macartney, his most bitter landlord critic.

Graph 6.1 demonstrates that, by 1906, Russell was heavily dependent on Catholic votes. There is a strong relationship between areas containing a concentration of Catholics, and areas yielding high Russellite polls at the general election (as is indicated by the correlation coefficient for these two variables: $R = 0.76$). Minor distortions are caused by unusual constituencies (North Antrim, with a strong Protestant Liberal tradition), or by the relative merits of the candidates (a weak Russellite in North Derry—an English journalist—polled badly). Reliable figures for the numbers of Catholic voters in each division are not available, so slight distortion

---

[106] *BNL*, 7 Feb. 1902, 5. Also St John Ervine, *Craigavon: Ulsterman* (London, 1949), 99.

[107] Peel Papers, D 889/4C/2, 742, Peel to Lonsdale, 10 Feb. 1903.

[108] *BNL*, 23 Mar. 1903, 11.

[109] Moore Papers, Joseph Wilson to Moore, 9 Feb. 1902.

[110] *BNL*, 22 Jan. 1903, 4.

[111] T. J. Campbell, *Fifty Years of Ulster, 1890–1940* (Belfast, 1941), 263.

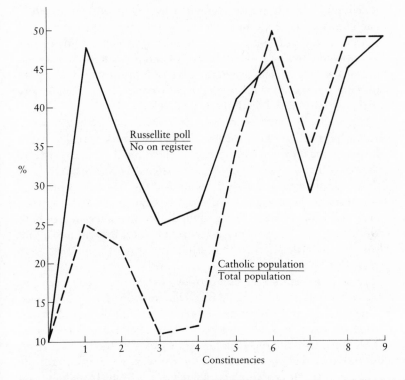

FIG. 6.1. Russellites and the Catholic vote, 1906
Sources: Census Returns (1901), Province of Ulster (1902), ccxxii and ccxxvii; Returns of Electors, 1906, xciv. 837; Walker, Parliamentary Election Results.
Note: The constituencies are: 1. N. Antrim 2. Mid-Antrim 3. E. Antrim 4. N. Down 5. E. Down 6. N. Fermanagh 7. N. Londonderry 8. S. Londonderry 9. S. Tyrone

may be caused by variations in relative sectarian enfranchisement levels: the evidence of sectarian voting strengths which does survive, suggests, however, that there is no significant variation.

In 1906 Russell was more reliant than ever on Nationalist votes, and he recognized this both publicly (in his South Tyrone victory speech), and privately: writing to the defeated Russellite candidate, Arnold White, he revealed the extent of this dependence: 'I was very sorry at N.D.[erry], and East Antrim. The N[ationalist] vote went badly astray in both places, owing to lack of organisation. But we polled out magnificently where it was organised.'[112] In 1900, standing against both independent and Nationalist candidates, Russell had captured over 2,400 Unionist votes in his South Tyrone constituency. But by 1906 all but 150 Unionists voted against him, and he was only elected, as he admitted, by a strong Nationalist poll: 'Coming out unscathed I owe my safety first to the unswerving loyalty of the entire body of Catholic voters'.[113]

It seems likely that this dependence on Nationalist support partly explains Russell's failure in 1906. Table 6.1 shows a breakdown of the poll in the only two constituencies where comparison of the 1906 failure with the 1902-3 success is possible. This reveals, in both North Fermanagh and East Down, that the Russellite poll (as a proportion of the total number of electors) held up fairly well between 1902 and 1906. Since there is a slight decline in the registers of both constituencies, mirrored in the Russellite vote, it is probable that Russellites polled at maximum possible strength in 1902-3, and were weakened by subsequent registration work.

There is a slight increase in turn-out within both constituencies, and this is reflected in the magnified Unionist vote. Unionists seemed to be able, not only to capture all the increase in the poll, but also to call on other electoral resources. In North Fermanagh the increase in Unionist vote is largely explained by the large turn-out in 1906; but in East Down the increase in the Unionist vote far exceeds the increase in turn-out. Unionists gained votes from Russellites, and may also have consolidated their position through successful work in the registration courts. The conclusion suggested by these calculations is that, though the Russellite vote fell slightly, Unionist success in 1906 was largely due to an improved ability to mobilize support. Unionist victories did, however, rely on a small—but significant—amount of Russellite defection.

The MacDonnell affair, carefully exploited by Unionist politicians, inspired old fears of Catholic political ascendancy; it also precipitated a campaign of electoral organization, the need for which had been highlighted by the Unionist failures of 1902-3.[114] Against this background, Russell's land and consensus politics ceased to have relevance. He ran candidates in Unionist seats where normally no

---

[112] National Maritime Museum, Arnold White Papers, WH1/80, T. W. Russell to White, 30 Jan. 1906. I am grateful to Dr R. H. Williams, St Peter's College, Oxford, for this reference.   [113] Campbell, *Fifty Years*, 264.
[114] Cf. Lyons, 'Irish Unionist Party', 22.

TABLE 6.1. *The Unionist Counter-Attack, 1902–1906*

(i) East Down

Year	No. on Register	Total Poll	Percentage of Poll		Party Vote/Register	
			Russellite	Unionist	Russellite	Unionist
1902	8184	7005	51	49	44	42
1906	8072	7352	46	54	41	50

(ii) North Fermanagh

| 1903 | 5213 | 4662 | 52 | 48 | 46 | 43 |
| 1906 | 5083 | 4750 | 49 | 51 | 46 | 48 |

Sources: Census Returns (1901); House of Commons Electoral Returns; Walker, *Parliamentary Election Results*.

Nationalist would have stood—and in these constituencies, Catholics registered their support. But Russell was dependent, too, on a limited number of Protestant farmer votes. In 1902–3, he was able to capture these, and his candidates were elected by a Protestant–Catholic rural coalition. In 1906 this coalition seems to have collapsed, and Protestant Russellites defected to Unionism, even if in one constituency, Mid Antrim, the landed MP, R. T. O'Neill, still got 'a much stiffer contest than anyone had supposed at first . . . Colonel Verschoyle [the Russellite] having got such a hold on the farmers'.[115] Renewed fears of Home Rule meant that a party so obviously dependent on Catholic votes could no longer exercise an appeal to Protestants—even to those who, against a different political background, had been prepared to offer support.

6.   The 'Young Men' of a Loyalist 'Radical Right'

In F. S. L. Lyons's article on the devolution controversy the direct connection between the creation of the UUC and the devolution debates was apparently confirmed by the contribution of William Moore and C. C. Craig to the development of each. Craig and Moore

---

[115] Private Possession, R. T. O'Neill Papers, H. A. White to Miss O'Neill, 24 Jan. 1906.

were the two Ulster members 'most responsible' for the establishment of the Council—and for inspiring the attack on MacDonnell and Wyndham. It seemed that these men were merely extending their work against MacDonnellism by promoting the new central Unionist agency.[116]

Yet Moore and Craig had also led the attack on T. W. Russell: Craig was the first 'official' loyalist candidate to defeat a Russellite opponent—and he had been given considerable aid by William Moore. Joseph Wilson, Craig's election manager, offered profuse thanks, contrasting Moore's assault on Russell with the reticence of his Party colleagues: 'Your speeches were most effective, and infused new blood into the fight. I only wish we had a few more members with your courage.'[117] E. S. Finnegan, the veteran Belfast Conservative boss, offered more telling approbation: 'Tell William Moore', he commanded Wilson, 'that they all swear by him in the [South Antrim] division, and that he has improved his position enormously by the bold-blooded way he went for T. W. [Russell]. He turned hundreds of votes . . .'.[118] In subsequent contests against Russellism, Moore, with his new colleague, Craig, led the official campaign, securing the defeat of a Russellite sympathizer in West Down. By 1905, the Provost of Trinity, Anthony Traill, could claim that 'there is no doubt that Mr. Moore and Mr. Craig are the two members for the North of Ireland who are able to combat Russellism successfully'.[119]

When, in the last weeks of the Balfour ministry, Moore was being considered as a stop-gap Solicitor-General for Ireland, his Ulster Party supporters remembered, not his contribution to the devolution debate, but rather his fight against Russell. Canvassing Walter Long, as Chief Secretary, Harry Liddell, member for West Down, James Craig, candidate for East Down, and the Party secretary, John Lonsdale, all drew attention to Moore and the Russellite threat: Liddell attributed his own recent election victory to Moore's intervention; Craig agreed, claiming that 'no one [has] contributed more' than Moore to 'saving' West Down and South Antrim from

---

[116] Lyons, 'Irish Unionist Party', 10–13.

[117] Moore Papers, Joseph Wilson to William Moore, 9 Feb. 1903.

[118] Moore Papers, E. S. Finnegan to Joseph Wilson, [Feb. 1903].

[119] Trowbridge, Walter Long Papers, 947/115, Anthony Traill to William Moore, 27 Nov. 1905.

Russellism.[120] Only Lonsdale mentioned Moore's work in exposing MacDonnell and Wyndham—but as an afterthought to a more characteristic account of the assault on Russell.[121]

In the minds of many contemporaries, therefore, Moore and Craig's political reputation rested squarely on their campaign to topple T. W. Russell: the architects of the UUC were also commonly regarded as the architects of Russell's decline. This connection is at least as significant as their link with devolution; and it confirms that the evolution of the UUC may be viewed in the context of the campaign against Russell, and not solely as an epilogue to devolution. The Unionist Council may have been precipitated by the devolution scare, but it was designed by politicians who had been occupied for years in buttressing an increasingly shaky constituency base. Russell, and not MacDonnell, haunted the minds of Edwardian Irish Unionists: the MacDonnell issue ultimately only mattered in so far as it could be employed to stem the defections inspired by the land agitation.

More generally, Moore and C. C. Craig were among a number of younger Ulster Unionist MPs who were coming to prominence at this time, displacing and replacing the veterans of the Party. Their political development had taken place in the more complex conditions of the later 1890s, with the fervour and unanimity of 1886 and 1893 often only an adolescent memory. Thus they were sometimes more flexible and responsive than the heroes of the campaign against Parnell, and while their faith in the Union remained immovable, they were interested in a broader range of issues. The Craig brothers, for example, especially James, dabbled in a variety of imperial and social concerns, proponents of Empire Day, the compulsory flying of the Union Jack, reform of the Irish poor law, better conditions in the National Schools. William Moore and James Craig were also among the chief architects of Ulster Unionist resistance to the third Home Rule Bill. More socially aware and more effectively militant than an earlier generation of Unionist politician, these 'young men' of Edwardian loyalism have some claim to be treated as the 'radical right' of their movement.[122]

---

[120] Trowbridge, Walter Long Papers, 947/115, H. Liddell to Long, 2 Nov. 1905; James Craig to Lord Londonderry, 2 Nov. 1905.

[121] Ibid. 947/115, J. B. Lonsdale to Long, 10 Nov. 1905.

[122] Ervine, *Craigavon*, 131-75.

7. *Walter Long and the Ulstermen, 1905*

If Irish Unionists effectively used MacDonnell for independent electoral reasons, they, in turn, were exploited at a higher level of the political hierarchy—again for reasons which had little to do with what were apparently the key issues of the February debates. At the constituency level, Unionist MPs used the scandal to achieve a broader condemnation of the record of the Wyndham regime, and also for their own political ends—to thwart the threat of Russellism. This strategic dimension was relevant to the high politics of the episode, for the devolution scandal developed into a debate on Unionist policy in Ireland, and was exploited by leading Unionists for reasons of personal rivalry.[123]

Wyndham's tragedy was only one personal aspect of the broader repercussions of the loyalist campaign. In principle, his resignation need not have had policy implications; in practice, Irish Unionists had deliberately broadened the terms of the MacDonnell debates by projecting their doubts about Wyndham's Unionism onto his conciliatory record as Chief Secretary. The Ulster Party's brief ascendancy in the wake of his resignation gave these doubts an unprecedented significance, and they dictated the immediate future of government policy in Ireland.[124]

After the resignation of Wyndham, the cabinet minister most closely associated with a moderate Irish policy was Gerald Balfour. His name was canvassed as a possible successor to Wyndham, and an influential Liberal Unionist cabal, headed by Horace Plunkett, pressed for his appointment.[125] But the encouragement given to loyalist militancy by Wyndham's fall meant that the Unionist leadership could not risk the appointment of a well-known moderate. Balfour confessed privately to Plunkett his dependence on loyalist quiescence; he confessed this publicly through the elevation of Walter Long to the Irish Office.[126]

---

[123] Ronan Fanning, 'The Unionist Party and Ireland, 1906-1910', *IHS*, xv. 58 (Sept. 1966), 152-5; Richard Murphy, 'Walter Long and the Conservative Party, 1905-1921', Ph.D. thesis (Bristol, 1984), 55-6.

[124] Cf. Gailey, 'Policy Towards Ireland', 284.

[125] Whittingehame, Gerald Balfour Papers, TD 83/133/113, Plunkett to Betty Balfour, 13 Mar. 1905. Plunkett Diaries, 9, 11, 12 Mar. 1905.

[126] Plunkett Diaries, 9 Mar. 1905.

Walter Long had been associated for some time with the Unionist faction generally sympathetic to Irish loyalism. He had family connections among the Protestant Irish. He was married to a daughter of the ninth Earl of Cork, and his grandfather had been a Wicklow squire, who had represented the county at Westminster as an Orange Tory.[127] During the devolution debates, Long had supported in cabinet the justice of the Irish Unionist case.[128] His personal and political credentials were, therefore, admirably tailored to mollify a suspicious loyalist audience.

Yet, even he had not been Balfour's first choice as replacement to Wyndham, for Edward Carson and John Atkinson had each been offered the Chief Secretaryship.[129] Both were leading Irish Unionists; both had been significantly involved in presenting the loyalist case against MacDonnell and Wyndham. Within parliament, Carson and Atkinson had, as junior ministers, avoided any explicit condemnation: both voted for the government in the two divisions on Redmond's amendment and motion. But their commitment to their Irish colleagues had been otherwise indisputable—which is largely why Balfour considered them as suitable appointees. In the event, both declined office for personal reasons, and Balfour therefore turned to the Englishman most in accord with militant Irish Unionist opinion. The appointment of Walter Long was consciously intended, as Balfour admitted, to 'give the Orangemen great satisfaction'.[130]

'Satisfaction of the Orangemen' had an immediate and sweeping effect on the British regime in Ireland. Walter Long would later claim, in his *Memories* (1923), a very great esteem for Wyndham—yet, on arriving in Ireland, he set out to encourage those who had been Wyndham's most unrelenting opponents.[131] Long's allies in Ireland were almost exclusively Unionist: indeed, his closest friends—Saunderson, Abercorn—were leading members of the Orange Order. Saunderson was Long's most important loyalist confidant: his views on, for example, the timing of the general election were ferried to the cabinet, and great stress was laid on his broader political value

---

[127] Murphy, 'Walter Long', 21.

[128] BL, H. O. Arnold-Forster Diaries, Add. MS 50345, 1 Mar. 1905. ABP, Add. MS 49776, fo. 46, Long to Balfour, 21 Feb. 1905.

[129] Bodleian Library, J. S. Sandars Papers, c749, fo. 100a, John Atkinson to Balfour, 11 Mar. 1905; Horace Plunkett Diaries, 11 Mar. 1905.

[130] ABP, Add. MS 49763, fo. 70, Arthur Balfour to J. S. Sandars, 4 Jan. 1905.

[131] Viscount Long of Wraxall, *Memories* (London, 1923), 142.

in Ireland. Long was prepared even to travel the eighty miles between Dublin and Saunderson's Cavan home (driven by the redoubtable Henry Robinson) in order to obtain the loyalist's advice.[132]

This reliance on loyalist leaders restored more perfectly than ever Irish Unionist access to central decision-making. Under Wyndham, Irish Unionists had come to be denied this access, and by 1904 they could only register their grievances by political agitation, and not, as hitherto, through discreet, internal party pressure. Long, unlike Wyndham, regarded Irish Unionists as integral elements of his own party: Irish Unionist opinions were consequently made available to government through the medium of the Irish Office—this for the first time since Arthur Balfour's Chief Secretaryship.

Loyalist influence emerged in Walter Long's concentration on traditional areas of their concern. Suspicions of sectarian discrimination had inspired much of the opposition to Wyndham— and the two most controversial cases (Anderson and Ballinasloe) were personally investigated by Long. He was able to convince Saunderson and many of the Ulster members—not all—that their allegations concerning MacDonnell's involvement had been unfounded.[133] Correcting old patronage grievances had a corollary in a new strategy of public appointments. Long was impressed by the depth of feeling which Wyndham's allocation of jobs and grants had created, and he was sympathetic to the gut loyalist view that Irish administration, in patronage, as in all else, should be conducted on strict party lines. 'Policy', Long wrote in one of many prim correctives inflicted on Dudley, 'is often indicated by the appointments made; this is especially the case in Ireland'.[134] Since 'policy' was to be unerringly Unionist, 'appointments' would follow suit: Long had no time for Wyndham's conviction that the loyalist community possessed insufficient talent for all the key posts within the Castle bureaucracy.[135]

---

[132] See e.g. ABP, Add. MS 49776, fo. 150 Long to Balfour, 29 Nov. 1905. Long, *Memories*, 171-4. Sir Henry Robinson, Bart., KCB, *Memories: Wise and Otherwise* (London, 1923), 172. Long, *Memories*, 172.

[133] Long, *Memories*, 147. WLP, Add. MS 62409: Long to Saunderson (copy), 10 Nov. 1905; Add. MS 62409: Edward Saunderson to Long, 11 Nov. 1905.

[134] Trowbridge, Walter Long Papers, 947/65, Long to Dudley (copy), 7 Aug. 1905.

[135] Trowbridge, Walter Long Papers, 947/126/15, Long to George Wyndham (copy), 2 Sept. 1906.

Two leading Ulster opponents of Wyndham were chosen for special promotion, and were the objects of peculiarly tortuous negotiation. William Moore, who continued to agitate for MacDonnell's dismissal—even under Long—was offered the Irish Solicitor-Generalship. Broad hints were given, through Edward Saunderson, that this promotion was contingent on a more enthusiastic acceptance of the Long regime: the prospective appointee fell into line with immodest haste, writing to the Chief Secretary in order to pledge his loyalty.[136] Walter Long's personal political interest lay in creating a semblance of Irish Unionist unity, supporting both himself and the government. It was professionally advantageous to be able to show that he could lead dissident Irish Unionist opinion back under the umbrella of the Unionist alliance—that he could succeed in restoring order to the party confusion which Wyndham had created. From this perspective, minority extremists, like Moore, were worth appeasing.

John Atkinson was also singled out for attention. Like Moore, Atkinson had been prominently associated with the campaign against Wyndham; like Moore, he was an able and influential Irish Unionist.[137] He was a consistent supporter of Long's policies in Ireland, and sustained a friendship with him which outlived their professional relationship. Atkinson was created Lord of Appeal in December 1905—a unique jump from comparatively junior legal office in Ireland to one of the most senior posts in the British judiciary. His main competitor in the promotion stakes had been a moderate, out of sympathy with Long, who hankered after the return of Wyndham: Lord Justice Fitzgibbon was, however, one of the most experienced judges on the Irish bench. Atkinson, thus, had not been appointed for his judicial expertise, since he had never sat as a judge: rather his contest with Fitzgibbon embraced a clash between the two Unionist policies of Irish government. Long regarded Atkinson's candidature, both as a test of relative political strength, and as a means by which to gain a tangible expression of approval from Arthur Balfour. He was successful, but only after prolonged and heated debate.[138]

---

[136] WLP, Add. MS 62409, William Moore to Long, 7 Dec. 1905.

[137] Lyons, 'Irish Unionist Party', 12.

[138] See the extensive correspondence relating to the problem of Atkinson's promotion in WLP, Add. MS 62409.

Championing individual Irish Unionists, Walter Long also upheld the policy which had been their perennial community concern: law and order. Wyndham had tried to pare policing costs in order to direct the saving into what he regarded as a more constructive security policy—creating a contented rural population through land purchase. Irish loyalists (like William Ellison-Macartney) had been embittered by what they deemed the neglect of conventional law enforcement. Walter Long, characteristically, shared their perceptions—both of the primacy of law and order among administrative priorities, and of the efficacy of traditional policing; and he reacted to the failing security situation with an aggression designed to allay their unease. He piloted a recruitment programme for the Royal Irish Constabulary, with the aim of increasing its strength from the Wyndhamite trough of 7,500 to 10,000. Saturation policing in County Galway brought to an end a campaign of agrarian disturbance. Sporadic rent strikes throughout the southern counties of Ireland were ended using RIC force.[139]

In employing a heavy-handed security policy, Long was seeking not only to restore order, but also to restore loyalist confidence both in Castle government and the Unionist leadership. In combination with his emollient line on patronage, high-profile policing achieved its principal purpose: by November 1905, Irish Unionists, who only eight months before had been conspiring to undermine the government, pleaded now for an extension of its life.[140] This was a measure of Long's party achievement as Chief Secretary.

Through his devotion to the interests of loyalism, Walter Long had rejected the legacy of constructive Unionism sustained and developed by Wyndham. Two differing Irish Secretaries destroyed the possibility of an unambiguous party orthodoxy on Ireland. Sympathy for either policy implied distaste for the other; sympathy for neither, or both, implied lack of commitment: this was the essence of Arthur Balfour's dilemma over Ireland between 1906 and 1910. Walter Long, backed by Irish loyalism, maintained a demand for a statement of preference—which Balfour could not give, without

[139] Long, *Memories*, 149-59; Long's reputation as a tough law enforcer is questioned by Richard Murphy in his 'Walter Long', 37-9.

[140] Murphy, 'Walter Long', 42; the address which Murphy refers to came only from Dublin Unionists. See also WLP, Add. MS 62409, Abercorn to Long, 7 Nov. 1905; Saunderson to Long, 24 Nov. 1905.

being seen to sacrifice Wyndham. In the short term, therefore, Balfour strove to avoid any unequivocal commitment; in the long term the distrust generated by the devolution affair ensured that Wyndham was edged out of any worthwhile influence over the Party line on Ireland.[141]

At a time when national interest was waning, Walter Long was able, with relative ease, to control the Irish policy of the Unionist opposition. His Union Defence League brought a hard-line case into British constituencies; as the leader of the Ulster Party (following Saunderson's death in 1906), he directed the loyalist assault on Bryce and Birrell.[142] When, after 1910, Ireland returned to the forefront of political debate, and the Unionist party needed an Irish platform, the most immediate precedent was the uncompromising stand of Walter Long and the Irish loyalists. It was the legacy of Long's Chief Secretaryship, and not that of Wyndham, which dictated the nature of Unionist opposition in 1912.

8. *Summary*

In 1904 Unionism had been in power for over eight years and the Home Rule menace had never been more feeble. Lacking an effective threat, the fragility of the Unionist alliance in Ireland was exposed. Divisive constituency pressures, uncovered and exploited by T. W. Russell, racked many Ulster constituencies, and brought defeats for official Unionism in North Fermanagh and East Down. Irish Unionists members—pre-eminently Moore and Craig—toured Ulster constituencies in the wake of the Russellite menace, attempting to shepherd support; but defaming Russell, and questioning his Unionism, had only a limited electoral value. Reorganizing the Party offered, in the short term, no better strategy; for reorganization could achieve little in the context of the demoralization, inspired by

[141] Long retained a pathological jealousy of Wyndham, though. In Nov. 1909 Acland-Hood, the Unionist Chief Whip, asked Carson and Wyndham to open and close the Unionist contribution to a debate on Birrell's Land Bill. Long, excluded, responded bitterly. See DRO, Theresa, Lady Londonderry Papers, D/Lo/C/666, fo. 98, Long to Theresa Londonderry, 19 Nov. 1909. For Long's jealousy of Wyndham in more personal matters see Theresa Londonderry Papers, D/Lo/C/666, fo. 20, Long to Theresa Londonderry, 29 Oct. 1907, and also Vincent (ed.), *Crawford Papers*, 133, 182.

[142] Murphy, 'Walter Long', 139–42.

Russell's victories. The Ulster Party needed first to find a political initiative.

Within the House of Commons, an equally fragile Unionist consensus had begun to weaken. Conservative Irish members, especially landlords, had been offended by the reforms of the late 1890s, and embarked on a campaign of dissent. A honeymoon period at the beginning of Wyndham's reign had seen a slight easing of tensions; and for some months Ulster die-hards believed that they had found a second Arthur Balfour in his former private secretary. But local unrest and parliamentary neglect soon disabused loyalist members of their early illusions. Already by 1904, they had attempted—several times—to reform the Irish administration: in 1902, through bewailing the crime figures, and through complaining about alleged employment discrimination in 1903-4. Yet, by the autumn of 1904, despite restrained but unmistakable loyalist opposition, George Wyndham was still resolutely opposed to the forms of partisan administration which they craved. Irish Unionists had come to feel that, having been excluded from a Unionist Castle administration, they were absolved from any commitment of loyalty to their British leaders. When the devolution scandal broke, they therefore exploited it in order to force a change in government policy, regardless of the consequences for internal Unionist relations.

What worried the Ulster Party in 1905 was not Home Rule, then, but rather the threat of Russellism, and the problems created by being excluded from the Irish government. What worried Unionist voters was not so much Home Rule as the long-term failings both of their representation, and of the Wyndham regime. The political fears of Irish loyalist MPs explain the intensity of their concern over devolution; their supporters' material and sectarian fears explain the very broad nature of the parliamentary indictment of Wyndham. It was ironic, therefore, that, though their suspicions concerning the Chief Secretary's integrity may have had substance, these, ultimately, were only a secondary interest.

The devolution affair restructured Ulster representation. It contributed to an older process of alignment, described in chapter 5, whereby MPs were brought down from their social pedestal, and rendered more accountable and susceptible to local pressure. It inspired an unprecedented campaign of parliamentary sniping; indirectly, and in connection with the Russellite threat, it led Irish Unionists to develop the local structures of independence. Thus devolution marked the close of the first stage of Unionist development—an era dominated by the parliamentary Ulster Party, and by its swashbuckling chairman, Colonel Edward Saunderson.

Constituency ties had conflicted with loyalty to the national alliance. After an age of innocence, Ulster members came to understand that they could exploit the divergence between local and central opinion for their own political profit. Their self-reliance was given, therefore, its fullest opportunity—and Irish Unionists drifted further beyond the failing grasp of British Conservatism.

The affair also altered George Wyndham's self-perception. Befuddled by drink, his political values grew increasingly arcane: the Middle Ages supplied a utopian vision, free from business rapacity, and servile—loyalist—contumacy. His imagination focused on knights, picturesque peasants, and Holy Mother Church; the spectre of plutocratic conspiracy and Jewish intrigue distorted an older and cooler political perspective.

He had always balanced a career in politics and in letters. Once he had resigned, romance dictated a political ideal. Devolution, which thrust the grim reality of modern popular politics onto Ulster Unionism, provided George Wyndham with a sunnier, medieval illusion.

7

The Emergence of Ulster Unionist Militancy, 1905-1911

1. The McNeill Hypothesis

The extremity of Ulster Unionist opposition to the third Home Rule Bill has for long been explained in the context of the Parliament Act of 1911. This interpretation originated with Ronald McNeill's *Ulster's Stand for Union*, an important work of Unionist historiography, published in 1922, in the immediate aftermath of the Anglo-Irish Treaty, and angrily dedicated 'To the Memory of the Unionist Party'. For McNeill, as for his successors, Ulster's 'stand' effectively began with 'the entirely novel situation arising from the passing of the Parliament Act'—a situation which demanded (and won) a correspondingly novel political reaction.[1] Thus Ulster militancy evidently only truly developed after August 1911, a period characterized by unique constitutional insecurity, intense local organization, and by a reaffirmation of the historic bond between British and Irish Unionism.

The strength of this hypothesis lay partly in the fact that it offered no challenge to conventional Unionist self-perceptions. Thus, by portraying Ulster militancy as a direct sequel to Liberal constitutional chicanery, McNeill and his successors were merely reiterating contemporary Unionist apologetic. Moreover, the hypothesis had the complementary merit of plausibility. It is true, as McNeill asserted, that the peak of loyalist militancy followed the removal of the House of Lords' veto. It is also true that earlier threats of armed action, made when the veto was still intact, were never carried into effect: and it might be urged, therefore, that the power and sympathy of the Lords represented an influential restraint.

And yet, judged within a broader context, the McNeill hypothesis appears more problematic. For example, the powers of the House

---

[1] Ronald McNeill, *Ulster's Stand for Union* (London, 1922), 45. A. T. Q. Stewart, *The Ulster Crisis* (London, 1967), 25. Edward Marjoribanks and Ian Colvin, *Life of Lord Carson* (3 vols.; London, 1932-6), ii. 76-7.

of Lords had rarely been a subject for party consensus (as evidenced by the attitude of Gladstone and Rosebery in 1892–5) and thus the veto was always a questionable source of security.[2] In any case, Ulster Unionism could not credibly rely on the Lords while proclaiming a commitment to the will of the British democracy, and describing itself as a popular movement. Ulster Unionists' security, and therefore their commitment to formal constitutional politics, lay rather in the stability and usefulness of their bond with British Unionism. Only with evidence of British treachery or systematic ineffectiveness—and this last would be a threat in a prolonged period of Unionist opposition—did loyalists turn to the cultivation of their own organizational resources.

The fundamental difficulty with McNeill's interpretation, therefore, lies in the narrowness of his vision—in his sketchy treatment of Ulster Unionist development before 1911. Perhaps there was consolation for McNeill, an opponent of the Anglo-Irish Treaty and its signatories, in returning to consider a period both of uncomplicated Tory fidelity to Unionist principles and of apparent party unity. If so, then the character of British and Irish Unionist party relations before 1910–11 would have been uncomfortable evidence. For loyalism was in flux at this time, its external relations and internal structure both undergoing considerable alteration. The nature of these developments—declining sympathy between the British and Irish Unionist parties, intensive local reorganization—suggests that loyalism was growing more embattled and self-reliant. This, in turn, might be related to the apparently unprecedented self-reliance of 1912 which was McNeill's central theme. McNeill, however, chose not to make this connection, assuming that the combination of a Home Rule threat and the Parliament Act was wholly sufficient to explain the apparent revolution in loyalist behaviour which occurred after 1911. Here his assumption is re-examined; the main themes of Ulster Unionist development between 1905 and 1911 are isolated and discussed, and an alternative perspective on the revolt of 1912 is suggested.

[2] See e.g. Peter Stansky, *Ambitions and Strategies: The Struggle for the Leadership of the Liberal Party in the 1890s* (Oxford, 1964), 37 ff., 135 ff., 175–8. James Loughlin, *Gladstone, Home Rule and the Ulster Question, 1882–1893* (Dublin, 1986), 282.

2.   Tory Patrons and Ulster Unionism, 1906-1911

Visiting Belfast in February 1907, David Lloyd George addressed himself to the developing character of Ulster Unionism. He identified the existence of change, isolated several features for comment, and noted in particular the new inability of loyalists to call on the leading talent of British Unionism ('the old Ulster Unionism, when it imported men to Belfast, *did* import men . . .').[3] Able and demotic politicians like Churchill and Joseph Chamberlain were replaced by an inferior type of import—'Mr. Walter Long, an amiable Wiltshire Orangeman, Lord Londonderry, a wild Durham Orangeman—and Captain Craig'.[4] He might have added that Arthur Balfour had paid no visit to Unionist Ireland since 1893, and that the most active intervention which even the most significant loyalist gathering might now expect was a telegram of encouragement from their national leader. Furthermore, few other ex-ministers of the Unionist administration ventured over to Ireland; and even those with formal Irish affiliations, like Walter Long, were increasingly captivated by the demands of British politics.

But the relationship between loyalism and the British leadership in these years was at once more fluid than Lloyd George suggested, while broadly conforming to his perception of drift. Thus, while loyalism and a significant section of the national party command viewed each other with, at best, indifference, this might graduate into apparent mutual affection or disdain. Traditionally one of the fundamental determinants of the parties' intimacy had been the relevance and significance of the Home Rule issue; and indeed after 1911, with the dual threat of the Home Rule and Parliament Bills, the bond between Irish and British Unionism was swiftly renewed. But the more general demands of opposition to Liberalism had encouraged Unionist unity in 1886 and 1892 to 1895—and thus a restoration of internal harmony could have been predicted for the years between 1906 and 1911. In fact, though an active and aggressive Liberal administration might have inspired a more coherent opposition, considerable tension developed between the Unionist parties. And this can be traced to the devolution controversies of 1904-5 and 1906, and their aftermath of British impatience and Irish distrust.

[3] *BNL*, 9 Feb. 1907.   [4] Ibid.

The direction of change within internal party relations is recognizable among the leaders of British Unionism—Arthur Balfour, and the two most plausible contenders for his crown in 1911, Austen Chamberlain and Walter Long. The rigour of Balfour's Chief Secretaryship had been universally approved in Unionist Ireland; and, discounting his habitual and rhetorical sarcasm, Balfour had on the whole returned this affection (at any rate until 1896). The growth of Conservative loyalist resistance towards aspects of constructive Unionism had soured relations, but it was only in 1905-6 that a new and comprehensive hostility was fully aired. The circumstances of the devolution affair of 1904-5, and of its re-run in 1906, need not be rehearsed at length here.[5] As was argued in the preceding chapter, in 1905 many Ulster Unionists believed not only that George Wyndham had been culpably involved with a scheme of devolved government for Ireland, but that Wyndham had had the sanction of Balfour himself. There is no indisputable evidence to suggest that Ulster Unionist suspicions were justified; but, whatever the truth of their accusations, they won a significant amount of support within a section of British Toryism.

In October 1906, following the lead of their parliamentary chairman, Walter Long, Irish Unionists pressed for the publication of letters in Balfour's possession which allegedly shed new and damaging light on Unionist policy in Ireland between 1902 and 1905.[6] Despite the leader's anger and intransigence—he resolutely refused to countenance publication—Irish Unionists pursued their demand with aggression, deploying their considerable political resources to the full. Alexander Acland-Hood, the Tory Chief Whip, was in contact with loyalist feeling through his brother-in-law, who served on the staff of the *Irish Times*; and he largely sympathized with their case, if only because he recognized that, for the sake of party morale, 'the Chief should be cleared of any idea of complicity in devolution'.[7] Austen Chamberlain warned Balfour that 'indignation' over the matter was not confined to the Irish Unionists

[5] The best accounts remain F. S. L. Lyons, 'The Irish Unionist Party and the Devolution Crisis of 1904-1905', *Irish Historical Studies* vi. 21 (Mar. 1948), Ronan Fanning, 'The Unionist Party and Ireland, 1906-1910' *IHS*, xv. 58 (Sept. 1966); and Andrew Gailey, 'The Unionist Government's Policy Towards Ireland, 1895-1905', Ph.D. thesis (Cambridge, 1983). See ch. 6.

[6] Fanning, 'Unionist Party', 152-3.

[7] Bodleian Library, Oxford, J. S. Sandars Papers c748, fo. 184, Alexander Acland-Hood to Sandars, 11 Sept. 1906.

alone, and that 'a disastrous hesitation' was afflicting the broader Unionist party.[8] J. S. R. Philips, editor of the *Yorkshire Post*, while more loyal to Balfour's stand, offered similar impressions of party feeling.[9] And *The Times* and the *Spectator* unequivocally stated that Balfour should comply with loyalist demands, the latter going so far as to suggest that, were Balfour to persist, Colonel Edward Saunderson would be justified in broaching the matter in the House of Commons.[10]

Balfour's initial response to the loyalist agitation was to draft a coruscating rebuke which he circulated among the leaders of the party, and which was ultimately intended for publication. He tackled Irish Unionist suspicions with a dismissive irony:

if such professions of [Unionist] faith are a mere cloak for intrigue, then no doubt I am quite unworthy to lead the Irish Unionist party: but I must be permitted respectfully to add that if the Irish Unionist party regard this as a possible hypothesis, then in my opinion, they are quite unworthy to be led by me. These are ills for which, if they be real, no publication of documents, however indiscreet, can provide a remedy.[11]

Though Balfour at last bowed to the advice of his colleagues and suppressed this response, it only palely reflected the hostility which he felt for the rumour-mongering Irishmen nominally under his command. Their suspicions were, he wrote to Long, 'contemptible'.[12]

In the event the controversy died as swiftly as it had grown, Balfour having mollified his loyalist critics through a speech given at Manchester on 23 October 1906. But the bitterness of the agitation at its height would colour all subsequent relations between the party leader and Irish Unionists. In November 1906 several leading Dublin Unionists were anxious to offer a gesture of conciliation; and a proposal was floated to invite Balfour to Ireland once the Liberal government's Devolution Bill had been introduced. Balfour's Manchester statement had silenced all but his most confirmed critics:

[8] Birmingham University Library, Austen Chamberlain Papers, AC 7/4/15, Austen to Balfour, 7 Oct. 1906. Fanning, 'Unionist Party', 158-9.

[9] Sandars Papers, c752, fo. 119, Phillips to Sandars, 19 Oct. 1906.

[10] Sandars Papers, c751, fo. 76, Phillips to Sandars, 1 Oct. 1906. Fanning, 'Unionist Party', 154, n. 26.

[11] WLP, Add. MS 62403, Balfour to Long, 5 Sept. 1906.

[12] Blanche E. C. Dugdale, *Arthur James Balfour, First Earl of Balfour, KG, OM, FRS, &c* (2 vols.; London, 1936), i. 317.

'his last speech has put things on a better basis here', A. W. Samuels wrote from Dublin on 3 November 1906, 'and a few more bits of straight-out talking like it would soon quicken the old spirit among many who had believed they were being given away'.[13] But the proposal came to nothing: Balfour fended off such invitations with a frosty courtesy. Later, when he was directly approached by Walter Long to address an annual plenary session of the Ulster Unionist Council, he replied bluntly that 'Belfast is out of the question'.[14] And there is evidence to suggest that, despite the loyal gestures of certain influential Irish Unionists, Balfour's attitude was heartily reciprocated by many northern Unionists.[15]

Long's Irish connections and raw political sensitivity dictated a certain caution—but Balfour was capable of providing a less restrained revelation of his anger. In the light of their leader's tetchy refusal to come to Belfast in 1908, Irish Unionists had set their sights on a more modest source of British patronage, and Earl Cawdor, a former First Lord of the Admiralty, was invited to address the Ulster Unionist Council gathering of January 1909. Faced with such a flattering, if somewhat intimidating request, Cawdor turned to Balfour for help. Other leading Unionists whom he had consulted had been divided over the Belfast visit, those with Ulster and UUC connections like Londonderry being warmly in favour, while more disinterested Tories like Acland-Hood counselled caution (judging presumably that a Belfast audience would only be satisfied by an extreme and therefore compromising speech).[16] Balfour, at any rate, was only too aware of the susceptibilities of a loyalist gathering, and of the need for extremism, though his reply to Cawdor was characterized by a self-indulgent vilification of 'these foolish northern Unionists' rather than by any clearer guidance.[17] Significantly, Balfour revealed that he was still stung—two and a half years after the event—by the devolution furore, and that his opinion of loyalism had not significantly mellowed; indeed rather the reverse:

They chose a year or two ago (confound them) to suspect us of somewhat weakening in our attitude upon that subject [Home Rule]—a most insolent

[13] WLP, Add. MS 62410, A. W. Samuels to Long, 3 Nov. 1906.
[14] WLP, Add. MS 62403, Balfour to Long, 4 Dec. 1907.
[15] Patrick Buckland, *Irish Unionism, 1885-1923: A Documentary History* (Belfast, 1973), 202-3.
[16] ABP, Add. MS 49709, fo. 59, Balfour to Cawdor, 7 Jan. 1909.
[17] Ibid.

and unworthy suspicion, but extremely characteristic of the Irish mind. I remember its making me very angry at the time . . . it is like a man suspecting you of forging a cheque. It is beneath your dignity even to take the trouble to repudiate the charge, still less to explain to him that you think forgery wrong![18]

Years earlier, in May 1899, Lady Frances Balfour had accused Arthur of failing to 'suffer contradiction gladly' and had cited three old disputes as evidence of his unreasonableness.[19] Replying, he had effectively conceded the truth of Lady Frances's case through his own ill-disguised irritation and anger. Evidently he had a long memory for certain types of criticism; and while this may not have significantly diverted his political judgement, it affected personal and political relations at a more superficial level. Thus Balfour's Unionism never wavered, even when some of his friends and colleagues were prepared to reconsider their constitutional creed (as in 1910). And, while he never forgot Ulster Unionists' disloyalty, he recognized their significance, especially when the powers of the Lords and, by implication, Home Rule emerged as major issues. He offered no public correction; rather he preferred to exhibit the apparent unity of the British and Irish parties. While before 1910 he had remained politely aloof, in April 1910 when the active allegiance of loyalism was a clearer priority, he emerged as guest of honour at a major Ulster Unionist function in the House of Commons.[20] And in the autumn of 1910, when reports of federalist trimming at the Constitutional Conference were circulating, the most influential Irish Unionist leaders, though perturbed, retained confidence in Balfour's Unionism.[21] Indeed his reassurance was a crucial salve during the difficult period in October–November 1910 when federalism was receiving a sympathetic airing in a section of the Tory press, and when the flexibility of figures like F. E. Smith was common

---

[18] ABP, Add. MS 49709, fo. 59, Balfour to Cawdor, 7 Jan. 1909.
[19] ABP, Add. MS 49831, fo. 227, Balfour to Frances Balfour, 23 May 1899. Other examples of Lady Frances's lack of regard for her brother-in-law are to be found in Dugdale, *Balfour*, ii. 67; and also John Vincent (ed.), *The Crawford Papers: The Journals of David Lindsay, Twenty-Seventh Earl of Crawford and Tenth Earl of Balcarres, 1871–1940 during the years 1892 to 1940.* (Manchester, 1984), 231.
[20] Buckland, *Documentary History*, 277. *BNL* 15 April 1910.
[21] PRONI, Papers of Theresa, Marchioness of Londonderry, D 2846/1/1/57, Carson to Lady Londonderry, 6 Nov. 1910. Partly printed in H. Montgomery Hyde, *Carson: The Life of Sir Edward Carson, Lord Carson of Duncairn* (London, 1953), 280–1.

knowledge among leading Ulster Unionists.[22] And yet, though loyalists now accepted Balfour's good faith, they still bemoaned his lack of fire, and contrasted their own vitality and sense of urgency with his insouciance.

This equivocal loyalty is both a measure of how far the relationship between Balfour and his Irish party had developed since November 1906—and also of the new, pragmatic and perfunctory, nature of their bond. Balfour and loyalism remained united by the narrow and unemotional tie of Unionism: but there was no sentimental dimension to their understanding, such as could be said to have existed in 1893. And pragmatism was no less a part of the Irish Unionist attitude towards their British leader than vice versa.

The bond between loyalism and Birmingham had perhaps a broader foundation, though this was never used to create any lasting political alliance. A generation of landlord leaders within Irish Unionism (Saunderson, Deramore, Londonderry) had viewed Joseph Chamberlain with caution, at least until his succession to the Colonial Office.[23] But where Saunderson, for example, had resented the influence of Birmingham Unionism over Tory land policy, he proved an uncritical admirer of the radical Colonial Secretary— and became a convert to tariff reform. Indeed, more generally, there was no significant 'little England' or free trade lobby within loyalism, and by the late Edwardian period even the formerly Cobdenite manufacturing interest of Belfast had declared for colonial preference.[24] Moreover, the sympathy between Orange Ulster and Orange Lancashire existed in spite of separate attitudes towards free trade (though it would be wrong to exaggerate the predominance of free trade among even Lancashire Unionists).[25] Chamberlainite rhetoric linking colonial preference to the longer-term need for imperial confederation had a ready appeal to loyalists given that one of their oldest arguments against Home Rule had been that it would precipitate the disintegration of Empire. Thus Joseph Chamberlain,

[22] PRONI, Theresa Londonderry Papers, D 2846/1/155, Carson to Lady Londonderry, 27 Oct. 1910. Hyde, *Carson*, 279. Theresa Londonderry Papers, D 2846/1/1/71, Carson to Lady Londonderry, 7 Oct. 1911. The Hon. George Peel, *The Reign of Sir Edward Carson* (London, 1914), 205–7.

[23] Reginald Lucas, *Colonel Saunderson M.P.: A Memoir* (London, 1908), 125. KRO, Papers of Aretas Akers-Douglas, U 564/C167/4, Deramore to Akers-Douglas, 2 Nov. 1889.

[24] *BNL*, 4 July 1908, 7 Oct. 1908, 20 Nov. 1909, 1 Jan. 1910.

[25] Alan Sykes, *Tariff Reform in British Politics, 1903–1913* (Oxford, 1979), 167.

whether as selfless convert to Unionism, or as the champion of imperial interests, became a focus of affection for even the most crusty Irish Tory. Chamberlain's stroke and incapacity demanded that the relationship between Birmingham and Belfast be re-examined—but the loyalty which he had inspired was such that Austen automatically and briefly inherited Ulster Unionist support. Characteristically, Austen neglected this opportunity to cultivate personal allegiance (where Walter Long, and earlier Tories on the make were less discriminating). And thus here, as in other aspects of Anglo-Irish party relations, the authority of loyalism over the leadership appeared to be weakening.

Nevertheless, between 1905 and 1911 a number of leading Irish Unionist politicians actively promoted tariff reform. Edward Saunderson publicly aligned himself with Joseph Chamberlain, and stood committed to preference at the election of January 1906.[26] Five Ulster Unionist MPs, including three of the most influential figures of the Edwardian party—J. B. Lonsdale, William Moore, and C. C. Craig—attended a tariff reform meeting at the House of Commons on 13 April 1905.[27] Four years later, in April 1909, George Wyndham noted the presence of 'extreme Ulstermen' at a tariff reform function in the Commons where he was delivering a speech.[28] Given the intense hostility which had been long felt by Ulster Unionists for Wyndham, their presence was seen—at any rate by Wyndham himself—as a gesture of reconciliation. In fact tariff reform was chief amongst a number of issues which helped to promote a limited *rapprochement* between the ex-Chief Secretary and his Orange critics between 1909 and Wyndham's death in 1913.

But the outstanding proponent of tariff reform within late Edwardian Unionism was undoubtedly James Craig, Carson's lieutenant between 1911 and 1914 and a future Prime Minister of Northern Ireland. On 13 February 1907 Craig 'spoke strongly for action' on tariff reform at a meeting with Austen Chamberlain; in September he was elected as one of the Vice-Presidents of the Tariff Reform League, and in January 1909 he was appointed to sit on

[26] Lucas, *Saunderson*, 348-9.

[27] JCP, JC 20/4/20, 'list of the names of 142 members present at the tariff meeting held in the House of Commons on 13 April [1905]'.

[28] J. W. Mackail and Guy Wyndham (edd.), *The Life and Letters of George Wyndham* (2 vols.; London, [1924]), ii. 633.

the parliamentary Tariff Reform Committee.[29] Inevitably Craig's political priorities were Irish; but, at a time when Home Rule was not an active political issue, he demonstrated that even a comparatively junior loyalist back-bencher could contribute to non-Irish controversies within Unionism.

For some months after the Unionist election defeat of 1906 it seemed that this sympathy between loyalism and Birmingham might evolve into a more substantial alliance. Edward Saunderson was courted by Austen Chamberlain in preparation for what promised to be a clash between Balfour and the Chamberlains at the party meeting planned for 15 February 1906. The famous exchange of letters between Joseph Chamberlain and Balfour on St Valentine's Day averted the threat of confrontation, so that Saunderson's support lost even a marginal value: nevertheless he pledged his fidelity to Austen, and spoke to this effect at the party convocation.[30] When Saunderson died later that year Austen was genuinely moved, describing the Colonel in a private letter to his stepmother as 'a real loss'.[31] Significantly, the reaction of the Balfour clan to the loyalist's death was much less charitable.[32]

The climax to this short-lived alliance came as early as November 1906. In the autumn Austen had supported Walter Long against Balfour over the 'MacDonnell Mystery'; and, primed with this evidence of good faith, Carson and James Campbell had asked him to open the Irish Unionist winter campaign.[33] He successfully fulfilled this obligation in Dublin on 7 December 1906. Austen's stay saw his induction into the sanctuaries of Irish loyalism: he lunched on 7 December with the Provost of Trinity, dined at the Kildare Street Club, and had supper with Campbell, a rising star of southern Unionism, and one of the architects of Ulster Unionist resistance in

[29] PRONI, Diary of Lady Craigavon, D 1415/B/38, 7 Sept. 1907, 28 Jan. 1909 Austen Chamberlain (ed.), *Politics from Inside: An Epistolary Chronicle, 1906–1914* (London, 1936), 51.

[30] Lucas, *Saunderson*, 369. PRONI, Edward Saunderson Papers, T 2996/3/3, A. Chamberlain to Saunderson, 7 Feb. 1906. Austen Chamberlain Papers, AC 7/2/8, Saunderson to A. Chamberlain, 8 Feb. 1906—printed partly in Fanning, 'Unionist Party', 150.

[31] Austen Chamberlain Papers, AC 4/1/11, Austen to Mary E. Chamberlain, 27 Oct. 1906.

[32] Whittingehame, Gerald Balfour Papers, TD 83/133/273, Lady Betty Balfour to Gerald, [Oct. 1906].

[33] Austen Chamberlain Papers, AC 4/1/11, Austen to Mary E. Chamberlain, 27 Oct. 1906.

1912. On 8 December he dined at the St George's Yacht Club with John Ross, a leading Presbyterian Unionist, and formerly MP for Londonderry City.[34]

But despite these auguries, Chamberlain rapidly lost interest in Ulster Unionism; and by 1908 impatient references to loyalist truculence were appearing in his correspondence.[35] His irritation also embraced the static Unionism which was a fundamental of Edwardian loyalism. By the time of the Constitutional Conference, Chamberlain was inclining towards federalism—and he was deeply impressed by the work of F. S. Oliver, 'my intimate friend since our College days, and a publicist of notable originality and distinction'.[36]

In part this change of attitude may be explained by the developing demands of the campaign for tariff reform. Even at the height of his sympathy, in 1906, Austen had felt that 'a speech on Home Rule is like flogging a dead horse'; and by February 1909 he scandalized the loyalist partisan, Henry Chaplin, by proclaiming that the country 'was not interested' in Ireland, and that the Unionist party could not win an election primarily on an Irish issue.[37] Only tariff reform offered the prospect of victory, 'for it was the only thing the country cared for'.[38]

But perhaps the most significant wedge between Austen and loyalism lay in the chairmanship of the parliamentary Ulster Party. When Saunderson died in October 1906 his office was inherited by the MP for South County Dublin, Walter Long. Long, though a tariff reformer, emerged as a comparative moderate, and as a leading opponent of Chamberlain's campaign to win Unionism for Birmingham.[39] While Long's lieutenants in the Ulster Party were less devoted to Balfour and more sympathetic to the legacy of Joseph Chamberlain, they were for all practical purposes bound to their parliamentary chairman. If there is a sense in which Long and Chamberlain were competing for the affections of loyalism in 1906,

[34] Chamberlain, *Politics from Inside*, 41-2.

[35] Austen Chamberlain Papers, AC 4/1/249, Austen to Mary Chamberlain, 31 Mar. 1908. Chamberlain, *Politics from Inside*, 102-3.

[36] David Dutton, *Austen Chamberlain: Gentleman in Politics* (Bolton, 1985), 72-3. Chamberlain, *Politics from Inside*, 193.

[37] Chamberlain, *Politics from Inside*, 140-1.

[38] Ibid.

[39] Richard Murphy, 'Walter Long and the Conservative Party, 1905-1921', Ph.D. thesis (Bristol, 1984), 58-9.

then this contest ended with Long's succession to the Ulster leadership in November 1906. Thereafter as relations between Long and Austen cooled, so too relations between Austen and Long's Ulster clients cooled. Linked, as they were, to a personal adversary, Ulster Unionists lost all practical relevance to Austen's ambitions.

Yet, though he was the most consistently sympathetic and the most influential ally of loyalism within the Unionist front rank, even Long's commitment was wavering by 1909–10. Like Balfour a generation earlier, Long was venerated in Ulster both for his uncompromising Unionism and for his achievement as Chief Secretary for Ireland. And, as with Balfour, Irish Unionists sought a more formal bond with their British patron through the offer of a loyalist constituency. Where Balfour had rejected a similar invitation in 1892, circumstances compelled Long to a more careful consideration; and in January 1906, having been defeated in Bristol, he stood, and was elected for, South County Dublin.[40] In November he was selected to succeed Saunderson as chairman of the parliamentary Ulster Party; and, in January 1907, the constitution of the movement having been changed for that purpose, Long was elected as vice-president and effective head of the Ulster Unionist Council.[41]

His activity as Ulster leader was variable, periods of intense agitation giving way to diversion into major British issues. Between 1906 and 1907 he was certainly active for the loyalist cause, articulating extremist disquiet over the devolution affair, and founding the Union Defence League as an Ulster missionary agency in England.[42] He was received with acclaim at the first annual meeting of the Ulster Unionist Council, held in Belfast in January 1907; and he returned to Ulster in April in order to bless the candidature of George Clark at the crucial North Belfast by-election.[43] In October 1907 he attended a golfing dinner in Portrush, County Antrim, and was pleased with his reception here, as more generally in Ulster: 'the loyalty and kindness of the whole party over here to me is really very remarkable'.[44] And throughout

---

[40] ABP, Add. MS 49849, fo. 102, H. L. Barnardo to Balfour, 2 Oct. 1891. The request came from South County Dublin.
[41] McNeill, *Ulster's Stand*, 38. *BNL*, 31 Jan. 1907.
[42] Murphy, 'Walter Long', 139–40.
[43] *BNL* 5 April 1907.
[44] DRO, Papers of Theresa, Marchioness of Londonderry, D/Lo/C/666/19, Long to Lady Londonderry, 6 Oct. 1907.

the years 1906–7, and beyond, he maintained close contact with leading Irish Unionists like Abercorn and John Atkinson, and with sympathetic Irish civil servants like J. J. Taylor and Henry Robinson.[45]

But by 1908, despite his titular commitment, Walter Long's interest in Ulster Unionism was waning. He was largely absent from Ulster between 1908 and January 1910; and he was unable to attend the annual meetings of the UUC in 1908 and 1909 (a painful dereliction from the point of view of loyalists, for whom these party festivals assumed an exaggerated importance in the politically lean years between 1906 and 1910).[46] Similarly painful was the rarity of his attendance at the sessions of the parliamentary Ulster Party, of which he was nominally chairman.

Moreover, like Balfour and Austen Chamberlain, Long could be irritated by the demands of his loyalist clients (though, as always, it is difficult to distinguish ritual abuse among senior politicians from conviction). In August 1907 he affirmed with Balfourian hauteur that 'Ireland and Irishmen are not grateful recipients of one's efforts'; in November, after an embarrassing dispute among the Unionists of West Down, he complained that 'Irishmen are not easy to manage'.[47] Each of these sweeping indictments was delivered within a context of loyalist misdemeanour, and Long was prepared to expand on his irritation to confidants like Theresa Londonderry. While he had been delighted by his reception at Portrush, he did not need to look further than Balfour to find that loyalist commitment might prove ephemeral; and, having described the enthusiasm of his audience to Lady Londonderry, he added morosely: 'I hope it will last!'.[48] Furthermore, there is evidence to suggest that, like Balfour, he was enraged by the independent behaviour of loyalist extremists. When Chief Secretary the pressure of a section of loyalist MPs against his Under-Secretary had caused offence, and Long had tried to purchase the allegiance of William Moore through the offer of the Irish Solicitor-Generalship.[49] But even as late as February 1910,

---

[45] Murphy, 'Walter Long', 136, 138 n. 1. There is an extensive correspondence between Long, John Atkinson, and Henry Robinson among both Long archives—in Wiltshire and in the British Library.

[46] BNL, 23 Jan. 1908, 28 Jan. 1909.

[47] DRO, Theresa Londonderry Papers, D/Lo/C/666/ 9, 23:, Long to Lady Londonderry, 6 Aug. 1907; 21 Nov. 1907.

[48] DRO, Theresa Londonderry Papers, D/Lo/C/666/19, Long to Lady Londonderry, 6 Oct. 1907.

[49] WLP, Add. MS 62409, William Moore to Long, 7 Dec. 1905.

when a more uncritical judgement of loyalism was again in vogue, Long could still be apologetic about the 'broad mindedness' of the Ulster Unionist representatives.[50]

Other factors encouraged a drift from an Ulster commitment. Like Chamberlain, Long had been caught up in the battle for tariff reform; but, while there was a limited congruity between the principles of the two men, Long was fundamentally opposed to the aggression displayed against Unionist free traders like the Cecils.[51] Chamberlain viewed the pressure and agitation of the Tariff Reform League with equanimity, thereby alienating Long. But the dispute over the persecution of the free traders diverted Long from Ireland in 1907-8; and between June and December 1909 he was similarly preoccupied with the Budget Protest League.[52] In addition, recurrent illness through the period compelled him to surrender all political activity: this was the explanation for his absence from the UUC meeting of January 1908, for example.[53] A lengthy period of convalescence between January and June 1909 also removed Long from both British and Ulster politics.[54]

The comparative irrelevance of Irish affairs before 1910 affected him, though not so forcefully as Austen Chamberlain. In 1906 English colleagues had warned him against 'sinking yourself in the Irish stew . . . you have a harder and bigger game'.[55] The tepid response of many leading English Unionists to his Union Defence League must have underlined the liabilities of a purely Irish platform. Moreover, while the support of Irish Unionists was potentially of broader, British value, this was most conspicuously true when Irish matters dominated popular or parliamentary debate. Otherwise the cost of maintaining this support—farming a constituency physically and politically far removed from Wiltshire and Westminster—was very great, and ultimately proved to be insupportable.

Long's commitments to Unionism, and secondarily to Irish Unionism, were never abandoned. But when active engagement in loyalist politics looked set to affect his British stature, he was forced to reconsider the balance of his activities. This recognition was

---

[50] DRO, Theresa Londonderry Papers, D/Lo/C/666/107, Long to Lady Londonderry, 1 Feb. 1910.

[51] Murphy, 'Walter Long', 58-60.

[52] Ibid. 68-9.   [53] *BNL*, 23 Jan. 1908.

[54] Murphy, 'Walter Long', 68; Long, *Memories* (London, 1923), 181.

[55] WLP, Add. MS 62410, Gretton to Long, 26 Oct. 1906.

achieved as early as April 1908. By June of that year Long had announced his intention of contesting the Strand constituency at the next general election.[56] Having left South County Dublin and Ireland in January 1910, he resigned from the chairmanship of the Irish Unionist Parliamentary Party, and thus from the vice-presidency of the Ulster Unionist Council.[57] He continued to attend meetings ·of the parliamentary party, and was present at many of the major celebrations of Unionism between 1912 and 1914.[58] But his importance to Unionism was now secondary, where at one time he might have played the role of Carson. Within the space of twenty months, between February 1910 and November 1911, Long had effectively declined two opportunities for party leadership, probably thwarting thereby the last chance for unity between the commands of Irish and British Unionism.

Loyalism had more committed sympathizers within the rop rank of the Unionist command; but here, too, as with Balfour, Chamberlain, and Long, their effective value was waning by 1909-10. H. O. Arnold-Forster, Liberal Unionist MP for West Belfast between 1892 and 1906, and a former Secretary of State for War, was described by George Wyndham as an 'Orangeman'.[59] While this judgement was extreme, Arnold-Forster's death in 1909 removed an influential Ulster Unionist partisan from the ranks of the British party. Other Unionist leaders had Irish family or property ties. The eighth Duke of Devonshire and fifth Marquess of Lansdowne had significant Irish estates; but neither desired to patronize Irish loyalism and in any case Devonshire died in 1908.[60] Of the remaining ex-ministerial Irishmen, St John Brodrick had been defeated at the general election of 1906, and, though he returned to parliament as an Irish representative peer, his influence within the British leadership was impaired. Lord Ashbourne, the former

---

[56] WLP, Add. MS 62413, James Henderson to Long, 1 June 1908; John Arnott to Long, 3 June 1908; R. Blennerhassett to Long, 3 June 1908; A. W. Samuels to Long, 4 June 1908; Long to Percy Bernard, n.d. (copy).

[57] WLP, Add. MS 62415, Long to J. B. Lonsdale, 8 Feb. 1910 (copy). *BNL* 5 Jan. 1910.

[58] Murphy, 'Walter Long', 198-207, for a summary of Long's attitudes and activity at the time of the third Home Rule Bill.

[59] Eaton, Papers of George Wyndham, Wyndham to Sibell Grosvenor, 20 Feb. 1906.

[60] Patrick Buckland, *Irish Unionism*, i. *The Anglo-Irish and the New Ireland, 1885-1922* (Dublin and New York 1972), pp. xvi-xvii.

Unionist Lord Chancellor for Ireland, was on the list of Bonar Law's shadow cabinet in 1912; but he was ageing (seventy in 1907) and had little influence over Balfour.[61] Only Lord Londonderry and Edward Carson balanced positions of significance within British Unionism and intimate connections in Irish loyalist politics—and even with these most successful exponents, the problems of sustaining a dual career were only too apparent. Thus as Londonderry devoted himself to Ulster politics between 1906 and 1910, chairing most of the public meetings of the Ulster Unionist Council, his English career suffered. In any case it is not altogether clear whether Londonderry was widely regarded as a credible Tory patriarch: Lord Balcarres deemed him to be one of 'the two stupidest men in Britain'.[62] On the other hand Carson, whose ability was universally acclaimed, played a comparatively insignificant part in Irish politics, devoting himself to the law courts and to English platforms and controversies. In fact, judged on the evidence of his public commitment to loyalism in the late Edwardian period, Edward Carson was an extremely odd choice as Ulster leader. It would thus be wrong to suppose that his succession to Walter Long was inevitable, for there were other, more obvious candidates. And it may be that Carson was no less a compromise choice than Bonar Law, with James Craig playing Austen Chamberlain to William Moore's Walter Long.[63]

A variety of circumstances coalesced between 1906 and 1910 to reduce the influence of Irish Unionists over the leadership of the British party. The comparative insignificance of Home Rule reflected on the standing of loyalists; while the narrow aggression which they displayed over the MacDonnell controversies—even though it had been condoned by many British Unionists—angered and bewildered moderates. The ranks of loyalist ex-ministers were being thinned out through old age, death, or demotion. Thus on the one hand the dominance of alternative causes diverted long-time sympathizers like Long (and, indeed Carson) from loyalism; while the actions of loyalists, particularly over the MacDonnell affair, actively repelled

[61] L. P. Curtis, *Coercion and Conciliation in Ireland, 1880-1892: A Study in Conservative Unionism* (Oxford and Princeton, 1963), 188.

[62] Vincent (ed.), *Crawford Papers*, 277.

[63] J. C. Beckett, 'Carson: Unionist and Rebel', in his *Confrontations: Studies in Irish History* (London, 1972), 160-1. The oddness of the choice of Carson was noted by contemporaries: St John Ervine, *Sir Edward Carson and the Ulster Movement* (Dublin and London, 1915), 61. Craig, Moore, and Lonsdale were the northern Unionist leaders who attracted the greatest notice and approval from the loyalist press.

those leaders like Balfour who had regarded them with a hitherto passive contempt. And though in the mid-term loyalists benefited little from the leadership of Walter Long, they may have suffered in Birmingham through being identified so closely with the Chamberlains' chief party antagonist. By 1909, such was the isolation of Belfast, that the Ulster Unionist Council could only attract the comparatively undistinguished Cawdor to its annual meeting—and even he had had doubts about attending. Lloyd George's caricature of a friendless and inflexible loyalism was coming near to reality.

There were, however, mitigating elements within this otherwise gloomy perspective from Belfast. Though Carson only returned to popular loyalist politics in 1909-10, the years of opposition were seeing his rise to the front rank of national Toryism. Another lawyer in the ascendant was soon identified by loyalist leaders as a useful, and potentially invaluable sympathizer. F. E. Smith pledged his allegiance to Ulster Unionism as early as April 1907, when he spoke at UUC meetings in Belfast and Newtownards.[64] As MP for Liverpool Walton, Smith was subject to local pressure for Unionist orthodoxy; but his extravagant public support for loyalism may have had more to do with the tactical need to return to party fundamentals when out of office. He delivered an important indictment of Birrell's Irish administration in January 1909, which echoed Irish Unionist arguments and was reported in the Belfast loyalist press.[65] Furthermore, he and Carson had campaigned together in 1906, and they shared a public platform at Putney in February 1909—early symptoms of what would blossom into an even more important political relationship by 1912-14.[66]

At the opposite end of the career scale, Henry Chaplin, dropped from Salisbury's cabinet in 1900, staged a political come-back by means of tariff reform and the Union in 1906-7. As for Smith, loyalism was a useful and undemanding tool for personal advancement—though the 'Squire's' faith was probably less pragmatic, for he had close family connections in Tory Ulster (his

[64] BNL, 5 April 1907.
[65] BNL, 9 Jan. 1909. It should be noted, however, that Smith was not so conscious of constituency difficulties that he repudiated the Lloyd George coalition proposals of 1910: P. J. Waller, Democracy and Sectarianism: A Political and Social History of Liverpool, 1868-1939 (Liverpool, 1981), 267.
[66] Lord Birkenhead, Frederick Edwin, Earl of Birkenhead: The First Phase (London, 1933), 143. BNL. 11 Feb. 1909.

son-in-law was Viscount Castlereagh). Chaplin unreservedly backed Walter Long and the loyalists over the 'MacDonnell Mystery'; and, campaigning in 1907, he concentrated on the lamentable state of Birrell's Ireland.[67] He repeated this emphasis within the shadow cabinet, irritating Austen Chamberlain with his simple devotion to Irish affairs.[68]

3. Missionaries in England, 1906–1910

It had been Chaplin's experience in November 1907 that Ireland and Irish loyalists had gone down well with his audiences; indeed he could write patronizingly to Long that 'your Irish friends . . . [have] made an excellent impression'.[69] Between 1906 and 1909 Irish Unionists appeared regularly on English platforms, and, with certain audiences at any rate, they could win an extremely sympathetic reception.[70] But the ultimate success of these campaigns was far from clear, particularly given the more impressive achievements gained by similar efforts in the 1880s and early 1890s. Before 1910 most Irish Unionists felt that their missionary work was making little impression on English electoral opinion.

Irish Unionist speakers and the paraphernalia of their mission— slides, broadsheets, pamphlets—had been a familiar element of the British electioneering trail between 1886 and 1895; but a decade of Tory administration, allied with the Boer War and the tariff controversy, had quelled the zeal both of the missionaries and of their prey, the British voter. The loyalist presence in England was wound down—the Irish Unionist Alliance closed its London office in 1902; and northern politicians confined their agitation to the House of Commons, and focused their concern on apparently wayward ministers like George Wyndham.[71]

[67] WLP, Add. MS 62406, Henry Chaplin to Long, 5 Sept. 1906; Chaplin to Long, 12 Nov. 1907; Chaplin to Long, 15 Nov. 1907. Edith, Marchioness of Londonderry, *Henry Chaplin: A Memoir* (London, 1926), 178, 196.
[68] Chamberlain, *Politics from Inside*, 141.
[69] WLP, Add. MS 62406, Chaplin to Long, 15 Nov. 1907.
[70] See e.g. Patrick Buckland, *Irish Unionism,* ii. *Ulster Unionism and the Origins of Northern Ireland* (Dublin and New York, 1973), 72 (though see also p. 91 for a general assessment).
[71] Irish Unionist Alliance, *Report for 1902* (Dublin, 1903), 9.

Irish Unionists had been resigned to the indifference of British electors between 1895 and 1906; but the defeat of Balfour's government, even though it had not occurred on the Home Rule issue, restored English support as a loyalist priority. Walter Long's Union Defence League was partly a response to this new insecurity, and it co-operated with the Ulster Unionist Council and the Irish Unionist Alliance to form a new co-ordinating body, which would be the chief agent of loyalist endeavour in Great Britain. The Joint Committee of the Unionist Associations of Ireland was formed in December 1907; and by March 1908 it was ready to launch an assault on the British electorate.[72]

The existence of the Unionist Associations of Ireland was mute testimony to the lack of faith felt by loyalist activists in English Unionist voters. In the absence of any conspicuous success, and with the evidence of formidable internal opposition, both the UDL and the UAI illustrate the growing gulf separating British and Irish Unionism. Certainly at the launching of the campaign of 1908, it emerged that loyalist leaders felt considerable disquiet at the ignorance and infidelity of the British, and especially of the British Unionist, electorate. Lord Londonderry complained that

political memories are very short . . . their friends on the other side of the channel were dead to the danger because they believed Home Rule was dead. It was therefore the duty of their friends to state that the reasons put forward in the past still held good and it should be their privilege to warn the English people with regard to the danger that confronted them. They had been lulled into a sense of false security . . .'[73]

S. H. Butcher, a southern Irish Unionist and MP for Cambridge University, registered a similar argument more succinctly and petulantly:

at this moment the English democracy was preoccupied with hopes and fears of its own, but it was all the more necessary that before the next general election that democracy should be instructed on the Irish question. England was partly ignorant and partly forgetful of Irish affairs.[74]

[72] Buckland, *Ulster Unionism*, 69. PRONI, UUC Papers, D 1327/2/1, Minute Book of the JCUAI.
[73] *BNL*, 21 Mar. 1908.
[74] Ibid. Similar doubts were expressed at the first meeting of the Joint Committee: Minute Book of the JCUAI, D 1327/2/1, 19 Dec. 1907. See also Buckland, *Documentary History*, 288-9.

The experience of the campaigns would prove the reasonableness of these qualms. However, if Irish Unionists had accurately perceived the distance between themselves and English opinion, then the means they chose to overcome this barrier reflected less certain judgement. Inaugurated in distrust, these campaigns would compound the fears of desertion increasingly felt by Irish loyalists before 1911.

The extent of the missionary task had been brought home to Walter Long as early as the winter of 1906–7. In November 1906, fresh from their bitter confrontation with Balfour over the MacDonnell letters, Long and Londonderry began to canvass support for the Union Defence League—a body which, while designed for a specific missionary purpose, also reflected a distrust of the will and capacity of the Unionist party. Leading Unionists reacted sourly to the proposals of Long and Londonderry: Lords Balfour of Burleigh, St Aldwyn, Jersey, and Milner all offered qualified disapproval, while the Duke of Devonshire was unequivocally hostile.[75] St Aldwyn, Balfour of Burleigh, and Jersey each claimed to support gradualist reform for Irish government, and consequently doubted whether this would be compatible with the immobile Unionism of the new League.[76] Balfour of Burleigh and the Earl of Cadogan (the latter of whom proved comparatively enthusiastic) each condemned militant loyalism: 'I am anxious not to be connected with . . . the extreme "Orange" position' warned Balfour, while Cadogan rejoiced that, through the UDL, the defence of the Union would be 'in better hands. Between ourselves the Irish Unionist Alliance and the Ulster Unionist Council are not to be relied upon'—an ironic confidence, given the prominent role played by Long in both these organizations.[77] Though Long put on a brave face ('my League is doing very well indeed . . . people seem really pleased'), the tepid response of his former colleagues must have been a bitter revelation.[78] In fact the role of the UDL was secondary to that of the largely Irish-based missionary organizations, though it briefly came to prominence in the campaign against the third Home Rule

[75] WLP, Add. MS 62410, Devonshire to Long, 9 Nov. 1906; Jersey to Long, 30 Dec. 1906; Devonshire to Long, 25 Nov. 1906. Also Add. MS 62411, Balfour of Burleigh to Long, 23 Jan. 1907; Goschen to Long, 24 Jan. 1907; St Aldwyn to Long, 30 Jan. 1907.
[76] WLP, Add. MS 62411, Balfour of Burleigh to Long, 2 Feb. 1907.
[77] Ibid. 23 Jan. 1907; Cadogan to Long, 4 Jan. 1907.
[78] DRO, Theresa Londonderry Papers, D/Lo/C/666/6, Long to Lady Londonderry, 15 Jan. 1907.

Bill.[79] And Walter Long, nominally president of the League, in reality soon lost interest, moving on to new areas of controversy and leaving its direction in the hands of Ian Malcolm.[80]

If the response from ex-ministers to loyalist endeavours was disappointing, then the missions themselves threw up further problems. In March and April 1908 the Unionist Associations of Ireland organized its first campaign, with public meetings in Bristol, Cheltenham, Reading, Colchester, Lincoln, Scarborough, North Shields, and Glasgow.[81] These gatherings appear to have passed off quietly—but this did not necessarily mean that Irish Unionist campaigners were universally welcome, or that they were always regarded as an electoral asset by provincial Tories. In May 1908 loyalists intervened in the by-election in Manchester North West, a contest made necessary through the promotion of Churchill to the cabinet. The division contained an Irish Catholic population, to whom Churchill addressed Home Rule sentiments: thus the appearance of exuberant loyalists represented both an obvious Unionist reaction, and at the same time created difficulties for their party's candidate, who of course was seeking every possible vote. However, Jack Sandars believed that the resentment felt against loyalist missionaries had a wider grounding than the particular circumstances of Manchester North West: 'as things are going now they don't seem to be in much request with our regular Party organisations'.[82] Irish Unionist waywardness in the division lobbies, and particularly over the Licensing Bill, was 'not calculated to recommend their advocacy of Unionist interests in Ireland to the English electorate'; that they should vote against the party whip over an English bill was nothing less than 'outrageous'.[83]

A similar, if more bitter, controversy developed from a by-election in Newcastle in the autumn of 1908. George Renwick, the Unionist candidate, had been reluctant to import loyalist speakers for his campaign, because, as in Manchester, there was a significant number of Irish Catholic voters in the division. In these circumstances anti-

---

[79] Buckland, *Ulster Unionism*, 74. Richard Murphy, 'Faction in the Conservative Party and the Home Rule Crisis, 1912–1914', *History*, lxxi. 232 (1986), 223–4.

[80] ABP, Add. MS 49859, fo. 205, Ian Malcolm to Balfour, 2 Dec. 1907; Add. MS 49859, fo. 207: Malcolm to Balfour, 15 Dec. 1907.

[81] Minute Book of the JCUAI, D 1327/2/1, 7 May 1908. Buckland, *Documentary History*, 295–6.

[82] ABP, Add. MS 49765, fo. 148, Sandars to Balfour, 5 May 1908.

[83] Ibid.

Home Rule drum-beating was likely to prove a liability where development of the education question, in the wake of Birrell's controversial and abortive Bill, held out greater possibilities.[84] Such apparent trimming by Renwick inflamed Walter Long—and particularly because it had involved an affront to his own campaigners. But Renwick obtained the tacit approval of Balfour, who would neither censure the Newcastle Unionists, nor offer them any form of instruction.[85] This characteristically ambiguous course proved in fact to be justified, for, left to his own devices, Renwick patched up a compromise with the loyalist zealots, accepting two of their missionaries, while promising to stand firmly on a Unionist platform. But this *was* a voluntary agreement, for Balfour had laid down the dictum that 'these North of Ireland worthies must wait for the invitation of the candidate or his association' before intervening in a contest.[86] Moreover, he as leader 'could not be the means of forcing them on a constituency which did not desire their services'.[87]

Such conflicts may have been confined to a minority of the constituencies worked by the missionaries, but they were more widely counter-productive. Loyalists might be demoralized by the evidence of British party pragmatism; while the Tory hierarchy, through which the process of arbitration percolated, conceived an exaggerated notion of the missionaries' trouble-making powers. Certainly Sandars, once sympathetic, even when Irish Unionists had been at their most irritating, grew increasingly impatient of the 'gang of noisy Irish protestants'.[88]

But there was another sense in which these campaigns and their successors in 1910 ran counter to the intentions of their promoters. They revealed 'gross incompetence and indifference' on the part of English party organizers, and not merely the offensive, but comprehensible, opposition of candidates like Joynson-Hicks in Manchester or Renwick in Newcastle.[89] After the second UAI

[84] ABP, Add. MS 49777, fo. 7, Long to Balfour, 27 July 1908; Add. MS 49777, fo. 10, Hood to anon. [Long], 9 May 1908. WLP, Add. MS 62403, Long to Balfour, 16 Sept. 1908 (copy).

[85] WLP, Add. MS 62403, Balfour to Long, 18 Sept. 1908.

[86] ABP, Add. MS 49765, fo. 175, Sandars to Balfour, 20 Sept. 1908.

[87] Ibid.   [88] Ibid.

[89] Minute Book of the JCUAI, D 1327/2/1, reports of the Election of December 1910 from F. E. Ball, R. D. Bates, and R. J. H. Shaw. Also Buckland, *Documentary History*, 301, 303-7.

campaign, held in 1910, Dawson Bates, secretary of the Unionist Council, lamented 'the extraordinary ignorance of the home rule question on the part of the electorate'—exactly the complaint which had been made by Londonderry, Butcher, and others in 1907, before the campaigns had been organized.[90] Walter Long, on the other hand, felt that the general election of January 1910 had revealed a rather greater popular grasp of the Unionist case, but he too was now aware of the resistance faced by loyalist missionaries.[91] These revelations, while they did not altogether discourage further campaigning (entrenched infidelity could only be a spur to further evangelism), provided a rational basis for fears of English rejection. Rather than educating the English, or cementing the national alliance, the missions taught loyalist activists the extent to which they depended upon their own resources.

The campaigns illustrated a further weakness. The leaders of Ulster Unionism participated only very reluctantly, and even then they rarely ventured outside the heartland of English loyalist support— Merseyside, Lancashire, and Clydeside.[92] James Craig and W. J. Allen, a prominent Orange leader, generally confined their British campaigning to Glasgow (though Craig did offer one speech to a Lincoln audience in the UAI campaign of 1908, and Allen made a successful appearance at the annual meeting of the National Union of Conservative Associations held in Manchester in November 1909).[93] Of eleven speeches delivered by William Moore in Britain in the years 1907–11, and recorded by the *Belfast News Letter*, only two were given outside Merseyside and Clydeside—one to an Orange gathering in Preston, and the other to an audience in Croydon, a seat held by the former West Belfast MP and 'Orangeman', H. O. Arnold-Forster.[94] Only Irish Unionists like Carson and James Campbell with English careers and undemanding constituencies (each sat for the University of Dublin), could campaign widely in England. Most MPs devoted their energies to their own Ulster seats—and this

[90] Ibid.
[91] Stanley Salvidge, *Salvidge of Liverpool: Behind the Political Scene, 1890–1928* (London, 1934), 103. Though even the sanguine Long recognized that 'in many parts of the country the view was accepted by our people that Home Rule had fallen into abeyance and that there existed no longer any need to expatiate upon its dangers'.
[92] See the list of speakers in Buckland, *Documentary History*, 295-7.
[93] *BNL*, 18 Nov. 1909. Ulster Unionist Council, *Annual Report for 1909* (Belfast, 1910).
[94] *BNL*, 11 May 1907, 2 Feb. 1909.

was hardly surprising as a choice of priorities, given the internal dissent which had afflicted the early Edwardian movement.

Nevertheless, this parochialism contrasted with the tendency, in the 1880s and 1890s, for Ulster MPs to neglect their constituencies in favour of parliament and of the English campaign trail: this more peripatetic Unionism was a particular feature of the career of the Orange leader, Edward Saunderson.[95] At the same time, parochialism was not unique to the late Edwardian period as a feature of loyalist development. On each of the earlier occasions when a Liberal party committed to Home Rule had been in power, Irish Unionists had looked to their own resources. But in 1886 and 1893 the bond with British Toryism had been stronger and the threat of Home Rule much less ambiguous than between 1906 and 1910. Paradoxically, the uncertainty among their opponents helped to break down the bonds between Irish and British Unionism. As has been shown, the condition of the British party in the later period offered very little reassurance to loyalist qualms, whether at the level of high politics or in the constituencies. And while loyalists could not afford to surrender the struggle within British Unionism, and even retained influence there (especially in the Commons, during the passage of the third Home Rule Bill), local resources assumed a disproportionate and unprecedented significance. Where once exaggerated reports of Ulster organization and militancy served as a complement to a parliamentary and British campaign, it now appeared that local action was the principal, if not the sole, loyalist defence against Home Rule.

4. Isolation and Armaments, 1910-1911

The sense of isolation which was developing within loyalism after 1906 took a variety of political forms, rhetorical and, above all, organizational. The relationship with British Unionism altered. This development has already been examined from the British and high-political point of view—but the gradual repulsion of the parties was mutual. Irish Unionists had experienced or perceived betrayal at the hands of their British allies in the past, but relations had always been

---

[95] See my *Edward Saunderson and the Evolution of Ulster Unionism, 1865-1906* (Belfast, forthcoming).

speedily restored (as in 1885–6). Now, while the alleged association of Wyndham with devolution had shattered unity in 1905, there was little comprehensive reconciliation. Instead, the devolution controversy was exhumed in 1906 and thereafter loyalist unease was never fully allayed. Disquiet graduated into hostility with the evidence of local British indifference, and the temporary threat of a general conversion to federalism in the autumn of 1910. Loyalty to Balfour never fully recovered from the events of 1905–6: his popularity at the end of his Chief Secretaryship, in 1891, was never regained, and it was a telling detail at the time of his retirement in 1911 that the *News Letter* chose to illustrate the story with a twenty-year-old photograph of the ex-leader.[96] Irish Unionists preferred to remember the vigorous Chief Secretary rather than the pragmatic party leader. Even among firmer allies there was evidence of drift: Walter Long's passion for loyalism became inexplicable with his move from South County Dublin to the Strand, by which he not only deserted his Irish friends but also exposed a highly vulnerable Unionist seat to Nationalist conquest.[97] And Londonderry's reputation fell when he voted with Lord Lansdowne for the Parliament Bill in August 1911.[98] Irish Unionists were left with only the Irish and middle-class elements of their leadership unsullied by misdeed or suspicion.

If a new and frosty relationship with British Conservatism heightened loyalist isolation, then this was also related to the internal condition of northern Irish politics. A variety of local constituency tensions had discredited the narrowly parliamentary policy of the late Victorian Unionist party; and local unrest had focused in particular on the residual landed element within loyalist parliamentary representation.[99] These revolts, combined with the

[96] *BNL*, 31 Oct. 1911.

[97] One of Long's reasons for moving was the fear of being defeated in Dublin, WLP, Add. MS 62413 : Long to Hood, 14 April 1908 (copy); Long to Bernard, n.d. (copy). The abrupt circumstances of Long's announcement angered the Orangemen. See WLP, Add. MS 62413 : Wallace to Long, 10 Dec. 1908.

[98] Hyde, *Carson*, 287. *BNL*, 27 July 1911. McNeill, *Ulster's Stand*, 44–5. McNeill rather underestimates the bitterness which Londonderry's action caused.

[99] Henry Patterson, 'Independent Orangeism and Class Conflict in Edwardian Belfast: A Reinterpretation', *Proceedings of the Royal Irish Academy*, lxxx, sect. c, 1–27 (1980), 27. Richard McMinn's work on North Antrim emphasizes the vitality of the Liberal tradition in that division. See J. R. B. McMinn, 'The Myth of "Route" Liberalism in County Antrim, 1869–1900', *Eire-Ireland*, xvii. 1 (Spring 1982), and 'Liberalism in North Antrim, 1900–1914', *IHS*, xxiii. 89 (May 1982), 19–20.

effects of agricultural depression and land purchase, reduced the numbers and influence of landlords within the parliamentary party, and—more gradually—within the other power centres of the movement (the executive committee of the Ulster Unionist Council, for example). New leaders and a new parliamentary profile affected the balance of local and national political commitments. The old landed leadership, represented by figures like Saunderson, Lord Arthur Hill, and Thomas Waring, had pioneered a parliamentary focus for loyalism. But both Saunderson and Waring were dead by 1907, and Hill was out of parliament by 1908. None of these men had been publicly active in local politics after 1886, and Saunderson's tenure of the North Armagh constituency was characterized by recurrent apologies for neglect.[100] A new generation of parliamentary representatives—the Craig brothers, Lonsdale, Moore, H. T. Barrie—differed both in occupational background and in choice of political arena. They were generally from the commercial and legal classes, and where they possessed land (as in the case of James Craig) it was not as a staple source of income but rather as a status symbol or as a recreational asset. All these men, with the questionable exception of Lonsdale, were highly active local politicians (Lonsdale was secretary to the parliamentary party and had therefore a peculiarly great parliamentary commitment). All received testimonials from their constituents in contradistinction to the complaints which had been the rewards of their predecessors in the 1890s.[101] This is not to suggest that there was any *systematic* rejection of parliament before 1911 (or indeed before 1914); but it is true that the relative significance of parliament was being decisively reduced through the more intensive local political activity of Unionist politicians. And this was occurring not just as a consequence of the paramilitary activity of 1912–14, but also earlier in the Edwardian period.

This new, comparative isolation registered both on the self-perception of loyalists (and indeed on the perceptions of others), and on the structures of the movement. As early as January 1907 Lonsdale had told the Ulster Unionist Council that 'they must not rely entirely upon their members of parliament; they must be

---

[100] See my *Edward Saunderson*.

[101] PRONI, H. B. Armstrong Papers, D 3727/E/46, Lonsdale to Armstrong, 5 May 1910. Diary of Lady Craigavon, D 1415/B/38, 30 May 1911. *BNL*, 30 May 1911, 1 Dec. 1911.

prepared to adopt other means of reaching the electors of England and Scotland'.[102] Years of comparatively unprofitable constitutional opposition confirmed Lonsdale's prognosis, bringing home the inadequacy of any narrow parliamentary strategy. By 1910—and thus before the Parliament Bill—Irish Unionist MPs were publicly expressing their despair at the futility of Commons debate. Robert Thompson, newly elected member for North Belfast, complained to the London correspondent of the *News Letter* about the limited opportunities for achievement in the House of Commons.[103] While other, British Unionists were angered by the 'dictatorial' nature of the Liberal regime, the dismissive attitude of Birrell towards loyalist grievances reduced the Ulster Party to a peculiar rage: 'government by flippancy and jest' was Moore's indictment of Birrell's record.[104] Unrest within the parliamentary party filtered through to the loyalist press, and editorial reference was made to the 'disabilities under which the Ulster Unionist members are laid by the attitude of ministers towards them'.[105] Ultimately the Parliament Bill precipitated an apparently logical resolution to these grievances—but it brought no fundamental alteration in loyalist attitudes, or in their behaviour. The removal of the Lords' veto offered further justification for a drift towards local resources which had a much longer history.

Organizationally this self-reliance had its roots in opposition to the first and second Home Rule Bills which had inspired an independent parliamentary party and various representative and missionary organizations like the Templetown Clubs and the Ulster Loyalist Union.[106] But, without exception, these bodies were either oriented towards English evangelism, or were short-lived. None could claim to be broadly representative of loyalist popular opinion. The formation of the Ulster Unionist Council in 1905 was a much more decisive rejection of the British political forum—because it represented the first popular co-ordinating body for northern loyalism, and because it developed without significant patronage

---

[102] *BNL*, 31 Jan. 1907.   [103] *BNL*, 23 April 1910.
[104] Birrell's record has been the subject of favourable reappraisal: Patricia Jalland, 'A Liberal Chief Secretary and the Irish Question: Augustine Birrell 1907–1914', *Historical Journal*, xix. 2 (1976), 421–51.
[105] *BNL*, 30 July 1910.
[106] See D. C. Savage, 'The Origins of the Ulster Unionist Party, 1885–1886', *IHS*, xii. 47 (Mar. 1961) 185–208. Buckland, *Ulster Unionism*, 8–14.

from British politicians. Moreover, it was created in the difficult circumstances of local political weakness, and developed as a response to apparent British treachery over the MacDonnell affair. It was more popularly based than its precursors, and it gradually expanded its representative capacity, the crucial Standing Committee being enlarged in 1911 and 1918.[107] Thus it was designed to channel local feeling into a formal Unionist structure; but, while the hierarchy of the Council may have muffled some unrest, it was more than a blandly Tory organ.[108] It was the most powerful body to which Irish Unionist political representatives had ever been responsible—and this inevitably encouraged a more gritty and a more populist articulation of faith. Certainly Cawdor left the Ulster Unionist Council convocation of 1909 under no illusion that he had been addressing a conventional Tory gathering: 'they all seem to be radicals at Belfast', he remarked, wide-eyed, to Jack Sandars.[109]

The Council also represented an encouragement towards local reorganization and in the later Edwardian period a number of important refinements were made. The origins of these local developments, like the origins of the Council itself, lay partly in the fissile state of the late Victorian party. But reorganization developed extensively after 1906, and under the aegis of the Council. Its claim to represent the Ulster Unionist democracy in practice meant that it goaded local party elders like Charles Falls in North Fermanagh or Joshua Peel in Mid-Armagh to reactivate largely dormant party machinery—and to produce delegates for the Council sessions.[110] Similarly, at the end of 1906, a long disorganized and divided party in North Armagh agreed to form a divisional Unionist association. A variety of pressures had dictated this course, most prominently from the Ulster Unionist Council, and through the need to find a parliamentary candidate to replace Edward Saunderson. Thereafter one of the principal functions of the association's twice-yearly meetings was to produce delegates for the Council.[111] With

---

[107] John Harbinson, *The Ulster Unionist Party, 1882-1973: Its Development and Organisation* (Belfast, 1973), 23-4.

[108] Harbinson, *Ulster Unionist Party*, 36.

[109] ABP, Add. MS 49709, fo. 63, Cawdor to Sandars, 1 Feb. 1909.

[110] See e.g. PRONI, Joshua Peel Papers, D 889/4C/3/211, Peel to Lonsdale, 24 Nov. 1904 (copy). PRONI, Falls and Hanna Papers, D 1390/26/6/65, Falls to T. H. Gibson, 14 Jan. 1905 (copy).

[111] PRONI, Minute Book of the North Armagh Unionist Association, MIC 34, *passim*.

encouragement from the UUC, and under the pressure of events, Unionist associations were formed or re-formed in East Donegal, North Monaghan, Newry, and Mid-Tyrone by the end of 1909; and in that year a major reorganization of Belfast Unionism took place.[112] The veteran Belfast Conservative Association, which had controlled Tory politics in the city for over fifty years, was broken down into three autonomous divisional associations (a popularly constituted association had long existed in the western and most fiercely contested division of the City). This *was*, as the Ulster Unionist Council Year Book for 1910 commented, 'one of the most important features in local Unionist politics during the past year'; but it was also merely the most conspicuous aspect of a much more deeply-rooted movement within Unionism.[113]

Complementary to the revitalization of official Unionism after 1905 was the renaissance of Orangeism. In part the spectacular growth of the late Edwardian movement represented the reacquisition of members lost to the schismatic Independent Orange Order.[114] Prominent Unionist MPs like William Moore led a counter-attack on the briefly successful Independents, and this, combined with an effective amnesty to former Orange dissidents, provided the foundations for the regrouping and expansion of the official movement: 'to the dupes I have always been in favour of the "open door"', declared a less than magnanimous R. H. Wallace.[115] There was a considerable investment in the construction of new halls and the purchase of new banners; the laying of foundation stones, ceremonial openings, and the unfurling of banners became familiar tasks even for non-Orange MPs. Orange charities like the City of Belfast Loyal Orange Widows' Fund flourished.[116] Just as in 1885-6, the vitality of Orangeism offered a path to leadership within

[112] Ulster Unionist Council, *Year Book for 1910* (Belfast, 1911).

[113] Ibid.

[114] Henry Patterson, *Class Conflict and Sectarianism: The Protestant Working Class and the Belfast Labour Movement, 1868-1920* (Belfast, 1980), 64-6. It should be noted that John Gray in his *City in Revolt: James Larkin and the Belfast Dock Strike of 1907* (Belfast, 1985), 50, disagrees with Patterson about the rapidity of IOO decline—though not about its existence.

[115] PRONI, R. H. Wallace Papers, D 1889/1/2/3/44, Wallace to Lyons, 15 Feb. 1909 (copy). Private Possession, Papers of Nina Patrick (daughter of William Moore, MP), Moore to Nina, 'Thursday evening' (Oct. 1907): 'I am going over to give Lindsay Crawford and the Independents in Birkenhead a touch . . .'.

[116] *Annual Reports of the City of Belfast Loyal Orange Widows' Fund: with Lists of Donations and Subscriptions* (Belfast, 1907-15).

Irish Unionism: James Craig, like Edward Saunderson before him, came to political prominence through harnessing his career to recrudescent Orangeism, tirelessly addressing Orange meetings, and exploiting Orange contacts like Colonel Robert Wallace.[117] When Craig was portrayed by *Vanity Fair*, in 1911, the caption given to his cartoon was, appropriately enough, 'Orangeman'.

This expansion was certainly encouraged by the renewed possibility of Home Rule and, more generally, by an unsympathetic Liberal supremacy. But it was also founded on the restored credibility of conventional organized Unionism, which in turn had been achieved through the Ulster Unionist Council and local party renewal. Together, the development of Orangeism and Unionism drew out the distinction between the local party and its national leadership. A vital local organization exacted a greater commitment from loyalist representatives than hitherto. Through the creation of the Council and the encouragement of local Unionism, MPs like Moore and the Craig brothers fashioned both a constituency and a restraint. The massive popularity of these and other MPs at the end of the Edwardian period was founded on their commitment to party democracy; but this, in turn, implied a commitment to loyalist fundamentalism.[118] If the weakness of late Victorian Unionism was created through the compromises demanded by a parliamentary policy, then the strength of the late Edwardian party lay in its effective rejection of parliament and its return to political and sectarian basics. This was simultaneously a measure of the stability of the leadership and of its growing separation from British political opinion.

A combination of circumstances in the winter of 1910–11 translated this creeping and tacit rejection of the British parliamentary process into open militancy. By the end of 1911 plans had been laid for a provisional government in Ulster, while Orangemen were parading in military fashion and Unionist leaders communed with a gunsmith. The Parliament Bill became law in August 1911. During the last stage of its passage James Craig had laid the plans for the display of force at Craigavon House which was once thought to have 'determined the policy and the methods to be followed during the

[117] Craig's Orangeism is discussed in Patrick Buckland, *James Craig, Lord Craigavon* (Dublin, 1980), 19–20. Wallace Papers, D 1889/3/18, James Craig to Wallace, 31 Jan. 1910; D 1889/6/6, James Craig to Wallace, 5 Dec. 1906.
[118] Patterson, *Class Conflict*, 65. Patterson. 'Independent Orangeism', 26.

next three years'.[119] A martial display by a group of Tyrone
Orangemen on the day of the demonstration suggested, 'almost by
accident', the idea and value of a citizen army.[120] Through this
interpretation, offered by McNeill and inherited by subsequent
commentators, a turning point in loyalist political behaviour was
identified in the late summer of 1911, with further independence and
militancy being related to the removal of the Lords' veto and the
effects of one monster meeting.[121]

It has been suggested here, on the other hand, that the rejection
of conventional constitutional politics which occurred in 1911 was
the continuation of a process of isolation and a programme of reform
dating back at least to 1905. The Parliament Act served merely to
underline a need for self-reliance which had been recognized ever
since the onset of chill into the relationship with British Unionism
and the British leadership. While the Craigavon demonstration and
the plans for a provisional government *were* timed to follow the
promulgation of the Act, the framework for such a government had
long been present in the Standing Committee of the Ulster Unionist
Council; and in fact there was a significant overlap in personnel
between this Committee and the Commission of Five appointed in
September 1911 to prepare for a provisional government. Finally,
and crucially, Orange paramilitary activity was *not* a feature peculiar
to the aftermath of the Parliament Act and Craigavon. Confidential
schemes for Orange arming and drilling were laid at least as early
as November 1910—predating, therefore, both the second Liberal
victory of that year and the passage of the Parliament Bill.[122]

The year 1910 gave point to the gamut of loyalist suspicion. Fears
of English indifference were corroborated by two election defeats

[119] Stewart, *Ulster Crisis*, 48.

[120] Stewart, *Ulster Crisis*, 69; McNeill, *Ulster's Stand*, 56–7; St John Ervine,
Craigavon: Ulsterman (London, 1949), 192.

[121] Stewart, *Ulster Crisis*, 25. Of the passage of the Parliament Act Stewart writes:
'the last obstacle to Home Rule was removed. The time had come, it seemed,
for the trumpets to sound, and the walls of Jericho would fall down of their own accord . . .'.

[122] Stewart, *Ulster Crisis*, 48. The Commission consisted of Carson, James Craig,
R. G. Sharman-Crawford, R. H. Wallace, T. Sinclair, and Edward Sclater. Of these
Carson was Vice-President of the UUC, Sharman-Crawford was Honorary Treasurer
and the remainder were members of the powerful Standing Committee: Ulster Unionist
Council, *Year Book for 1912* (Belfast 1913), 6–7. In fact the arming of Ulster was
suspected as early as January 1911: *Daily Mail*, 11 Jan. 1911. Peel, *Reign of Carson*,
210.

for Unionism: in the aftermath of the December contest Robert
Wallace wrote that he had been saddened 'by the way we
have been treated in England', while Carson confided to Lady
Londonderry that he had felt 'seedy and depressed since the
elections'.[123] On the other hand, fears of British Unionist treachery
had been enlivened by the favourable attitude of some leaders
to a scheme of federal Home Rule. The sympathy of Unionist
organs like *The Observer* was of course apparent; but rumours
of leadership betrayal, having no firm foundation, were all the
more disquieting.[124] Carson believed that there might be truth
in such rumours, and he left no doubt of his own response
to any betrayal: should this occur, 'I earnestly hope the Conservatives will never again be in office during my life'.[125]
Finally—and only in the context of the preceding doubts—the threat
of Home Rule regained substance in the light of Asquith's new
enthusiasm for Redmond, and his revised attitude towards the Lords'
veto.

It was against this background, and in the context of a more
prolonged organization, that the Ulster Unionist Council took the
initial steps towards a military defiance. At the end of November
1910, when some Unionists still believed in the possibility of an
election success, the Council formed a secret committee which was
to oversee approaches to arms dealers, and to select weapons for
an Ulster army. The membership of this Committee is unclear,
though the gunrunner F. H. Crawford claimed that it comprised 'the
leading men in this part of Ulster [Belfast] and men who have
practically unlimited means to carry this [arming] through (if they
will)'.[126] On 22 November 1910 Crawford, acting apparently under
the instructions of this Committee, wrote to five munitions works
in England, Austria, and Germany, and invited a quotation for
20,000 rifles and one million rounds of ammunition: 'the rifles need
not be very latest pattern—second hand ones in good order

[123] Wallace Papers, D 1889/1/2/3, Wallace to A. Pickering, 20 Dec. 1910;
PRONI, Theresa Londonderry Papers, D 2846/1/1/59, Carson to Lady Londonderry,
23 Dec. 1910. Ervine, *Craigavon*, 202-3.
[124] A. M. Gollin, The Observer *and J. L. Garvin, 1908-1914: A Study in a Great
Editorship* (Oxford, 1960), 223-34; Peel, *Reign of Carson*, 203-10.
[125] PRONI, Theresa Londonderry Papers, D 2846/1/1/55, Carson to Lady
Londonderry, 27/28 Oct. 1910. This is partly quoted in Hyde, *Carson*, 279.
[126] PRONI, F. H. Crawford Papers, D 1700/10/1/1, 860, Crawford to Charles
Playfair, 1 Dec. 1910 (copy).

preferred'.[127] On 1 December he wrote to several continental newspapers, requesting tenders for a similar quantity of arms and ammunition.[128] By 12 December—again, before the final polling in the election—sample weapons were before the Council's committee; but, to Crawford's chagrin, a decision to purchase was temporarily postponed in order to pursue a secret enrolment of names for the Ulster fighting force.[129]

The militants focused their attention on the German arms dealers, Gatchstuck of Berlin and Spiro of Hamburg—but, after problems with the former and suspicions of treachery, Benny Spiro became the main armourer to to the Ulster Council. By March 1911 the Council had voted the first major cash allocation for the importation of guns; and by the early summer of 1911 at least 2,000 weapons had already been imported.[130]

Two central problems of interpretation emerge from this outline account of the first arming activities of the UUC. First, the importation of weapons in 1910-11 does not in itself prove that Ulster Unionists were preparing for civil war: the precedents of 1886 and 1893—empty rhetoric and inconsequential invitations for weapons tenders—might suggest that the later activity was similarly designed for English consumption. This view has some plausibility, for there was a movement within the UUC in early 1911 to stage publicly the purchase of 1,000 weapons as a publicity stunt: provoking the government in this way would have almost certainly meant the seizure of the arms—but the effect on English opinion, it was calculated, would be dramatic and favourable.[131] Any residual confidence in this policy of bluff did not, however, sway key leaders like James Craig and influential secondary figures like Crawford. Indeed, Crawford brought pressure to bear on Craig in order to obtain a statement of militant intent; and the latter obliged, indicating his unequivocal commitment to effective—secret and continuing—importation: 'I am convinced that unless a steady supply [of rifles] is started', he affirmed on 20 April 1911, 'we will be caught

---

[127] Crawford Papers, D 1700/10/1/1, 854, Matthews (pseudonym for Crawford) to R. S. A., Birmingham and London, Small Arms Manufactory, Steyr, and Deutsche Waffen und Munitionsfabriken, 22 Nov. 1910 (copies).

[128] Crawford Papers, D 1700/10/1/1, 851, Crawford to various continental papers, 1 Dec. 1910 (copies).

[129] Ibid. 871, Crawford to Playfair, 12 Dec. 1910 (copy).

[130] Ibid. D 1700/5/17/2/3, Crawford Diary of Gunrunning.

[131] Ibid. D 1700/10/1/1, 932, Crawford to Craig, 8 April 1911 (copy).

like rats in a trap'.[132] For his part Crawford seized on this evidence of sympathy in order to press home his financial claims, and to increase the number of weapons under order.[133]

The second difficulty with the outline account arises from inconsistencies within the evidence, and from the nature of the key witness—Crawford himself. Crawford's love of intrigue, and his heavy-handed precautions to secure secrecy, do not inspire confidence in his published and autobiographical testimony. Nevertheless his own account of the early purchase of weapons, published in a modified form as *Guns for Ulster*, has provided the foundation for some of the most influential analyses of the episode.[134] *Guns for Ulster* was partly constructed from memory rather than from detailed research, or from the evidence of Crawford's own papers: these appear to have been mislaid in the 1930s, and probably remained missing when Crawford was revising his memoirs in 1946–7.[135] Unsurprisingly, given the haphazard nature of its origins, *Guns for Ulster* conflicts with the evidence of Crawford's own correspondence, which has since re-emerged. The sequence of gun-running episodes is confused, and key events—such as Crawford's first advertisements for weapons—are apparently misdated. Fortunately the account provided by Crawford in his letterbooks and diaries is confirmed by the evidence of his in-correspondence—and, in certain crucial details, by the evidence provided in the papers of another loyalist conspirator, the Orange leader Colonel Robert Wallace. Wallace's archive confirms that loyalist militancy was well-advanced before August 1911, and that the Orangemen were mobilizing as early as December 1910. For example, on 22 December 1910, Wallace was able to provide confidential reassurance to a Canadian sympathizer: 'at the present', he wrote, 'we are quietly organising. The various [Orange] lodges have received enrolment forms and will be taught

---

[132] Ibid. D 1700/5/6/1, Craig to Crawford, 20 April 1911.

[133] Ibid. D 1700/10/1/1, 940, Crawford to Craig, 21 April 1911.

[134] Stewart, *Ulster Crisis*, 90–1. See F. H. Crawford, *Guns for Ulster* (Belfast, 1947), 16. The only other published account of the gun-running written by a participant is R. J. Adgey, *Arming the Ulster Volunteers* (Belfast, n.d.). Unfortunately, this too was written from memory—and appeared 40 years after the events.

[135] PRONI, Additional Crawford Papers, D 640/30, Crawford to C. C. Craig on the disappearance of his memoirs of the gun-running. Adgey claimed that Crawford did not actually write *Guns for Ulster*: Adgey, *Arming the Ulster Volunteers*, 71.

simple movements'.[136] This chimes exactly with an account provided by Crawford for a colleague only ten days earlier.[137]

There can be no doubt then that the groundwork for civil war was being laid in the winter of 1910–11, with the first attempts at arming and drilling. Furthermore, northern Unionist opinion was being mobilized in other, less controversial ways. Already in December 1910 plans for the revitalization of the old Templetown Unionist clubs were under way, the intention being to recruit 'men who would never identify themselves with the Order'.[138] As is well known the Unionist Clubs were publicly relaunched in January 1911, and enjoyed an immediate and rapid expansion—well before the collapse of the Unionist peers and the enactment of the Parliament Bill. And in April 1911, five months before the martial appearance of the Tyrone Orangemen so much emphasized in the McNeill hypothesis, Wallace confided to a fellow Colonel and Boer War veteran that he had been encouraging the Orangemen of Belfast to adopt military formation:

I am trying to get my Districts in Belfast to take up a few simple movements—learning to form fours and reform two deep, and simple matters like that. I suggested some time ago the advisability for the men to march on the 12th in fours, and not to straggle along in the way that they have become accustomed to . . .[139]

Given this groundwork, the aftermath to the Parliament Bill was comparatively undramatic. Indeed William Moore, who had cogently defended the loyalist right to armed resistance as early as January 1911, publicly described the House of Lords as being merely 'one of their outposts in the [Unionist] fortress'; while Carson suggested in July 1911 that even the unreformed Lords could not be depended upon to throw out a Home Rule Bill.[140] The Parliament Act underlined the need for weapons—but its true significance in the history of Ulster militancy was less as a motivating force than as a means by which the militants could bring their measures of resistance into the open. For them, the Act and eventually the Home

[136] Wallace Papers, D 1889/1/2/3, 127, Wallace to Sproule, 22 Dec. 1910 (copy).
[137] Crawford Papers, D 1700/10/1/1. 871, Crawford to Playfair, 12 Dec. 1910.
[138] Wallace Papers, D 1889/1/2/3. 127, Wallace to Sproule, 22 Dec. 1910.
[139] Ibid. D 1889/1/2/3, 162, Wallace to Maxwell, 18 April 1911 (copy).
[140] BNL, 13 July 1911. PRONI, Theresa Londonderry Papers, D 2846/1/1/66, Carson to Lady Londonderry, 30 July 1911.

Rule Bill represented a suspension of the constitution; and such a radical departure provided a quasi-legal foundation for even their most extreme activity.[141]

Though the peak of loyalist aggression came after the Parliament Bill, the contrast with earlier activity was more apparent than real—because it was a contrast between private and public activity. Nevertheless, there was a perceptible hardening of attitudes, and Carson appears to have sanctioned militant activity for the first time: hitherto it had been Craig who had treated with the grubby extremes of loyalism.[142] Thus at the very end of July 1911 Carson confided to Craig that 'I am not for a game of bluff, and unless men are prepared to make great sacrifices which they clearly understand, the talk of resistance is no use'.[143] Craig had demonstrated his own extremist convictions some months before, through his attitude to the gun-running—but there is nothing to indicate that Carson had as yet been informed of this early evidence of hardline commitment. However, at the great Craigavon demonstration of 23 September 1911, the movement for weapons was made public: even the menu cards at Craig's luncheon party on this occasion bore an illustration of crossed rifles and the motto—'The Arming of Ulster'.[144] Thereafter, at a series of private and public meetings of the Ulster Unionist Council, detailed plans for resistance were laid and, as Ronald McNeill implied in a speech at Canterbury, these probably included an outline for a more coherent military response.[145] Certainly by December 1911 Craig had discreetly visited a gunsmith 'on an important matter'—so important that he did not commit any details to paper.[146] And by January 1912, its legality having been established, public paramilitary activity began in earnest.[147] An Ulster army was evolving; and if it remained largely unarmed, then the activities of Crawford in 1910-11 had demonstrated that this would only be a temporary obstacle in the path of a northern holy war.

[141] See e.g. *BNL*, 23 Oct. 1911.
[142] e.g. PRONI, Theresa Londonderry Papers, D 2846/1/1/60, Carson to Lady Londonderry, 13 Jan. 1911.
[143] Hyde, *Carson*, 286-7.
[144] Lady Craigavon Diary, D 1415/B/38, 23 Sept. 1911.
[145] *BNL*, 23 Oct. 1911.
[146] Lady Craigavon Diary, D 1415/B/38, 8 Dec. 1911; Ervine, *Craigavon*, 205.
[147] Stewart, *Ulster Crisis*, 69-70; McNeill, *Ulster's Stand*, 59.

5. *Summary*

Between 1905 and 1911 Ulster Unionism had developed from an essentially parliamentary movement into an army of resistance, retaining a residual and peripheral parliamentary presence. Attendance in House of Commons divisions dropped appreciably for the period between 1905 and 1910, while the local role of Irish Unionist MPs and leaders grew correspondingly more significant.[148] Contributing to, and developing from, this local drift was a new and more frosty relationship with British Unionism. British leaders, both Tories like Balfour and Liberal Unionists like Austen Chamberlain, were diverted from Home Rule by other issues; and thus progressively less priority and less patience were awarded to loyalist demands. The succession of Andrew Bonar Law and the introduction of the third Home Rule Bill restored a passionate but transient unity between 1912 and 1914.

Yet the structure of independent Ulster Unionist resistance had been laid down well before November 1911: indeed, the basis for such resistance was already significantly advanced by the end of 1910, when the beginnings of a *rapprochement* with the British party are perceptible. Bonar Law's Ulster Protestant ties were speedily unearthed at the time of his succession, and the *News Letter* carried a feature on 14 November 1911 which proudly and soothingly detailed this background.[149] Yet Bonar Law was not so prominent as a proponent of conventional Unionism that loyalist leaders like Carson did not have to offer public reassurance on this score.[150] Perhaps such reassurance was needed, given that Law had been identified with F. E. Smith as an advocate of settlement at the Constitutional Conference. Certainly loyalist leaders like Lonsdale privately bemoaned the elevation of Bonar Law, on the grounds of his inexperience.[151]

---

[148] Alvin Jackson, 'The Irish Unionist Parliamentary Party, 1885–1906', D.Phil. thesis (Oxford, 1986), 105.

[149] *BNL*, 14 Nov. 1911.   [150] *BNL*, 27 Nov. 1911.

[151] H. B. Armstrong Papers, D 3727/E/46, Lonsdale to Armstrong, 11 Nov. 1911 ('in my opinion he is wanting in knowledge of statecraft . . . he has never been a cabinet minister, and is nothing like as able a parliamentarian as Mr. Long or Mr Chamberlain . . .', Austen Chamberlain, *Politics from Inside*, 193. For the shift to approval in 1912–13, see Wallace Papers, D 1889/1/2/3, 219, Wallace to Scott, 11 April 1912; Vincent (ed.), *Crawford Papers*, 303, n. 20.

The Parliament Bill appeared when the distillation of Ulster Unionist opinion—its isolation from former British sympathizers, its local redevelopment—was far advanced. The passage of the Bill certainly hardened attitudes, as evidenced by the Craigavon demonstration; but it did not create the zeal for independent action. The possibility of an end to the Lords' veto was merely one of a variety of circumstances which was propelling hardline leaders like Robert Wallace and F. H. Crawford towards militant activity before the election of December 1910. And the local political preconditions for such militancy—isolation, anger, and a heightened sense of an organized loyalist community—long ante-dated 1910.

Threats of an armed rising had for years been a feature of loyalist political rhetoric.[152] But before 1906 the campaign against Home Rule was largely parliamentary, and the groundwork for military resistance was only developed much later. Where the loyalist commander of 1886 and 1893, Edward Saunderson, was exclusively a parliamentary combatant, Carson, his successor, presided over the preparations for civil war. Thus the political revolution, or counter-revolution, which McNeill described was as much a rejection of previous loyalist strategy as a defiance of Asquithian Liberalism: above all, it embodied a recognition of the comparative failure of the relationship with Toryism.[153] But where McNeill identified the novelty of loyalist action in 1911, he miscalculated its broader context and chronology. There *was*, arguably, a revolution in loyalist political behaviour—but its roots and development were more intricate than has hitherto been understood.

---

[152] Loughlin, *Gladstone*, 274–83.
[153] W. S. Rodner, 'Leaguers, Covenanters, Moderates: British support for Ulster, 1913–1914', *Eire-Ireland*, xvii. 3 (1982), 68–85, emphasizes the far from unanimous support elicited by northern Irish extremism within British Toryism.

8

Conclusion

Unionist resistance to the third Home Rule Bill was different both in form and in scope to any earlier endeavour. In 1886 and 1893 local agitation on behalf of the Union varied little from the types of pressure politics adopted in contemporary Britain: there was certainly much talk of an armed struggle, but no evidence has survived to suggest that such talk was ever seriously translated into action. Rather, the chief forum for Irish Unionist endeavour before 1911–12 was Britain and the British House of Commons, and the most conspicuous displays of local political activity, such as the Ulster Convention of June 1892, were often designed with a view to their impact upon British public opinion. If this was ever true of the forms of resistance adopted in 1912, then the mass importation of weapons, allied to the crescendo of popular anxiety, ensured that British preoccupations were ultimately relegated.

In acting as they did, Irish Unionists were rejecting what had amounted to a parliamentary policy. This is not to say that Irish Unionist MPs, either individually or collectively, ceased to have weight; but, with the development of local organization after 1905 it is beyond dispute that the general significance of the parliamentary party within the Unionist movement was weakened. The formation of the UUC, in combination with a renaissance of organized Unionism in the counties and boroughs of Ulster, meant that, effectively for the first time, the Irish Unionist parliamentary party was formally responsible to local opinion. It would be idle to pretend either that this represented a democratic revolution, or that there had been no earlier local movement superintending the conduct of loyalist MPs. But the significance of the UUC lay in its capacity to survive, while its expansion over the years meant that the role of parliamentary representation was gradually diminished.

The Council was perhaps the most conspicuous aspect of a broader localization in Ulster Unionist politics. The need to respond to Home Rule had temporarily upset the politics of class and local grievance within Ulster, and a fragile solidarity characterized Unionist politics before 1894. Given the absence of any serious internal threat, Irish Unionist MPs could fight their battles in England and Westminster without much reference to the state of local politics. By helping to reactivate the land debate in 1894–5, and again after 1900, the South Tyrone radical T. W. Russell not only imperilled the Unionist consensus; he also compelled Unionist MPs to descend from the ethereal heights of the constitutional debate to a grittier, local arena. His campaigns in Ulster and electoral success demanded an equivalent response from Irish Unionists; his identification of the Ulster Party's inactivity and inefficiency demanded a demonstration of local endeavour. The Presbyterians of the PUVA and independent candidates in Belfast contributed to this provocation, but Russell's role was of paramount importance. It was largely to combat the threat created by him that the UUC was launched in 1904.

The debate on land had other political repercussions, and furthered the localization of Unionist politics in other ways. The unpopularity of landlordism meant that landed MPs within the Ulster Party were under continual pressure; and allied with financial vulnerability, this pressure resulted in a fall in their numbers. The retreat of the squire from the Ulster Party not only involved the loss of what was, by all accounts a comparatively well-integrated parliamentary body; it also opened the way for a younger breed of politician, better equipped for political debate, both in terms of profession and aptitude. In many cases the departure of a landed MP was a spur to local organization; and indeed the squire was occasionally as much a threat to the vitality of local organization as vice versa. Deference to landed magnates had certainly emasculated the Unionist parties in some divisions (East Down, North Armagh, Mid-Antrim), although the MPs for such seats were generally the targets of farmer criticism elsewhere in Ulster. The new MPs—the 'young men' of the Ulster Party, to borrow Jane Ridley's designation—appear to have been subject to closer local scrutiny than their predecessors, and this may be explained by their comparative youth, their particular social standing, and the different and more challenging political context against which their rise took place.

If Unionist MPs were being brought back to Ulster through the pressure of local events, then there was a high political dimension to this realignment. The paradox of the relationship between the Ulster Party and parliamentary Conservatism was that, while the Party had been born out of the fear of Tory treachery, the effective political survival of loyalist MPs came to depend upon sustained good relations between the parties. The compromises imposed upon the Ulster Party by British parliamentary politics were only worth bearing if its members could demonstrate substantial achievement. Thus popular perceptions of the Ulster Party's usefulness tended to hinge upon the tractability of Tory government; and when government seemed unresponsive, the viability of a loyalist presence in parliament came under suspicion.

That the relationship between Toryism and the Ulster Party had failed in 1905 was beyond doubt. Nor was there much scope for a restoration of confidence in 1912–14, if only because of the suspicions of leading British Unionists regarding the electoral usefulness of Ulster's plight. Indeed, the public unity of Bonar Law and Carson, F. E. Smith and Craig, has tended to obscure the fact that the forms of political activity embraced by loyalists reflected a lack of confidence in British Toryism as much as a distrust of Asquith. Leading Ulster Unionists in 1910, no less than in 1892, had been shocked by Liberal victory at the polls: successive Conservative defeats, allied with the Parliament Act, underlined the value of independent local organization.

This is not to suggest that the débâcle of Unionist relations was an inevitability. On the contrary, Irish Unionist MPs were generally socially and financially well-equipped to win friends within the Tory party. There is much evidence to suggest that this potential was realized, and that many Irish Unionists were assimilated within the various political and social networks of parliamentary Toryism. Moreover, the hostility of leading British Unionists towards their Ulster allies has been frequently exaggerated, and treated out of context.

Nor were Irish Unionists systematically hostile to constructive Unionism. Certain key issues—allocation of government funding, the Catholic university question—raised sectarian hackles, but even here there was no single, definable loyalist attitude. Other reforms, whether over land or local government, could not be unequivocally rejected by the Ulster Party, given that these benefited the Unionist democracy no less than the Nationalist. Thus to assume that there was a spiral of loyalist anger, beginning with Gerald Balfour's arrival in Ireland, and culminating in the devolution revelations is to oversimplify an exceedingly difficult relationship between the Ulster Party and constructive Unionism. Wyndham did not fall victim to loyalist wrath in 1905 because of his general commitment to amelioration: indeed his Land Act of 1903 had helped to rescue Ulster Unionism from what seemed an impending electoral cataclysm. Rather it was because he aroused sectarian emotions, specifically through the appointment of MacDonnell, and through the shadiness of his own political methods, without offering any palliative in the areas of patronage or security policy. Unionist MPs could show their supporters little by way of tangible achievement; and, by the last months of Wyndham's reign, for the sake of their local credibility, they badly needed a spectacular parliamentary coup. Wyndham's resignation and the elevation of Long briefly supplied these needs; but the memory of Wyndham's 'treachery' proved to be enduring, and coloured subsequent relations between the parties.

The retreat of Irish Unionism was not simply the concomitant of a changing relationship with British politics. The eclipse of the Irish Unionist Parliamentary Party by local organization also implied a reassessment of the bond between northern and southern Unionism in Ireland. The strength of the Ulster Party of the 1890s had been derived from the very fact that that it was *not* wholly an 'Ulster' Party. Apart from the temporary hold of Unionism over several southern seats (South County Dublin, St Stephen's Green, and Galway City), southern loyalists sat for British seats, and worked within the Party; southern peers and industrial magnates lent their prestige and financial support. Southern organizations, like the IUA, had helped to finance northern constituency work: indeed, the Alliance had provided the 'Ulster' Party with London committee rooms and an information service. There were certainly fears of an independent Ulster stand; but it was tacitly accepted that the credibility of the loyalist case against Gladstone rested upon an illusion of homogeneity.

Thus the polarity of northern and southern loyalist, perceptible at a local level from the mid-1880s, did not at first have any particularly profound parliamentary effect. Throughout the last decade of the century, Ulster members persistently bolstered their own standing by claiming to represent the southern minority. Many retained strong ties with the southern provinces, and even in 1906 a substantial proportion of the Party were resident in the south, and had southern connections through Trinity College, Dublin.

Yet, whatever the personal bonds, the Party had come to depend upon a progressively Ulsterized political base. The Irish Unionist

Alliance had scaled down its northern operations by the beginning of the century; and the creation of the Ulster Unionist Council completed the process by which Belfast emerged as a natural focus for Ulster constituency organization. By December 1910 the last popular Unionist seat in southern Ireland (South County Dublin) had fallen into Nationalist hands. Excepting Trinity College, the Ulster Party had come, at last, to represent only Ulster constituencies.

But, by 1910, who was, or was not, represented by the Party mattered little—for the Party itself had become an irrelevance. The whole process of Ulsterization had reflected a failing confidence in parliamentary resistance, since it involved a sacrifice of parliamentary for local strength. After 1910 Westminster was more fully relegated in loyalist priorities; and it became a secondary theatre of a phoney war, whose front line lay, appropriately, in Ulster itself.

When, on an autumn morning in 1906, they buried Edward Saunderson, the conventional pieties were observed. His heroism was attested: he had been the saviour of his people in their grimmest struggle—an uncompromising antagonist, who held to his Orange faith with tenacity. In due course a statue—in appropriately defiant post—was erected to his memory; by the time of its unveiling, a tendentious 'Life' had appeared. Unionist Ireland seemed prepared for a cult of its fallen commander.

Yet, it was Carson, and not Saunderson, who enjoyed apotheosis. For all the unctuous rhetoric of colleagues like William Moore, Saunderson, at the end, had been privately written off as a deadweight. Political initiative, as over the UUC, had been snatched from his hands by younger and more bitter men. Saunderson was above all a parliamentarian; beyond a seigneurial presence, and a facility for Protestant rhetoric, he had been peculiarly ill-equipped in responding to popular political appetites. When Unionism shifted out of Westminster into local meeting halls, his leadership was exposed as anachronistic. Thus when he died, he was mourned; none the less, a subsequent loyalist generation destroyed his legacy.

BIBLIOGRAPHY

1. PRIMARY SOURCES

A. Manuscripts

(i) Private Papers
Birmingham University Library

Austen Chamberlain Papers.
Joseph Chamberlain Papers.

Bodleian Library, Oxford

Antony MacDonnell Papers.
Alfred Milner Papers.
J. S. Sandars Papers.
Papers of the second Earl of Selborne.

British Library

H. O. Arnold-Forster Diaries.
Arthur Balfour Papers.
Walter Long Papers.
Stafford Northcote Papers.

Chatsworth House, Derby

Papers of the eighth Duke of Devonshire.

Churchill College, Cambridge

Lord Randolph Churchill Papers.

Durham Record Office

Papers of Theresa, Lady Londonderry.
Papers of the sixth Marquess of Londonderry.

Hatfield House, Herts.

Papers of the third Marquess of Salisbury.

House of Lords Record Office

Papers of the first Lord Ashbourne (Edward Gibson).
Papers of the fifth Earl Cadogan.

Kent Record Office, Maidstone

Papers of the first Viscount Chilston (Aretas Akers-Douglas).

National Maritime Museum, Greenwich

Arnold White Papers.

Plunkett Foundation, Oxford

Diaries of Sir Horace Plunkett.

Public Record Office of Northern Ireland

Papers of the second Duke of Abercorn.
H. B. Armstrong Papers.
Papers of the fourth Earl of Belmore.
Papers of Carleton, Atkinson and Sloan, Solicitors.
Edward Carson Papers.
Henry Chaplin Papers.
Papers of the first Viscount Craigavon (James Craig).
F. H. Crawford Papers.
Papers of the first Lord Cushendun (Ronald McNeill).
Papers of the first Marquess of Dufferin and Ava.
Adam Duffin Papers.
C. W. Dunbar-Buller Papers.
Papers of the fourth Earl of Dunraven.
Papers of Sir William Grey Ellison-Macartney, MP.
Papers of the fourth Earl of Erne.
Papers of Falls and Hanna, Solicitors.
Diaries of William Johnston, MP.
Papers of the sixth Marquess of Londonderry.
Papers of the seventh Marquess of Londonderry.
Papers of Theresa, Lady Londonderry.
Papers of Hugh De Fellenberg Montgomery.
Papers of Joshua Peel, Solicitor.
Papers of Colonel Edward Saunderson, MP.
Papers of Colonel R. H. Wallace.
Papers of John and W. R. Young of Galgorm.

Trinity College, Dublin

H. O. Arnold-Forster Papers.
W. E. H. Lecky Papers.

Westminster City Library, London

Charles Gatty Papers.

Whittingehame, North Berwick (consulted in the Scottish National Register
  of Archives)

Arthur Balfour Papers.
Gerald Balfour Papers.

Wiltshire Record Office, Trowbridge
Walter Long Papers.

Private Possession

Diaries of Margot Asquith (in the temporary possession of Michael and Eleanor Brock).

Papers of Sibell, Lady Grosvenor (in the possession of the Duke of Westminster).

Papers of Denis Hyde (in the possession of the Duke of Westminster).

Typescript Memoir of Henry Liddell, MP (written by, and in the possession of, his nephew).

Papers of William Moore, MP (in the possession of Sir William Moore). A few, rather important, letters—and a vast hoard of 'Durrant's' cuttings—survive.

Additional Papers of William Moore, MP (in the possession of Dr Amanda Shanks). Some perfunctory letters from leading politicians to Moore, and a more interesting correspondence between Moore, his wife, and his daughter.

Papers of R. T. O'Neill, MP, (in the possession of Mr J. McClintock, Carrickfergus, Co. Antrim). Only a very few letters and cuttings survive from what must have been an extensive correspondence between O'Neill and his mother and unmarried sister.

Diaries of Nina Patrick, based on a record by Sidney Blanche Moore (in the possession of Dr Amanda Shanks). An important narrative, written by William Moore's daughter and wife.

Papers of George Wyndham (in the possession of the Duke of Westminster).

(ii) Institutional Records
Public Record Office of Northern Ireland

Papers of the East Down Unionist Association.
Papers of the East Tyrone Unionist Association.
Minute Book of the Parliamentary Consultative Committee of the Irish Unionist Alliance.
Minute Book of the Executive Committee of the Irish Unionist Alliance.
Minute Book of the General Council of the Irish Unionist Alliance.
In-Correspondence of the Irish Loyal and Patriotic Union/Irish Unionist Alliance.
Papers of the North Armagh Unionist Association.
Papers of the Ulster Unionist Council.
Papers of the Joint Committee of the Unionist Associations of Ireland.
Minute Book of the South Antrim Constitutional Association.

Private Possession
Minute Book of the Fortwilliam District Unionist Club.

B. Printed Primary Sources

(i) Newspapers and Periodicals
Belfast News Letter
Coleraine Chronicle
Irish News
Irish Times
National Review
Northern Whig
Pall Mall Gazette
Punch
Quarterly Review
Vanity Fair

(ii) Published Autobiographies, Letters and Diaries
AMERY, L. S., *My Political Life* (3 vols.; London, 1953–5).
BLUNT, W. S., *My Diaries* (2 vols.; London, 1919–20).
BRABAZON of TARA, Lord, *The Brabazon Story* (London, 1955).
BRETT, M. V., and ESHER, OLIVER Viscount (edd.), *The Journals and Letters of Reginald, Viscount Esher* (4 vols.; London, 1934–8).
BROCK, MICHAEL and ELEANOR (edd.), *H. H. Asquith: Letters to Venetia Stanley* (Oxford, 1982).
BRUCE, H. J., *Silken Dalliance* (London, 1947).
BUCKLE, G. E. (ed.), *Letters of Queen Victoria, 1886–1901*, 3rd. ser. (3 vols.; London, 1932).
CALLWELL, Brigadier-General C. E., *Field Marshal Sir Henry Wilson, Bart., GCB, DSO: His Life and Diaries* (2 vols.; London, 1927).
CHAMBERLAIN, AUSTEN (ed.), *Politics from Inside: An Epistolary Chronicle, 1906–1914* (London, 1936).
CLARKE, ALAN, (ed.), *'A Good Innings': The Private Papers of Viscount Lee of Fareham, PC, GCB, GCSI, GBE* (London, 1974).
COLLES, R., *Castle and Court House: Being Reminiscences of Thirty Years in Ireland* (London, 1911).
COOKE, A. B., 'A Conservative Party Leader in Ulster: Sir Stafford Northcote's Diary of a Visit to the Province, October 1883', *Proceedings of the Royal Irish Academy*, lxxv, sect. c. 4 (Sept. 1975), 61–84.
—— and MALCOMSON, A. P. W., *The Ashbourne Papers, 1869–1913: A Calendar of the Papers of Edward Gibson, First Lord Ashbourne* (Belfast, 1974).
—— and VINCENT, JOHN, 'Ireland and Party Politics, 1885–1887: An Unpublished Conservative Memoir', *Irish Historical Studies*, xvi. 62 (Sept. 1969), 154–72.
—— —— *Lord Carlingford's Journal: Reflections of a Cabinet Minister, 1885* (Oxford, 1971).

CRAWFORD, F. H., *Guns for Ulster* (Belfast, 1947).

DAVID, EDWARD, (ed.), *Inside Asquith's Cabinet: From the Diaries of Charles Hobhouse* (London, 1977).

DESART, The Earl of, and LUBBOCK, Lady S., *A Page from the Past: Memories of the Earl of Desart* (London, 1936).

DUGDALE, BLANCHE E. C., 'The Wyndham–MacDonnell Imbroglio, 1902–06', *Quarterly Review* cclviii. 511 (Jan. 1932), 15–39.

DUNRAVEN, The Earl of, *Past Times and Pastimes* (2 vols.; London, [1922]).

FITZROY, Sir ALMERIC, *Memoirs* (2 vols.; London [1925]).

GLADSTONE, H., *After Thirty Years* (London, 1928).

GRIFFITH-BOSCAWEN, A. S. T., *Fourteen Years in Parliament* (London, 1907).

HALDANE, R. B., *An Autobiography* (London, 1929).

HAMILTON, Lord ERNEST, *Forty Years On* (London [1922]).

HAMILTON, Lord GEORGE, *Parliamentary Reminiscences and Reflections, 1868–1885* (London, 1916).

—— *Parliamentary Reminiscences and Reflections, 1886–1906* (London, 1922).

HEALY, T. M., *Letters and Leaders of My Day* (2 vols.; London, [1928]).

INGLIS, B., *West Briton* (London, 1962).

JOHNSTON, NANCY E., *The Diary of Gathorne Hardy, later Lord Cranbrook, 1866–1892: Political Selections* (Oxford, 1981).

LANG, ANDREW, *The Life, Letters and Diaries of Sir Stafford Northcote, first Earl of Iddesleigh* (2 vols.; Edinburgh and London, 1890).

LONG of WRAXALL, Viscount, *Memories* (London, 1923).

MACKAIL, J. W., and WYNDHAM, GUY (edd.), *The Life and Letters of George Wyndham* (2 vols.; London [1924]).

MACKNIGHT, THOMAS, *Ulster as it is, or Twenty Eight Years' Experience as an Irish Editor* (2 vols.; London, 1896).

McMINN, J. R. B., *Against the Tide: A Calendar of the Papers of Rev. J. B. Armour, Irish Presbyterian Minister and Home Ruler, 1869–1914* (Belfast, 1985).

MANCHESTER, Duke of, *My Candid Recollections* (London, 1932).

MIDLETON, Earl of, *Records and Reactions* (London, 1939).

MORLEY, Viscount, *Recollections* (2 vols.; London, 1917).

O'BRIEN, G. (ed.), *The Reminiscences of the Rt. Hon. Lord O'Brien* (London, 1916).

O'CONNOR, T. P., *Memoirs of an Old Parliamentarian* (2 vols.; London, 1929).

O'NEILL, TERENCE, *The Autobiography of Terence O'Neill* (London, 1972).

OXFORD and ASQUITH, Earl of, *Fifty Years in Parliament* (2 vols.; London, 1928).

PEASE, ALFRED, E., *Elections and Recollections* (London, 1932).

RENTOUL, J. A., *Stray Thoughts and Memories* (Dublin, 1921).

ROBINSON, Sir H., *Memories: Wise and Otherwise* (London, 1923).

ROBSON, R. B., *Autobiography of an Ulster Teacher* (2nd edn., Belfast, 1937).

ROSS, Sir JOHN, *The Years of My Pilgrimage: Random Reminiscences* (London, 1924).

ROSSMORE, Lord, *Things I can tell* (London, 1912).

VINCENT, JOHN, (ed.), *The Crawford Papers: The Journals of David Lindsay, Twenty-Seventh Earl of Crawford and Tenth Earl of Balcarres 1871–1940, during the Years 1892 to 1940* (Manchester, 1984).

WINTERTON, Earl, *Orders of the Day* (London, 1953).

WYNDHAM, GUY, (ed.), *Letters of George Wyndham, 1877–1913* (2 vols.; Edinburgh and London, 1915).

(iii) Works of Reference
The Annual Register.

BATEMAN, JOHN, *The Great Landowners of Great Britain and Ireland* (4th edn., London, 1883).

FOSTER, J. (ed.), *Alumni Oxoniensis: The Members of the University of Oxford, 1715–1886* (4 vols.; London, 1887–8).

FOWLER, THOMAS, *The History of Corpus Christi College, Oxford, with Lists of its Members* (Oxford, 1893).

GASKELL, E., *Ulster Leaders: Social and Political* (London, 1914).

GIBBS, VICARY, DOUBLEDAY, H. A., HOWARD DE WALDEN, Lord (edd.), *The Complete Peerage of England, Scotland, Ireland and the United Kingdom, extant, extinct or dormant, By G. E. C.*, (13 vols.; London, 1912–59).

HANHAM, H. J., *Bibliography of British History, 1851–1914* (Oxford, 1976).

Irish Loyal and Patriotic Union/Irish Unionist Alliance, *Annual Reports.*

MAIR, R. H. (ed.), *Debrett's Illustrated House of Commons and the Judicial Bench* (London, 1867–1931).

Pall Mall Gazette Extra: 'The New House of Commons, 1910' (London, 1910).

STENTON, M, and LEES, S., *Who's Who of British Members of Parliament, 1832–1979*, (4 vols.; Hassocks and Brighton, 1976–9).

Ulster Unionist Council, *Annual Reports.*

WALKER, BRIAN M., 'The Irish Electorate, 1868–1915', *Irish Historical Studies*, xviii. 71 (Mar. 1973), 359–71.

—— *Parliamentary Election Results in Ireland, 1801–1922* (Dublin, 1978).

Who's Who.

YOUNG, R. M., *Belfast and the Province of Ulster in the Twentieth Century* (Brighton, 1909).

(iv) Parliamentary Papers

Hansard, *Parliamentary Debates*.

Parl. *Papers 1894*, xiii. 1, (Report from the Select Committee on Land Acts (Ireland) together with the Proceedings of the Committee).

Parl. *Papers 1902*, ccxii, ccxxvii (Census Returns, Province of Ulster).

Parl. *Papers 1906*, xciv (Returns of Electors).

Cabinet Papers (microfilm in the Public Record Office of Northern Ireland).

(v) Contemporary Pamphlets and Political Comment

ADGEY, R. J., *Arming the Ulster Volunteers* (Belfast, n.d.).

Anon. [LINDSAY CRAWFORD?], *Orangeism: Its History and Progress: A Plea for First Principles* (Dublin, n.d.).

BONN, M. J., *Modern Ireland and her Agrarian Problem* (Dublin and London, 1906).

CARSON, E. H., 'Mr Birrell's Record in Ireland', *Quarterly Review*, ccviii. 414 (1908) 283–92.

CHAMBERLAIN, JOSEPH, *Speeches on the Irish Question: A Collection of Speeches delivered between 1887 and 1890* (London,1890).

COYNE, W. P. (ed.), *Ireland: Industrial and Agricultural* (Dublin, 1902).

DICEY, A. V., *A Leap in the Dark: A Criticism of the Principles of Home Rule as Illustrated by the Bill of 1893* (London, 1911).

—— *A Fool's Paradise: Being a Constitutionalist's Criticism on the Home Rule Bill of 1912* (London, 1913).

DOWDEN, E., 'Irish Unionists and the Present Administration', *National Review*, xliv (Oct. 1904).

DOWSETT, C. F., *Land: Its Attractions and Riches* (London, 1892).

DUNRAVEN, The Earl of, *The Crisis in Ireland: An Account of the Present Condition of Ireland and Suggestions towards Reform* (Dublin and London, 1905).

—— *The Outlook in Ireland: The Case for Devolution and Conciliation* (Dublin and London, 1907).

ELLIS, Revd T., *The Actions of the Grand Orange Lodge of the County of Armagh (and the Reasons thereof) on the 6th of July 1885* (Armagh, 1885).

ERVINE, ST JOHN, *Sir Edward Carson and the Ulster Movement* (Dublin and London 1915).

[FISHER, J. R.], *The Ulster Liberal Unionist Association: A Sketch of its History, 1885–1914* (Belfast, 1914).

GOOD, J. W., *Irish Unionism* (Dublin and London, 1920).

IWAN-MULLER, E. B., *Ireland: Today and Tomorrow* (London,1907).

[KENNEY, P. D.], *Economics for Irishmen* (Dublin, 1907).

KERR-SMILEY, P., *The Peril of Home Rule* (London, 1911).

LOUGH, THOMAS, *England's Wealth: Ireland's Poverty* (3rd edn., London, 1897).

LOW, S., *The Governance of England* (rev. edn., London, 1914).

LOWELL, A. L., *The Government of England* (rev. edn., New York, 1924).

LUCY, HENRY, W., *A Diary of the Salisbury Parliament* (London, 1892).

—— *A Diary of the Unionist Parliament, 1895–1900* (Bristol and London, 1901).

—— *Peeps at Parliament: Taken from behind the Speaker's Chair* (London, 1903).

—— *Later Peeps at Parliament: Taken from behind the Speaker's Chair* (London, 1905).

—— *The Balfourian Parliament* (London, 1906).

LYSAGHT, E., *Sir Horace Plunkett and his Place in the Irish Nation* (Dublin and London, 1916).

McCARTHY, M. J. F., *Rome in Ireland* (London, 1904).

McELROY, S. C., *The Route Land Crusade* (Coleraine, n.d.).

McNEILL, RONALD, *Ulster's Stand for Union* (London, 1922).

MIDLETON, Earl of, *Ireland: Dupe or Heroine?* (London, 1932).

MORRISON, H. D., *Modern Ulster: Its Character, Customs, Politics and Industries* (London [1920]).

[OLIVER, F. S.], *Federalism and Home Rule, by Pacificus* (London, 1910).

OSTROGORSKI, M., *Democracy and the Organisation of Political Parties* (2 vols.; London, 1902).

PEEL, Hon. GEORGE, *The Reign of Sir Edward Carson* (London, 1914).

PLUNKETT, Sir H. C., *Ireland in the New Century* (London, 1904).

ROSENBAUM, S. (ed.), *Against Home Rule: The Case for the Union* (London, 1912).

RUSSELL, T. W., 'A Resumé of the Irish Land Problems', Nineteenth Century, xxvi (Oct. 1889), 608–21.

—— *Compulsory Purchase: Five Speeches Made by Mr. T. W. Russell* (London and Dublin, 1901).

—— *Ireland and the Empire: A Review* (London and New York, 1901).

SAMUELS, A. W., *Home Rule: What is it?* (Dublin and London, 1912).

SAUNDERSON, E. J., *Two Irelands: Loyalty versus Treason* (London and Dublin, 1884).

SMITH, G. H., *Rambling Reminiscences: Being Leaves from my Notebook as a Public Political Speaker* (Newry, 1896).

—— *The North-East Bar: A Sketch, Historical and Reminiscent* (Belfast, 1910).

STEAD, W. T., *Coming Men on Coming Questions* (London, 1905).

TAYLOR, J. W., *The Rossmore Incident: An Account of the Various Nationalist and Counter-Nationalist Meetings held in Ulster in the Autumn of 1883* (Dublin, 1884).

2.SECONDARY SOURCES

A. Articles, Biographies, and Monographs

ALCOCK, ANTHONY, et al., Ulster: An Ethnic Nation? (Lurgan, 1986).

ANDERSON, R. A., With Plunkett in Ireland: The Co-op Organiser's Story (2nd edn., Dublin, 1983).

ASKWITH, Lord, Lord James of Hereford (London, 1930).

BAKER, S., 'Orange and Green', in J. H. Dyos and M. Wolff (edd.), The Victorian City (2 vols.; London, 1973), ii. 789–814.

BALL, F. E., The Judges in Ireland, 1221–1921 (2 vols.; London, 1926).

BARKER, M., Gladstone and Radicalism: The Reconstruction of Liberal Policy in Britain, 1885–94 (Hassocks, 1975).

BARTON, D. P., Timothy Healy: Memories and Anecdotes (London and Dublin, 1933).

BECKETT, J. C., The Anglo-Irish Tradition (London, 1976).

—— 'Carson: Unionist and Rebel', in Beckett (ed.), Confrontations: Studies in Irish History (London, 1972).

—— The Making of Modern Ireland (1603–1923) (2nd edn., London, 1981).

BELL, G., The Protestants of Ulster (London, 1976).

BENTLEY, M., Politics without Democracy, 1815–1914: Perception and Preoccupation in British Government (London, 1984).

—— and STEVENSON, J., High and Low Politics in Modern Britain: Ten Studies (Oxford, 1983).

BERRINGTON, HUGH, 'Partisanship and Dissidence in the Nineteenth-Century House of Commons', Parliamentary Affairs, xi. 4 (Autumn 1968), 338–74.

BEW, P. A. E., 'The Problem of Irish Unionism', Economy and Society, vi. 1 (Feb. 1977), 89–109.

—— Land and the National Question in Ireland, 1858–1882 (Dublin, 1978).

—— GIBBON, P., and PATTERSON, H., The State in Northern Ireland: Political Forces and Social Classes (Manchester, 1979).

—— C. S. Parnell (Dublin, 1980).

—— 'Politics and the Rise of the Skilled Working Man', in J. C. Beckett (ed.), Belfast: The Making of the City, 1800–1914 (Belfast, 1983).

BIGGS-DAVISON, JOHN, George Wyndham: A Study in Toryism (London, 1951).

BIRCH, A. H., Small-Town Politics: A Study of Political Life in Glossop (Oxford, 1959).

BLAKE, ROBERT, The Unknown Prime Minister: The Life and Times of Andrew Bonar Law, 1858–1923 (London, 1955).

BLEWETT, N., 'The Franchise in the United Kingdom, 1885–1918', Past and Present, xxxii (Dec. 1965), 27–56.

BOLAND, J., *Irishman's Day: A Day in the Life of an Irish M.P.* (London [1946]).

BOTTOMLEY, P. M., 'The North Fermanagh Elections of 1885 and 1886: Some Documentary Illustrations', *Clogher Record*, viii. 2 (1974), 167–81.

BOURNE, J., *Patronage and Society in Nineteenth-Century England* (London, 1986).

BOYCE, D. G., *Englishmen and Irish Troubles: British Public Opinion and the Making of Irish Policy* (London, 1972).

BOYLE, J. W., 'The Belfast Protestant Association and the Independent Orange Order 1901–1910', *Irish Historical Studies*, xiii. 50 (Sept. 1962), 117–54.

—— 'A Fenian Protestant in Canada: Robert Lindsay Crawford', *Canadian Historical Review*, lii. 2 (1971), 165–76.

BREUILLY, JOHN, *Nationalism and the State* (2nd. edn., Manchester, 1985).

British and Irish Communist Organization, *The Birth of Ulster Unionism*, (5th edn., Belfast, 1984).

BUCKLAND, PATRICK, *Irish Unionism*, i. *The Anglo-Irish and the New Ireland, 1885–1922* (Dublin and New York, 1972).

—— *Irish Unionism*, ii. *Ulster Unionism and the Origins of Northern Ireland* (Dublin and New York, 1973).

—— *Irish Unionism: 1885–1922* (Historical Association Pamphlet, London, 1973).

—— *Irish Unionism 1885–1923: A Documentary History* (Belfast, 1973).

—— 'The Unity of Ulster Unionism, 1886–1939', *History*, lx (1975), 211–23.

—— *The Factory of Grievances: Devolved Government in Northern Ireland, 1921–1939* (Dublin, 1979).

—— *James Craig, Lord Craigavon* (Dublin, 1980).

CALLWELL, Brigadier-General C. E., *The Memoirs of Major-General Sir Hugh McCalmont, KCB, CVO* (London, 1924).

CAMPBELL, JOHN, *F. E. Smith, First Earl of Birkenhead* (London, 1983).

CAMPBELL, T. J., *Fifty Years of Ulster: 1890–1940* (Belfast, 1941).

CECIL, Lady GWENDOLEN, *Life of Robert, Third Marquess of Salisbury* (4 vols.; London, 1921–32).

—— *Biographical Studies of the Life and Political Character of Robert, Third Marquess of Salisbury*, (London [1948]).

CHADWICK, M. E. J., 'The Role of Redistribution in the Making of the third Reform Act', *Historical Journal*, xix. 3 (1976), 665–83.

CHILSTON, ERIC, Viscount, 'Lord Salisbury as Party Leader, 1881–1902', *Parliamentary Affairs*, xiii. 3 (1960), 304–17.

—— *Chief Whip: The Political Life and Times of Aretas Akers-Douglas, First Viscount Chilston* (London, 1961).

—— *W. H. Smith* (London, 1965).

CLARKE, EDITH M., *Round About Rathfriland* (Rathfriland, 1981).

CLARKE, P. F., 'British Politics and Blackburn Politics, 1900–1910', *Historical Journal*, xii. 2 (1969), 302–27.

—— *Lancashire and the New Liberalism* (Cambridge, 1971).

CLARKE, S., and DONNELLY, J. S. (edd.), *Irish Peasants: Violence and Political Unrest in Ireland, 1780–1914* (Manchester, 1983).

COMFORT, G. O., *Professional Politicians: A Study of the British Party Agents* (Washington, 1958).

COOKE, A. B., and VINCENT, JOHN, *The Governing Passion: Cabinet Government and Party Politics in Britain, 1885–6* (Brighton, 1974).

CORNFORD, J. P., 'The Transformation of Conservatism in the late Nineteenth Century', *Victorian Studies*, vii (1963), 35–66.

—— 'The Parliamentary Foundations of the Hotel Cecil', in R. Robson (ed.), *Ideas and Institutions of Victorian Britain: Essays in Honour of George Kitson Clark* (London, 1967).

CROMWELL, V., 'The Losing of the Initiative by the House of Commons, 1780–1914', *Transactions of the Royal Historical Society* (1968), 1–23.

CURTIS, L. P., *Coercion and Conciliation in Ireland, 1880–1892: A Study in Conservative Unionism* (Oxford and Princeton, 1963).

—— 'Incumbered Wealth: Landed Indebtedness in Post-famine Ireland', *American Historical Review*, lxxxv. 2 (Apr. 1980), 332–67.

D'ALTON, Father E. A., *A History of Ireland from the Earliest Times to the Present Day* (3 vols.; London, 1910).

D'ALTON, IAN, 'Southern Irish Unionism: A Study of Cork Unionists, 1884–1914', *Transactions of the Royal Historical Society*, xxiii. 3 (Jan. 1973), 71–88.

—— 'Cork Unionism: Its Role in Parliamentary and Local Elections, 1885–1914', *Studia Hibernica*, xv (1975), 143–61.

DAVIS, PETER, 'The Liberal Unionist Party and the Irish Policy of Lord Salisbury's Government', *Historical Journal*, xviii. 1, (Mar. 1975), 85–104.

DAVIS, RICHARD, *Arthur Griffith and Non-Violent Sinn Fein* (Dublin, 1974).

—— 'Ulster Protestants and the Sinn Fein Press, 1914–1922', *Eire-Ireland*, xv. 4 (1980), 60–85.

DELANY, V. T. H., *Christopher Palles: His Life and Times* (Dublin, 1960).

DERRY, JOHN W., *Castlereagh* (London, 1976).

DIGBY, MARGARET, *Horace Plunkett: An Anglo-American Irishman* (Oxford, 1949).

DUGDALE, BLANCHE, E. C., *Arthur James Balfour, First Earl of Balfour, KG, OM, FRS &c* (2 vols.; London, 1936).

DUTTON, DAVID, 'Unionist Politics and the Aftermath of the General Election of 1906: A Reassessment', *Historical Journal*, xxii (1979), 861–76.

—— *Austen Chamberlain: Gentleman in Politics* (Bolton, 1985).

EGREMONT, MAX, *The Cousins: The Friendships, Opinions and Activities of Wilfrid Scawen Blunt and George Wyndham* (London, 1977).

ELLIOT, A. R. D., *The Life of George Joachim Goschen, First Viscount Goschen* (2 vols.; London, 1911).

ENSOR, R. C. K., *England, 1870–1914* (Oxford, 1936).

ERVINE, ST JOHN, *Craigavon: Ulsterman* (London, 1949).

FANNING, RONAN, 'The Unionist Party and Ireland, 1906–10', *Irish Historical Studies*, xv. 58 (Sept. 1966), 147–71.

FITZPATRICK, DAVID, *Politics and Rural Life: Provincial Experience of War and Revolution, 1913–1921* (Dublin, 1977).

—— 'The Disappearance of the Irish Agricultural Labourer, 1841–1912', *Irish Economic and Social History*, vii (1980), 66–92.

FOSTER, R. F., 'Parnell and his People: The Anglo-Irish Ascendancy and Home Rule', *Canadian Journal of Irish Studies* (June 1980), 105–34.

—— *Lord Randolph Churchill: A Political Life* (Oxford, 1981).

FRASER, P., 'The Growth of Ministerial Control in the Nineteenth-Century House of Commons', *English Historical Review*, lxxv (1960), 444–63.

—— 'The Liberal Unionist Alliance: Chamberlain, Hartington and the Conservatives, 1886–1904', *English Historical Review*, lxxvii. 302 (Jan. 1962), 53–78.

FRY, AGNES, *The Life of the Rt. Hon. Sir Edward Fry GCB*, (Oxford, 1921).

GAILEY, ANDREW, 'Horace Plunkett's New Irish Policy of 1905', in Carla Keating (ed.), *Plunkett and Co-operatives: Past, Present and Future* (Dublin, 1983).

—— 'Unionist Rhetoric and Irish Local Government Reform, 1895–9', *Irish Historical Studies*, xxiv. 93 (May 1984), 52–68.

—— *Ireland and the Death of Kindness: The Experience of Constructive Unionism, 1890–1905* (Cork, 1987).

GARDINER, A. G., *The Life of Sir William Harcourt* (2 vols.; London, 1923).

GARVIN, J. L., and AMERY, J., *The Life of Joseph Chamberlain* (6 vols.; London, 1932–69).

GATTY, C., *George Wyndham: Recognita* (London, 1917).

GEARY, LAURENCE M., *The Plan of Campaign, 1886–1891* (Cork, 1986).

GIBBON, PETER, *The Origins of Ulster Unionism: The Foundation of Popular Protestant Politics and Ideology in Nineteenth-Century Ireland* (Manchester, 1975).

GOLLIN, A. M., The Observer, *and J. L. Garvin 1908–14: A Study in a Great Editorship* (Oxford, 1960).

GRAY, JOHN, *City in Revolt: James Larkin and the Belfast Dock Strike of 1907* (Belfast, 1985).

GRIBBON, S., 'The Social Origins of Ulster Unionism', *Irish Economic and Social History*, iv (1977), 66–72.

GUTTSMAN, W. L., *The British Political Élite* (London, 1963).

GWYN, W. B., *Democracy and the Cost of Politics in Britain* (London, 1962).

HAMER, D. A., *John Morley: Liberal Intellectual in Politics* (Oxford, 1968).

—— *Liberal Politics in the Age of Gladstone and Rosebery* (Oxford, 1972).

HAMMOND, J. L., *Gladstone and the Irish Nation* (London, 1938).

HANHAM, H. J., *Elections and Party Management: Politics in the Time of Disraeli and Gladstone* (2nd edn., Hassocks, 1978).

—— 'Political Patronage at the Treasury, 1870–1912', *Historical Journal*, iii. 1 (1960, 75–84.

—— 'The Sale of Honours in Late Victorian England', *Victorian Studies*, iii. 3 (Mar. 1960), 277–89.

—— 'Opposition Techniques in British Politics, 1867–1914', *Government and Opposition*, ii. 1 (Nov. 1966), 35–48.

—— 'Politics and Community Life in Victorian and Edwardian England', *Folk Life*, 4 (1966), 5–14.

HARBINSON, JOHN, *The Ulster Unionist Party, 1882–1973: Its Development and Organisation* (Belfast, 1973).

HARDINGE, Sir A. E. H., *Life of Henry Howard Molyneux, Fourth Earl of Carnarvon, 1831–1890* (3 vols.; London, 1925).

HARKNESS, D. W., *The Restless Dominion: the Irish Free State and the British Commonwealth of Nations, 1921–31* (London, 1969).

HEPBURN, A. C., 'The Irish Council Bill and the Fall of Sir Antony MacDonnell', *Irish Historical Studies*, xvii. 68 (Sept. 1971), 470–98.

HICKS-BEACH, Lady V., *The Life of Sir Michael Hicks-Beach, First Earl St Aldwyn* (2 vols.; London, 1932).

HOBSBAWM, E. J., and RANGER, T. (edd.), *The Invention of Tradition* (Cambridge, 1983).

HOLLAND, B., *Life of Spencer Compton, Eighth Duke of Devonshire* (2 vols.; London, 1911).

HOPPEN, K. T., 'Landlords, Society and Electoral Politics in Mid-Nineteenth-Century Ireland', *Past and Present*, 75 (May 1977), 62–93.

—— *Elections, Politics and Society in Ireland, 1832–1885* (Oxford, 1984).

HOW, F. D., *William Conyngham Plunket, Fourth Baron Plunket and Sixty-first Archbishop of Dublin: A Memoir* (London, 1900).

HOWARD, C. H. D., 'Joseph Chamberlain and the Irish Central Board Scheme' *Irish Historical Studies*, viii (1953), 324–61.

HOWARTH, JANET, 'The Liberal Revival in Northamptonshire, 1880–1895: A Case Study in Late Nineteenth-Century Elections', *Historical Journal*, xii. 1 (1969), 78–118.

HYDE, H. MONTGOMERY, *Carson: The Life of Sir Edward Carson, Lord Carson of Duncairn* (London, 1953).

JACKSON, ALVIN, 'Irish Unionism and the Russellite Threat 1894–1906', *Irish Historical Studies*, xxv. 100 (Nov. 1987).

JACKSON, ALVIN, *Edward Saunderson and the Evolution of Ulster Unionism, 1865–1906* (Belfast, forthcoming).

JALLAND, PATRICIA, 'A Liberal Chief Secretary and the Irish Question: Augustine Birrell, 1907–1914', *Historical Journal*, xix. 2 (1976), 421–51.

—— *The Liberals and Ireland: The Ulster Question in British Politics to 1914* (Brighton, 1980).

JAY, RICHARD, *Joseph Chamberlain: A Political Study* (Oxford, 1981).

JEFFERSON, H., *Viscount Pirrie of Belfast* (Belfast, n.d.).

JONES, ANDREW, *The Politics of Reform, 1884* (Cambridge, 1972).

JONES, G. A., 'Further Thoughts on the Franchise, 1885–1918', *Past and Present*, xxxiv (July 1966), 134–8.

JOYCE, P., *Work, Society and Politics: The Culture of the Factory in Later Victorian England* (Brighton, 1980).

KENNEDY, A. L., *Salisbury, 1830–1903: Portrait of a Statesman* (London, 1953).

KENNEDY, L., and OLLERENSHAW, P., *An Economic History of Ulster, 1820–1939* (Manchester, 1985).

KINGHAN, N., *United We Stood: The Official History of the Ulster Women's Unionist Council, 1911–1974* (Belfast, 1975).

KIRKPATRICK, R. W., 'Landed Estates in Ulster and the Irish Land War, 1879–1885', *Economic and Social History*, v (1978), 73.

LAFFAN, MICHAEL, *The Partition of Ireland, 1911–1925* (Dundalk, 1983).

LAWRENCE, R. J., *The Government of Northern Ireland: Public Finance and Public Services, 1921–1964* (Oxford, 1965).

LECKY, ELIZABETH, *A Memoir of the Rt. Hon. W. E. H. Lecky* (London, 1910).

LEE, J., *The Modernisation of Irish Society* (Dublin, 1973).

LEE, J. M., *Social Leaders and Public Persons: A Study of County Government in Cheshire since 1888* (Oxford, 1963).

LEIGHTON, S., *The History of Freemasonry in the Province of Antrim, Northern Ireland* (Belfast, 1938).

LONDONDERRY, EDITH, Marchioness of, *Henry Chaplin: A Memoir* (London, 1926).

LOUGHLIN, JAMES, *Gladstone, Home Rule and the Ulster Question, 1882–1893* (Dublin, 1986).

LUCAS, REGINALD, *Colonel Saunderson, M.P.: A Memoir* (London, 1908).

LYONS, F. S. L., 'The Irish Unionist Party and the Devolution Crisis of 1904–1905', *Irish Historical Studies*, vi. 21 (Mar. 1948), 1–22.

—— *The Irish Parliamentary Party, 1890–1910* (London, 1951).

—— *Ireland Since the Famine*, (2nd edn., London, 1972).

—— and HAWKINS, R. A. J. (edd.), *Ireland under the Union: Varieties of Tension* (Oxford, 1980).

MCCAFFREY, PATRICIA, 'The Wyndham University Scheme, 1903–1904', *Irish Ecclesiastical Review*, cx. 6 (Dec. 1968), 329–49.

McCLELLAND, A., 'The Later Orange Order', in T. D. Williams (ed.), *Secret Societies in Ireland* (Dublin, 1973).

McDOWELL, R. B., 'Edward Carson', in C. C. O'Brien (ed.), *The Shaping of Modern Ireland* (London, 1960).

—— *The Church of Ireland, 1869–1969* (London, 1975).

McMINN, J. R. B., 'Presbyterianism and Politics in Ulster, 1871–1906', *Studia Hibernica*, xxi (1981), 127–46.

—— 'The Myth of "Route" Liberalism in County Antrim, 1869–1900', *Eire-Ireland*, xvii. 1 (Spring 1982), 137–49.

—— 'Liberalism in North Antrim, 1900–1914', *Irish Historical Studies*, xxiii. 89 (May 1982), 17–29.

MAGEE, J., 'The Monaghan Election of 1883 and the "Invasion of Ulster"', *Clogher Record*, viii. 2 (1974), 147–66.

MANSERGH, N., *The Government of Northern Ireland: A Study in Devolution* (London, 1936).

—— *The Irish Question, 1840–1921* (rev. edn., London, 1965).

MARJORIBANKS, EDWARD, and COLVIN, IAN, *Life of Lord Carson*, (3 vols.; London, 1932–6).

MARSH, PETER, *The Discipline of Popular Government: Lord Salisbury's Domestic Statecraft, 1881–1902* (Hassocks, 1978).

MATHESON, J. B., 'Orangeism in Ballymacarrett', *Journal of the East Belfast Historical Society*, ii. 1 (Nov. 1985), 23–37.

MAXWELL, Sir H., *Life and Times of the Rt. Hon. William Henry Smith, M.P.* (2 vols.; London, 1893).

MILLER, DAVID W., *Church, State and Nation in Ireland, 1898–1921* (Dublin, 1973).

—— *Queen's Rebels: Ulster Loyalism in Historical Perspective* (Dublin, 1978).

MOODY, T. W., 'The Irish University Question in the Nineteenth Century', *History*, xliii (1958), 90–109.

MOXON-BROWNE, EDWARD, *Nation, Class and Creed in Northern Ireland* (Aldershot, 1983).

MURPHY, D., *Derry, Donegal and Modern Ulster, 1790–1921* (Londonderry, 1981).

MURPHY, RICHARD, 'Faction in the Conservative Party and the Home Rule Crisis, 1912–1914', *History*, lxxi. 232 (1986), 222–34.

MURRAY, ALICE, E., *A History of the Financial and Commercial Relations between England and Ireland from the Time of the Restoration* (London, 1903).

NEWTON, Lord, *Lord Lansdowne* (London, 1929).

O'BRIEN, C. C., *Parnell and His Party, 1880–1890* (2nd edn., Oxford, 1964).

O'BROIN, LEON, *The Chief Secretary: Augustine Birrell in Ireland* (London, 1969).

O'DAY, ALAN, *The English Face of Irish Nationalism: Parnellite Involvement in British Politics, 1880–1886* (Dublin, 1977).

—— *Parnell and the First Home Rule Episode, 1884–1887* (Dublin, 1986).

O'HALLORAN, CLARE, *Partition and the Limits of Irish Nationalism: An Ideology under Stress* (Dublin, 1987).

O'HALPIN, E., *The Decline of the Union: British Government in Ireland, 1892–1920* (Dublin, 1987).

OLNEY, R. J., *Lincolnshire Politics, 1832–1885* (Oxford, 1973).

PATTERSON, HENRY, 'Conservative Politics and Class Conflict in Belfast in the 1890s', *Saothar: Journal of the Society for the Study of Irish Labour History*, ii (1976), 22–32.

—— 'Redefining the Debate on Unionism', *Political Studies*, xxiv (1976), 205–8.

—— 'Independent Orangeism and Class Conflict in Edwardian Belfast': A Reinterpretation', *Proceedings of the Royal Irish Academy*, lxxx, sect. c (1980), 1–27.

—— *Class Conflict and Sectarianism: The Protestant Working Class and the Belfast Labour Movement, 1868–1920*, (Belfast, 1980).

PELLING, H., *Social Geography of British Elections, 1885–1910* (London, 1967).

PETRIE, Sir CHARLES, *Walter Long and His Times* (London, 1936).

—— *The Life and Letters of Sir Austen Chamberlain, KG, PC, MP* (2 vols.; London, 1939–40).

—— *The Carlton Club* (London, 1955).

PHILLIPS, G. D., *The Diehards: Aristocratic Society and Politics in Edwardian England* (Cambridge, Mass., 1979).

PINTO-DUSCHINSKY, M., *British Political Finance, 1830–1980* (London, 1981).

PUGH, MARTIN, *The Tories and the People, 1880–1935* (Oxford, 1985).

QUINAULT, R. E., 'Lord Randolph Churchill and Home Rule', *Irish Historical Studies*, xxi. 84 (Sept. 1979), 377–403.

RAMSDEN, J., *A History of the Conservative Party: The Age of Balfour and Baldwin* (London, 1978).

RICHARDS, PETER, *Honourable Members: A Study of the British Backbencher* (London, 1959).

ROBB, J. H., *The Primrose League* (Columbia, 1942).

ROBERTS, D. A., 'The Orange Order in Ireland: A Religious Institution', *British Journal of Sociology* (Sept. 1971), 269–82.

ROBINSON, LENNOX, *Bryan Cooper* (London, 1931).

ROBSON, R. (ed.), *Ideas and Institutions of Victorian Britain: Essays in Honour of George Kitson Clark* (London, 1967).

RODNER, W. S., 'Leaguers, Covenanters, Moderates: British Support for Ulster, 1913–1914', *Eire-Ireland*, xvii. 3 (1982), 68–85.

ROEBUCK, PETER, (ed.), *Plantation to Partition: Essays in Ulster History in Honour of J. L. McCracken* (Belfast, 1981).

RUSSELL, A. K., *Liberal Landslide: The General Election of 1906* (Newton Abbot, 1975).

SALVIDGE, STANLEY, *Salvidge of Liverpool: Behind the Political Scenes 1890-1928* (London, 1934).

SAUNDERSON, H., *The Saundersons of Castle Saunderson* (London, 1936).

SAVAGE, D. C., 'The Irish Unionists: 1867-1886', *Eire-Ireland*, ii. 3 (1967), 86-101.

—— 'The Origins of the Ulster Unionist Party, 1885-6', *Irish Historical Studies*, xii. 47 (Mar. 1961), 185-208.

SEARLE, G. R., *The Quest for National Efficiency* (London, 1971).

SHANNON, CATHERINE, 'The Ulster Liberal Unionists and Local Government Reform, 1885-1898', *Irish Historical Studies*, xviii. 71 (Mar. 1973), 407-23.

SHEARMAN, HUGH, *Not an Inch: A Study of Northern Ireland and Lord Craigavon* (London, 1942).

SMITH, ANTHONY, D., *Theories of Nationalism* (2nd edn., London, 1983).

SOLOW, BARBARA, *The Land Question and the Irish Economy (1870-1903)* (Cambridge, Mass., 1971).

SOMMER DUDLEY, *Haldane of Cloan: His Life and Times, 1856-1928* (London, 1960).

STANSKY, PETER, *Ambitions and Strategies: The Struggle for the Leadership of the Liberal Party in the 1890s* (Oxford, 1964).

STEWART, A. T. O., *The Ulster Crisis* (London, 1967).

—— *The Narrow Ground: Aspects of Ulster, 1609-1969* (London, 1977).

—— *Edward Carson* (Dublin and New York, 1981).

SYKES, ALAN, *Tariff Reform in British Politics, 1903-1913* (Oxford, 1979).

THOMAS, J. A., *The House of Commons, 1832-1901: A Study of its Economic and Functional Character* (Cardiff,1939).

—— *The House of Commons, 1906-1911: An Analysis of its Economic and Social Character* (Cardiff, 1958).

THOMPSON, FRANK, 'The Armagh Elections of 1885-6', *Seanchas Ardmhacha: Journal of the Armagh Diocesan Historical Society*, viii (1977), 360-85.

—— 'Attitudes to Reform: Political Parties in Ulster and the Irish Land Bill of 1881', *Irish Historical Studies*, xxiv. 95 (May 1985) 327-40.

—— 'The Landed Classes, the Orange Order and the anti-Land League Campaign in Ulster, 1880-1', *Eire-Ireland*, xxii. 1 (1987), 102-21.

TOWNSHEND, C., *Political Violence in Ireland: Government and Resistance since 1848* (Oxford, 1983).

URWIN, D. K., 'The Development of the Conservative Party Organisation in Scotland until 1912', *Scottish Historical Review*, xliv. 138 (Oct. 1965), 89-111.

WALKLAND, S. A. (ed.), *The House of Commons in the Twentieth Century: Essays by Members of the Study of Parliament Group* (Oxford, 1979).

WALLER, P. J., *Democracy and Sectarianism: A Political and Social History of Liverpool, 1868–1939* (Liverpool, 1981).

WEST, TREVOR, 'The Development of Horace Plunkett's Thought', in C. Keating (ed.), *Plunkett and Cooperation: Past, Present and Future* (Dublin, 1983).

—— *Horace Plunkett, Cooperation and Politics: An Irish Biography* (Gerrard's Cross, 1986).

WHYTE, J. H., 'Landlord Influence at Elections in Ireland, 1760–1885', *English Historical Review*, lxxx. 317 (Oct. 1965), 740–60.

WRENCH, J. E., *Alfred, Lord Milner: The Man of No Illusions* (London, 1958).

WYNNE, M., *An Irishman and His Family: Lord Morris and Killanin* (London, 1937).

YOUNG, KENNETH, *Arthur James Balfour: The Happy Life of the Politician, Prime Minister, Statesman, and Philosopher 1848–1930* (London, 1963).

B. Theses

BARTON, B. E., 'Sir Basil Brooke: The Making of a Prime Minister', Ph.D. thesis (Belfast, 1986).

BUCKLAND, PATRICK, 'The Unionists and Ireland: The Influence of the Irish Question in British Politics. 1906–1914', MA thesis (Birmingham, 1965).

—— 'Southern Unionism, 1885–1922: With Special Reference to the period after 1914', Ph.D. thesis (Belfast, 1969).

FOY, M., 'The Ulster Volunteer Force: Its Domestic Development and Political Importance in the Period 1913–1920', Ph.D. thesis (Belfast, 1986).

GAILEY, ANDREW, 'The Unionist Government's Policy Towards Ireland, 1895–1905', Ph.D. thesis (Cambridge, 1983).

JACKSON, ALVIN, 'The Irish Unionist Parliamentary Party, 1885–1906', D.Phil. thesis (Oxford, 1986).

LYONS, F. S. L., 'Irish Parliamentary Representation, 1891–1910', Ph.D. thesis (Dublin, 1947).

MCCLELLAND, AIKEN, 'Johnston of Ballykilbeg', M.Phil. thesis (Coleraine, 1978).

MCKEOWN, P., 'The Land Question and Elections in South Antrim, 1870–1910', M.S.Sc. thesis (Belfast, 1981).

MCMINN, J. R. B., 'The Reverend James Brown Armour and Liberal Politics in North Antrim, 1869–1914', Ph.D. thesis (Belfast, 1979).

MEGAHEY, A. J., 'The Irish Protestant Churches and Social and Political Issues, 1870–1914', Ph.D. thesis (Belfast, 1969).

MORGAN, A., 'Politics, the Labour Movement and the Working Class in Belfast,1890–1914', Ph.D. thesis (Belfast, 1981).

MURPHY, RICHARD, 'Walter Long and the Conservative Party, 1905–21', Ph.D. thesis (Bristol, 1984).

RIDLEY, JANE, 'Leadership and Management in the Conservative Party in Parliament; 1906–1914', D.Phil. thesis (Oxford, 1985).

RODNER, W. S., 'Lord Hugh Cecil and the Unionist Opposition to the third Irish Home Rule Bill: A Conservative's Response', Ph.D. thesis (Penn. State, 1977).

THOMPSON, F., 'Land and Politics in Ulster, 1868–1886', Ph.D. thesis (Belfast, 1982).

WALKER, BRIAN M., 'Parliamentary Representation in Ulster, 1868–1886', Ph.D. thesis (Dublin, 1976).

—— 'Pride, Prejudice and Politics: Society and Elections in Ulster, 1868–1886' (unpublished MS).

INDEX

Abercorn, 2nd Duke of 31, 40, 46,
  77, 155, 169, 172, 173, 203,
  205, 218, 277, 296
Acland-Hood, Alexander 106, 107,
  287, 289
Aitken, Max 206
Akers-Douglas, Aretas 75, 77, 105,
  135, 205, 213
Allen, W. J. 306
Amery, L. S. 72
Andrews, Thomas 232
Anglo-Irish Treaty 87, 284, 285
Antrim, 6th Earl of 205, 232
Archdale, E. M. 94, 206, 227
Arnold-Forster, H. O. 68, 72, 76,
  80, 86, 91, 200, 306
  and southern Unionism 90
  and contribution to parliament 98
  and Land Bill (1896) 149–50
  elected for West Belfast 201, 223
  appointed to Admiralty 246
  death of 298
Arnold-Forster, Mary 118, 199, 223
Arrears Bill (1882) 25
Ashbourne, 1st Lord *see under*
  Gibson, Edward
Asquith, H. H. 3, 79, 97, 101 n.,
  315, 324
Asquith, Margot 254
Atkinson, H. J. 179
Atkinson, John 97, 122–3, 162,
  164, 227, 247, 254, 261, 266,
  277, 279, 296
Atkinson, T. J. 199

Bagwell, Richard 173
Balcarres, 10th Earl of 79–80, 107,
  111, 299
Baldwin, Stanley 76
Balfour, A. J. 78, 80, 81, 117, 118,
  135 n., 192, 217, 262, 263, 282,
  287–91, 293, 296, 298, 299–300,
  302, 303, 305, 308, 320
  and land reform 137, 138–41,
  145, 147–8, 150–1, 156, 160,
  163, 167, 194

and local government reform 170,
  172–3
and Catholic university
  proposals 176, 178–86, 187,
  190, 191
and Irish election contests 211,
  212, 215–16, 218
and T. W. Russell 216
and Wyndham 244, 253, 258,
  264–6, 280–1
and Walter Long 276–7, 278, 280
Balfour, Lady Betty 76, 254
Balfour, C. B. 213
Balfour, Lady Frances 290
Balfour, Gerald 76, 88, 145, 154,
  186, 212, 214, 217, 246, 276,
  324
  and move from Irish Office 156,
  195
  and Local Government Bill (1898)
  172–3, 175
Balfour of Burleigh, 6th Lord 303
Ball, F. E. 202
Ballinasloe Affair 248–9, 261, 278
Baptist Union of Great Britain 179
Barrie, H. T. 61, 309
Barton, D. P. 58, 72, 97, 126, 149,
  150, 206
Bates, R. Dawson 240, 306
Bateson, Thomas (1st Lord
  Deramore) 31, 232, 291
Beattie, Andrew 232
Belfast Conservative Association 140,
  222–3, 312
Belfast News Letter 37, 38, 45, 95,
  124, 133, 135–6, 139, 140, 159,
  161, 178, 226, 228, 246, 308,
  310, 320
Belfast Telegraph 68
Bellingham, Henry 77–8, 243
Berrington, Hugh 108, 109
Birch, A. H. 197
Birmingham, George (Canon
  Hannay) 14, 58 n., 91 n., 110
Birrell, Augustine 191, 281, 300,
  305, 310

348 INDEX

Bloomfield, J. C.   203
Blunt, Wilfrid Scawen   258
Blythe, Ernest   87
Bonar Law, Andrew   111, 299, 324
  at Blenheim Palace   117, 118
  elected leader   320
Boraston, John   209, 210
Bowra, Maurice   76
Brabazon of Tara, 1st Lord   99
Breuilly, John   7
Bristol Protestant League   180
Brodrick, St John (9th Viscount
  Midleton)   243, 263, 298
Bruce, Henry   33, 101
Bryce, John   129, 281
Buckland, Patrick   1, 6, 267
Budget Protest League   297
Burdett-Coutts, Baroness   76
business interests:
  in Unionism   59–61, 70, 88,
    168–9, 231, 235, 309
  in Nationalism   67–8
Butcher, J. G.   56
Butcher, S. H.   76–7, 302, 306

Cadogan, 5th Earl of   100, 128, 154,
  155, 156, 163, 247, 303
Cairns, 1st Earl   23
Cambridge University   72, 76
Campbell, James (1st Lord Glenavy)
  74, 94, 97, 157, 214, 293,
  306
  his ambition   110–11
  and devolution debates   261, 265–
  6
Carlton Club   16, 32, 46, 73, 74,
  224
Carnarvon, 4th Earl of   37, 38
Carson, Lady Annette   76
Carson, Edward   6, 16, 58, 73, 75,
  76, 78, 227 n., 244, 292, 298,
  306, 315, 318, 324, 326
  contribution to parliament   94, 97,
    100–1
  and Land Bill (1896)   148, 150
  and financial relations dispute   153
  appointed Solicitor-General   154,
    159
  and Land Bill (1903)   162
  and Catholic university proposals
    181, 185
  candidate for Trinity College seat
    213

and devolution debates   265, 266
and Russellism   269
offered Chief Secretaryship   277
as Ulster Unionist leader   299, 300
and loyalist militancy   319, 321
on Bonar Law   320
Castlereagh, Viscount (later 7th
  Marquess of Londonderry)   232
  see also Londonderry, 6th
  Marquess of
Castlestuart, 5th Earl of   233
Castletown, 2nd Lord   137
Catholic political opinion   4, 13, 25,
  29, 42, 77;
  and Catholic university proposals
    182, 183, 186
Catholic University of Ireland   177
Catholic university question   88,
  176–92, 324
Cawdor, 3rd Earl of   118, 289, 300,
  311
Cecil, Lady Gwendolen   50, 119
Cecil, Lord Hugh   99
Central Conservative Association
  (Belfast)   196
Central Conservative Society
  (Belfast)   18, 196, 197
Central Protestant Defence Association
  18
Chamberlain, Austen   55 n., 118,
  216, 287, 292–5, 296, 297, 298,
  299, 301, 320
Chamberlain, Joseph   97, 98, 120,
  129, 193, 220, 286
  Irish Unionist support for   112,
    291–2, 294
  and T. W. Russell   136, 166,
    194
  and Land Bill (1887)   136, 137
  and Land Bill (1896)   148
  and Wyndham's land reforms
    167 n.
  and 'A Unionist Policy for Ireland'
    170
  and Catholic university proposal
    180
  and party division in Ulster
    215–16
Chamberlain, Neville   251
Chambers, Thomas   201
Chaplin, Henry   294, 300–1
Church of Ireland opinion   4, 17,
  18–19, 21, 179

Cooke, A. B., and John Vincent 24, 26, 51-2
Cooke, Henry 18
Cooper, Bryan Ricco 66-7
Corbett, T. L. 66, 75, 86, 96, 103, 111, 200, 225-6, 228, 233
Cork, 9th Earl of 277
Corrupt Practices Act (1883) 204
Corry, James Porter 29, 32, 127
Craig, Charles Curtis 3, 233, 234, 265, 292, 309, 313
  and Land Bill (1903) 162, 163
  and Catholic university proposals 187
  and Ballinasloe case 248, 249
  and Constable Anderson case 250, 251, 252
  and devolution affair 264, 266, 269, 273-5
  and formation of UUC 273-4
  campaigns against Russell 273-5, 281
Craig, James (1st Viscount Craigavon) 60, 76, 286, 299, 309, 313, 324
  his education 62
  and clubs 74
  and North Fermanagh 206
  support for William Moore 274
  and loyalist 'radical right' 275
  and tariff reform 292-3
  and Orangeism 313
  and gun-running 316, 319
Craigavon Demonstration (1911) 313, 314-15, 319, 321
Cranbrook, 1st Earl of 47
Crawford, F. H. 315, 316, 317, 318, 319, 321
  and Guns for Ulster 317
Crawford, R. Sharman 225, 233
Crawford, Robert Lindsay 224
Crichton, Viscount (later 4th Earl of Erne) 19, 20, 128, 218, 245

Dane, J. W. 204
Dane, Richard M. 86, 96, 126, 165
De Vesci, 4th Viscount 172
Department of Agriculture Act (1899) 156
Deramore, 1st Lord see Bateson, Thomas
Derby, 14th Earl of 23
Deutsch, Karl 12

Devlin, Joseph 252
devolution affair 85, 97, 243-4, 252-66, 267, 268, 269, 272, 276, 282, 283, 286, 299, 308, 311, 324
  and Unionist reorganization 236-40
  revival in 1906: 286, 287-8, 289-90, 295, 308
Dickson-Poynder, John 257 n.
Dillon, John 89
Disraeli, Benjamin 23, 177
Dixon, Daniel 59
Downshire, 6th Marquess of 220
Dudgeon, A. J. 202
Dudley, 2nd Earl of 254, 257, 258, 266, 278
Dufferin and Ava, 1st Marquess of 152, 219-20
Dugdale, Blanche 253
Dunraven, 4th Earl of 189, 244, 253
  and devolution affair 254, 255, 256, 257, 258, 264

Eccentric Club 75
elections, general:
  (1880) 57, 67
  (1885) 39-40, 56, 57, 64, 65, 67, 73, 215
  (1886) 64, 66
  (1892) 58, 65, 68, 69, 143, 144, 210-11
  (1895) 66, 143, 144, 208, 211, 223
  (1900) 55, 157-8, 211, 225-6, 246, 272
  (1906) 55, 58, 73, 268, 269, 272, 273, 292, 302
  (Jan. 1910) 66, 68, 69, 73, 306, 311, 324
  (Dec. 1910) 310, 311, 314, 315, 316, 324
  (1918) 57, 64, 65, 68, 73
elections, regional:
  Northwich (1887) 143
  North Bucks (1889) 180
  Cork (1891) 213
  North Belfast (1896) 223
  East Down (1902) 159, 227, 270, 272-3, 281
  South Belfast (1902) 224
  South Antrim (1903) 159, 270